WORKING AT PLAY

Working at Play

———◆—◆·———

A HISTORY of VACATIONS
in the
UNITED STATES

———◆—◆·———

Cindy S. Aron

New York   Oxford
OXFORD UNIVERSITY PRESS
1999

Oxford University Press

Oxford   New York

Athens   Auckland   Bangkok   Bogotá   Buenos Aires
Calcutta   Cape Town   Chennai   Dar es Salaam   Delhi
Florence   Hong Kong   Istanbul   Karachi   Kuala Lumpur
Madrid   Melbourne   Mexico City   Mumbai   Nairobi   Paris
São Paulo   Singapore   Taipei   Tokyo   Toronto   Warsaw

and associated companies in
Berlin   Ibadan

Copyright © 1999 by Cindy S. Aron

Published by Oxford University Press, Inc.,
198 Madison Avenue, New York, New York 10016

Oxford is a registered trademark of Oxford University Press

Library of Congress Cataloging-in-Publication Data
Aron, Cindy Sondik, 1945–
Working at play : a history of vacations
in the United States / Cindy S. Aron.
p. cm.   Includes bibliographical references and index.
ISBN 0-19-505584-5
1. United States—Social life and customs.
2. Vacations—United States—History.   I. Title.
E161.A75   1999
973 — dc21   98-25552

3 5 7 9 8 6 4 2

Printed in the United States of America
on acid-free paper

For Mark and Samantha

Contents

———•◆•———

CONTENTS

Acknowledgments

—————•◆•—————

M any people have helped me with this book, and it is a great pleasure
now to acknowledge and thank them.

The cooperative and dedicated staff of numerous repositories, both
large and small, offered critical assistance in locating documents and pho-
tographs. I would like to thank the reference librarians and archivists at the
New-York Historical Society, the New York Public Library, the National
Museum of American History, the Virginia Historical Society, Alderman
Library at the University of Virginia, the U.S. Department of Labor, the
Prints and Photographs Division of the Library of Congress, the National
Archives, the Dukes County Historical Society, and the Saratoga Springs
Historical Society. I would like to offer thanks more specifically to Dr.
Martha Stonequist, City Historian of Saratoga Springs; Jean Stamm, Assis-
tant Director of the Saratoga Springs Public Library; Jane Smiley, archivist
at Mohonk Mountain House Archives; and Bill West and Elton White at the
National Cash Register Company. Alfreda Irwin, historian-in-residence at
Chautauqua, was nice enough to copy important documents from the
Chautauqua collection and to lend me microfilm. Hope Nicely and Brian

Critz at the Catherwood Library at Cornell University found and sent me material from the records of the ILGWU.

Many years ago Robert Conte, historian at the Greenbrier, helped to spark my interest in the history of vacations. He has continued to be of great assistance, making the collection of documents and photographs in the Greenbrier's archives available to me. Field Horne has provided a stellar example of an altruistic and magnanimous scholar, offering me use of the remarkable collection of first-person accounts of Saratoga Springs that he has assembled. He has, moreover, always been ready to answer the numerous questions with which I periodically have bothered him. Jean Langston not only located photographs of Highland Beach, but arranged to have them reproduced for me. The late Evelyn Distelman was kind enough to lend me two of her family photographs. Janet Distelman made sure that the photographs found their way into my hand. I express my thanks to the Distelman family and my sincere regrets that Evelyn Distelman died before she could see the picture published in the book. Thanks, as well, to Mrs. Ted Sharp for permission to use and quote from the diary of Eva Moll. The Greenbrier Hotel and the Highland Beach Historical Commission have obligingly granted permission for use of photographs from their collections.

I have received invaluable assistance from students who took on a variety of often onerous tasks. Thanks go to Peter Kastor, Rebecca de Schweinitz, and James Van Hook. Amy Feely deserves special recognition and thanks for doing an incredible amount of work—often under serious time constraints.

Friends, family, and colleagues at the University of Virginia and elsewhere have invested considerable time and energy reading and commenting upon my work. Many thanks to Laurel Berger, Pamela Berger, Lenard Berlanstein, Eileen Boris, Alon Confino, Rebecca Edwards, James Gilbert, Michael Holt, Field Horne, Robert Kohler, Charlene Lewis, Stephen Innes, Ann Lane, Gloria Moldow, Anne Schutte, Carole Srole, and Susan Ware. I shudder to think what this book would have looked like had I not had the benefit of their thoughtful, wise, yet always gentle suggestions. Edward Ayers, Grace Hale, and Joseph Kett gave the manuscript a particularly close reading and prodded me to refine, reshape, or recast the argument. This book is a great deal better for their efforts.

Thanks go as well to the people at Oxford University Press. Thomas LeBien, my editor, has more than lived up to his title, disproving the now familiar complaint that editors no longer edit. His careful and intelligent editing of my manuscript improved the final product enormously. Regina Knox did a remarkable job of copyediting the manuscript in a very short period of time. Susan Ferber and Helen Mules have gracefully and effi-

ciently overseen and managed the many tasks associated with turning manuscript into book.

My greatest debts are to Samantha and Mark. Over the many years that I
have been working on this book, Samantha gave me first the joy of watching
her become a grown-up and then the exquisite pleasure of having an adult
daughter. Mark read drafts of chapters, offering encouragement and smart
suggestion. But much more importantly, he remains my center—the person
whose love and support has, for more than thirty years, sustained me.

Introduction

———◆———

Some of my earliest memories are of the beach. In 1944 my grandparents bought a summer house in New London on the Connecticut shore. For years thereafter the entire extended family—grandparents, parents, aunts, uncles, and cousins—fit, a little tightly, into the seven bedrooms. The women and children remained from mid June until Labor Day. The men came only for the weekends. They drove down from the city on Friday nights, often arriving in time for a swim before dinner, and departed on Sunday nights.

Summers at the beach were wonderful for the children, less so for the adults—especially the women. The beach house was large and airy, but it had far fewer conveniences than our middle-class suburban homes. Rather than an up-to-date washer and dryer in a conveniently placed laundry room, the beach house offered an old fashion wringer machine in a very damp and musty basement and a clothesline in the backyard. One and a half bathrooms serviced more than three times as many people as the two and a half bathrooms of our regular houses. A constant parade of sandy feet made housekeeping difficult. And then there were the joys and tensions of living in a multigenerational home containing the elder matriarch, two daughters, one daughter-in-law, and numerous small children.

1

The last half of the twentieth century is far removed from the last half of the nineteenth, but I can locate the origin of my family's yearly trek to the beach in the experiences of middle-class vacationers from more than a century ago. Much about my childhood experience differs of course from that of pioneering nineteenth-century vacationers, but some similarities connect us.

On the most basic level, we are connected by place. Where my family's house sits is about a mile from where a summer hotel, by the mid-1850s, welcomed visitors. Those people were primarily wealthy WASPs who traveled by rail from New York City, and we were a family of Jews from Hartford—the eldest of whom still felt more comfortable speaking Yiddish than English. But the fact that we shared the same place—albeit a century apart—testifies to how customs and habits of vacationing endured even as the nature of the vacationing public changed. When my father and uncles arrived late on Friday and left on Sunday night they too were participating in a ritual begun by men a century earlier. By the early 1870s men were depositing their wives and children at resorts and summer homes and returning to their work in the hot city.

What links my family's vacation experiences to a longer history is, perhaps most importantly, the other functions that summers at the beach served. For the last fifty years the family beach house has offered more than a place to relax. It brought generations together, allowing American grandchildren to know their immigrant grandparents far more intimately than they otherwise would have. At the beach house we found marriage partners, birthed children, mourned deaths, celebrated birthdays, and cemented family ties. If vacations provided my family the opportunity to engage in such important social and cultural work, what functions—both real and symbolic—might vacations have served as they became an integral part of the American landscape?

Think, for a moment, of the range of vacations that we indulge in today: the grueling week-long backpacking trek, the trip to Disney World, the quiet week at a rented seashore cottage, the European tour, the hunting and camping expedition, the splurge at a posh resort, the visit to relatives in another part of the country, the golfing holiday, the road trip in the Winnebago, the time at a health spa. Vacations announce much about the vacationer—not only class status and economic standing, but personal aspirations and private goals. More than just yearly rituals in which we connect with friends and family, vacations are also exercises in self-definition. In affording time away from the demands of everyday life, vacations disclose what people choose to do rather than are required to do.

But, of course, such choices are never entirely free. Cultural directives, social constraints, and economic limitations influence even our most liberating experiences. So too in the past. The history of vacations reveals a constant tension between the desires and needs of would-be vacationers and what the culture, at any specific moment, determined acceptable. It is, indeed, this tension that informs and shapes the history that follows.

This book tells two stories. One concerns how, when, and why vacationing came to be part of American life, charting this cultural and social institution as it grew from the custom of a small elite in the early nineteenth century to a mass phenomenon by the eve of World War II. It is, in part, a story of change. As such the history of vacations is embedded in a familiar history of the United States—the transformation of an agricultural into an urban–industrial nation, the growth of a transportation network, the creation of a large middle class, the increase in prosperity and free time. Such changes allowed both vacation places and a vacationing public to develop and take shape. At the same time, vacation resorts themselves became sites of change—creating environments in which vacationers not only could enjoy new sorts of pleasures but could also experiment with new, often less restricted, rules of conduct and behavior.

The other story concerns American cultural anxieties about vacations. It records extraordinarily little change. Indeed, what is compelling about the history of vacations is the constancy with which Americans have struggled with the notion of taking time off from work. Despite the dramatic transformations in American life from the middle of the nineteenth to the middle of the twentieth centuries, concerns about vacationing remained remarkably consistent. Americans engaged in a love/hate battle with their vacations—both wanting to take them and fearing the consequences. Relaxing did not come easily to American men and women who continued to use their leisure in the performance of various sorts of work—religious work, intellectual work, therapeutic work. Leisure and labor remained complicated and troubling categories—in some ways polar opposites, in other ways closely connected.

———— •◆• ————

Vacationing began as a privilege of the early nineteenth-century elite—southern planters and wealthy northerners who journeyed in search of health and pleasure. Over the last half of the century men and women from the emerging middle class, enjoying intervals set aside for rest and recreation, began to become part of a growing throng of vacationers. During these decades a vast variety of summer resorts took shape across the nation, catering to the increasing crowd of American vacationers. Seashore, mountains, springs, country towns, and rural farmhouses all became vacation destinations. Although many vacationers elected to frequent such resorts, others opted to become tourists—taking advantage of the expanding network of railroads to visit cities, historic and cultural markers, and natural wonders. Still others preferred the outdoors, choosing to spend their vacations camping in tents or shacks and enjoying the benefits and beauty of nature. The spread of vacationing knew no regional boundaries. It was a nationwide phenomenon.

The early decades of the twentieth century witnessed the expansion of vacationing beyond the privileged middle class. Reformers concerned with the plight of poor women and children along with businessmen interested in increasing the efficiency of their workforce began to champion vacations for working-class people. By the 1920s some working-class men and women joined the vacationing public, enjoying periods set aside specifically for the pursuit of leisure. The decade of the Great Depression, ironically enough, saw a majority of working-class Americans finally gaining the right to an annual paid summer vacation.

While this book charts the democratization of vacationing from the early nineteenth through almost the middle of the twentieth century, it focuses considerable attention on the ways in which middle-class Americans "invented" vacations for themselves in the decades after the Civil War. The sorts of vacations that many of us are familiar with today took shape during the last four decades of the nineteenth century as middle-class men and women embarked on what, for many, was a new kind of experience. Understanding the history of vacations thus requires a close look at the nineteenth-century middle class.

Numerous historians have examined the growth of a self-conscious American middle class as it formed in the 1820s and 1830s and reshaped itself during the last half of the century. Where the antebellum middle class had been composed of small businessmen, professionals, farmers, and artisans, the middle class of the last half of the century began to include increasing numbers of employees—women and men who worked in the offices of America's expanding corporations. Indeed, the term "middle class" masks important changes, central to the development of vacationing, that took place in the lives of American men and women over the course of the nineteenth century. In the early part of the century a key component of being middle class, at least for a man, was the probability that one day he would be independent and self-employed—either as a professional or as a small businessman. But as the century wore on, more middle-class men found themselves working permanently as salaried employees in America's growing corporate economy. Moreover, the large and bureaucratic companies in which such men worked made it unlikely that many would ever achieve the independence and autonomy that had once served as hallmarks of middle-class status.[1]

For women, middle-class status meant something else, particularly being freed from the necessity of either wage-earning labor outside the home or productive domestic labor within it. Female school teachers and (by the late decades of the century) clerical workers managed to pursue gainful employment and maintain their position within the middle class. But for the vast majority of women, marriage to someone who allowed them to preserve at least the facade of leisure remained an important hallmark of being middle class. Thus, over the last half of the nineteenth century the American middle class embraced a vast, amorphous array of people: self-employed skilled artisans and farmers; men who worked as professionals and small businessmen; an expanding corps of male white-collar clerks and midlevel managers; the women who were married to such men and who, by virtue of that fact, were relieved of the necessity of paid employment; single women who worked as school teachers or as clerical employees in government or private offices.

During these decades the middle class was creating itself not only economically, but socially and culturally as well. Historians have determined various ways in which middle-class Victorians distinguished themselves from members of the working class: the nature of their nonmanual employment, their urban residential patterns, their adoption of a set of values that privileged domesticity and privacy, their embrace of refined manners and the trappings of respectability, and their behavior as consumers.[2] I argue that vacationing became another critically important marker of middle-class status. Middle-class men and women not only claimed the privilege of vacationing, but made that privilege into a middle-class entitlement. By the turn of the twentieth century the middle class had established vacationing as a requirement for its physical health and for its spiritual and emotional well-being as well.

But taking vacations did not come easily to the middle class. Throughout the nineteenth century vacations presented middle-class men and women with a number of problems and dilemmas. And herein lies the second story this book will tell. Even as middle-class people created modern vacations, they simultaneously engaged in a discussion about the dangers that this new cultural institution presented. Vacationing generated fear and anxiety among the nineteenth-century middle class, because vacationers were people at leisure and leisure remained problematic. Work, discipline, and industry were the virtues that allegedly counted for the success and well-being not only of individuals, but of the nation itself. Conversely, leisure and idleness could be sources of moral, spiritual, financial, and political danger. Reconciling their need and desire for extended periods of rest and recreation with their commitment to work remained a central struggle for middle-class Americans. Historians have seen leisure as a locus of class conflict—a terrain on which working and middle-class people battled for control over culture.³ I suggest that leisure was contested as well within the middle class, and that the conflict may, in fact, not yet be completely resolved.

In part, nineteenth-century Americans' distrust of leisure derived from the legacy of Puritan ancestors. Those who hoped to build a "city upon a hill" knew that work, not play, was the key to their success. Puritans never offered labor as a route to salvation, for Puritans maintained a strict belief in the inability of human beings to influence an already predestined divine plan. But Puritans believed, nevertheless, in the importance of hard labor. Work was, for Puritans, a means of glorifying God. Even if people could not "labor" their way to salvation, they nevertheless believed that in performing daily, productive labor they were following God's plan, doing "God's work."⁴

Those who fashioned the Puritan commonwealth in colonial New England tried their best not only to put the force of law and convention behind such beliefs, but to make them an integral part of the Puritan psyche. Puritan ministers exhorted their congregants to be disciplined. "God's precious time" should not be wasted. Puritan officials discouraged not only idleness and sloth, but amusements that were "unproductive or morally suspect." Courts and magistrates monitored closely the habits of their citizens and chastised those who were profligate or extravagant. Most forms of amusement—cards, theater, dancing—were forbidden.⁵ Not that colonial New Englanders never relaxed or played. Even Puritans had understood that people needed time for legitimate "recreation," time to restore mind and body so that work and religious devotion could continue. At house-raisings and on militia days devout Puritans found occasional opportunities for socializing and relaxation. And, no doubt, those who were less than devout tried to circumvent the laws and enjoy even some of the proscribed pleasures.⁶

Puritan distrust of leisure remained a crucial component of Protestant thought long after Puritans had lost control of both the politics and the culture of New England. Moreover, Puritan glorification of work persisted even after many Protestants had rejected the strict predestinarianism that was once so central to Puritan thought. By the nineteenth century many Protestant ministers were willing to embrace a more liberal philosophy. Righteous behavior, which included hard work, might help pave the way to salvation. But work continued to be more than "merely a painful means to moral health and redeeming grace." It was, rather, "a blessing."⁷ Work could bring earthly success in this life and salvation in the next. Play could threaten both.

Nineteenth-century fears of leisure stemmed from political as well as religious sources. The American Revolution had created a republic that depended upon an independent and virtuous citizenry for its success. Disinterestedness and self-sacrifice provided the cement which, the revolutionary generation maintained, would hold the republic together. Revolutionary leaders believed that leisured gentlemen would assume the reins of government in the new republic. Leisure—meaning freedom from the necessity of making a living—was celebrated as a way for rich men to become disinterested public servants. Southern slaveholders readily endorsed this leisure ideal, using it as another justification for the continuing enslavement of African American men and women. Not birth and lineage but merit, talent, and dedication to the public good distinguished the American republican gentleman.[8]

Faith in the abilities and importance of this leisured aristocracy eroded in the half century that followed the American Revolution. During much of the eighteenth century work had been perceived not as a potential source of wealth, but as the necessary alternative to starvation and poverty. In the early nineteenth century, however, common men began to affirm the value and honor of their productive labor. As Gordon Wood has explained, "productive labor now came to be identified with republicanism and idleness with monarchy."[9] As mechanics, traders, and businessmen took the opportunities made available to them by the new republic, they increasingly heaped scorn upon leisured gentlemen who lived off profits from their land rather than from honest daily effort. What once had been celebrated as leisure became condemned as idleness. The deepening sectional crisis of the antebellum period bolstered these beliefs, as northern antislavery advocates deplored the corrosive effects of slavery on white men made dissipated by the absence of work. A leisured aristocracy threatened the republic, while a population of hardworking, useful men ensured its success.[10]

The work ethic—shaped by both Puritan and republican doctrines—dominated the nineteenth-century social and intellectual landscape. Indeed, the celebration of work persisted even as the growth of an industrial economy exchanged the ennobling labor of the skilled artisan for the monotonous, even dehumanizing labor of the factory worker.[11] Champions of the "New South Creed," promoted the "gospel of work" as one tool in their campaign to rebuild the postbellum south. In the process, they rejected the antebellum ideal of the leisured plantation gentleman and embraced the "hardworking, busy, acquisitive individual."[12] Throughout the century social critics and intellectuals—both from the North and South—continued to wrestle with the problems of work and leisure as they confronted both the rich who did not have to work and the poor who appeared unwilling to work. Thorstein Veblen's 1899 attack on "conspicuous consumption," *The Theory of the Leisure Class*, indicted the idle rich.[13] At the same time the labor unrest and strikes of the Gilded Age raised the specter of the idle poor. That middle-class Americans resisted the temptations of leisure, whether presented as the indulgence of the rich or the disruptive tendencies of the poor, remained a central concern to those who cared about the future of the nation.

Middle-class men and women could find other more mundane but still compelling reasons to be wary of leisure. Only work, not leisure, could bring the promise of financial gain and dispel the fear of financial ruin. The possibility of enjoying the bounties of an expanding economy spurred industrious mechanics and artisans in the new republic and motivated much of the emerging middle class throughout the nineteenth century. Working hard brought not only religious and patriotic satisfaction but material rewards. Although the consumer economy of the nineteenth century paled compared to what would follow in the twentieth, middle-class people could still hope that hard work would yield numerous material benefits: pianos for their parlors, education for their children, and the help of a domestic servant, for example. The accoutrements of middle-class refinement required arduous labor—not only to earn income sufficient for the purchase of the amenities, but to acquire the education and knowledge demanded by middle-class respectability.[14] These acquisitions, in turn, became symbols of middle-class status, embodying the discipline and hard work that had gone into securing them.

By the same token, sloth and idleness could threaten not only the niceties but the very fabric of life itself. Those who aspired to middle-class status in the nineteenth century may have enjoyed a comfortable lifestyle, but few felt secure from the vagaries of a cyclical economy that brought depressions about every twenty years. Leisure presented not only moral or political dangers but real economic risks to a middle class that operated without an economic safety net. Cultural dictates to work and save fit an economy within which even the middle class could not be sure of economic security.

Such directives reveal a decidedly gendered view of the perils of leisure and the benefits of work. Puritan warnings about idleness affected men and women equally in an economy in which the labor of both was recognized as critical for survival and in a religious system that offered or withheld salvation without regard to sex. But the republican celebration of work concerned the labor of men—the work that brought profit and potential wealth. Women lacked economic independence, the central requirement for citizenship in the republic, and women's domestic labor did not acquire the moral authority and worth that redounded to the work of mechanics and tradesmen.[15] The endorsement and celebration of work that dominated the nineteenth century took men's work as the measure.

Ideas about work and leisure, then, operated differently for women. On the one hand, both women and men were discouraged from being idle or wasteful. But as productive labor moved out of the homes of an emerging middle class, women in those homes assumed leisure as one of the badges of ladyhood. Victorian women acquired middle-class status not only by being relieved of the necessity of wage work, but by having a domestic servant to lighten household chores. The converse was also true. Wage-earning women and domestic servants became, by definition, working class. There were exceptions: Middle-class women worked as school teachers and, by late in the century, as office workers. Moreover, many middle-class women found themselves with little domestic help and spent long hours performing domestic duties. But the majority of middle-class women—especially those who were married—were absolved from the necessity of entering the labor force.[16]

For such women being "at leisure" was not a condition fraught with either moral or political risks but rather a culturally sanctioned requirement. Victorian culture assigned these women other duties—the care and socialization of children, the creation and maintenance of a refined domestic unit that would soothe and revitalize their overworked and harried husbands, and responsibility for those unfortunates in their communities who needed moral, spiritual, or material assistance. Although the nineteenth century did not designate such tasks "work," the middle-class women who performed them remained exempt from any of the negative associations with leisure. Indeed, few people questioned the fact that such women, along with their husbands, both needed and deserved vacations. But women's connection to vacationing was not entirely unproblematic. Vacation resorts could provide women unusual opportunities to exercise both autonomy and influence. From swimming in the surf to parading in their best finery, some female vacationers challenged conventional norms. That women predominated both numerically and culturally at many fashionable resorts appeared, to some nineteenth-century critics, to heighten the dangers and temptations that leisured places presented.

The political, religious, and economic mandates to work weighed heavily on would-be nineteenth-century vacationers. Anxieties about vacations persisted even as middle-class Americans began to define themselves, in part, by their right to take vacations. Along with parlors, pianos, and the other accoutrements of status, hard work had bought middle-class men and women the privilege of some time spent not working. Vacationing thus exposed the contradictions at the center of the middle class: industriousness and discipline helped to make people middle class and thus entitled them to vacations, but vacations embodied the very opposite of what the middle class most valued. The irony notwithstanding, middle-class people were left with a persistent dilemma. How to enjoy leisure without jeopardizing the commitment to work? This tension pervaded and shaped the history of vacations in the nineteenth century.

The problem became more complex as the twentieth century altered the makeup of the vacationing public. During the 1910s and 1920s working-class whites, immigrants, and middle-class African Americans began to participate in vacation experiences that had once belonged predominantly to the white middle class. Although vacationing rarely united people across racial, ethnic, or class lines, it did create a cultural experience that a wide cross-section of the population came to share.

Public discussion about vacationing clearly reflected the presence of these new vacationers. Echoing the nineteenth-century belief that working-class people needed the threat of poverty to keep them at work, skeptical twentieth-century commentators feared that vacations would ruin a labor force already prone to self-indulgence. Even the more enlightened social critics wondered whether these new vacationers could find the balance with which the middle class struggled—to enjoy vacations without falling prey to the dangers inherent in leisure. The presence of working-class vacationers brought renewed efforts by social commentators, reformers, and business-men to link vacations to work. As a result, Americans across the social spectrum continued to hear a decidedly ambivalent but, by the twentieth century, familiar message—one that simultaneously sanctioned and resisted vacationing.

———— •◆• ————

A short warning about definitions and boundaries seems in order. First, I have defined vacations as pleasure trips that last at least a few days. In other words, one-day excursions do not count. My goal was to understand how the custom and practice of extended trips away from home became part of American life, and what those trips came to mean both for the participants and for the culture at large. As such, excluding daily excursions seemed reasonable.

Second, I have omitted any discussion of vacations abroad. Only very wealthy individuals could have afforded European travel during this period. Since I was trying to explain how vacationing became a customary part of first a middle-class and later a working-class experience, I chose to concentrate on those sorts of vacations that were financially possible for the majority of vacationers.

Third, I end the book in 1940. By then vacationing had become firmly entrenched as part of "the American way of life," and thus the story that I had set out to tell was over. At the same time, significant changes after World War II made the United States a dramatically different place and altered vacationing in important ways. The expansion and availability of air travel, for example, shrank the globe, making international travel a reality for people who once could never have contemplated a trip abroad. Winter vacationing—whether skiing in the mountains or escaping the cold for the beaches of the Caribbean—became an increasingly important component of America's vacation culture, at least for those with sufficient economic resources. I leave to another scholar the fascinating job of investigating and explaining these developments. I would venture, however, that even as people created and explored new vacation possibilities, familiar doubts continued to trouble American vacationers. Indeed, as the Epilogue suggests, the legacy of the nineteenth century reaches into the very last years of the twentieth, often influencing both our choices of vacations and our feelings about those vacations.

PART ONE

Inventing Vacations

∂ 1 ℘

Recuperation and Recreation

—— •◆• ——

THE PURSUIT of HEALTH
and GENTEEL PLEASURES

In early August of 1827 Elihu Hoyt arrived in Saratoga Springs from his home in Deerfield, Massachusetts. His diary records his surprise at what he discovered there: "One would suppose that we should find everybody here on the sick list—but it is far from being the case. . . . Many of the visitors come here probably in good sound health, for amusement, & for the sake of spending a week or two among the fashionable to see & to be seen. . . . We have fashionable balls, . . . concerts, and all descriptions of amusement."[1] Both Hoyt's expectation and the reality he encountered at Saratoga reveal much about the early history of vacations in the United States. Curing sickness and securing good health certainly motivated many of those who visited Saratoga during the summer. But the quest for amusement was also a critical part of the story.

This chapter charts the beginnings of American resorts, the development of the first American vacationing public, and the debate over leisure that emerged toward the middle decades of the nineteenth century. It explores how elite Americans sought health and pleasure at springs and seashore and how more middling folks used religious camp meetings as sources of both recreation and spiritual restoration. Significantly, neither of these groups would have used the word "vacation" to characterize their ventures. Not until midcentury did the word "vacation" come to be used as a description for such journeys—at roughly the same time that ministers, doctors, and journalists began to devote considerable attention to the problems of leisure and amusement.

The debate that ensued echoed persistent and enduring tensions within American culture over whether, how much, and under what conditions men and women might allow themselves time away from work for the purpose of recreation. During the 1840s and 1850s a range of voices tentatively questioned America's long-standing celebration of work and argued the benefits of leisure. These new ideas about the values of leisure and play, while far from uncontested, served nevertheless as an intellectual rationale that would help to make vacationing a widespread middle-class phenomenon in the decades that followed.

The first American vacationers, however, were not middle class. The story begins, in fact, before much of an American middle class existed at all, as a tiny number of the eighteenth-century colonial elite made their way to a handful of springs and seaside watering places.

———————————— • ◆ • ————————————

In 1744 when Dr. Alexander Hamilton, a prosperous Maryland physician, embarked on a four-month journey "intended only for health and recreation," he was undertaking an unusual venture for his time. Few people traveled for pleasure in eighteenth-century America. The dearth of good roads, bridges, maps, or places to stay enroute made travel slow, onerous, and sometimes dangerous. Since many roads could not accommodate carriages and few colonies offered public coaches, Hamilton journeyed on horseback. The taverns and private homes at which he stayed ranged from the comfortable to the flea-infested.[2]

Although traveling remained difficult, the later decades of the eighteenth century did see slight improvements—the initiation of public stage service, the building of bridges over a few important rivers, and the publication of a handful of regional road maps.[3] Equally important for the history of vacations, however, was the development of a colonial elite with the time, financial resources, and interest to make life more genteel, pleasurable, and healthful.[4] By the 1760s a few members of the gentry were making their way to some of America's first vacation places.

A small number of South Carolina planters, for example, escaped the heat and disease of their plantations and sailed with their families up the coast to Newport, Rhode Island. They were joined by a handful of wealthy merchants from Philadelphia and some travelers from Jamaica. These early sojourners often spent as many as four or five months on the Rhode Island coast, where they benefited not only from the salubrious air but enjoyed concerts, dances, boat rides, and the company of congenial friends and acquaintances. But getting to Newport was still a long, arduous, expensive, and often dangerous venture. Little wonder that Newport's summer visitors remained few in number, ranging from twenty-nine to ninety-nine people a year in the decade before the American Revolution.[5]

During the late eighteenth century a smattering of other vacation resorts opened their doors to small groups of summer travelers. Wealthy merchants, planters, and politicians began to make their way to a few primitive watering places, primarily mineral springs, hoping to find health-restoring waters and agreeable company. Stafford Springs in Connecticut, Berkeley Springs in Virginia, and Bristol on the outskirts of Philadelphia were among the eighteenth-century springs that attracted members of the gentry.[6]

The elite Americans who initiated vacation travel in the late eighteenth century no doubt knew that they were partaking of a well-established European tradition. Europeans had been traveling to various spas since the late Middle Ages, pursuing both health and pleasure as they drank the waters, soaked in the baths, and enjoyed a variety of both innocent and illicit amusements.[7] In England both royalty and members of the upper class began patronizing spa towns in the seventeenth century. As on the continent, such places drew not only the infirm, but elite visitors searching for amusement and entertainment.[8] By the eighteenth century English watering places had begun to assume a more genteel and sober demeanor. In 1702 Queen Anne visited Bath, bringing the court, London society, and a veneer of respectability with her. Over the next decades impressive public buildings and more refined amusements attracted fashionable members of London society. Guests at Bath enjoyed sumptuous balls, concerts, dinners, and theatricals.[9]

Traveling to mineral springs may have provided a way for elite eighteenth-century Americans to ape the British upper class, but American watering places offered considerably less in the way of luxuries or even amenities than their English counterparts. When George Washington arrived at Berkeley Springs in 1761 he found that lodgings could "be had on no terms but building for them." He continued, "Had we not succeeded in getting a tent and marquee at Winchester, we should have been in a most miserable situation here."[10] Conditions at Berkeley improved over the next few decades, but American watering places remained few in number and primitive in nature throughout the eighteenth century.

The first half of the nineteenth witnessed a slow but significant increase in the numbers of vacationers and of vacation resorts. Seashore, springs, and mountains began receiving guests, many of whom sought to protect or improve their health. The scourges of cholera and yellow fever that swept through cities in the summer frightened many into fleeing their homes. Philip Hone, a member of the New York elite, took his family from New York City to Rockaway, Long Island, during the summer of 1832 to escape from cholera.[11] Residents of Boston faced similar problems that year. Charles Francis Adams protected members of his family by sending them to their country home in Medford.[12] Heat and humidity brought a variety of afflictions to those living on southern plantations as well. As a result, planters and their families often repaired in the summer to more healthful, up-country homes or to various springs.[13]

Escaping disease proved only part of the incentive to travel. People were also intent upon seeking health. Doctors often recommended traveling to locations where their patients would benefit from the climate, air, and water. Nineteenth-century physicians understood ill health to result from an imbalance—either an excess or deficiency—of various bodily fluids. Seeing the body as a closed system with a finite reserve of energy, doctors also posited that people possessed an essential but limited amount of "vital force." Most doctors agreed that stimulation and excitement were particularly liable to deplete the system. Orthodox medical practice aimed to maintain this delicate balance of energies and fluids, often by most unpleasant methods. Bleeding, leeches, blistering, and the use of powerful chemical purgatives formed part of the arsenal of "heroic" treatments of regular physicians. Discharging enough quantities of blood, sweat, feces, or partially digested food would, doctors maintained, restore patients to health.[14]

Beginning in the 1820s and persisting throughout the following decades, a variety of health reformers, unhappy with the dangerous and painful remedies of "regular" or "allopathic" doctors, searched for more benign techniques. These popular health movements spawned a variety of "irregular" physicians—Thompsonians, homeopaths, hydropathists, and electromagnetists among others. Looking to less violent and painful treatments, irregular physicians often substituted natural and vegetable remedies for the chemicals and poisons of the orthodox practitioners. While still holding to the belief in the importance of maintaining a balance of fluids and conserving "nervous energy," irregular doctors also began to discuss the benefits of hygiene, fresh air, vegetarian diets, and exercise.[15] Nature, many believed, could be enlisted in the cure and prevention of disease. After the 1830s, even orthodox physicians—partly in response to competition from irregulars—began to moderate their practices and put more store in the power of nature. By midcentury some of the more extreme heroic measures fell into disfavor, bloodletting became a more infrequent practice, and doctors relied upon smaller doses of medicines.

Traveling in search of air or water fit the prescription of both regular and irregular doctors. Both believed that change of climate could alter the balance of bodily fluids and that mineral waters, operating as powerful diuretics and laxatives, could produce the same effects. As irregulars, health reformers, and later traditional doctors advocated fresh air, temperate climate, sunlight, bathing, and exercise, the salubrious benefits of various summer resorts became increasingly apparent.[16]

Change of air—particularly the move from an intemperate to a more moderate climate—could, some physicians felt, mitigate or even cure some diseases, among them consumption, asthma, gout, and rheumatism. In 1835 Robley Dunglison, medical professor at the University of Maryland, published a textbook on *Elements of Hygiene,* the long title of which is revealing: *On the Influence of Atmosphere and Locality; Change of Air and Climate; Seasons; Food; Clothing; Bathing; . . . &c &c. on Human Health.* Dunglison maintained that many people who claimed to have been cured by the waters at various mineral springs were, in fact, helped primarily by the air. "Long before the citizen of our Atlantic towns reaches the Alleghany springs of Virginia," Dunglison asserted, "he has an earnest of the advantage he is about to derive from change of air; and many a valetudinarian finds himself almost restored during the journey, fatiguing as it is, through the mountain regions, which have to be crossed before he reaches the White Sulphur [Springs]." Dunglison understood as well that trips to watering places could work their magic on the body through the mind and spirit. The "varied scenery and society, absence from cares of business" helped patients recover. While not denying the potential benefits of the water, Dunglison still claimed that "taking invalids in general, we are satisfied that more is dependent upon change of air than on the administration of waters."[17]

Despite Dunglison's skepticism, by the 1830s American doctors were devoting considerable attention to the healing and restorative powers of water. Hydropathy would not become a distinctive branch of American medicine until the 1840s, but doctors were endorsing the benefits of water decades earlier.[18] Although physicians took interest in water in all forms— sea water, fresh water, and mineral water—the latter seemed to claim particular attention. In 1831 Philadelphia physician John Bell, for example, took specific notice of the curative possibilities of various thermal and mineral springs in his *Treatise on Baths and Mineral Waters.* Bell explained that mineral waters contained many of the same ingredients found in the apothecary shops, but that "mineral waters . . . produce the therapeutical effects . . . with more ease, and with less perturbation, and even in a painless manner."[19]

The list of diseases that mineral waters allegedly cured was legion—gastrointestinal problems, respiratory infections, skin eruptions, rheumatism. These claims sometimes came from physicians with a financial interest in the springs who may have exaggerated a tad. In 1846 Dr. Thomas Goode, the proprietor of the Virginia Hot Springs, published *The Invalid's Guide to the Virginia Hot Springs* in which he included testimonials from patients who professed that the waters cured not only gastrointestinal and rheumatic problems, but deafness and paralysis as well.[20]

The continued endorsement of the medical profession no doubt helped to encourage the opening of more springs and seaside resorts during the 1820s and 1830s. At the same time improvements in transportation—roads, canals, and the introduction of steamboat service along inland rivers—made journeying to such places somewhat less onerous.[21] And while conditions at many resorts remained primitive and travel continued to be slow, the number of guests began to increase.

Saratoga began to develop as a resort during the 1820s. Until then Ballston Spa, just a few miles away, had attracted most of the visitors to the area—some of whom had taken short trips into Saratoga to try the water there.[22] By 1821 the two largest hotels in Saratoga, the Pavilion and Congress Hall, held from 150 to 200 people each.[23] Philip Stansbury visited Saratoga in July of 1822 and found 800 "strangers" there.[24] Elihu Hoyt, who was so surprised to find healthy people at Saratoga, reported in 1827 that "1200 strangers" were currently "at the Springs, & that 12,000 in all have visited during the present season."[25]

In the years after 1820 new resorts also sprang up around the numerous mineral springs that dotted the western part of Virginia.[26] Most of these springs began as small, modest establishments, but the demand for rooms often surpassed the supply. Travelers frequently reported arriving to find no place for them. William Stabler in 1838 wrote to his cousin Sallie of his trip to the Red Sulphur, where he was going for "restoration." Along the way, however, he had "been repeatedly informed that they were full to overflowing . . . and that many had to lodge on the floor of the Dudley room." He decided that he had traveled too far "to be put back by any but insuperable difficulty." The rumors, he soon learned, were true. "Immediately on getting out of the stage I entered my name in the Register and inquired if I could get a room? The manager informed me that he intended to put 4 of us in the room . . . until the next day when he would try to do better for me."[27]

Seaside resorts, as well, were beginning to attract visitors during the 1820s and 1830s. The sea had not always presented a benign or welcoming image. Indeed, as Alain Corbin has brilliantly explained, up until the middle of the eighteenth century much of Western culture regarded the ocean as a dangerous, forbidding place. It represented the abyss, called up remembrance of the flood, and suggested uncontrollable and even demonic forces. Over the course of the eighteenth century the "fear and repulsion" of the ocean was replaced by a growing belief in the therapeutic potential of cold sea baths and an aesthetic appreciation of the sublimity of sea and shoreline. Romantic artists and poets helped to make the seashore a place for contemplation—a "favorite spot for self-knowledge."[28]

By the early nineteenth century Americans were making their way to a variety of spots along the coast. Cape May, which had begun to receive visitors from Philadelphia in the 1810s, boasted two hotels in 1823. When William Brobson, a Wilmington lawyer, visited Cape May in August of 1825 he was among the forty guests at "the largest and most pleasant" of the houses that he found there. Ten years later a third hotel had been built, and by 1840 a fourth was in operation. Numerous boardinghouses, some of them reputedly "very large," also accommodated lodgers.[29] Nahant, along the Massachusetts shore, catered to a Boston clientele during the 1820s. Josiah Quincy, mayor of Boston, sent his wife and daughters there in August of 1824 despite warning that "Boston was absolutely emptied, and that every house in Nahant was absolutely crammed, and that as to our getting lodgings at the Hotel, it was perfectly absurd to attempt it."[30] Newport continued to host Southern planters and their families, many of whom spent the entire summer at the Rhode Island resort.[31]

Diaries and letters of visitors to these springs and seaside retreats recorded detailed descriptions of their maladies, hopeful bulletins of improvements, and discouraging reports of relapses. Nor were these casual references of the "I'm fine" or "feeling better thank-you" variety. Traveling invalids reported to loved ones back home on the amount of water drunk, food ingested, wastes expelled, and pounds gained or lost.

Jane Cary Randolph, for example, journeyed in 1829 to some of the Virginia springs in search of health. In a letter to her mother from the Salt Sulphur, she apologized for not having written earlier, claiming ill health as her excuse: "I have not mended so rapidly since the first week—frequently suffering with pain in the side and debility. We staid a fortnight at the White Su[lphur] & yet, although I drank freely of the water, it had but little effect." Her husband suggested that they move on to the Salt, where, he claimed, "the waters are considered more active."[32] Many invalids journeyed from one Virginia spring to another in search of the water that would best cure their specific problems.

Although watering places often made extravagant claims for the vast range of diseases that their waters could cure, doctors and patients alike believed that waters varied in their effectiveness and that certain springs could cure certain ailments but were useless for others. Thus the nature of their complaints often determined the destination of summer travelers. In the early 1830s George Harrison wrote to his sister from Warm Springs explaining that he and his wife were comfortably accommodated there while waiting for suitable quarters to become available at the nearby Hot Springs. He had chosen the Hot because he had "reason to believe the baths there eminently useful in afflictions of the stomach" and he wished "Isabella to use them under the most favorable circumstances."[33] Mrs. E. M. Grosvenor wrote in July of 1833 from Saratoga informing friends about her and her husband's cure:

> Everything is very pleasant and I think these waters may promote health, if they do not restore ours. We commence cautiously. Mr. G. takes both Congress and Empire, with advantage. I take Empire water. The Physician does not encourage me much about drinking the water as it is not considered good for consumptives. . . . The air strengthens my lungs, and the rest and quietness do me more good than any kind of medicine. I have not taken the water yet long enough to test its benefits in regard to my case. My cough is not worse than it has been.[34]

Most watering places provided scales, because patients kept close track of and reported on their weight. Many diseases, specifically consumption, left the patient thin and wasted; gaining weight signaled a hopeful return to good health. Susan Blain, for example, had accompanied her ailing brother to White Sulphur in 1831 and wrote their father informing him that "Brother Archie has fattened very much since we left home; he weighed at Sweet Springs the other day 192 pounds and bid me say he is fattening hourly."[35]

Those who visited these places were often compelled to witness the unappealing, sometimes even repugnant, afflictions of their fellow sufferers. Charles Irving visited the Red Sulphur in August of 1834 where he counted about one hundred guests, two thirds of whom were "invalids" and most of those suffering with consumption: "To see the poor creatures coughing and spitting is a sight which I assure you is by no means pleasant—a great many are low—one died here on yesterday . . . as for my health I hope I am better my friends say I am better but I feel not much changed. I have fattened some two or three pounds!"[36] Irving decided to remain one more week at the Red Sulphur before moving on to the White Sulphur. His decision may have been sparked, at least in part, by a desire to flee the melancholy environment of the Red for the more cheerful company at the White Sulphur.

Following doctors' advice in some instances meant heading for springs or seashore. But physicians had also prescribed travel itself as a cure for illness. The advice of British physician James Clark, appearing in an 1843 article in the *Democratic Review*, claimed that "the mere act of travelling over a considerable extent of country is itself a remedy of great values, and, when judiciously conducted, will materially assist the beneficial effects of climate."[37] Some patients apparently took such suggestions to heart. Daniel Safford, a man who parlayed a blacksmith shop into a successful iron manufactory and then devoted himself to various reform causes, learned from his doctor that travel would help to maintain his health. His wife explained: "The difficulty in his heart, from which he had suffered more or less for many years, had increased to an alarming degree, owing, it was thought, to protracted sittings in a crowded house, without proper ventilation. . . . His physician advised that he should spend his summers thereafter in traveling, as the means most likely to prolong his life."[38] The young Rutherford B. Hayes received similar advice. In 1847, still a young, struggling lawyer in Ohio, he found himself suffering from "a sore throat, brought on, as the physicians say, by confinement, etc., in my office. . . . [T]he doctor says . . . that to effect a perfect cure I must leave the office for a year or two and try an entire change of habits of life, diet, climate, etc." Hayes settled for a two-month trip to New England where he visited friends and relatives, fished, sailed, and climbed Mt. Washington. He returned to Ohio well enough to resume his law practice.[39]

There is little doubt that many of the early nineteenth-century Americans who traveled either to specific watering places or simply to escape the confines of home and work did so in hopes of recuperation and restoration. A third "r," however, accompanied the other two. "Recreation" was an important part of this story.

The letters and diaries of those who visited these watering places commented not only on the health imperatives that sent the writer there, but also on the numbers of *other* visitors whose primary motivation for visiting was *not* health, but rather pleasure or fashion. Invalids frequently took note of the amusements and activities of the healthy. For example, Mrs. Read, the wife of a Bedford whaling captain, asserted that health had necessitated her visit to Saratoga in 1826, but also recorded in her diary: "The pleasure parties and balls every evening in this village engross the attention of the old and young, sick and well. . . . "[40] Jason Russell, in the last stages of consumption, traveled to Saratoga in 1839 on recommendation of his doctor. His journal recorded that the "various" amusements of the visitors included "rifling, concerts, assemblies, cotillion parties every evening except Saturday, and games of all descriptions from tossing coppers to the billiard tables." Saratoga, he concluded, could "hardly be termed a resort for invalids but rather of wealth and fashion, there being in all probably forty people in health to one that is sick."[41] It is impossible to know the exact proportion of the fit to the ailing. Certain watering places attracted more of the former and others more of the latter. Mineral springs probably included a higher percentage of invalids than did seaside resorts, although the springs certainly drew their share of pleasure seekers.

The infirm usually did not travel to these watering places alone. Frequently one or more relatives accompanied the seriously ill member of the family. The primary purpose of the visit was the cure of the invalid, and those who attended him or her might also hope to benefit from the water or the air. But such escorts were usually ready to engage in recreation and entertainment. Samuel Hoffman, for example, accompanied his father from Baltimore to White Sulphur for two months during the summer of 1832. His father was quite ill, "surprisingly weak" and unable to "sit up for any length of time at once." Still, Hoffman noted that he was "improving" and hoped that a few days would find him "about." Hoffman assured his wife that "I pass nearly all my time with him of course, giving an hour in the morning and in the afternoon to riding." Hoffman's description of a typical day's activity revealed that, despite the demands of his role as invalid's companion, life at White Sulphur was far from unpleasant for him:

> I rise at 6 and appropriate the time up to 8 to drinking the waters—lounge for half an hour after breakfast, when I mount my Horse for an hour or more then betake myself to my room, say about 10 1/2 o'ck—read—write and sleep a little till 2—dine—return to my room to read—at 6 ride either on Horseback or in a Barouche—Sup at 8—and though we have a fine band, and dancing-room, I leave it for my room—which, by the by, is particularly comfortable.

Not a bad way to spend a few months, as Hoffman himself agreed: "I have never known time at a watering place to pass so rapidly or so agreeably. So much so that I find it difficult to accomplish all I desire."[42]

Even the people who sought health were not necessarily invalids. They had journeyed to such places hoping either to improve their already satisfactory health or to avoid the harmful summer climate of their homes. Savvy resort proprietors learned quickly to cater to clients who hoped to combine recreation with recuperation. It was not difficult for health resorts to serve, equally well, as pleasure spots.

Guests at most resorts seemed to follow similar rules about who could indulge in what pleasures. From Saratoga to the Virginia Springs billiards quickly became a staple of resort life, but only for men. Some men played an occasional game, others spent many hours around the billiard table.[43] Men also gambled, often at cards. Blair Bolling found himself bored at White Sulphur in 1839, in part because he was "averse to participating in what forms a pretty general source of amusement for the company, viz.

card playing in one way or another, from the genteel game of whist to the farobank."[44] By the late 1840s men visiting Saratoga could frequent a room off the bowling alley where "there were faro tables, roulette, card games, and many other gambling jimracks."[45]

But most amusements were not gender-specific. Indeed, the extent to which male and female guests engaged in the same sorts of activities reveals that different, more relaxed codes of conduct prevailed at resorts than at home.[46] Women who sojourned at these watering places engaged in forms of amusement that would have been forbidden elsewhere. Both male and female guests, for example, played nine pins. William Stabler wrote to his cousin Sallie from Red Sulphur Springs in 1838 reporting that he had "found ladies and gentlemen including a couple of clergymen at nine pins." The game was, he felt "a pretty robust exercise for the ladies."[47] Not all people approved of women's participation. Elihu Hoyt was a little shocked to find two women, daughters of a local farmer, competing with guests at Saratoga in 1827.[48] Not only locals, but female guests played nine pins. On the second morning of his 1837 visit to Saratoga, Samuel Dawson, a young cadet from West Point, visited the nine pin alley and found there "a party of Ladies who seemed to enjoy the Game very much." Dawson reported to his friend being "considerably amused at the manner in which they rolled the ball."[49]

While most watering places offered billiards for men and nine pins for members of both sexes, specific resorts became known for distinctive forms of entertainment. Resort owners tried various strategies to keep their patrons happy and entertained. During the 1830s Saratoga installed a miniature circular railroad "with a car, where two persons can sit together and propel themselves."[50] If new technology offered one of the attractions at Saratoga, the Fauquier White Sulphur tried enticing visitors with more historical forms of entertainment. The Fauquier boasted yearly medieval festivals, complete with jousting and other competitions.[51] In the 1840s White Sulphur allowed a company of actors to convert an unused stable into a theater and charge fifty cents to guests for the performances. The theater apparently held 400, "including the gallery in which the colored people sat." But one guest remembered that "it was never very full whilst I was there."[52]

Those who visited the seashore spent time bathing in the ocean. William Brobson, the Wilmington lawyer who visited Cape May in August of 1825, found that the "principal amusements" there were "bathing and dressing." Both men and women bathed in the "morning, noon and evening," although not at the same time. The bathing hours were, he explained, "separate for ladies and gentlemen; saving the privilege of *married* men, who attend their wives."[53] There were, apparently, limits to how much codes of conduct could be relaxed. In the 1820s the notion of ladies and gentlemen bathing together remained beyond that limit.[54]

Although bathing may well have been segregated by sex, what distinguished most resort activities was the extent to which men and women enjoyed them together. During the very decades when prescriptive literature was mandating separate spheres for men and women, those who frequented early resorts were spending considerable time with members of the opposite sex. Young Samuel Dawson described the "routine of pleasures" of a typical day at Saratoga in 1837:

> Breakfast at eight o'clock, and then all retire to the drawing room and the Ladies and Gentleman for an hour or so promenade, then a party either takes a ride out to a very beautiful little Lake called Saratoga, situated 4 miles from the village, or go down to the nine pin alley and play until they get tired. . . . They dine at two, promenade up and down the drawing room for an hour and then take an evening walk or go to the circular railway and ride round for a while. . . . Sup at six; promenade and then at eight the dancing commences and continues until twelve or one. . . . It is almost impossible to give you any idea of the high enjoyment a person may have there for two or three days.[55]

A structured informality seemed to characterize resort life. Each place had its own routine—times for drinking the water, times for meals, times for promenading and visiting, times for bathing (in either mineral waters or ocean), times for carriage rides, times for specific games and entertainments. Those who so desired could keep apart from the crowd.[56] But most visitors—at least the healthy ones—seemed to want to join the throng.

Evenings were the premier time for socializing. Guests sometimes got up *tableaux vivants* and charades to entertain themselves.[57] Diaries and letters repeatedly mention the dances and parties that took place—often nightly. Hops, balls, and cotillions were regular occurrences. An anonymous diary described the evenings spent "either with balls[,] music or conversation or something better" at Saratoga in 1825.[58] Susan Blain, staying at White Sulphur Springs in August of 1831, informed her mother that balls occurred "every night."[59]

Balls and dances encouraged courting, another important amusement for which watering places quickly became known. Resorts, even those initially renowned for their health-giving possibilities, offered arenas for men and women to meet, socialize, play, and sometimes find mates. In his 1833 book, *A Moral and Political Sketch of the United States of North America,* Achille Murat described Saratoga this way: "The papas and mamas are ready to die with ennui all the day; the young ladies play music, the young gentlemen make love to them; . . . in the evening comes dancing."[60] A male visitor to the Red Sweet Springs in Virginia reported on the "great many elegant, pretty and agreeable ladies" who enjoyed "charming beaux to wait upon them." He enjoyed being included among the latter, explaining, "I am constantly going from morning till night, first with one & then another. . . ."[61]

The amusements available at early nineteenth-century resorts befitted the class and status of the clientele. These were, for the most part, genteel people pursuing genteel pleasures. Visitors would not have found the raucous entertainments of frontier culture or the seedy pleasures of the urban underworld. There is little evidence of either goose pulls or rat baiting finding their way to watering places in the few decades after 1820.[62] Gentlemen were permitted to gamble and play cards, only so long as ladies were not present. Men and women took care to bathe (in either mineral springs or ocean waters) at separate times. And even when visitors engaged in unusual sorts of activities, they always did so in the most refined manner. Mrs. Read had traveled to Saratoga in August of 1825 in the hopes of recovering her health. While there she received a "polite invitation" to accompany a group to the lake: "We made a little fishing party and I found it a very pleasant amusement as I had the good fortune to catch four. . . . We passed some time in admiring this truly beautiful collection of water; the boat we went fishing in had an awning on top, which made it very comfortable."[63] Fishing was not a customary sort of entertainment for ladies. Mrs. Read's description of the event, however, reveals her efforts to render the outing genteel. The "polite invitation," "very comfortable surroundings," and opportunity to enjoy "truly beautiful water" turned an unusual activity into an acceptable form of female amusement.

The people who frequented these places would have expected no less. Those who patronized resorts and watering places came, primarily, from the more settled parts of the country and the more well-heeled sections of society. The elite had the time and resources to travel, whether for health or for pleasure. William Brobson, himself a respected lawyer and businessman, remarked in his diary in 1825 on the recent "increase" in the "fashionable propensity for tours of pleasure and visiting watering places and sea shore, during the summers when relaxation from the labour of business is desirable." The "wealthy and the fashionable," he observed, had begun to devote part of the summer to traveling to places like Niagara, Saratoga, and Cape May.[64]

Brobson was right. During the second quarter of the nineteenth century wealthy Americans escaped unhealthful cities or plantations, sought cures for ailments, or simply enjoyed themselves at a variety of new summer watering places. Elite southern planters—the Lees of Virginia, the Singletons of South Carolina—regularly took or sent their families, for example, to the springs.[65] Guests at early nineteenth-century resorts came, as well,

The Columbian Spring, Saratoga Springs, New York, c. 1860s. Drinking the water was often a daily ritual. Note the presence of the African-American nursemaid at far right. (Library of Congress, U.S. Geographic File, LC-USZ62-43053.)

from northern families like that of Josiah Quincy, the mayor of Boston who became president of Harvard in 1829.[66] Catharine Sedgwick—member of another well-placed Massachusetts family and, by the 1830s, a well-known literary figure—enjoyed visits to Saratoga, Warm Springs, and White Sulphur.[67] Sidney George Fisher of Philadelphia, someone who could live quite nicely off the income from his family's property, enjoyed himself for a few weeks during summers of the late 1830s at Newport and Long Branch.[68] And elite New Yorker Philip Hone—while claiming he hoped to avoid cholera or other diseases plaguing New York during the summer months—was clearly seeking and finding a variety of pleasures in his yearly summer visits to Saratoga, Ballston, and Long Island.[69]

It was primarily people like the Quincys, Sedgwicks, and Hones, along with southern planters and their wives, who frequented watering places during the first half of the century. While not members of an idle aristocracy, neither were they people whose days were consumed with the problems of earning a living. Able to leave their investments, plantations, domestic responsibilities, or business affairs for extended periods of time, many visitors to early nineteenth-century watering places were not so much taking a vacation from work as changing their location in a search for health and enjoyment.

People with limited or even moderate economic resources found little opportunity for such extended holidays. Diaries of lawyers, school teachers, businessmen, and farmers in the first half of the nineteenth century rarely mention anything resembling a vacation. Adolphus Stern, for example, was a German Jewish immigrant who lived in Texas, married a Catholic woman, and became active enough in both business and politics to be elected to the Texas House of Representatives in the late 1840s. A man of some means, the owner of a few slaves, Stern's diary still revealed no evidence of anything remotely resembling an extended respite from work—either for health or for pleasure.[70] Half a continent away, Sally and Pamela Brown, school teachers in Plymouth Notch, Vermont, in the mid-1830s, also found no time for anything but work. When they were not teaching school they were busy mending, sewing, and spinning.[71] In the late 1830s John Peters worked as a merchant and an agent. He traveled from Mississippi to New York and back again trying to drum up business or, when that failed, find employment. But he never visited the springs or seashore.[72] The poorest members of society, of course, lacked both the time and the resources for such ventures. Day laborers, struggling journeymen, and domestic servants could not have taken off on "tours" to Newport or "jaunts" to the springs. Neither were farmers able to leave their land for extended summer excursions to summer resorts.

Occasionally evidence surfaces of someone with less than substantial means embarking on something like the sort of trip we have been describing. Hezekiah Prince was a young man who worked first as a customs inspector and then as an insurance agent in a seaport on the coast of Maine. In July of 1826 he traveled with a friend to "old Capt. Bradford's in Herring Gut" where they remained "for a week or more . . . to try the sea air, bathing, &c for the benefit of our health." While health was his stated purpose, his description of the week clearly made it sound like a pleasure trip. He spent his time walking about the island, fishing, lobstering, and bathing. Only once did ill health appear to crimp his style, resulting in his decision not to join a fishing expedition because "they wished to remain out all night which would not have done for invalids."[73]

Prince was not a member of the elite. Neither, of course, was he journeying to a fancy watering place. "Old Capt. Bradford's in Herring Gut" probably did not appear on the Quincy's, Sedgwick's, or Hone's list of destinations. That he was able, however, to spend the week at the shore would have distinguished him from most of his contemporaries. Not until midcentury would people like Prince begin to form a middle-class, vacationing clientele. In the meantime, the ability to leave home for an extended stay remained primarily the preserve of people with substantial means.

——————— •◆•———————

With one important exception. During these decades considerable numbers of people from the middling and lower orders engaged in activities that in some ways resembled vacationing. They attended camp meetings. If the search for health brought the wealthy to springs and seashore, the search for salvation brought many people of meager means to yearly camp meetings. These events were, of course, organized for religious not recreational purposes. But most scholars agree that camp meetings played a critical social function for those who participated.[74] As such, these camp meetings became some of the first nonelite vacation destinations—places where ordinary folk fashioned institutions and conventions that suited both their spiritual and their recreational needs. Not surprisingly, the sites of a few of the early nineteenth-century camp meetings became enduring middle-class vacation resorts in the decades after 1850.[75]

The earliest camp meetings began as Presbyterian revivals on the Kentucky frontier during the last years of the eighteenth century. Presbyterians quickly became disenchanted with the displays of emotionalism that attended camp meetings and within a few years abandoned them to Methodists. Throughout the next four decades Methodists enthusiastically embraced and promoted camp meetings as a means of encouraging religious fervor and increasing the number of their adherents. Methodist encampments grew in number and spread throughout the United States. From Martha's Vineyard to the Minnesota Territory, through Ohio, Indiana, and Pennsylvania, and into the slave states of the South, thousands of Americans flocked to yearly encampments.[76] Camp meetings usually lasted from four to eight days, although a few continued as long as twelve, and drew anywhere from a few hundred to many thousands of people from as far away as fifty miles.[77]

The comments of observers and participants reveal that these camp meetings served more than a religious function. Rural people, especially those living on the frontier, often led lonely lives. A trip to the yearly camp meeting may have been one of the few opportunities to break the monotony, get some relief from the labor of farm and household, meet new people, and socialize in a large group. In 1822 a visitor to a camp meeting in Warrenton, Virginia, estimated that as many as five thousand people attended on Saturday and Sunday, with the number dropping to one or two thousand for the remainder of the week. He described the varied sorts of people who congregated there—some were penitent in their prayer, while others "made great parade about religion with no other view than to exhibit themselves as object of admiration before men." Still others, "disdaining such hipocrisy [*sic*], yet entirely neglectful of the avowed cause of the meeting, gave themselves up, with much zest and glee to the social enjoyment which the large assembly afforded."[78]

Camp meetings attracted not only the pious. Observers—many of them critical of the revivals—frequently mentioned the rowdiness, the immorality, and the people selling and drinking whiskey on the fringes of the encampments. Organizers, too, recognized that large crowds of people often provoked unacceptable sorts of behavior. By the 1830s Methodists were establishing rules and posting a watch to try to keep socializing and unruliness from interfering with religion.[79]

The social nature of camp meetings was apparent not only in the disorderly and sometimes inebriated crowds, but in less egregious sorts of behavior. Young people, for example, took the opportunity of camp meetings to scout out potential mates. Remarks of many who attended sound not unlike those who observed the goings-on at fashionable watering places. Lucien C. Boynton, the president of the Northumberland Academy, visited a Baptist Camp Meeting in Westmoreland, Virginia, in 1842. He recorded in his diary: "On Saturday and Sunday there was not a little prominading [*sic*] and courting on the part of the beaux and belles, somewhat to the vexation of the preachers and the annoyance of the attentive part of the audience."[80] Her experience at an 1846 Georgia Camp Meeting prompted one young woman to record in her diary: "I have attended the Houston camp meeting and enjoyed myself well in one respect. We had beaux in abundance, which always gratifies the vanity of girls—too much for their spiritual good."[81]

Most camp meeting participants lived in tents, often arriving in wagons loaded with all they would need to make themselves comfortable during their stay. The visitor to the 1822 Virginia camp meeting described the tents pitched there as "placed close together," but noted that "about 40 or 50 . . . were very commodious and quite elegant establishments."[82] By the 1830s many encampments, especially in the Midwest, were becoming permanent campgrounds. According to historian Charles Johnson, some of these places had "wooden cottages, some two stories high, substituted for the simple cloth tents."[83] Captain Frederick Marryat described in 1838 a campground near Cincinnati encompassing "an acre and a half . . . surrounded on the four sides by cabins built up of rough boards." A preacher's pulpit at the center was encircled by "hundreds of tents pitched in every quarter." Marryat discovered that these tents included many amenities: "Every article necessary for cooking; mattresses to sleep upon, etc; some of them even had bedsteads and chests of drawers which had been brought in the waggons [*sic*] in which the people in this country usually travel."[84]

Neither did attending camp meetings require abstaining from good food. At Warrenton "the cooks and waiters were all busy (in the rear of the tents), as . . . at a barbecue, or at a tavern on a court day, the former preparing, the latter arranging on the tables the most abundant & choice fare." After dinner those who "strayed about in the surrounding wood" would find there "immense piles of watermelons, barrels of various kinds of cakes, and several sorts of confectionery for sale."[85]

Certainly not all camp meetings offered either commodious accommodations or tasty fare. Many people lived in simple tents and cooked over campfires. Even spartan conditions, however, proved no deterrent to the thousands of people who journeyed yearly to camp meetings throughout the country.

The experience of those who attended camp meetings obviously differed from that of wealthy guests at springs and seaside. Visitors lived primarily in tents rather than in hotels or boarding houses. Camp meetings did not provide the same sorts of opportunities for recreation that elite watering places offered. No fancy balls or bowling alleys. The sociability and occasional rowdiness at camp meetings were by-products rather than the prescribed purpose of the event. Still, the two experiences shared some important characteristics. Attending a camp meeting afforded a trip away from home for a number of days and nights, an opportunity to leave the cares of farm or household behind, and the chance for any number of new social experiences. Just as the wealthy sought physical health at watering places, people of lesser means pursued spiritual restoration at summer camp meetings. If the elite left the springs with renewed health, camp meeting participants may well have returned home in a state of spiritual rebirth, or at least relaxed enough to face chores of farm and homestead.

———————— • ◆ • ————————

In the period, then, between about 1820 and the middle of the nineteenth century a variety of Americans—invalids in search of health, members of the northern elite, southern planters and their families, and folks of limited means pursuing salvation—began to indulge in behavior that resembled vacationing. None, however, would have used the word vacation to describe the experience.

Prior to the 1850s most Americans used the word vacation not to designate a time set aside for travel or recreation, but to refer to students' or teachers' break from school or college.[86] Even *Appleton's Illustrated Hand-Book of American Travel*, a large compendium of information about travel published in 1857, never mentioned the word "vacation." The book claimed to be a guide to the "cities, towns, waterfalls, battle-fields, mountains, rivers, lakes, hunting and fishing grounds, watering places, summer resorts." The author, T. Addison Richards, encouraged Americans to travel, to explore, and to spend as little as a week or as much as the whole summer visiting new places: "Go somewhere, if you can, all of you, and wherever and whenever you go, God speed you on your way and send you duly back wiser, better, and healthier and happier men and women." He used numerous words to describe the people and the experience—traveler, tour, resort, summer stay. But not vacation.[87]

During the 1850s, however, the word vacation slowly crept into both private writing and published works. Richard Henry Dana Jr. took vacations of some sort almost every summer beginning in the early 1840s, referring to them as "excursions" rather than "vacations." But in 1856 he recorded in his diary, "Sailed for England, in the Steamer America, to spend a short vacation." Thereafter he always called his various summer trips vacations.[88]

Dana and others may have started calling their trips "vacations" because articles about vacations began to appear in newspapers and magazines by the 1850s. For example, an 1855 editorial in the *New York Times* entitled "Vacations for Business Men," urged men to put aside their unending quest for wealth and to remember other needs—good health, long life, enjoyment, and a vigorous progeny. Businessmen ought to take a vacation from their labor and allow themselves rest, sport, and recreation; they ought to "grasp at less and enjoy more." Incessant work, the article warned, would result in a life "sans health, sans stomach, sans capacity for all better and higher things."[89] The use of the word vacation signaled a heightened effort to promote the idea of vacationing.

By the early 1850s readers of newspapers and magazines were increasingly likely to hear advice about the advantages of a vacation. In August of 1855 the *New York Times* described the pleasures and benefits of passing time on the still undeveloped shore of northern New Jersey. City people who felt "worn and weary with their Winter's watching" could find "relaxation from the toil of gathering up riches. During the season they revel in these waters of life, or dream away the passing hours on the wooded hillsides—and then when Autumn comes they are back again to the busy mart, when they renew their old contests with the world, and feel again the old heart-burnings, the old cares and the old thirst for money-getting."[90] An article on "The Wilds of Northern New York" that appeared in an 1854 issue of *Putnam's Monthly Magazine* recommended "much in this region to draw hitherward the pleasure-loving." Able to "retire from the busy world, away from its noise and tumult, its cares and perplexities," the traveler to these spots would enjoy not only the healthful influence of "pure air and fresh breezes" but would discover how sublime scenery and sights fed the intellect and the imagination.[91]

Moreover, medical advice about the importance of respite from work and the benefits of travel to various watering places was finding its way from the pages of medical texts to the mainstream press. In 1843 the *Democratic Review* ran an article called "The Medical Philosophy of Traveling" detailing the arguments of physicians who warned of "the wear-and-tear" complaint. Victims of this malady—often characterized by a variety of nervous and digestive problems—were likely to be those urban dwellers who had strained "the thinking faculties." Particularly at risk were "merchants engaged in deep and involving speculations." Such people could, however, find relief "in the relaxation and corporeal exercise sought in a pure rural atmosphere." Citing a number of medical texts, the article maintained that not only ruralizing, but the experience of travel itself, along with beneficial changes in climate, could work wonders for mood, digestion, and appetite.[92] Physicians had been making such claims for a number of decades and advising their patients accordingly. But midcentury began to see such recommendations quoted, summarized, and repeated in the popular press.

As these examples suggest, Americans in the 1850s were being offered new reasons for taking a summer respite from work even as old admonitions about health continued. Where the search for a cure or the protection of the body from disease had motivated many of those who traveled to seashore or mountains in the early nineteenth century, by the 1850s vacationers sought other goals. First, mental and spiritual renewal were becoming as important as physical regeneration. Taking a vacation would make the businessman not only healthier, but more fit for his daily tribulations. The message was, at this point, addressed specifically to men. Middle-class women were, in theory, permanently at leisure and therefore had no "work" from which they needed a vacation. Second, pleasure and amusement were becoming more than an enjoyable by-product of a trip planned for other purposes. Recreation was increasingly an end in itself.

———— •◆• ————

Both the incorporation of the word vacation into public and private discourse and the more frequent endorsement of the benefits of vacationing signaled the beginnings of an important shift in attitudes toward work and leisure. In the early nineteenth century, widely held cultural norms regarded work as the core of a moral and stable social order. Church-going Protestants, especially those living in the Northeast, were likely to spend Sundays listening to sermons on the virtues of work and the potential dangers of play.

Such admonitions perhaps seemed all the more necessary since, in the words of one religious publication, "the fast habits of our modern life" had begun quickly "crowding in."[93] While America was still overwhelmingly rural, the numbers of people living in urban communities grew measurably over the first half of the century. Early industrialization and the growth of commerce were creating numerous smaller cities like Lowell, Massachusetts, and Rochester, New York. By 1850 New York City and Philadelphia could count their residents in the hundred thousands.[94] Such cities hosted a growing variety of commercial amusements. Theaters, "museums" that featured various sorts of entertainment, circuses, and minstrel shows welcomed substantial numbers of paying customers. At the same time prizefighting, horse racing, and a variety of other blood sports attracted an audience of predominantly working-class men.[95]

While much commercial leisure originated in the cities, it reached far beyond the population of urban dwellers. Roads, canals, and early railroads were not only making urban pleasures and dangers more available to rural people, they were also bringing a variety of entertainment—itinerant jugglers, acrobats, menageries, and circuses—into the hinterlands. Like it or not, growing numbers of people had the time, inclination, and money to play.

And many—particularly religious leaders—did not like it. As a range of new commercial amusements started to become available, religious men found themselves faced with "the necessity for some solution" to the "Amusement problem."[96] Where once community surveillance and the dread of divine retribution had kept people on the straight and narrow, a more anonymous urban culture and the decline of strict Calvinist ideas made pleasures both more available and less frightening. As the process of secularization encouraged Americans to "embrace the world," God-fearing Christians and their moral leaders were left with an important question. What sorts of leisure activities were morally acceptable and what were not?[97]

The extremes were pretty clear. At one end, leisure spent in the pursuit of intellectual or spiritual self-improvement fell in the permissible column. Attending lectures and reading moral literature (many still found fiction suspect) were allowed. The other end of the spectrum was equally clear. Bawdy houses, taverns, and blood sports were beyond the pale. But a vast and expanding range of pleasures remained between these two extremes.

Critical in determining acceptable from forbidden pleasures was the distinction between "recreation" and "amusement," a distinction that the Puritans had established centuries earlier. Puritans, for all their celebration of work, were not ascetics. They had recognized the human need for relaxation, endorsing as appropriate recreations like "walking, riding, fishing, fowling, hawking, hunting, ringing, leaping, vaulting, wrestling, running, shooting, singing of Psalmes and pious Ditties." Recreations were uplifting; they refreshed and readied a person for work. Amusements, however, left people enervated and drained. Puritans counted the theater, for example, as one of the worst and most dangerous sorts of amusement. The theater allegedly incited extreme emotions and left the spectators exhausted. It also encouraged degeneracy among the actors who, rather than following an "honest occupation," were "making a profession out of a recreation."[98]

More than two hundred years later many Protestants still clung to the distinction between recreation and amusement as their moral guide, condoning the former and condemning the latter. A contributor to the Congregationalist publication, *The New Englander*, explained in 1851: "A recreation . . . is something which recruits, restores, and prepares the man for better service, and should be engaged in, always, with this end in view." But an amusement left people "wasted," "exhausted," and "with an aching head." Amusement was "pleasure for *pleasure's sake.*" Scripture endorsed recreation but forbad amusement.[99]

It was, however, not always so easy to tell which was which. By the middle of the nineteenth century the distinction between recreation and amusement had grown increasingly muddied. Dancing at a ball might be sinful amusement, but dancing in your home could be healthful and invigorating recreation. Were square dances (cotillions and quadrilles) a form of beneficial and innocent exercise but round dances (waltzes and polkas) an example of disgraceful and promiscuous behavior?[100] Attending the theater could fall in either category, depending on the composition of the audience and the play being presented. With an audience cleansed of rowdies and a carefully chosen playbill, the theater, some maintained, might be an uplifting experience.[101]

In antebellum cities respectable men and women engaged in a variety of amusements—some of which the clergy would have condoned, but others of which remained suspect. Isaac Mickle, a young man reading law in Philadelphia in the 1840s, attempted to negotiate a comfortable course between the array of urban pleasures and his personal moral convictions. Mickle came from a wealthy Quaker family and moved in important circles. He spent much of his leisure time (of which he managed to find a good bit) going to lectures and visiting at the homes of respectable young ladies. But he also engaged in less proper forms of amusement. On New Year's of 1842, reflecting on the year past, he admitted that he had "acquired a knowledge of some games of skill, among which that of billiards is the most interesting and therefore the most dangerous." The danger lay partly in the sort of people whom the game attracted: "A junto of young men more respectable for their birth than their lives—a bevy who move at once in the highest and lowest circles of society." He resolved "to forsake it altogether." While recognizing the moral dangers of billiards, Mickle had few qualms about attending the opera, the theater, and even a "grand ball" where "the company numbered about four hundred, and was very brilliant." Although Mickle himself never danced, he noticed and enjoyed the "many very pretty girls there, and some very good dancers" and "found inducements nevertheless to remain until the end—which was about five o'clock in the morning."[102]

The gradual acceptance of various forms of enjoyment resulted from a complex process by which American culture became more urban and more worldly. In part, the presence and participation of elite people helped to elevate and to bestow gentility and legitimacy upon some amusements. But religious leaders also played an important role. Rather than ceding the realm of leisure to the enemy, some ministers began to argue in favor of amusements, provided they were regulated and controlled by people with religious and moral sensibilities.[103]

The earliest challenge came from liberal denominations, particularly Unitarians. Eschewing the notion of human depravity in favor of a belief in the basic goodness of human nature, Unitarians found little difficulty in embracing the notion that life should afford pleasure. As early as the 1830s William Ellery Channing, the dean of American Unitarianism, began to question the orthodox Protestant distrust of play. In 1837 Channing delivered an address on temperance in which he held that "man was made to enjoy as well as to labor, and the state of society should be adapted to this principle of human nature." He reminded his listeners that God had "implanted a strong desire for recreation after labor" and had "made us for smiles more than for tears." Play was important because it served to preserve a moral order. Unless "innocent pleasures" were available, Channing warned, people would choose dangerous and even "criminal" ones.[104]

Although Channing looked more kindly on the idea of enjoyment, he still drew a distinction between recreation and amusement with which most orthodox ministers would have been comfortable. Pleasures should "refresh, instead of exhausting the system" and not produce "boisterous mirth." The difference came in the sorts of things that, for Channing, counted as acceptable forms of recreation. Such pleasures included not only music, recitations, and lectures but dancing (as long as the dancing did not occur at balls) and a theater that, if reformed, "would take a high rank among the means of refining the taste and elevating the character of a people."[105]

Channing's celebration of play reaffirmed its important relationship to work. The right sorts of amusement would ultimately serve rather than undermine the value of work, because they would "send us back to our daily duties invigorated in body and spirit."[106] Even if Channing's ultimate goal remained the preservation of "invigorated" workers, his endorsement of widely condemned amusements—especially his willingness to countenance the possibility of theater—represented an important challenge to orthodox Protestant thought.[107]

By midcentury the Unitarian magazine *Christian Examiner* was prepared to go well beyond Channing's earlier attempts to redeem certain enjoyments. An 1848 article rehabilitated the notion of amusement itself, arguing that "amusements, under the plan of Providence, form an essential part of the great system of influences by which human faculties are trained." Claiming that pleasures need no longer serve a purpose, the writer implicitly rejected the orthodox distinction between recreation and amusement: "A sufficient reason for participating in them [amusements] is that they give pleasure." The article also challenged traditional Puritan directives against the wasting of time, holding that there was "no better way of spending time than in enjoying what God has given to be enjoyed."[108]

Liberal ministers and religious writers remained a minority voice, but continued to endorse innocent amusements as a means of discouraging harmful and vicious ones—"driving out bad entertainment by providing good."[109] A theater that Christianity had helped to reform and purify, dancing that occurred in the homes of moral and religious people, and a military band that played on the public square at public expense could all help to reform the tastes and guard the morals of pleasure seekers. Even sinful amusement could turn beneficent when put to innocent purpose. A bowling alley, for example, was "a public nuisance" when it attracted "the idle and dissipated . . . for the purpose of gambling." But "a bowling alley made use of in a large city, as the best kind of exercise within their means, by men who spend ten or twelve hours a day leaning over desks in offices and counting-rooms, may be to them the source of health and lengthened days and useful labors."[110] While never discarding the notion that leisure activities could be useful, liberal religious thinkers tried to bestow the virtue of usefulness on a range of ordinarily proscribed amusements even as they made the case for pleasure being its own reward.

These notions issued primarily from Unitarians, a tiny minority of antebellum Christians. Most Protestant ministers, less convinced of the righteousness and virtue of their flock, would have warned their parishioners to stay out of theaters and bowling alleys. But by midcentury a few important ministers within mainstream denominations also began to confront the questions of work and leisure. It was becoming increasingly clear that the growth of commercial culture, especially in the urban Northeast, put numerous temptations in the paths of good Christians. Some ministers realized that simply exhorting their parishioners to work and railing against the evils of amusements would not suffice. Somehow they would have to reckon with the needs and desires for entertainment of even God-fearing Christians. Many resisted, adhering to the orthodox line and preaching prohibition. But others accommodated the more secular culture in the hopes of being able to shape and influence it.

Horace Bushnell's 1848 speech before the Phi Beta Kappa Society of the University of Cambridge reveals how some religious leaders were rethinking the issue. Bushnell, a widely known and controversial Congregationalist minister from Hartford, entitled his speech "Work and Play." He emphasized the importance of both, calling them "the universal ordinance of God for the living races." "No creature lives that must not work and may not play." People work, he held, because they "must, because prudence impels." But play came from "a fund of life that wants to expend itself." Bushnell saw work as an "activity *for* an end," while play was an "activity *as* an end."[111] Bushnell thus challenged those ministers who found play acceptable only when it "prepare[s] for new scenes of labor and usefulness."[112] In fact, Bushnell claimed the reverse—that people worked so that they could play. Work was the "temporary expedient," not life's goal:

> To imagine a human creature dragged along, or dragging himself along, under the perpetual friction of work, never to ascend above it; a creature in God's image, aching for God's liberty, beating ever vainly and with crippled wings that he may lift himself into some freer, more congenial element—this, I say, were no better than to quite despair of man.

He quickly added, however, that he meant not to "derogate thus from the dignity of work." Rather, work was ennobled and honored by serving as preparation for "a state so exalted." In the end, Bushnell saw in play the place where poetry was created, where genius was cultivated, and ultimately where Christian religion resided.[113]

Bushnell's elevated notion of play fit his efforts to make gentility and refinement a part of Christian culture. Good taste and beauty, Bushnell maintained, were "attributes of God." Those who had secured and enjoyed the trappings of refinement—by building lovely houses for example—were not wasting their efforts in frivolous pursuits but were contributing to God's plan: "Architecture, gardening, music, dress, chaste and elegant manners—all inventions of human taste—are added to the rudimental beauty of the world, and it shines forth, as having undergone a second creation at the hand of man."[114] Historian Richard Bushman has explained how during the first half of the nineteenth century refinement became "virtually an expression of godly morals."[115] Some of the pleasures of genteel refinement seemed not unlike the pleasures of genteel play—the beauty of opera, the splendor displayed at a ball. Indeed, Protestantism's embrace of refinement may have helped make acceptable the sorts of leisure—opera, theater, and balls—that wealthy, genteel people enjoyed.

Perhaps no nineteenth-century religious figure reveals both the changing ideas about and continuing conflict over work and leisure as well as does

Henry Ward Beecher. Beecher had imbibed the ethic of hard work from his well-known father, Lyman, who had "vented his nervous energies by exercising on parallel bars and shoveling sand from one corner of his basement to another."[116] In the mid-1840s Beecher, then a struggling young minister in Indianapolis, delivered a series of sermons, published as *Addresses to Young Men*, that sounded the strictest of orthodox Christian admonitions to work hard and shun play.[117] Beecher warned against idleness of any sort, even "reading for the relief of ennui."[118] While he ceded the "*necessity* of amusement" and believed that "gaiety of every degree . . . is wholesome to the body, to the mind, and to the morals," he counseled young men to look to nature and the beauty of God's work for enjoyment. Other sorts of amusements—gambling, horse racing, theater, cardplaying, taverns—bred pools of sin and depravity.[119]

But within a few years Beecher began to alter his message. By the early 1850s he was ministering to the wealthy parishioners of the Plymouth Church in suburban Brooklyn—people who could afford the time and money for relaxation. Beecher quickly came to understand the conflicts his parishioners faced—knowing the importance of work, thrift, and discipline but lured by the pleasures of wealth, luxury, and status.[120] Influenced by the romantic love of nature that had inspired Channing, Bushnell, and others, Beecher began to suggest that leisure and relaxation could be a route to God.[121] Writing in July of 1854 from Lenox, Massachusetts, where he and his family were spending their two-month vacation, Beecher extolled the virtues of leisure:

> Thus to walk, to read now and then some noble passage of some great heart, to fall off again to musing, to read again half aloud or in a murmuring whisper some holy poetry, this it is to be transcendently happy. . . . It is after long labor that such periods of rest become doubly sweet. For unwearied hours one drifts about among gentle, joyous sensations or thoughts, as gossamers or downy seeds float about in the air, moved only by the impulses of a coquetting wind.[122]

The Beecher family stayed on a farm—the very symbol of American industriousness. But for Beecher, the primary purpose of this specific farm was not to produce sweat and yield sustenance but "to lie down upon."[123] Three years later Beecher wrote again about his summer experience, explaining that to enjoy a vacation one must have a "decided genius for leisure." Those equipped with such a genius understood that "you must not be in a hurry to get up in the morning or to retire at night. You must regard it as quite the same, whether you look at a tree ten minutes or thirty."[124] For a culture bred on "early to bed and early to rise," such sentiments were, indeed, radical. Beecher was using language that hinted at the value not just of recreation, but of idleness.

Beecher would no doubt have denied that idleness was his goal. In fact, he would have maintained that the purpose of leisure was self-improvement and education.[125] Neither did Beecher disavow the importance of work. His sermons remained a mélange of often contradictory ideas—sanctioning work and excoriating laziness, then cautioning his parishioners about the hazards of too much activity and pleading the importance of rest and leisure.[126] Still, Beecher's ideas and his example (he regularly vacationed for two months in the summer) served notice that, even in the Protestant Northeast, leisure was gaining respectability.

The South had inherited a different legacy. The earliest southern colonists did not bring with them the divine command to work that had motivated their Puritan counterparts in New England.[127] Elite white southerners had been flirting with leisure long before a few northern ministers began tentatively to tout the virtues of repose. Slavery, of course, played a big part. Eighteenth-century southern planters from William Byrd to Thomas Jefferson recognized the importance of work and attempted to inculcate a work ethic in their children and their slaves.[128] But extolling the value of work was difficult in a society in which the bulk of the labor fell to slaves. For antebellum southerners, work was not necessarily the repository of all virtue. Before northern physicians and ministers had warned about the potential pitfalls of too much work, some southerners were pointing to the North's preoccupation with work as an example not of behavior to be emulated but of a "frenzied acquisitiveness."[129]

Leisure held a different place in the slave South than in the industrializing Northeast. Always wary of being accused of dissipation or laziness, southern writers began in the early nineteenth century to offer a defense of leisure. If work held the potential for degradation, its opposite—leisure—could be a sign of elevation and civilization. And some southerners did invoke this classical notion of leisure, maintaining that being relieved of the necessity for work freed white planters to spend their time in higher pursuits—learning, culture, and public life. The reality rarely matched the myth.[130] By the antebellum decades southern planters—often self-consciously aping the English elite—were more likely to spend their leisure gaming, hunting, or on an extended stay at the springs. The evangelical revivals of the early nineteenth century and the consequent spread of Methodist and Baptist ideas did temper some of the southern enthusiasm for play. Revivals left in their wake prohibitions of gambling, cardplaying, and dancing. Southern evangelicals, like their northern counterparts, found most amusements "suspect."[131] The fact remains, however, that southern planters had recognized leisure as a potential good at a time when most northerners still found virtue to reside almost exclusively in work and industry.

The shifting attitudes toward work and play that surfaced in the mid-nineteenth century found expression, as well, in the endorsement of what came to be known as "muscular Christianity." During the 1850s several ministers, most notably Thomas Wentworth Higginson and Edward Everett Hale, began to decry the then current notion that holiness of the spirit required weakness of the body. Writing for the *Atlantic Monthly* in 1858, Higginson argued that Americans needed strong bodies if they were to succeed in the challenges that contemporary life posed. Once, he explained, the demands of the frontier and the threat from hostile Indians had "created an obvious demand for muscle and agility." But urban Americans, wrongfully believing that "a race of shopkeepers, brokers, and lawyers could live without bodies," found themselves plagued by "the terrible records of dyspepsia and paralysis." Higginson's answer was physical exercise, but not shoveling sand from one corner of the room to another. He advocated, rather, various forms of athletics and play. Swimming, sailing, rowing, skating, baseball, and football would all serve to build healthy, "muscular Christians."[132]

Those who embraced physicality and strenuosity were responding to a host of problems that seemed to be troubling nineteenth-century Protestants. While Higginson had endorsed physical exercise for girls as well as for boys, those who endorsed "muscular Christianity" worried primarily about the health and status of Christian men. The influence of an increasingly large and vocal female constituency in many Protestant churches made some churchmen uneasy. At the same time urban luxuries, consumer goods, and the softness of city life seemed, to some, to be undermining the toughness and manliness of Christian men. Complicating this potential crisis of masculinity were the problems posed by class. Cities increasingly offered a host of urban amusements to serve the population of working-class men—prizefights, gambling houses, blood sports, brothels. Protestant ministers worried that such temptations would prove too great for some of their middle-class parishioners.

Given these concerns, wholesome athletics could serve a multitude of purposes. Athletics required self-discipline and control—virtues that Protestants encouraged as necessary for success in the world of work. Moreover, athletic participation helped to promote and to demonstrate the strength and manliness of Christian men. As importantly, athletics could offer upper-class and middle-class men an alternative to dangerous commercial entertainments and perhaps even lure some working-class men away from ratbaiting and gambling to more innocent sports. By the end of the 1850s numerous men's colleges were beginning to build gymnasiums for their students. During the postbellum decades the YMCA would offer middle-class men a safe place to indulge in sport, helping to make amusement and play acceptable parts of middle-class life.[133]

———— • ◆ • ————

As Americans encountered more leisure opportunities, they also faced a mélange of sometimes contradictory advice about whether and how to enjoy them. While no firm consensus was reached, by midcentury a few guidelines had been established. First, reputable medical opinion counseled the importance of respite from work and the benefits of traveling to places where water, air, climate, and enjoyable company could work some good. Second, some influential religious figures had begun to discover the value of certain kinds of leisure. Although certainly not discarding their commitment to the value of work, some ministers were arguing that play was part of God's plan. A few religious leaders were even tentatively challenging the long-standing Protestant proscription of pleasure for its own sake and, just as tentatively, redeeming a variety of amusements from the realm of sin to the world of morality and respectability. And all of these new ideas were making their way into the public press as popular magazines and newspapers explored the possibilities and advantages of a stay at the seashore, springs, or mountains.

What did all this mean for would-be vacationers? On the one hand, they might feel secure that a trip to a vacation spot rested safely at the moral end of the leisure spectrum. Summer resorts, because they promoted health, fit within even the narrowest definition of acceptable leisure. That more doctors were beginning to argue that sojourns to such places would leave the vacationer refreshed, reinvigorated, and ready to work only reinforced their value.

On the other hand, much that happened *at* summer resorts fell on the other side of the ledger. Dancing, billiards, bowling, cardplaying, and gambling occupied many of the guests. When Mrs. Read described the "pleasure parties and balls" that occurred nightly at Saratoga in 1826, she confided her fears that "this place . . . will prepare more souls for destruction than these efficacious waters will heal infirm bodies."[134] Guests who objected could and apparently did choose to remain aloof from unsuitable activities. Southern evangelicals, for example, frequented the springs of Virginia but never participated in the round of balls and parties.[135] Mrs. Read spent most of her month in Saratoga in quiet repose—drinking the water, attending church, chatting with the other sickly guests at her boarding house, and lamenting the profane and godless behavior of the multitudes around her.[136]

Not all guests shared Mrs. Read's qualms. In fact, large numbers of people apparently felt comfortable participating in what many Americans would have labeled morally questionable amusements. The quest for health, genuine to be sure, no doubt contributed to the ease with which guests enjoyed the pleasures around them. Bathing in mineral waters or ocean surf, for example, could be transformed from a sensuous indulgence to a legitimate cure. The air of legitimacy and respectability that the elite, genteel clientele bestowed upon these resorts may have deflected criticism and helped to assuage the misgivings of some visitors.[137]

But not entirely. Watering places remained on ambiguous moral ground, occupying a shifting and tenuous place on the spectrum of leisure-time pursuits. The endorsements of physicians and the tentative approval of liberal ministers did not totally dispel fears about leisure or play. Leisure remained contested. Indeed, the history of vacations over the next century is eloquent testimony to that contest. Americans struggled to fashion forms of vacationing that would allow them to reconcile their desire for leisure with persistent cultural dictates about the importance of work and the dangers of play. Vacation places became sites where these tensions were mediated and tested, if never entirely resolved.

What the religious debates, medical writings, and newspaper articles of midcentury had done, however, was to make recreation, amusement, and leisure respectable enough so that increasing numbers of the emerging middle class felt willing to contemplate the possibility of a vacation. What they needed were places to go and the means to get there.

❧ 2 ❧

"Summer hotels are everywhere..."

---•◆•---

A FLOOD of
VACATIONERS

In the summer of 1873 Louisa Roberts traveled with her husband, a dentist, from their home in Philadelphia to the Put-in-Bay Islands in Lake Erie near the mouth of the Detroit River. There she found "thousands" enjoying the boating, fishing, bathing, and sunshine. Roberts remarked in her diary that although easterners knew "little . . . of this island watering place, it is very popular with the west and southwest and is yearly growing in importance." She found all the hotels "full to overflowing."[1]

The crowds at places like Put-in-Bay testified to the increasing importance of vacationing among the emerging middle class. Beginning in the 1850s and only temporarily interrupted by the Civil War, the growth of vacationing proceeded rapidly in the three decades after 1870. Expanding numbers of vacationers demanded new resorts, and savvy entrepreneurs accommodated the growing vacationing public. Railroads played a critical role, providing not only the means of getting vacationers where they wanted to go, but the advertisements to lure them and the capital to build many resorts. Supply and demand worked in tandem, making vacationers and vacation spots more prevalent and more visible in the American social landscape.

Along the coasts, in the mountains, near rivers and lakes—summer vacation places sprung up throughout the country. No one region claimed a
monopoly. Rather, vacationing was one of the things that the middle class
came to share, regardless of where they lived. While the specific nature of
their vacations could vary considerably, members of the middle class
increasingly participated in the event called "taking a vacation." Indeed,
over the last half of the nineteenth century, part of what distinguished middle-class people from those lower down the social ladder was the possibility,
if not necessarily the guarantee, of a summer vacation.

———•◆•———

Reading in their newspapers and hearing from ministers and doctors that
recreation could be good for them, more men and women began during the
1850s to venture from home for at least short pleasure trips. They were able
to do so, in part, because of changes in the nature of middle-class work during the last half of the nineteenth century. The growth of large corporations,
mass retailers, and expanding government bureaucracies brought with
them the demand for an army of white-collar employees. Clerks, salespeople, bookkeepers, and midlevel managers joined the professionals, school
teachers, and small entrepreneurs who inhabited the ranks of an expanding
American middle class. Distinguished from the working class by their with-
drawal from manual labor and their more privileged educational back-
grounds, the middle class also shared a commitment to domesticity and
refinement.[2]

But economically, the middle class was a diverse group. People who
counted themselves members earned widely different salaries. At the high
end were successful male entrepreneurs and professionals. Those who
managed to create successful businesses and booming practices earned
comfortable incomes—as much or more than $3,000 a year—but they also
risked financial disaster should clients or customers stop coming in the
door.[3]

Middle-class employees, on the other hand, often earned less, sometimes
a lot less. Their incomes varied considerably, depending on such specifics
as occupation, industry, location, and gender. The women who clerked in
government offices in Washington, D.C., earned, on average, between $900
and $1200 per year—very good pay for a nineteenth-century woman. Male
federal clerks did better than the women, the majority making at least $1400
a year, and a few drawing salaries of $2,000 or more.[4] Government salaries,
especially for low-level clerks, often ran higher than those in the private sector. An 1875 study by the Massachusetts Bureau of Statistics of Labor found
that male salaried employees—defined as people in "occupations involving
chiefly mental and literary qualifications"—earned an average of $1016 per

year while their female counterparts averaged only $429.[5] But for some white-collar employees private industry held the potential for substantial salaries. Bank cashiers and accountants could make over $2,000 a year, and Macy's department store allegedly paid its male and female buyers from $1,300 to $1,500.[6] School teachers fared much worse. Urban male school-teachers averaged about $33 a week, while women made less than half that much.[7] Historian Stuart Blumin has aptly characterized the nineteenth-century urban middle class as people "living well but lacking great wealth." Middle-class men and women "represented a specific set of experiences, a specific style of living, and a specific social identity."[8]

In the years after the Civil War one characteristic of a middle-class "style of living" increasingly came to include the possibility of a summer vacation. The structure of much middle-class work helped to make such vacationing possible, as white-collar employees in private or government offices found themselves the beneficiaries of a designated period of paid vacation. During the postbellum decades many businesses, sensitive perhaps to both medical and popular warnings about the dangers of overwork, were making at least one week's paid vacation standard practice for "brain workers."[9] George Whitwell Parsons, a young bank clerk in San Francisco, noted in his diary in June of 1879: "Busy day as all the week is in fact for me, as Stombs is away this week on his vacation and I do his work and mine."[10] A few weeks later it was Parson's turn. He spent his week of vacation visiting friends, riding to Congress Springs, going to the beach near Santa Cruz, and enjoying the countryside. The bank for which young Parsons worked was not unusual. White-collar workers in federal government offices were routinely allowed a full month's paid vacation each year—a singularly generous amount of time. Most businesses were more likely to follow the policies of the bank in which young Parsons worked, a week off each year.[11]

The press took notice of both the increasing size of the vacationing public and its growing middle-class character. An article in the *New York Herald* observed as early as 1847 that "a large number of beautiful girls, evidently belonging to the middle classes as well as to the wealthy or fashionable families," were frequenting Saratoga that season.[12] Five years later an editorial in the *New York Times* explained that although "each year adds largely to the accommodations provided for tourists, and seekers of health, pleasure, gayety, or rural quiet, . . . the human tide seems to flood them more completely than ever." During the previous winter numerous existing resorts had expanded and new hotels had been built, but "these emphatic efforts to keep pace with the times proved unavailing. The reinforcements of the traveling public took all preparations by storm, and proved them inadequate to the occasion." As a result, many a "luckless" vacationer "has been compelled to make his couch upon a sofa, or hang up in the barber's office, until more comfortable quarters could be provided."[13]

Newspapers not only described but helped to foster the growing interest in vacationing. During the 1850s advertisements for "summer retreats" began to appear in big city newspapers, while regular society columnists, some with alliterative pen names like "Minnie Myrtle," began writing columns about the goings-on at various resorts, aiming to whet the appetite of city dwellers and prodding them to undertake a summer vacation.[14]

"Leo" (one of numerous pseudonymous contributors to the *New York Times*) described how he suffered in the sweltering city in the early part of the summer, gazing daily at newspaper pictures "of the serene and purified existence whereof others had a realization in the distance far away." Reading such reports "so raised [his] thirst for roaming" that he decided to make one attempt at "ruralizing": "I would forget for a month the fluctuations in breadstuffs, the siege of Sebastopol, the rise and fall of domestics, and the prices of stocks. . . . Where there's a will there's a way. I had enough, and to spare, of the will—the way was not so abundant—the means not at all superfluous." After reading about the various "Summer Retreats," he concluded that Newport, Saratoga, Sharon, Niagara, and the White Mountains were not suitable for "a new beginner." Rather he decided to try closer to home—"the banks of the Hudson, or at the farthest the sea-coast of the Jerseys" and settled on Navesink on the Jersey Shore.[15]

People like "Leo" faced an increasing number of vacation choices as numerous new summer resorts appeared on the horizon during the 1850s. Would-be vacationers could find destinations not only along the banks of the Hudson or on the New Jersey shore, but in the Catskill and Franconia Mountains.[16] While many of these resorts served large urban populations of the Northeast, other sections of the country also sprouted vacation places. Some southerners, perhaps finding the antislavery climate of the North increasingly inhospitable, looked to places closer to home.[17] Although the Virginia Springs remained popular, by the 1850s Georgia, Tennessee, South Carolina, and Louisiana could boast vacation sites.[18] Randal McGavock's experience reveals both the range of choices and the growth of vacationing in the South. In August of 1857 McGavock, a lawyer and a member of an important Nashville family, visited a "new hotel" on Lookout Mountain in Tennessee. Finding it difficult to make acquaintances at Lookout, McGavock and his wife left for Catoosa Spring in Georgia where they found "a great crowd." But Catoosa, too, had its drawbacks. Most importantly, no rooms were available. Consequently, "the ladies were put in the attic with three or four others and I was sent over to Buzzards Roost where I remained separated from my wife about one week." If that were not bad enough, McGavock was plagued "every night by the infernal noise kept up by Dr. Oliver and his drunken associates." It took a week before the McGavocks moved into more suitable quarters in the hotel.[19]

The expansion of vacation resorts had begun in earnest by the 1850s. The Civil War put a temporary damper on the enthusiasm for resort building, especially in the South. Many of the Virginia springs, for example, either closed or were converted to hospitals during the war.[20] But the postwar years saw a flood of new vacationers and new vacation places throughout the country.

The railroads fueled much of that expansion and contributed, as well, to the democratization of vacationing. The twenty-five years after the Civil War brought more than a fourfold increase in the number of railroad miles operating in the United States.[21] While some watering places had been accessible by steamship throughout the antebellum period, others could only be reached by long travel in uncomfortable coaches over bumpy and sometimes dangerous roads. A trip could take days, depending upon the destination. Railroads changed all that, making travel quicker, easier, more comfortable, and cheaper, and bringing seashore, mountains, and countryside closer to the population of American towns and cities.[22]

The railroads fed the vacation industry in a variety of ways. The growing demand for vacation places led residents of small towns along the railroad to market their villages and hamlets as summer resorts—even when the sites offered little in the way of natural beauty or amenities. Bethlehem, New Hampshire, for example, was by 1880 attracting "hay fever sufferers and exhausted brain-workers" although its attractions, a correspondent for the *New York Times* admitted, were few: it "[is] not beautiful, nor is it a town. It is simply a long street . . . lined with a few hotels and houses, all of them built with a due regard for cheapness and plainness." Bethlehem's only appeal lay in its situation on the rail line and its location "as a central point from which to visit all the places of interest in the White and Franconia Mountains." These were apparently sufficient to make it, according to this report, "crowded, chiefly . . . with Boston people."[23] Communities positioned along rail lines discovered that they could advertise themselves as places of "summer retreat" for those who wanted to escape the heat of the big cities. In the process barren country towns became vacation destinations.

Some railroad companies invested directly in the development of resorts along or at the end of their lines, seeing this as a good way to increase ridership. The Camden and Atlantic Railroad owned the land company that helped to build Atlantic City. As historian Charles Funnell has explained: "[I]t was a happy arrangement: the railroad would increase the value of the Land Company's holdings, and the sale of land would bring customers for the railroad."[24]

Other railroads built lines to service already existing resorts, speculating that demand for access to such places would make the lines profitable. In 1869 the Chesapeake and Ohio laid tracks directly to the front gate of White Sulphur Springs. A trip that in the 1830s took four or five days of uncomfortable travel from Washington, D.C., and that during the 1850s required at least one overnight stay, could now be made relatively comfortably within fifteen hours. Many of the investors in the railroad had been longtime visitors to White Sulphur, and they must have felt confident of the resort's ability to lure enough guests to fill railroad cars.[25] Proprietors of southern watering places no doubt hoped that rail service would make their resorts attractive to northern visitors, for within a year of the railroad's arrival at White Sulphur the resort was running ads in the *New York Times* that read: "Round trip tickets from New York, with ample allowance of time to the visitors, only $27.45."[26]

While the White Sulphur was the first Virginia spring to have a railroad stop directly at its front gate, by the mid-1870s both the Chesapeake & Ohio and the Virginia and Tennessee railroads brought travelers to a number of depots from which they could catch either stage or canal connections to other springs.[27] It took only a few years before additional springs enjoyed the advantage of direct rail service. Blue Ridge Springs in Botetourt County, Virginia, advertised in 1874: "No staging or jostling in discomfort and danger over mountain roads is necessary to reach this delightful resort. The visitor steps from the platform of the palatial coaches of the Atlantic, Mississippi & Ohio Railroad, to the beautiful piazza of the hotel."[28]

Railroad companies in other parts of the country also gambled that lines to summer resorts would pay. In 1871 the Sheboygan and Fond du Lac Railroad built a depot at Green Lake in Wisconsin to service those visiting Greenway's Hotel—a resort that had opened in 1866 and served vacationers from Chicago. The railroad helped to create a snowball effect: railroad service to the lake encouraged other entrepreneurs to build hotels. The result was an increase in both the number of riders and vacationers.[29]

Sometimes the connection between vacationer, resort, and railroad was even more direct. In 1874 "Diamond" Joe Reynolds, a resident of Chicago who had made his fortune in grain and steamboats, embarked on a visit to Hot Springs, Arkansas. He took the train as far as it went, but then had to transfer to a coach. The rest of the trip proved a nightmare; the coach broke down and Reynolds had to spend the night in a local farmhouse. The experience convinced Reynolds to build a line all the way to the springs.[30]

Whether or not railroad investors also had a financial interest in the resort that their lines serviced, they certainly wanted to keep the trains full. The equation was simple. The more visitors at summer watering places, the more revenue generated for the railroads that carried them there. Consequently rail companies actively promoted vacationing by advertising for the resorts along their routes. By the 1880s railroads were publishing booklets and guides that offered detailed information on excursion routes, hotels, summer cottages, and country farmhouses.[31]

Promotional brochures stressed the ease of train travel, but advertisements—then as now—often lied. Many vacationers discovered that rail travel could be an arduous experience. An early visitor to Atlantic City described the dust during the train trip as "something fierce." "Everybody wore a linen or alpaca duster, a very necessary adjunct when traveling in those days. Any passenger that reached Atlantic City without getting his or her eyes full of cinders was looked upon as a curiosity."[32] Not only the heat and the dust, but the behavior of fellow passengers could make rail travel a trial. One disgruntled male customer complained in 1865 that the company sheltered its female customers from unsavory conditions, but subjected male riders to decidedly substandard accommodations. This particular rider found the service from New York to Saratoga wanting:

> The railway routes are deficient . . . in commonest courtesies of life. . . . [T]he best of the old fashioned cars . . . are reserved for 'gentlemen accompanied by ladies,' and single gentlemen without crinoline are unceremoniously thrust into what is inappropriately known as a 'gentlemen's smoking car.' It should be called 'the loafers' groggery,' for smoking, drinking, tobacco squirting, profanity and gambling are indulged in to the fullest degree. The car or cars thus appropriated are generally crowded to excess, more or less full-fare passengers being compelled to stand in these pest-houses until room is made by the arrival of passengers at their places of destination, or by some more knowing than the rest, stealing an opportunity to secure a seat in one of the half-filled ladies' cars. Remonstrance is in vain.[33]

Rail travel varied from line to line and improved as the century progressed. An 1875 article in *Lippincott's* claimed—although no doubt with some exaggeration—that a traveler from Philadelphia to Cape May would experience "no trouble, no fatigue, no vexation about luggage" during the three-hour trip. While rail travel was not always comfortable or clean, passengers could be fairly sure that the iron horse would bring them to their destination faster than coach or stage. People from Philadelphia could get to Atlantic City or Cape May in three hours, New Yorkers could be in the Catskills within half a day.[34]

As more railroads snaked through the country, vacation places took shape along the seashores, in the mountains, and near rivers and lakes. Fittingly, many such spots appeared near large population centers. Northeastern newspapers began to report on a number of new places now available within a reasonable distance of New York, Boston, and Philadelphia. By the last half of the 1860s correspondents from the *New York Times* were visiting and writing from a variety of new resorts. An article in 1865, for example, reported on the people visiting the "gaily situated" Pequot House in New London, a Connecticut town on Long Island Sound, and asserted that Brattleboro, Vermont, had become "one of the most delightful of the smaller inland places of Summer resort."[35] That same year the *Chicago Tribune* touted the charms of the Mansfield House in Stowe, Vermont, a new hotel that accommodated three hundred guests and could be reached by a smooth ten-mile coach ride from a railroad depot of the Vermont Central.[36] Apparently pleasure seekers from as far away as Cleveland, Cincinnati, and Chicago were traveling to resorts along the New England seacoast.[37] Five years later Lake George in upstate New York, Watch Hill on the coast of Rhode Island, and Fire Island, six miles off the coast of Long Island, were receiving summer guests, as were a variety of spots along the Hudson River and the Connecticut shoreline, on Staten Island, in the White Mountains, and on Thousand Island in Alexandria Bay.[38] In 1855 a reporter had characterized Cape Cod as "interesting from its barrenness"; by 1883 Cape Cod was, according to *Century* magazine, becoming "like all the rest of the New England coast, . . . familiar with the aspect of the summer visitor."[39]

Not only the Northeast saw the expansion of summer resorts. Indeed, vacation places appeared throughout the country. Virginia, which had long been known for a score of antebellum springs added new names to its summer attractions—Coyner Springs, Yellow Sulphur, Locust Grove, Mountain Top, Cobb's Island.[40] In the last two decades of the century North Carolina, Tennessee, and Georgia began to develop more resorts. The *Southern Bivouac,* a southern literary magazine, devoted three articles in the mid-1880s to southern summer resorts. It noted the popularity and accessibility of places like the Cloudland House on Roane Mountain in North Carolina, Lookout Mountain outside Chattanooga, White Cliff Springs "on the promontory of the Chillowees, a Tennessee foot-hill chain of rather moderate elevation," and Tallulah in Northern Georgia.[41]

The Midwest, too, sprouted new resorts—some large and fashionable, others small and quiet. The expansion of rail lines throughout the country meant that even people living in small midwestern towns had access to the burgeoning variety of vacation places. Orville Browning, a former cabinet member in the administration of Andrew Johnson, could, in July of 1870, take the train from his home in Quincy, Illinois—a town on the western edge of the state—and arrive at Versaille Springs two and a half hours later. Other summers Browning visited Perry Springs, another resort within a short distance of his home. Perry Springs was a small resort, accommodating between thirty and eighty people, although it apparently drew guests from as far away as St. Louis and New Orleans.[42] Lakes in southern Wisconsin were also becoming popular vacation places by the late 1860s, attracting people from Chicago, Milwaukee, Memphis, and New Orleans. Mackinac Island, at the juncture of Lakes Huron and Michigan, was by the end of the nineteenth century among the largest and most fashionable midwestern resorts.[43]

During the same years vacationing also came into vogue in the West. In the early 1870s people from Carson City and Virginia City journeyed to Lake Tahoe for rest and recreation. By 1872 Colorado Springs had opened the Manitou House, described by one visitor as a "well furnished" new hotel with "spacious and very comfortable" rooms "and the accommodations in all respects excellent."[44] Residents of Portland vacationed at Clatsop Beach, "the great watering place of Oregon."[45] *Harper's* magazine did an article in 1882 on "Some Western Resorts," reporting that "thousands flock" to the lakes and forests of the Northwest.[46]

By the last decade of the century vacation places had so proliferated that *Century Magazine* declared: "Summer hotels are everywhere. They form an almost continuous line along the coast of New England and the Middle States. One mountain region after another has succumbed to their invasion."[47] And while not all summer resorts were financial successes, many welcomed growing numbers of vacationers. People who visited summer resorts often testified in their diaries and letters to their crowded conditions. During her 1873 trip to the Put-in-Bay Islands, Louisa Roberts and her husband stayed at a hotel that could "comfortably accommodate one thousand guests" but that "at present" housed "nearly fifteen hundred."[48] Charles Ellis wrote to his brother from Warm Springs, Virginia, in the summer of 1881, noting that the proprietor was "at his wits end to provide for new comers."[49] Another report that summer from Fannie Cocke, also staying at Warm Springs, confirmed that "We have a crowd here now, & it requires great management to room them. . . . John [the proprietor] does not like it to be said that there are no vacancies as it prevents others from coming & he can really accommodate them in the place of those who leave, tho' he really has had his rooms filled for some time. This is the best season he has ever had & I hope it will continue so all summer."[50] The following summer looked just as promising for the proprietor of Warm Springs, who apparently had decided it was no longer a good idea to receive guests for whom he had no accommodations. Fannie Cocke reported to her brother: "We have a great crowd & John has had to telegraph people they could not possibly get a room."[51]

The railroads thus helped to ensure the survival of well-known, established antebellum watering places and served, as well, as midwives for the birth of new vacation sites. By reducing the expense of travel and shorten-

The Boardwalk, Atlantic City, New Jersey, 1897. Railroads helped to keep resorts like Atlantic City crowded with vacationers. (Library of Congress, Stereopticon File, LC-USZ62-73677.)

ing its time, the railroad helped to increase the size and alter the demographic makeup of the vacationing public. One no longer needed months of free time or buckets of money to travel. The availability of moderately priced train service meant that people with only a week or two to spare and sufficient discretionary funds could entertain the idea of a summer vacation. As more members of the middle class found themselves working in environments that promised both a fairly steady salary and a short annual vacation, middle-class men and women swelled the population of American vacationers.

Reflecting the class from which they came, these middle-class vacationers included a varied and eclectic assortment of people. A closer look at the clientele of Mohonk Mountain House reveals the range of people who were finding their way to summer resorts and suggests the possible impact of the vacation experience on this diverse nineteenth-century middle class. In 1870 Alfred Smiley, a Quaker school teacher, bought a run-down tavern on three hundred beautiful acres of land and lake at Paltz Point in New York. That summer he and his twin brother Albert opened their resort to forty guests, most of them friends from Philadelphia. The Smiley brothers quickly went to work improving and expanding their property—adding a telegraph office, a dining room building, a bowling alley, and accommodations for more guests. Within a few years of its opening, Mohonk Mountain House was receiving hundreds of inquiries from potential customers.[52]

The Smiley family continued to own Mohonk for more than a century and saved mountains of records and documents. Guest correspondence from the earliest years of the resort's history shows the assortment of vacationers who were taking advantage of the opportunities that rail travel, the opening of new resorts, and the new middle-class work routines offered. While all Mohonk's guests could claim membership in the middle or upper class, the clientele formed a diverse group who fashioned an array of different summer experiences.

Professionals and small businessmen who sought a week or two in the country and could manage to leave their practices or companies for a short time found Mohonk a good prospect. Eugene Du Bois, a commission merchant, requested two rooms at Mohonk for nine days in August of 1873. One room was for himself and his wife, and another for his parents.[53] Similarly A. N. Luchs, a "Manufacturer of Lace and Mourning Goods," sought a place where he could fish and boat. He wanted "the best terms on which you will keep me for about two weeks, commencing next week. I want a good room although it need not command the best views, as I do not intend spending a great deal of time in it."[54]

Mohonk attracted others who would no doubt have considered themselves within the middle class. F. H. Romceine, for example, wrote to the proprietor of Mohonk in early July of 1871 asking for information about prices and accommodations: "What will you charge for two young gentlemen, want to room together, 1 bed in room, want a pretty decent kind of room, are your boats in the Lake free to Boarders of the House, have you any young folks coming to stay there this summer, want the room from 15th July until 1st August. . . . Make your terms as low as you can for a good room."[55] Walter Leech had considerably less time to spend, but still wanted to visit a resort: "Myself and friends are desirous of finding some place to spend the 4th, 5th, & 6th of July. Please send by return mail price of board per day, fare & means of reaching the hotel."[56] Both of these letters arrived on business letterhead on which neither Romceine's nor Leech's names appeared, suggesting that these men were clerks who had been granted

Mohonk Mountain House, New York, c. 1900–1906. Mohonk Mountain House opened in the early 1870s and by the turn of the century was a large, well-established resort. (Library of Congress, Detroit Publishing Company Photograph Collection, LC-D418-14544.)

vacation time and were looking for a place to spend it. Eliza J. Lee of Brooklyn wrote in June of 1872 asking whether she and "two friends (teachers like myself)" could be accommodated for a week in early July. She recalled the enjoyable week she had spent at Mohonk the previous year and wondered "whether your terms are the same as last year, $10."[57] Edward A. Casey, an employee at the "Fidelity Ins. Trust and Safe Dep. Co." in Philadelphia asked about finding rooms for himself and his mother "for two weeks from the first of August (about which time I desire to take my business vacation)." His mother was "elderly and not strong" and he wanted her to "be comfortable." He explained, however, that his salary would "not warrant me (if I take her with me on holiday) in too much expense."[58]

Mohonk's vacationers shared middle-class status, but guests' economic circumstances varied considerably. Vacation places like Mohonk may have helped give coherence to a middle class that by the last half of the nineteenth century was growing increasingly incoherent and diverse. Not only was vacationing becoming a shared middle-class experience, but the very sites at which middle-class people vacationed offered opportunities for a relatively disparate array of people to come together for enjoyment and relaxation.

Male clerks, for example, who could afford only a few days off vacationed next to the sort of businessmen for whom they worked. If many middle-class male employees could no longer realistically aspire to owning businesses of their own, they could at least frequent some of the same resorts, enjoy the same leisure activities, and indeed rub elbows with those who had become successful entrepreneurs and professionals. As well as affording the chance for rest and recreation, a vacation spent at Mohonk may have reaffirmed status for those men whose class standing felt ambiguous or insecure and provided some compensation for the wealth and autonomy that remained out of reach.

For middle-class women a stay at such resorts no doubt also served a variety of functions. Many simply enjoyed a break from the daily cares of running a household and the chance to relax and socialize. Arriving at the dining room for meals must have been a welcome change for women who oversaw and—in households with few servants—participated in the purchase, preparation, and serving of daily meals. Married women often brought servants and nurses who relieved them of the care of children. The presence of servants, however, also helped to advertise the status and wealth of the matron. Not all female vacationers traveled with servants in tow. Many young school teachers, for example, could barely manage a week's stay at a place like Mohonk, but found themselves vacationing alongside wealthier married women comfortably ensconced at the resort for weeks or even months. Were the former perhaps watching the latter with an eye toward what the future might hold if they "married well"? For some female guests such a vacation could have offered a glimpse of future possibilities.

Ironically, those businessmen and professionals on the higher end of the middle-class spectrum sometimes found it more difficult to take vacations than did clerks and employees. Leaving a business or practice was sometimes impossible even for those with the financial means to take a vacation. Such men did, however, make sure that their families enjoyed the benefit of a vacation. Many such families planned for wives and children to stay at vacation spots while husbands remained in the city, commuting to the lake, seashore, or country on the weekend and perhaps joining the family for a week or two as business permitted. As early as 1872 letters from families seeking just such arrangements deluged Albert Smiley, proprietor of Mohonk Mountain House. Mohonk could be reached from New York in about five and a half hours—four on the train, another hour and a half in a coach up the mountain.[59] The trip was too long for father to make daily, but not too onerous for a once-a-week visit.

Some railroads even established special lines that catered specifically to weekend commuters. Richfield Springs, an inland resort "nearly 300 miles" from New York City, succeeded in attracting male guests with the help of the "married men's" train. The *New York Times* explained: "This train is composed of sleeping cars, which leave the springs every Sunday night for New York and Philadelphia over the Lackawanna Road, and are generally filled with elderly gentlemen and young unmarried men who have been spending the Sabbath with their families and sweethearts."[60] Families from Chicago vacationing at the Fountain House in Waukesha, Wisconsin, followed similar patterns. Four daily trains made it possible for "gentlemen from Chicago . . . to spend Sunday . . . with their families, and return to the city in time for business on Monday morning."[61]

Some families devised various means of reducing the cost of such vacations. Occasionally papa, back in the city, moved out of the house and into cheaper, less commodious quarters while his family was away. Matthew Deady, a lawyer in Portland, Oregon, did this two summers during the 1870s. In early July of 1872 Deady recorded in his diary: "Moved my bed down to my chambers where I expect to lodge until Sept. . . . Had furniture moved out of house and stored upstairs in Parrish brick, No [90] Front Street." The following week he reported that he had "commenced boarding at widow Reeds."[62] The Deady family made similar arrangements in 1878. In late May of that year Deady recorded that they were "packing up and getting ready to leave our home. . . . On Thursday morning we bade good bye to our old home and Gen Sawtelle and family moved in." His wife and sons left for Salem and "on the evening of the same day I slept in Sawyers Chambers, having fitted them up for that purpose with his consent during the week. I am to pay $5 per month the first month and $4 thereafter for the use of a bed and bedstead, bureau and towel rack to Powers the furniture man. I pay $20 a month for board with corresponding deduction any whole days absence."[63] This arrangement apparently allowed Matthew to have the vacation *he* wanted. When his family returned at the end of August he and his son commenced a three-week trip to San Francisco, Virginia City, Lake Tahoe, and Sacramento that he called his "vacation."[64]

Many men chose to join their families for a week or two during the summer. James B. Bouck, a partner in a provision broker's business, wrote to Mohonk looking for a place for his wife and child "from the third week in July until the end of August. I desire that they be *comfortably located*. . . . I may possibly conclude to remain with them for a couple of weeks."[65] R. D. Fonda sought a place for his wife, their two children—ages six years and fourteen months—and a nurse: "I expect to remain with my family a fortnight, and shall then return to the city, and leave them to stay until Sept. 1st, or later, provided they are pleased."[66]

HO! for the SEA SHORE!

Hygeia Hotel,
Old Point Comfort, Virginia.

Harrison Phoebus,
Proprietor.

*188_*

Potomac Steamboat Co.'s
DAILY LINE
——FOR——
NORFOLK, FORTRESS MONROE,
(OLD POINT COMFORT,)
PINEY POINT and POINT LOOKOUT.

Steamers GEORGE LEARY and EXCELSIOR leave 7th Street Wharf daily, (except Sundays,) at 5.30 P. M. Saturdays at 6 P. M.

Fare to NORFOLK and FORTRESS MONROE, $1.00. Round Trip, $1.50.
Fare to PINEY POINT & POINT LOOKOUT, - 50. Round Trip, $1.00.

Special feature of the Line **Saturday Night Excursions**, enabling business men to spend Sundays at the sea shore without loss of time. Special boat leaves Old Point Sunday evenings, arriving at Washington Monday in time for business.

FOR PASSAGE AND ROOMS, APPLY TO

REED'S SONS, 1216 F st., N. W.; B. & O. TICKET OFFICE, 14th and Penn. Avenue; ST. MARE HOTEL; POLKINHORN'S, next to Post Office; KNOX EXPRESS, 6th and Penn. Avenue; and COMPANY'S OFFICE, 7th street Wharf.

☞ KNOX EXPRESS calls for and checks baggage.

L. M. HUDGINS, Gen. Supt.   **C. A. TAYLOR,** Gen. Ticket Ag't.
W. P. WELCH, Agent.

Not only railroads but steamboat companies also advertised special lines for men who wanted to join their families at summer resorts for the weekend. This specific advertisement dates from the 1880s. (CSX Corporation, Richmond, Virginia.)

Those who could not afford to send the family to a resort like Mohonk had other options in the years after 1870. "Summer boarding" had long been available to wealthy, elite families who had retreated for most of the summer to cottages, country homes, or hotels. In the postwar decades well-placed people continued to avoid the heat of cities or disease-ridden plantations, much as they had done in the antebellum years. What changed after the war, however, was that summer boarding, something that had once been reserved for the wealthy, became a possibility for middle-class people with modest resources.

The railroads made it feasible for families to find summer quarters close enough to the city so that husbands could commute daily for work and return in the evenings to their wives and children in the country or along the shore. An article in the *New York Times* in 1885 maintained, "No question is of more concern to the average city household just now than how to avoid the coming hot weather." New Yorkers, however, were lucky enough to have an "almost endless variety of ways and places that tempt a trial." This article listed numerous sites on Long Island where people could board at summer cottages or boarding houses "on terms remarkably low" and specifically noted that "the south shore of the island is almost lined with charming spots." Among other possibilities were Freeport, Rockville Centre, and South Oyster Bay. Such places offered "small but homelike hotels, enough cottagers and summer boarders to insure pleasant society, and contact with a wholesome class of residents." Moreover, according to this correspondent, "whether hotel or boarding house life may be preferred, terms can be made that will be within modest reach and which need not add materially to ordinary expenses." Thus, "one whose duties do not keep him in town in the evening can manage with little trouble to take his family out of town and to join them at night without running expenses above what they would be if the family remained in town." Not surprisingly, the reader would learn, the Long Island Railroad had "prepared a list of the hotels and boarding houses along its lines . . . and one can see for himself the wonderful resources of Long Island in this respect by sending for a list."[67]

Summer boarding was somewhat different from, if still related to, vacationing. Most notedly, summer boarding did not necessarily afford the entire family a vacation. Men who commuted daily to jobs in the city were not, of course, on vacation, although they could enjoy the benefits of country air or cool sea breezes in the evenings and on Sundays. Regardless of whether husbands returned each evening or only on the weekends, summer boarding ostensibly benefited wives and children. Just as more prosperous members of the middle class installed women and children in places like Mohonk, those on the lower end of the middle-class ladder looked to this proliferation of inexpensive summer lodgings. But women stuck in stuffy boarding houses with uncooperative landlords and cranky children, or those whose summer accommodations were more primitive than their city houses, may not have considered the experience much of a vacation.

One disgruntled guest wrote a letter to the editor of the *New York Times* in June of 1870, complaining that the newspapers were "writing up the country watering places" and luring innocent victims to less-than-acceptable summer abodes. His wife, child, and baby had made arrangements to board at a country farmhouse, at the cost of $17 a week for one room. They expected "fresh vegetables, an abundance of milk and fruit, good butter, good bread, white sugar." What they got was "a vile mess of flour baked with soda, ... hard, dry, alkaline, and in no sense good bread." The landlord allotted them only one pitcher of milk at breakfast "that had the best part of the cream, if not the whole of it, skimmed off." And they were served "hash, and poor hash at that, three to five times a week." They stuck it out for three weeks, "until seeing that endurance of it was destroying our health and pleasure, we left."[68] An editorial in *The Nation* maintained that problems with summer boarding often originated in class and cultural differences between rural boarding house keepers—often farmers or fishermen—and urban guests. Not only ignorant of the "the habits and diets of 'city folks'," the landlord often objected "that what was good enough for himself and his wife [was] not good enough for these 'citified' people who descend[ed] on him once a year."[69]

The decision—hotel or boarding house, cottage or farmhouse—depended partly on the needs, desires, and expectations of the vacationers. But it also rested on money. Vacation places came at all prices. The affluent were prepared to pay a lot. At the high end of the scale, "cottages" in Newport were going at the rate of $2000 to $3000 for the season in the summer of 1874.[70] Andrew D. White, a man of independent means and president of Cornell University, spent the summer of 1873 at Newport with his family. They rented "Cliff Cottage" at $300 per week, "7 persons board and all."[71]

The well-heeled, as distinguished from the fabulously rich, often found suitable accommodations at large, fashionable hotels that offered amenities at a price. In 1874 the Grand Union Hotel at Saratoga was advertising its rooms at $28 per week.[72] But even this could be moderate in Saratoga. A bill to a Mr. G. H. Scribner and his wife at the Congress Hall in Saratoga Springs showed that he was charged $20 for only two days board.[73]

Prospect House opened on the southeastern shore of Blue Mountain Lake in the Adirondacks in 1882, offering luxury to wealthy guests at the cost of $25 per person a week, meals included. Among its other attractions, the Prospect House was, according to historian Frank Graham, "the first hotel in the world to equip each of its rooms with electric lights."[74] The Grand Hotel on Mackinac Island charged $3 to $5 a night, with meals

Grand Hotel, Mackinac Island, Michigan, c. 1900–1906. Grand Hotel on Mackinac Island was one of the most fashionable midwestern resorts by the end of the nineteenth century. (Library of Congress, Detroit Publishing Company Photograph Collection, LC-D4-19027.)

extra, when it opened in 1887. By 1890 a single guest could have paid $35 a week for the most desirable room (a front room with a bath); the best double in the house went for $54 per week.[75]

Congress Hall, Prospect House, and the Grand Hotel on Mackinac charged what the rich could afford to pay. People of more moderate means had other choices. Those who wanted to stay at hotels usually had to pay for the privilege—one that cost anywhere from $10 to $20 per week per person. Mohonk Mountain House advertised rates in its 1874 brochure of $20 a week for a single room, $36 to $40 for a double. The price included meals. This might have been a bit too steep for the clientele Mohonk was hoping to attract, because in 1877 Smiley dropped the rates for some single rooms to $15. The brochure asserted, moreover, that "liberal arrangements will be made with families wishing to make a prolonged stay at the Lake." Thus, families who could commit to a month—or a whole season—were likely to get a reduction in rates. By the early 1880s Mohonk had dropped its prices again, charging $25 to $35 per week for a double during the high season.[76]

Many of Mohonk's prospective guests, however, anticipated spending less. In an era when "the best table d'hote dinner in New York" cost $1.25, a lady's watch was advertised for just under $30, tuition at a select women's seminary ranged anywhere from $125 to $360, and a piano went for about $300, many potential middle-class vacationers hoped to pay no more than $10 a week per person (half price for children and servants) for a stay at a summer resort.[77] Mr. and Mrs. C.C. Kelsey of Brooklyn, for example, expected to spend "a month or more in the country" during the summer of 1871. They anticipated "quiet comfort, not style" and felt that Mohonk would suit if "the terms are not too steep for our limited means." For the Kelseys, $20 per week for two represented the upper limit of their vacation budget.[78]

The sorts of middle-class vacationers who contemplated a stay at Mohonk apparently were used to finding places in the $10 to $15 per week range. Mrs. William Gilfillan explained that "at Lake Luzerne for two large double rooms I only paid $40 per week." She was willing, however, to "give 50 or 55 at your house for good accommodations."[79] Another prospective Mohonk guest wrote that he and his wife intended to engage a room for the month of June 1888 "at the rate of $30 per week," noting that "this is as much as we are accustomed to pay at Bar Harbor & Campobello."[80] Even at a fancy watering place like Saratoga it was possible for the "bachelor of modest means and frugal mind who [was] out for an airing" to find "'peace with honor' in the narrow quarters of some humble boarding house at a weekly stipend of $10 and no extras."[81]

Prices at southern and western resorts resembled those in the North. In the mid-1870s a vacationer could stay at Millboro House in Bath County, Virginia, for $13 a week or at Warm Springs for $17.50. Most southern watering places charged half price for children and for "colored" servants.[82] Westerners also apparently found comfortable vacation accommodations in the $10 to $15 per week range. Alf Doten, an up-and-coming newspaperman from Virginia City, visited Lake Tahoe in 1872 for the first of many visits over the next ten years. He noted in his diary: "All the guests and pleasure seekers live in little houses or shanties scattered about at random, and all eat in the main house where McKinney himself [the proprietor] lives—A Chinaman does the cooking—Board and house rent, or lodging, $10 a week."[83] And when Portland lawyer Matthew Deady accompanied his wife to Grimes Hotel in Clatsop Beach on the Oregon shore, they invariably paid $10 per person a week.[84]

Even $10 to $15 a week, however, was out of range for many of those with little money but sufficient time for a vacation. Such people sought, and found, other alternatives. Large hotels with fancy amenities were out of the question. But scads of small hotels, boarding houses, and farmhouses advertised summer accommodations—by the day, week, or month. An 1882 booklet published by the Norfolk and Western Railroad listed a vast assortment of places that charged as little as $6 or $7 a week, $20 a month per person. Doubtless some of these were nothing more than an extra room in someone's farmhouse. Such "resorts" often could advertise nothing more than "two acres of well shaded yard."[85] S. G. Wood, for example, owned a place only a mile from Bonsack's Depot in southwest Virginia. He offered accommodations for twelve to fifteen people and hack service to pick up guests at the railway station. Visitors to Mr. Wood's would also find "hunting and fishing abundant, and good shade and play-ground for children." All this could be had for as little as $4 per week, $15 per month.[86] Rockingham Springs, Virginia, however, was a substantial enough resort to welcome one hundred guests and to publish its own twelve-page promotional brochure. In 1880 it charged only $8 a week, $30 a month; children and black servants paid half, "white servants according to accommodations required." Besides providing "shaded verandas," hunting, and fishing, the resort came equipped with a bowling alley and baths, both of which were "free."[87] Promotional booklets and brochures like these suggest that Virginia was filled with a wide range of places offering varying degrees of comfort for a relatively modest cost.[88]

The South was not the only region that offered cheap vacations. By the 1870s the *New York Times* was editorializing about the myriad inexpensive possibilities for people looking for summer retreats. From Mount Desert on the coast of Maine to Old Point in Virginia, prospective vacationers could find "houses or cottages, where the economical can live cheaply, and yet enjoy the real pleasures of the sea and seaside." The writer maintained that "a few weeks of salt-water bathing and sea air can be obtained anywhere on our coasts for less than it costs most families to live at home." Rather than a room in a "big, costly hotel," thrifty vacationers could "live in farm-houses, or cheap cottages, or economical boarding houses."[89]

The availability of growing numbers of inexpensive vacation spots extended the possibility of vacationing to people on the lower end of the middle-class spectrum. Indeed, these places offered such people reassurance that, despite their limited financial means, middle-class status had not eluded them. The nature of their vacations might have left much to be desired—the farmhouse hot and cramped, the food unappealing, the entertainment and amusements limited. Still, the ability to leave home and work, escape from the hot city, and perhaps enjoy some relaxation and recreation remained a privilege that many people of moderate means claimed as their own. As such they differentiated themselves from the working-class below them and reaffirmed their connection to that vast and diverse conglomeration called the middle class.

Not all middle-class people could indulge in the pleasures of a vacation. What proportion of the middle class did vacation in the late nineteenth century is difficult to determine. Many failed to find the time or money for even a week's stay at a cheap boarding house. Others could only muster the resources for an occasional vacation. Frank Trexler, a young lawyer trying to build up a successful practice in Allentown, Pennsylvania, managed only an infrequent pleasure trip. Over the decade of the 1880s Trexler, who was single and earning about $500 per year, took only two vacations—one a ten-day trip to Niagara, Montreal, Boston, and New York and the second a "short pleasure trip" of six days to Philadelphia, Luray, Natural Bridge, and Atlantic City. Other than these, he had to content himself with one-day excursions to Coney Island, afternoon picnics with friends, or a business trip to Milwaukee that afforded a little time for pleasure.[90]

The increasing importance of participating in a vacation experience led some middle-class people to try a variety of inventive strategies. Those who could not afford to leave their work sometimes tried to take their work with them. In 1886 J. M. Winfield, a physician, wrote to Smiley at Mohonk asking "if a physician could get enough practice in the hotel to warrant him to stay during the month of August & part of September." He explained, "I have been at Newport & Cape May & have done considerable practice in fact enough to defray all my expenses & would go there again but my sister is in need of mountain air." Mr. Smiley advised him that he had "better not depend on it."[91] The same year Laura Woodward, an artist, offered Smiley another proposition. She was hoping he would furnish her with a studio in which she could paint and from which she could sell her art to guests: "I have known instances where hotel proprietors have done so & it has worked nicely in being an additional attraction to the hotel & advantage to the artists."[92]

Others tried somewhat more subtle approaches. John Beekman, a physician, hoped that his wife and baby would be able to enjoy some "bracing mountain air" during the summer of 1886. He inquired about the rates at Mohonk: "Even if I cannot afford to stop at your place—send me what matter you have printed . . . telling of your situation. Everyday I have the question repeated many times, 'Doctor, where shall we all go this summer?' I would gladly tell them of 'Mohonk Lake.'"[93] Was Beekman hoping, perhaps, for a good deal on a summer vacation in exchange for his willingness to promote Mohonk amongst his patients?

It is impossible to know which people were more typical—the members of the middle class who swelled the population of American vacationers or those who remained home. What does seem certain, however, is that large numbers of middle-class women and men were doing what they could to

make vacationing an increasingly likely prospect. And they found some
assistance from the numerous business and professional organizations
emerging in the late nineteenth century.

The middle class, as Robert Wiebe's classic study has demonstrated,
organized itself into a variety of different groups, associations, and societies
in the late nineteenth century.[94] And organizations, then as now, held meetings and conventions. Increasingly throughout the late nineteenth century
the sites for such meetings included not only big cities, but summer resorts
and watering places. Vacationing for many middle-class people became
intertwined with the organizational or professional associations that structured and defined middle-class life. Boondoggles not only made it easier for
people to take vacations, but helped to integrate vacationing into the culture
of the middle class.

By the mid-1870s various professional, scholarly, and reform organizations—the National Temperance Convention, the American Philological
Society, the American Ophthalmological Society—were choosing places
like Newport and Saratoga to hold their meetings.[95] The numbers and variety of such organizations increased in the next decades, as did the sorts of
places at which they chose to meet. Long Branch, a seaside resort on the
New Jersey coast, hosted meetings of dentists and Presbyterians in July of
1880.[96] Those groups that met at Saratoga in 1885 included, among others,
the New York Medical Association, the National Council of Education, and
the National Association of Stove Manufacturers.[97] That same summer saw
the Massachusetts Press Association meeting at Martha's Vineyard.[98] By
June of 1895 the list of groups planning conventions at Saratoga ranged
from the American Congregational Home Missionary Society to the New
York State Pharmaceutical Association, the Sportsmen's Convention to the
Banker's Association, the Convention of Professors of Dancing to the American Social Science Association.[99]

It was not only elite professionals or wealthy businessmen who enjoyed
the benefits of these meetings. Conventions of school teachers regularly met
at Newport, and in June of 1890 the "colored Baptists who compose the
New England Missionary Convention" also held their meeting there.[100]
Mackinac Island was actively wooing the convention trade in the 1890s.
During the summer of 1898 130 school teachers from Pittsburgh, 100 insurance agents from the Mutual Life Company, and 135 newspaper editors
from Kentucky attended conventions at the Grand Hotel on Mackinac.[101]
For some attendees, these meetings may have provided not only an excuse
but the means for a vacation. Benjamin Atkins, a school teacher from North
Carolina who spent most summers visiting his family in Tennessee, managed one visit to a seashore resort where he and his wife "had some pleasant
sailing. . . ." The occasion was the North Carolina Teachers' Assembly.[102]

Like Atkins, many of those who attended these meetings took the opportunity to turn them into vacations for themselves and their families. The newspapermen who met on Martha's Vineyard in 1885 were "accompanied by their wives." The Sea View Hotel quartered the group, which, according to the newspaper, was "well entertained by Landlord Brownell." Neither was the whole time spent in meetings, for the newspaper reported that on Monday and Tuesday "the party visited Nantucket."[103] In 1873 when Louisa Roberts visited the Put-in-Bay Islands she was accompanying her husband to a meeting of the American Dental Association. The organization had, according to Roberts, decided on that spot "because there were ample accommodations and the place was everything that could be desired, even to moderation in the charges." Members of the organization were "invited to take wives and children and stay long enough to enjoy the boating, bathing and fishing" available on the island. Roberts found the stay there a great success, the time "made memorable by social intercourse with agreeable people from all parts of our country, including many gentlemen in the dental profession and their families, who like ourselves were attracted by inducements thrown out the year before."[104] The members of the American Institute of Instruction who were meeting at Newport in July of 1885 took time to visit the Casino "and also called at the torpedo station, where there were torpedo explosions for their benefit."[105]

The growing number of meetings that began to occur at watering places and resorts reveals that resort owners knew a good thing when they saw it. These conventions provided a way for resorts to attract a vacationing clientele and a way for middle-class people to facilitate the process of vacationing. Business, religious, and professional conventions boosted the vacation industry and helped to create a vacationing American middle class.

—————•◆•—————

Over the last half of the nineteenth century a vacationing infrastructure emerged in this country: a financially comfortable population whose work was structured to allow for short periods away, a range of resorts to receive would-be vacationers, and a transportation network to get people where they wanted to go. Together these circumstances allowed the American middle class to assume the privilege of vacationing—something that had once been reserved primarily for the elite.

But the process of making vacationing its own required that the middle class do more than ride the railroads to the newest vacation spots. Middle-class Americans, bred on a gospel of work, continued to be fearful of the consequences of idleness. While many voices were beginning not only to condone recreation but to advise time set aside for relaxation, finding a comfortable means of being at leisure remained problematic for the middle

❧ 3 ❧

"through the streets in bathing costumes"

────── ◆ ──────

RESORT VACATIONS, 1850-1900

Life is so much the same at all watering-places, except the few, like Saratoga and Long Branch, which are cursed with the crush of fashionables, that it is scarcely necessary to descend to details of how the days come and go.[1]

One July afternoon in 1872, newspaperman Alf Doten left his home in Carson City, Nevada, for a week's stay at Lake Tahoe. Upon arriving he and a female friend "took a nice little stroll together in the woods up the creek near by, & then took a sail on the Lake, paddling about in a skiff." His diary recorded that "other folks were out in other boats, fishing, etc." At about eight o'clock he returned to shore "& all hands sat in front of [a] house by [a] blaze of a big pan full of pine burrs, chatting etc—I played [the] harmonica—Bed at 9." The next day he fished, sailed, took a quick dip in the very cold lake, and enjoyed a concert by a National Guard Brass Band. In the evening he again "sat with family circle in front of house around pine burr fire. I played harmonica, & we had pleasant chat till 9½ when all hands retired. I [*sic*] Bed at 10."[2]

Contrast Doten's experience with a description of a typical summer day at White Sulphur Springs, West Virginia, in 1878. The visitor took the required pre-breakfast walk to the springs for a drink of the waters:

After breakfast the parlor is thronged, and the ten-pin alley, shooting-gallery, billiard-table, croquet ground, and at noon the 'German' [dance] in the ball-room, have their votaries. Promenades under the oaks on the lawn or to Lovers' Walk, drives, rides, the last newspaper or magazine, and every species of occupation consistent with the sweet do nothing of the time and place, then follow; and at half past two, with appetites sharpened by the mountain air . . . the company, numbering sometimes more than a thousand, have dinner served to them in the great dining room. . . . In the afternoon the programme of the forenoon is repeated, especially the riding, driving, and walking to pic-turesque points in the vicinity; and after tea the parlor . . . is the scene of inter-minable waltzes and Germans—on two nights of the week of full-dress balls.[3]

Far more than geography separated Lake Tahoe from White Sulphur Springs. Lake Tahoe in the 1870s was still a small, low-key vacation spot, while White Sulphur was the type of resort that a newspaper correspondent characterized as "cursed with the crush of fashionables."[4] Clearly, each resort offered vacationers different experiences; more profound were the different meanings that middle-class Americans attached to those experi-ences. A stroll in the woods, a dip in the lake, an evening concert at a small, unfashionable resort allegedly fostered renewal and health. But spending time at a fashionable watering place could, many feared, pose grave moral dangers.

The dangers stemmed, in part, from the fact that people at resorts—whether fashionable or not—were idle; they did no work. While busy and active, vacationers remained separated from the discipline of daily work. And work, many people believed, served as the glue that held the republic together and that kept middle-class people on the straight and narrow.

Over the last half of the nineteenth century hundreds of thousands of middle-class women and men found their way to the burgeoning number of summer resorts, where they had plenty of time on their hands and used it to indulge in a wide variety of sports and amusements. What transpired at these vacation spots was more than just fun. Indeed, important changes in middle-class behavior occurred, changes that loosened some of the restric-tions of Victorian propriety. Summer resorts seemed to allow, even encour-age, more relaxed rules of conduct. The ramifications were important, particularly for female vacationers. Women both discovered and helped to create a resort culture that freed them from some traditional middle-class constraints and allowed them to exercise new forms of personal autonomy.

But the absence of work-imposed discipline and the increased freedoms afforded to women at many resorts seemed to cultural critics to be a partic-ularly dangerous mix. The nineteenth-century public press devoted consid-erable attention to the subject of summer resorts and in the end offered a less than ringing endorsement. Journalists and writers repeatedly represented fashionable resorts as sites of deception, dissipation, and danger. Even as the numbers of resort visitors increased geometrically over the last half of the century, critics continued to warn against the potential moral hazards such places posed for respectable men and women.

———————•◆•———————

Nineteenth-century American resorts varied widely—in size, cost, location, clientele. Some resorts were small towns that swelled to crowded, mini-metropolises during the summer season—places like Cape May, Atlantic City, Saratoga Springs. By the summer of 1859 Cape May, for example, could accommodate several thousand people and sported "an infinite trail of restaurants, barber-shops, ice-cream saloons, bowling-alleys, billiard-rooms, pistol galleries, bathing-houses."[5] Other resorts presented a more rural demeanor. The *New York Times* described the Catskill Mountain House as "a refuge of civilization," offering "a hotel and good beds near the primeval forest."[6] But rural did not necessarily means spartan. In 1878, according to *Harper's New Monthly Magazine*, the main hotel at White Sulphur Springs was "a plain building 400 feet in length, with one of the largest and finest ball-rooms in America, and a dining-room 300 feet long and 140 wide, which seats at its round tables about 1200 guests." The hotel slept

Cottage "C," South Carolina Row, the White, White Sulphur Springs, West Virginia, 1878. This was one of the numerous cottages that housed guests at White Sulphur Springs. (The Greenbrier, White Sulphur Springs, West Virginia.)

about 700 patrons, but numerous cottages scattered about the grounds could "lodge 1200 or 1400 more." Within its forty acres White Sulphur also included baths, croquet fields, springs, "a bowling green . . . and innumerable pleasant walks and drives leading to points overlooking the beautiful and peaceful scene."[7]

Seaside resorts offered swimming; mountain resorts touted the pleasures of country walks and rides; inland springs added bathing to the pleasures of strolling or riding either through the town or countryside; lakes tendered the possibilities of fishing and sailing. Nearly all vacation spots had facilities for bowling and billiards. Vacationers at most resorts spent time lolling or loitering on the piazzas of hotels, chatting with friends, making new acquaintances, napping, and eating. Evenings were the time for dances, balls, or "hops."

Many historians have documented Americans' growing fascination in the late decades of the century with more active and competitive physical endeavors.[8] A variety of sports such as rowing and baseball began to claim the interest of middle-class men, while by the end of the century male college students were playing football at the nation's elite universities.[9] Middle-class women, however, found fewer opportunities to engage in vigorous physical activity. Newly opened women's colleges provided one of the few exceptions, daily physical exercise being thought a means of countering the debilitating impact of intellectual labor on the allegedly frail female body. And during the 1890s some women claimed the right to enjoy the new craze of bicycling.[10] But before the turn of the century most middle-class women had little familiarity with any strenuous sports.

Vacationers at summer resorts, perhaps reflecting the generalized and growing interest in competitiveness and physicality, participated in a range of sports and games. By 1880 newspaper correspondents were mentioning the increasing popularity of lawn tennis, and before long tennis tournaments became a part of resort life.[11] Some resorts built roller skating rinks and vacationers began to spend time riding bicycles.[12] A reporter writing from Cottage City on Martha's Vineyard in 1885 commented on the resort's bicycle and tricycle races, ball games, boat and tub races, swimming matches, tennis tournaments, and horseback riding.[13] The new "swimming tank," which opened at Long Branch on the Jersey shore in 1890, accommodated as many as 200 or 250 people a day and offered a "view room" with "comfortable chairs where a large number of spectators [could] look down on the swimmers." Those who swam in the tank "often play[ed] a sort of marine baseball."[14] During the 1890s Grand Hotel on Mackinac Island offered "a lively potpourri of sports, [including] . . . rugby, foot races, boxing, swimming and horse racing," as well as egg races on horses and a greased pole competition for young men.[15]

Swimming pool at the White, White Sulphur Springs, West Virginia, c. 1900. Note the spectators watching the swimmers. (The Greenbrier, White Sulphur Springs, West Virginia.)

At a time when middle-class cultural norms dictated a restricted range of activities for women and warned about the dangers of "promiscuous" (meaning mixed gender) entertainment, women at summer resorts willingly and eagerly participated in a variety of recreational activities. Moreover, they usually did so in the company of men. While middle-class standards recommended quiet and subdued amusements for women, resorts provided female vacationers the opportunity for competitive and sometimes strenuous physical recreation.

Bowling, for example, remained a universal of watering-place life. In a series of articles written for a weekly Washington, D.C., newspaper in 1859, a young woman described playing in a two-hour bowling match at Saratoga. She explained that the sport presented some problems: "Nothing can be more ill-contrived than crinoline, and twenty-six yards of silk or other material, in a dress for rolling balls. A swing of the arm at the side is easy for a gentleman, but not at all convenient for a lady, and all attempts at meeting the awkwardness of movement are not alike graceful." Despite such difficulties, her first roll of the ball brought down all ten pins, and her bowling skill helped her team to victory. Although initially not expecting "much from this pastime," she quickly learned "how exciting it may be."[16] For this young woman—and no doubt for many others—time spent at resorts brought not only a feeling of physical competence but an awareness of the pleasures of games and sport.

Newspapers reported stories of women playing tennis at Saratoga and golf on the Southampton Links on Long Island. One reporter, for example, advised "those who think fashionable young women do nothing but dance all night and sleep all day" to pay an early morning visit to "the quandrangle, where . . . the belles of the hop of the night before can be seen 'serving'

Ten pins, or bowling, party at the White, White Sulphur Springs, West Virginia, c. 1890s. Women and men bowled together at summer resorts. (The Greenbrier, White Sulphur Springs, West Virginia.)

On the links, Hotel Champlain, Bluff Point, New York, c. 1900–1915. By the turn of the century women were participating in sports like tennis and golf at summer resorts. (Library of Congress, Detroit Publishing Company Photograph Collection, LC-D4-500246.)

with a vigor than can only come from well-developed muscles."[17] Hiking also engaged female vacationers. Anne Mason, a visitor to Yellow Sulphur Springs, Virginia, in the summer of 1887, wrote to her husband describing her adventures: "Last evening we formed a party of twenty-two . . . & walked about four miles—started about 5:30 & did not get back until after 8 o'clock. We crossed one mountain & went to the summit of a second. . . . I did not feel the least bit tired. We all went right into supper just as we were & ate *enormously*—I feel splendidly with the exception of a right back pain. I think the walk must have brought me right—as soon as I can, I am going again & will try to take a walk every day. I never imagined I would enjoy anything as much." Neither were the pleasures of mountain hikes her only discovery. She also bowled, learning that she "enjoyed" the game "very much."[18] Ann Mason's trip to the springs brought with it the unintended discovery of the pleasures of physical exertion.

Women and men even competed against each other in some sports. In 1890 Asbury Park witnessed a boat race between Mr. Thomas G. Allan and Mrs. E. C. Shaw of New York. Having apparently "made a wager for a small supper," the two, "surrounded by a small number of friends . . . entered tidy little rowboats on Deal Lake and at the word began to pull bravely at the oars." The exciting contest ended with Mrs. Shaw a "full boat's length ahead of her competitor." Mr. Allan apparently paid up, having the supper "served on the banks of the Shrewsbury near Pleasure Bay."[19] That same year vacationers at Long Branch watched the "long swim by Mrs. Bortmer of New York and Mr. Charles Green and Mr. O. R. Lewis of Highland Beach. . . . The distance swam by the lady and the gentlemen was two and three quarters miles from Rocky Point to Spermaceti Cave. Time not given, but said to be remarkably fast for the distance made in open water."[20]

Even more daring, perhaps, was some women's participation in activities usually reserved exclusively for men. Female vacationers, for example, sometimes played billiards. An 1875 newspaper article lauded the Philadelphia women who vacationed at Cape May that summer not only for being "so pleasant and unaffected" but for their willingness to "bowl tenpins with such vigor, and shoot pistols with so much courage, handle a billiard cue so gracefully, and miss shots so cheerfully. . . ." Neither did such activities endanger the women's claims to propriety or womanly virtue. For not only, the reader learned, could the women from Philadelphia aim guns and shoot pool, they could also "play with the children so prettily, and talk with the men in such a sisterly fashion."[21]

Summer resorts provided middle-class women with a significantly wider range of amusements and pleasures than normally available to them. Take swimming, for example. Many women who visited the seaside braved the surf and swam in the ocean. Twenty-two year old Floride Clemson, a granddaughter of John C. Calhoun, visited Long Beach on the coast of New Jersey in 1864 and recorded her activities in her diary. She "learned to float like a cork, better than any man or woman there."[22] An article on Cape May in an 1875 issue of *Lippincott's* maintained that bathing was one of the main attractions of the resort. Even the "fashionable virgins" who came "to puff, . . . remain[ed] to bathe."[23]

By the last half of the century bathing protocol at seaside resorts had begun to change. Most noticeably, men and women were more frequently entering the surf together. Opinion varied on whether swimming was proper for respectable middle-class women, especially "promiscuous" swimming. Felicia Holt, writing for *Ladies Home Journal* in 1890, argued adamantly against the practice, even for men and women married to each other.[24] Others felt that learning to swim would increase women's enjoyment of the shore and help to ensure their safety on boats.[25] Despite the range of opinions, much evidence suggests not only that women swam, but that women and men frolicked in the waves together. In 1865 a correspondent writing from Long Branch described the scene in the surf: "There are honest lovers—married and other—who take their ladies valorously round the waist, in the water, and assist them with downright earnestness in the glorious sport of the hour."[26] Twenty years later the newspaper reported that "up and down the beach [at Long Branch] in the foaming surf are bathers of all sizes mingling happily in the water without reference to age, sex, or previous condition of servitude."[27]

But swimming, for female vacationers, was not necessarily simple, easy, or without consequence. The decision to enter the surf presented women with problems—particularly when it came to proper attire. Women's swimming clothes could both raise eyebrows and provoke ridicule. A description of the women swimming at Cape May in 1875 noted that "they don the various costumes . . . and convince themselves for the fiftieth time that bathing trousers cut to the knee, with blue striped stockings and a semiperceptible fastener thereto, are the correct thing for bathing in Cape May waters."[28] A reporter writing from Long Branch in 1870 marvelled that any women would choose to enter the surf, as there was nothing "more hideous than a woman in that horrible attire, clinging nervously to the life line or clasping her male protector with a death-grasp while the waves tumble her about." Those who chose not to bathe could "have the pleasure of sitting on the sand and making cruel remarks on the hideousness of their friends in the *outre* garments."[29] Others disagreed. One columnist, recognizing that "much has been said of the hideous sight the feminine world presents in its bathing costume," still found "a lady who is arrayed in a neat and tasty bathing dress . . . never more attractive than at that particular moment."[30]

While some women may have heeded the warnings and refrained from entering the surf, many others took the plunge. And when they did, the fabric of their "hideous" bathing costumes often clung to their bodies, revealing more than Victorian women usually chose to display. Felicia Holt held that "any one innately delicate, must feel shocked at the daily spectacle the bathing beach now presents."[31] Those who commented on female swimmers frequently mentioned their clinging clothes. The reporter at Long Branch maintained that "a lady whose beauty is a fact, and not a fiction, is beautiful when she once gets into the surf and the garments cling to [her] graceful form." He described one of the belles of the last night's ball emerging from the surf "and the embrace of this foamy lover has left her garments soaking, and outline the graceful curves of her luxuriant form with a distinctiveness which might serve a sculptor."[32] Similarly, a columnist writing from Newport the same year noted the difficulty of trying to hide any imperfections while bathing. Hence one woman emerged from the water looking "like a long wet stocking." On the other hand, the ocean could enhance a woman's appearance as it had "developed the charms" of a certain lady whose "wet clothes hug closely to her handsomely-chiseled limbs."[33] The sexual innuendo could not have been less subtle. Middle-class Victorians took great pains to restrain and inhibit female sexuality.[34] But the middle-class women who swam at seaside watering places revealed their bodies in ways that were not only unusual, but in other circumstances improper.

Not everybody approved. In 1900 James A. Bradley, the man responsible for building and promoting Asbury Park, a beach resort on the New Jersey Shore, began "a crusade against the revolting practice of parading through the streets of Asbury Park in bathing suits." Apparently "hundreds of women—and not a few of the sterner sex" tried to save the price of a bath house by walking from their hotels to the beach in their bathing costumes. Consequently, the streets of Asbury Park were filled "with scantily attired females, many of whom seem to take pride in displaying their anatomy." Although the town council had already passed an ordinance forbidding such behavior, the "law had never been enforced." Mr. Bradley decided to take action. He published an advertisement in the town newspaper alerting the public: "BATHING COSTUME NOTICE! DO NOT GO THROUGH THE STREETS IN BATHING COSTUMES. IT IS COARSE AND VULGAR." Bradley then directed the police to arrest any offenders.[35]

Swimming called attention to women's bodies not only because of the clinging, wet drapery of their bathing clothes, but because the power of the surf could expose parts of the body that would, under calmer conditions, remain hidden. In 1875 a newspaper correspondent described the unforeseen consequences of swimming in the heavy surf at Long Branch: "Fat women are seized by the advancing walls of transparent green, foam

Surf bathers, Atlantic City, New Jersey, 1896. Men and women enjoyed the surf together, even though rough waters and wet bathing costumes exposed female bodies to the gaze of onlookers. (Library of Congress, Stereopticon File, LC-USZ62-26574.)

crested, are whirled round and round like corks, and dashed into the reluctant arms of thin old bachelors, who seem horrified at the gifts of fortune. Manly forms that were proudly defying the coming waves, are suddenly inverted, and nothing is seen of them save wildly-agitated pedal extremities." The images of fat ladies colliding with thin old bachelors and "wildly agitated pedal extremities" were meant, no doubt, to amuse. The fact remained that the surf made men and women's bodies touch and exposed legs to the sight of the multitude.[36]

For many, women who braved the surf provoked disapproval. J. R. V. Daniels, a Richmond lawyer passing a few days at Old Point Comfort on the Virginia shore, related the following scene in an 1885 letter to his wife:

We watched the bathers among them Minnie Allen. She wore a tight fitting jacket with short sleeves and a skirt which did *not* reach her knees. Her legs, in pale red stockings, were almost too large, but beautifully shaped. Of course, every one in the water and out held their breath to look at this beautiful sinner as she emerged from the brine, laughing insolently. There she stood, a very Venus Libitina, the incarnation of Lust. She is getting bolder, and I think that ere long even Richmond society must throw her out. I cannot bear to see a virtuous woman talk with her.[37]

Minnie Allen surely must have committed worse sins than donning a short bathing skirt for her dip in the ocean. But Daniels's language suggests that by exposing herself in the water she had accentuated her sexuality and confirmed the image of herself as the "incarnation of Lust."[38]

Even a woman who dressed and behaved decorously could elicit "quite a little shock" when she engaged in seaside sports. Such was the case in 1890, for example, when a young woman from Philadelphia embarked on a crabbing expedition at Ocean Beach on the New Jersey shore. After alighting from her carriage she dismissed her driver and "procured a small batteau and a crab net" from the owner of the boathouse. Next she rowed herself out into the stream and "a moment later . . . stood upright, shook herself lightly, and then stepped easily over the side of the boat in a pretty Zouave costume of white and green silk." With the boat drifting nearby, the lady "moved along gracefully in the water a little more than ankle deep." She succeeded "now and then" in landing a crab in her net. This expedition, apparently, left "tongues of all those who saw her in her dainty costume wagging at will, some in praise and some in deprecation. . . ." The reporter concluded, however, by reminding the reader that "'that Philadelphia girl' . . . is one of the most modest and properly decorous of all the young ladies in the society of the Quaker City."[39]

Women bathers certainly knew that they were exhibiting their bodies to the gaze of male observers. Yet, the hapless Minnie Allen notwithstanding, most did so without incurring serious censure. Even James Bradley objected not to women donning bathing suits or entering the surf, but to those women who insisted upon wearing their bathing costumes "through the streets."

Summer resorts seemed to be providing space in which some of the rules of middle-class propriety were suspended, or at least relaxed. Women and men engaged in a wide range of sports and amusements, some of which brought them into close physical contact and called attention to their bodies. While members of both sexes no doubt enjoyed themselves, these resorts may have offered middle-class women a new taste of the pleasures of physical exertion and the chance at the sorts of amusements once reserved for men.

Certainly not all women engaged in all these activities. Neither did all resorts extend them the opportunity to do so. The possibility of frolicking in the waves at a Long Branch or Cape May presented greater potential for physical adventure than did, for example, a game of ten pins at Saratoga. But even those who visited inland spas or mountain resorts enjoyed pleasures and amusements that would have otherwise been unavailable to them. No proper woman, for example, would have passed through the doorway of an urban bowling alley. Those women who chose not to take part still witnessed other respectable women's participation in more vigorous, competitive, or physical sorts of endeavors. Most female vacationers met little overt disapproval as they hiked in the mountains, went fishing or crabbing, swam in the surf, and played billiards or ten pins. Vacations seemed to offer a license for unconventional behavior, as resorts sometimes served as laboratories in which men and women contested middle-class codes and experimented with new forms of social intercourse.

Perhaps nowhere was the potential challenge to middle-class rules of conduct so great as when it came to two other popular resort pastimes—flirting and courting. These, of course, had been staples of resort life since the early nineteenth century when the elite had hunted for mates at summer watering places.[40] Throughout the last half of the century flirting and courting continued to provide much of the entertainment at summer resorts and to help define the culture that emerged around these vacation spots. Some observers maintained that meeting attractive members of the opposite sex motivated both men and women to visit watering places. One reporter, describing Long Branch in 1865, remarked: "After deliberate cogitation, I have quite settled in my mind the fact that more people come here to 'flirt' (what a pretty word!) than for any other purpose."[41] A correspondent writing from Cape May in 1880 noticed that "the principal use of the piers seems to be love-making after dark. Then every seat is occupied by young couples who sit too close in proximity to be married, and talk to each other under their breath."[42] In 1900 James Bradley of Asbury Park, still perhaps peeved at the people parading down the streets in their bathing suits, ordered the "beach policemen to break up the 'kissing bees' held nightly in the dark corners of the pavilions and on the fishing pier."[43] The efforts of the Asbury Park police may have moved the "kissing bees" to a different location, but the flirtations doubtless persisted.

Evidence from letters and diaries confirms the reports of newspaper correspondents; lots of flirting occurred at summer resorts. Many men—both married and single—found the presence of pretty women one of the main attractions of watering places. During the summer of 1852 Edwin Jeffress made the rounds of the Virginia springs while his wife remained at home with their four daughters. Jeffress commented frequently in his diary about how much he was enjoying the company of the ladies, particularly his "favorite," the "very handsome, intelligent looking" Miss Quarles. He and Miss Quarles spent considerable time together at the White Sulphur; one evening they "rode out" on a two and a half mile trip to the top of the mountain. He noted in his diary: "Spent the most agreeable hour I have since I left home" and then added, "She dances exceedingly well." It is unclear whether Miss Quarles knew about Jeffress's wife and children, but he apparently had no misgivings about informing a Mrs. Saunders "that I was a married man with four little daughters. She informed me that she had no children."

Jeffress did not confine his flirtations to the White Sulphur and Miss Quarles. He moved on to the Rockbridge Alum, and then to the Healing Springs, where he "had a very good supper . . . & [spent] the balance of the evening with the old man's five pretty & interesting 'Daughters.' They played very well on the guitar & sang. . . . I passed as a young man I think very well until the next morning. . . . I talked about home, which probably led to the suspicion that I was a married man."[44] Flirting with pretty women clearly contributed to Jeffress's enjoyment at the springs.

Men often recorded in their diaries or wrote to their friends about the attractive women they met at vacation spots. A male student from the University of Virginia visited the White Sulphur in August of 1868 and found there considerable opportunity for flirting. He confided to his diary: "Soon became acquainted with most of the people there. Among those I liked were Miss Nina Cowardin, Miss Cochrane, Miss Poachman & several others." He attended "one of the finest and largest Fancy Balls which ever took place in the Mountains" with Miss Annie Maury, who was "dressed to perfection." Miss Maury's prowess on the dance floor did not keep him from dancing "also with Miss Jennie Caperton . . . a perfect little fairy, graceful, handsome & fascinating to a most dangerous degree." So much did he enjoy Jennie Caperton's company that "after taking Annie M. home" he returned to the dance, and through "a good deal of maneuvering" managed to escort the fascinating Miss Caperton to her cottage. Jennie's departure the following morning left him "in despair, for the light of those blue eyes had dazzled my vision & forced me to believe myself perfectly happy while under its influence." The despair lifted fairly quickly as he traveled from the White Sulphur to the Healing Springs "where I had a gay time with Miss Mattie Allen & the Dunlop girls." As almost an afterthought he added, "Spend a good deal of time in hunting and fishing."[45]

A man named Ned wrote to someone named "Caz" from White Sulphur in August of 1881 explaining that although the "table is poor[,] at night it is lively." The women dressed in their "best style" and "those men who are idiots put on dress suits & they dance, hug & *sweat.* Others promenade the long porch (1800 feet) & flirt." He claimed to be unaccustomed to such amusements: "I never knew how to flirt. Some gay damsels, attracted by my winning ways, tried to flirt with me but I promptly repelled their advances."[46]

As Ned's letter makes clear, women too enjoyed—and sometimes per-haps initiated—flirtatious encounters at vacation places. Ellen Turner spent some of the summer of 1857 at Cape Island, New Jersey, from where she corresponded with Dr. George Bagby. She was in her early twenties at the time and maintained that she did not "feel much interest in the crowd," but delighted in the bathing and was "enjoying myself as usual looking at the ocean." Her letter made it clear, however, that she also took pleasure from some of the male company: "I have nearly succeeded in captivating a Dutchman who sits next me at the table—he is quite handsome and polite. . . . I have not been introduced but nearly everyday I get a glance and a smile from him."[47]

Lucy Breckinridge, daughter of a well-to-do family from Virginia, clearly enjoyed her stay at the Montgomery White Sulphur in May of 1863 because of the presence of Drs. Archer and Holloway, "our most attentive gallants." Her diary recorded various amusements: "Sometimes we would take long walks to the top of the mountain and down on the banks of the Roanoke River. Sometimes we would play tenpins and at night play euchre and whist." Especially memorable was "being caught in a heavy rain at the top of the mountain, and having Dr. Archer run after me with a caterpillar, and going to gather wild strawberries, and some of the incidents at the tenpin alley. We had so much fun. It was very hard for us to tear ourselves away." The presence of Dr. Archer helped, no doubt, to turn getting drenched in a rainstorm into "fun."[48]

Even when they did not participate, vacationing men and women often noticed and commented upon the flirtations that they witnessed. Richard L. Burtsell, a Catholic priest from New York, confided to his diary that a friend and fellow priest had returned from Cape May "disgusted with the atten-tions paid to ladies by men, when both in the water."[49] Charles Ellis wrote to his brother from Warm Springs in August of 1876 informing him that Ran, a relative staying there as well, "spends most of his time with a large party of young ladies from Cincinnati, with whom he is a great favorite." Eleven years later Ellis, again at Warm Springs, wrote to his brother about the "two pretty serious flirtations going on here; one of them a Phila doctor, a widower, is devoting himself to the daughter of Genl. Terny."[50] An 1887 letter from Anne Harrison Mason at Yellow Sulphur Springs to her husband remarked that "the courting couples will be so thick that I'm afraid it will be hard work to keep out of the way."[51]

Dances and balls were, perhaps, the major sites for flirting and courting. Regardless of whether in the mountains, by the seashore, or near a spring, resorts held frequent dances. Some nights vacationers danced at informal "hops" and other evenings they attended fancy dress balls. Indeed, nothing appears so uniformly in the descriptions of summer resorts as the mention

A Ball at the White, White Sulphur Springs, West Virginia, 19 August 1897. Both informal dances and fancy dress balls were frequent occurrences at fashionable resorts. At this dance some of the attendees wore masks while others held hearts. (The Greenbrier, White Sulphur Springs, West Virginia.)

of these events. Nearly everybody who visited vacation spots commented upon them. Vacationers' letters to friends at home and journalists' reports to their newspapers detailed the size of the crowds, the nature of the music, the number of hours the event lasted, and the lavish dress of the female participants.[52]

Summer resorts provided space where middle-class men and women could meet and mingle, enjoy each other's company, and engage in a variety of mixed-sex amusements—a very different environment from that in which middle-class men and women passed most of their time. Although nineteenth-century middle-class women had moved outside of a narrowly defined domestic sphere, their world was still circumscribed by clear gender boundaries. Many women engaged, for example, in a range of reform, occupational, and educational ventures. Middle-class married women involved themselves in women's clubs, temperance organizations, and church activities. A small number of young women, primarily from the upper reaches of the middle class, were attending newly opened female colleges and recently integrated state universities. Many of the first generation of college-educated women, in turn, became involved in an array of late nineteenth-century reform efforts—living in settlement houses and lobbying to improve the lives of poor women and children. At the same time less privileged middle-class women were beginning to make their way into the expanding white-collar workplace.[53]

Although these activities brought women far beyond the boundaries of their homes, many such women still remained protected from contact with men, especially strangers. Most reform groups were composed primarily of other women. Women's colleges, of course, were primarily all female environments. The few women who did venture into a truly gender-integrated world were those who became students at coeducational universities and those who took white-collar jobs in government and corporate offices. Both found themselves, often uncomfortably, on male turf.

By the 1860s and 1870s not only the large midwestern state universities but some eastern institutions—Cornell and Boston University—had begun to admit women.[54] Some female college students, especially those who entered universities in the earliest experimental years, found opportunities to socialize informally with men. They sat next to male students in class and sometimes even lived in the same rooming houses. Others, fearing that too easy associations with men would challenge propriety, kept themselves apart from male undergraduates and confined their friendships to female students and families of professors. By the 1890s college became a more common if still not customary experience for middle-class women, and coeducational universities began to build dormitories and enact regulations to assure parents that their daughters would be protected.[55]

Female white-collar workers, perhaps more than other middle-class women, crossed the nineteenth-century divide between the male and female sphere—but not without incurring some disapproval. The first middle-class women to work in offices were employees of the federal government. Even though most worked in all-female departments, many found their morality impugned because they had placed themselves in an environment in which they could associate with unfamiliar men.[56]

The newer opportunities for men and women to mingle made middle-class people more rather than less wary of the potentially harmful consequences. By the last decades of the century, as new forms of urban commercial leisure tempted young people away from the watchful eyes of parents, etiquette books began to advise that chaperons accompany young women when they socialized away from home.[57] Despite considerable change in the circumstances of many women's lives, middle-class propriety still restricted the opportunities for heterosocial contact, especially when that contact might breed sexual possibilities. The nineteenth-century provided few places where middle-class people might mix and mingle freely with members of the opposite sex.

But at summer resorts men and women found almost unlimited chances to be together. They strolled along mountain paths, competed in games of tenpins, braved the surf, and danced at balls and hops. These watering places served as one locus for the formation of a heterosocial middle-class community, much the way urban dance halls and clubs did for young working-class people.[58] Middle-class women and men who vacationed at resorts apparently expected to enjoy themselves in the company of the opposite sex.

The successful development and viability of this new, heterosocial culture depended, first, upon resorts maintaining an even ratio of women and men. But many summer watering places found themselves with an abundance of the former and a scarcity of the latter. Newspaper and magazine accounts of life at resorts frequently commented on the shortage of men. In August of 1860 correspondents from the *New York Times* reported that men were scarce at both Saratoga and Newport. At Saratoga "there are more people . . . of the feminine persuasion than of the masculine. In consequence of this dearth of moustaches ladies have to escort each other to the Springs and whirl each other . . . on the piazzas."[59] Newport, the correspondent maintained, had never witnessed "more beauty, elegance and wit among its lady visitors than it boasts this season; but there is an absolute dearth of the other sex. What has become of all the young men? Are they swallowed up in the speculating vortex of Wall Street?"[60] According to an article in *Every Saturday* magazine, the absence of men at Saratoga during the summer of 1871 left "countless bevies of pretty girls . . . wander[ing] up and down the parlors with arms intertwining each others innocent waists." This observer feared that "the noble art of flirting would soon die out of our watering-places, simply for lack of material."[61] Reports of pretty young women dancing with each other graced the columns written from numerous watering places.[62]

While some newspaper correspondents may have been simply trying to entice more men to the resorts, their observations on the skewed sex ratio squared with reports from vacationers themselves who commented in their letters and diaries about the shortage of men. Mary Ann Lee, for example, wrote to her son, Robert E. Lee Jr., from White Sulphur in August of 1867, exclaiming, "How I wish you could have come up here—plenty of pretty girls and a scarcity of beaux—you would have been quite a lion."[63] By the early 1870s men were already depositing their wives and children at resorts, dashing up by rail or steamer on Saturday evening, and returning to the city on Monday mornings.[64] As a result, women may well have been the majority at many of these summer resorts.[65]

The presence of "too many women" had more serious consequences than the inhibiting of courting and flirting. For not only were women sometimes in the numerical majority, but, according to the press, they exercised a sort of cultural predominance as well. Not all resorts experienced this "problem." It was primarily "fashionable" resorts that allegedly suffered from the influence of female guests.

Fashionable watering places—whether located by the seaside or in the mountains—offered a vacation experience that differed in important ways from "not fashionable" summer resorts. Fashionable resorts were usually large, pricey, and known to attract a well-to-do, fashionable clientele. The goings-on at such places made the society pages of the city newspapers. Saratoga, Newport, and White Sulphur were, by the 1860s, already established fashionable resorts. Within a few decades Bar Harbor, Lenox, and Long Branch had joined the ranks. Of course not everyone at a fashionable resort was necessarily fashionable. Invalids, for example, continued to journey to such places in the hopes of recovering their health. Moreover, large resorts like Saratoga and Newport afforded a range of accommodations— large expensive hotels that housed the fashionable rich and smaller hotels and boarding houses where people of lesser means resided. The Reverend Theodore Cuyler was a frequent visitor to Saratoga in the late nineteenth century and described finding two classes of people there, one "devotees of fashion" and the other "made up of quiet business men and their families, clergyman, college professors and persons of impaired health."[66]

Visitors at fashionable resorts sometimes reported that they felt compelled to join the crowd and participate in an established routine of activities. Indeed, amusements and entertainments at some fashionable watering places seemed to assume an almost regimented quality. Guests at Saratoga, for example, often commented on the "sameness" of the routine they followed: the morning stroll to the springs, the afternoon ride to the lake, the loitering and lolling on the piazzas of the hotels, the bowling and billiard games, the ride on the circular railway, and the walk to a nearby "Indian encampment" where what passed for local Indians sold allegedly native wares.[67] A columnist visiting Saratoga in 1875 lamented the regimentation that accompanied a visit there. At Saratoga, he concluded, "there are well-established currents of happiness into which everyone is dragged as into an eddy, and we have now the exquisite satisfaction of being miserable in company and trying to believe that we are enjoying ourselves hugely. . . . [T]here are certain things to be done at certain times by people of well-regulated minds, without which happiness is deemed impossible." It was, he concluded "almost impossible not to go with the multitude."[68]

The culture and social life of a place like Saratoga allowed opportunities for middle-class vacationers staying at small hotels or boarding houses to consort with the wealthy patrons of large, expensive hotels. An 1880 article in the *New York Times* held that "one half of the summer population of

Broadway at the United States Hotel, Saratoga, New York, c. 1900–1915.
Broadway was a main thoroughfare for promenading in Saratoga, and
promenading was an important form of amusement at fashionable resorts.
(Library of Congress, Detroit Publishing Company Photograph Collection,
LC-D418-78045.)

Saratoga sit upon the hotel piazzas during the greater part of the day, actively engaged in loafing and lounging; the other half seem to be walking up and down Broadway."[69] Besides strolling down Broadway, vacationers could mingle while playing at tenpins, gambling in the casino, sipping water at the springs, or listening to the band concerts on the lawn. Middle-class vacationers could, if they chose, use the period of their vacation to try to emulate the lifestyle of the elite.

Activity, schedules, crowds—these were what filled descriptions of fashionable resorts. By contrast, visitors to less celebrated spots reported calmer surroundings and relaxed, easy-going days.[70] Illinois lawyer Orville Browning spent a week at Versailles Springs, Illinois, in August of 1871. He recorded in his diary: "I have indulged myself in almost total idleness, my only occupations being reading a volume of the British poets, and playing cards, the weather being quite too warm for much exercise. There was not much company, but I have enjoyed the week. It has been one of quiet and repose, and I feel refreshed and benefitted by the rest I have had." Six summers later he and his wife traveled to Elkart Lake in Wisconsin where their daughter and grandchildren were staying. Again he noted in his diary the almost total absence of activity: "Have done nothing since we came here but lie around and rest, reading a little and wandering a little in the woods." He appreciated not only the beauty of the "rural retreat" but the "exemption from the restraints and annoyances of fashionable society, and absolute quiet and freedom to do as you please."[71]

Fashionable resorts differed from their nonfashionable counterparts in significant ways. Although both provided some of the same sorts of amusements—bowling, hiking, billiards, fishing, swimming, tennis, croquet, dances (although usually informal "hops" rather than fancy dress balls), flirting, and courting—fashionable resorts offered more of everything and at a faster pace. Vacationers at fashionable resorts felt swept into a current of activity, while those at not fashionable resorts seemed content to rusticate and relax.

More important differences, however, separated fashionable from not fashionable resorts. First, fashionable resorts commanded considerable attention in the popular press, much of it negative or at best ambivalent. Second, female guests allegedly played an influential role at fashionable watering places. These two situations were not unrelated. Women's predominance at fashionable resorts contributed to the negative cast of much of the public discussion.

Throughout the last half of the nineteenth century newspapers and magazines devoted oceans of ink to the happenings at fashionable summer resorts. There was, undoubtedly, something of a circular relationship between a resort's claim to fashionableness and the articles about it in the papers. Newspapers felt compelled to publish frequent reports from those resorts considered fashionable; at the same time the presence of the journalists and the appearance of repeated articles helped to make the resort fashionable. As the century progressed, increasingly long, detailed, and regular reports of fashionable watering places appeared in city newspapers. In 1870 correspondents from the *Chicago Tribune* were reporting on the summer season at fashionable eastern resorts—Long Branch, Saratoga, Newport, and numerous watering places along Long Island Sound. By 1890 the *New York Times* was devoting whole pages of its Sunday paper to reports from summer resorts.[72]

Many of these accounts followed an almost formulaic pattern. Correspondents mentioned the lovely or rainy weather, the numbers of people who were pouring in as the season geared up or leaving as the summer ebbed, the names of the new arrivals or departures at each fashionable hotel, and the various entertainments and private parties that were occurring. These articles were probably meant to entice people to summer resorts, or to make those who had to remain in the city envious of the fortunate, fashionable people whose schedules and pocketbooks allowed them such pleasures. In fact, one critic claimed that proprietors specifically invited newspaper correspondents when their patrons seemed either unhappy or insufficient in number: "Of course, he is very handsomely treated for the one or two nights he remains, and accordingly, everything at the resort is perfection itself." Happy journalists then allegedly wrote glowing reports about the "first families" in attendance, particularly the ladies who were "endowed with attractions never dreamed of, even by themselves, before."[73]

Despite such claims, not all journalists offered glowing reviews of fashionable resorts. Indeed, an ambivalent tone pervaded much of the public discussion, reflecting the middle class's simultaneous enchantment with and suspicion of wealth and leisure. Embedded in the accounts of journalists and travelers was an evaluation of the nature, purpose, and consequences of resort life. And many who commented offered a decidedly negative appraisal. Fashionable resorts were not just places of innocent amusement. Dangers lurked therein, and many such dangers seemed associated with the habits and behavior of female vacationers.

Reporters and correspondents repeatedly characterized fashionable resorts as, first and foremost, places where women displayed their fashions. Women's clothes seemed to set the tone at vacation places. Fashionably dressed women were, in part, what made a resort fashionable and potentially profitable. Thus resort proprietors welcomed elaborately dressed women and gave them numerous opportunities to display their finery at dances and balls. The hotel owners at Long Branch in 1880 were, reputedly, "jubilant" not only because the hotels were crowded, but because the "ladies" were dressing "much more richly than for many years past. . . . The toilets displayed in the several miles of hotel parlors at the hops last evening were magnificent, and nearly every lady seemed to be the possessor of valuable diamond jewelry."[74]

Journalists described women's vacation wardrobes, commenting on the elaborateness of their *toilettes* and noting how frequently female vacationers changed their clothes. Many of these articles assumed either a mocking or critical tone. A reporter for the *New York Daily Tribune* wrote from Saratoga in 1865: "Poor bodies! [H]ow much pains in dressing, undressing and redressing do they take, day after day, night after night. . . . Poor souls! how they sit and fan, and pose and walk with all of an actor's care, but none of his love of Art!"[75]

The fashionably dressed women who frequented such places seemed little interested, according to journalists, in the rest and renewal that vacations were intended to bring. They sought, instead, opportunities to see and to be seen. Taking part in the spectacle, as either observer or participant, was a critical component of a fashionable vacation. And female vacationers apparently took every opportunity to show themselves—whether on the beach, the ballroom, or a country drive. Swimming at Cape May, for example, afforded more than the occasion for romping in the waves. Time in the surf also offered an opportunity for "sociability." One columnist described the scene this way: "People get acquainted in the water, have time for conversation, and can display their wit if they have any."[76]

Similarly, the drive to Saratoga Lake presented not just an opportunity for fresh air and scenery, but a chance to show off. A young woman who visited Saratoga in 1859 maintained that most people suffered rather than savored the outing: "Those who are so fortunate as to own carriages make up parties to drive out every fine day; not that they can by any possibility enjoy the same routine of driving, any more than any other ever-recurring occupation, but then it is a distinction here to ride out in one's own carriage, when so many stand to gaze and admire, and envy the fortunate ones who ride, while they must go on foot." It was not, she understood, the drive itself that was the attraction. In fact, the drive to the lake at Saratoga could be far from pleasant. The carriages were cramped, the company often unappealing, and the roads could become "so dusty as to be all but intolerable." The carriages "follow so close to each other that the sense of suffocation is ever present; and the entire route is one long-continued discomfort." She concluded by lamenting: "How imperious are the demands of fashion!"[77]

While showing off occupied both men and women at fashionable resorts, most agreed that women were the more egregious offenders. Women, particularly attentive to the "demands of fashion," gave too much time to their clothes. In so doing they were committing an offense more serious than vanity. These female vacationers were challenging important rules of Victorian respectability. Subjecting oneself to the public gaze remained in the nineteenth century something proper middle-class women did not do. Nineteenth-century etiquette books advised women to be inconspicuous in public. As historian John Kasson has explained, a proper woman "minimized eye contact with all but her acquaintances," wore a bonnet or veil that shielded her face, and made sure that her clothes did not attract attention. In so doing, she distinguished herself from working-class women and prostitutes who reveled in bright colored clothes and ostentatious hats (or worse, bare heads).[78] But at fashionable resorts, women's public display—either in bathing suits or ball gowns—formed a critical part of the entertainment.

Columnists and travel writers assumed not only that women determined the sartorial standards, but that men found meeting such standards onerous. A columnist writing from Newport in 1875 exclaimed: "Fashion indeed! [T]he mere thought of it in the hot Summer days is enough to make one flee away to some more congenial place, where a wearied father or husband may lie down in comfort and enjoy his hardly-earned rest." Men, according to this correspondent, wanted "to be easy, and disheveled and careless."[79] The subtext was clear—women were forcing their husbands and fathers to vacation unhappily at resorts where the rules of fashion prevailed. The landlords at Long Branch apparently understood full well which sex determined the vacation destination. An 1885 article explained that despite hard economic times proprietors at Long Branch remained unconcerned about the season: "Not this summer, he [the proprietor] said, 'We know that times are hard, but there are a certain number of people who must go to the country every summer. The men would gladly economize by going to some quiet out-of-the-way place, but women would rather squeeze along at a fashionable place."[80]

The fashionable resort experience was, according to the popular press, gendered female. A snobbish, gossipy atmosphere reputedly prevailed at some resorts, allegedly the result of women's influence. An 1883 article in *Harper's* discussed the daily gossip at hotels in the Catskills: "There is the usual 'I hear,' or 'Would you believe' . . . which is the floating coin of all summer hotel piazzas, and each new-comer is scanned as critically as if he or she were of real importance, instead of being only one of the moving gaily colored, eager eleven hundred." Nevertheless, he continued, new guests arrived nervously, aware that "the eyes . . . are upon them."[81]

Visitors and journalists alike commented upon the cliques that formed at places like White Sulphur and Newport.[82] An 1889 article on summer resorts in *Lippincott's* suggested the unfriendly situations that some vacationers encountered: "There is no loneliness so pathetic as that which a stranger feels in a large circle of people who know each other very well. Such cases of loneliness often occur at our summer resorts." Women, according to this writer, were particularly culpable. "We once heard a lady, at a mountain resort, say, in a tone of great self-satisfaction, 'I've been here for weeks, but I really don't know a soul in the house. I don't even know their names. You see, we have had our own party, and did not need other society.'" The problem could be remedied, the author continued, if only someone would extend a "hand . . . , a smile, a word" to the outsider. But not anyone would do: "It must be a woman's hand that is reached forth, for women are, to an almost unlimited extent, the arbiters of fate in social circles. A word or a glance from them often settles the status of some stranger for the entire season."[83]

Gossip and snobbery were not, according to the press, the worst consequences of women's influence at fashionable resorts. Journalists not only characterized fashionable resorts as places controlled by women, they also spoke about them as sites where artifice and immorality prevailed. Moreover, many of the articles left little doubt about the connection between the former and the latter. Correspondents, for example, wrote of women's vacation clothes as instruments of deceit. One described how the women at Long Branch in 1875 appeared in the afternoons dressed in "attire . . . worn with an effort to appear easy and unconstrained. Loose white dresses cover corsets that were never tighter, and slippers pinch toes as painfully as any gaiters could."[84] Ten years later another columnist, also writing from Long Branch, commented on "the withered old crones who try to conceal the ravages of time by plentiful applications of enamel and rouge and to distract the eyes from what cannot be hidden by blazing displays of diamonds."[85]

While clothing and cosmetics allowed women to disguise themselves anywhere, fashionable resorts offered the perfect arena for such deceptions. And women were certainly not the only culprits. *Harper's* magazine depicted Saratoga in 1859 as a place where "you will see the milliner sitting by the side of the wife of the millionaire, and the swarthy and dwarfed Creole from Cuba reputed to be a Don of Castile descent, talking bad English to both. Indeed the finest looking fellow on the portico of the 'States' one evening and the most reserved, was a barber from Broadway, with a lady on his arm."[86] At fashionable resorts, these observers warned, both men and women sometimes pretended to be who they were not.

The problems of pretense and disguise, according to historian Karen Halttunen, had troubled middle-class Americans throughout the first half of the nineteenth century. Those who followed fashion and put on airs, social commentators warned, threatened the sincerity necessary for a moral social order. But the demands of a more mobile, urban society increasingly required that people adhere to elaborate rules of decorum and etiquette, and such rituals undermined rather than promoted sincere or genuine social interaction. As a result, by the 1850s and 1860s, Halttunen explains, "the sentimental demand for perfect sincerity was losing its tone of urgency and being replaced by a new acceptance of the theatricality of social relationships." Middle-class Americans came to accept dress as a form of disguise and to endorse formal social rituals, what she calls "polite hypocrisy," as a necessity for successful social intercourse.[87]

Perhaps nowhere was this more evident than at fashionable resorts. What newspapers described taking place at these spots was a form of "theater"— the promenading of the guests, the grand entrance at balls, the emphasis on costume and dress. Indeed, resorts functioned, in some ways, like the parlor theatricals that became so popular around the middle of the nineteenth century.[88] But the "acting" had moved from the parlor to the streets, piazzas, and ballrooms, thereby creating a host of new problems. Parlors had contained only invited guests, while fashionable resorts brought strangers together. Anyone who could follow the rituals might be included, thereby giving potentially unsavory characters access to respectable society. In such an environment, many argued, "polite hypocrisy" was not necessarily harmless and innocent amusements could become risky.

Newspapers and magazines cautioned that dissipation and corruption frequently accompanied the pretense so common to resort culture. Fashionable resorts encouraged extravagance and excess, especially amongst people of moderate means. *Harper's* magazine explained that "young clerks, with their cigars and ratans" swelled the population of Saratoga in 1859:

> Their place at the dinner table is usually indicated by the shooting of a Champagne cork. They put on quite a wealthy air, and obviously make the most of the little they have. Poor fellows, . . . they imbibe a taste for the extravagant here which often interferes with their honesty, and with their subsequent prosperity in business. Economy and frugality are essential to success in life; these are simply mean vices at Saratoga, and are not to be named in the presence of the glorious virtue of prodigality which here reigns triumphant.[89]

Vacations, proponents argued, were intended to renew and refresh, refueling vacationers for the challenges of middle-class life. But a stay at a fashionable resort, these critics maintained, would do just the opposite. This was, of course, exactly what those who railed against various forms of recreation had feared. Traditional Protestant ministers had warned of the numerous dangers that could befall those who indulged in amusements.[90] Idleness was, after all, the devil's tool. Extended periods without the discipline of work could wreak havoc on a middle class struggling to live morally upright and financially successful lives. An apparently innocent quest for relaxation could end in ruin, teaching instead bad habits that left vacationers unfit for their daily work. Vacationing at a fashionable resort could be dangerous.

Gambling presented one of the most visible hazards. Fashionable resorts often contained gambling houses that, columnists warned, lured young men. An 1870 article cautioned that at Saratoga "there are several 'Club houses,'—i.e. gambling saloons clustered about the central part of the place which receive an extensive patronage from the fast men who congregate here."[91] Ten years later another columnist discussed the "drawbacks and corruptions of Saratoga life," offering his own "humorous and involuntary experience" of being "gracefully decoyed and fleeced." He described how a "well-dressed, good looking young fellow, who pretended to be, or may be, for aught I know, a clerk off on his vacation . . . sat down besides me, and in the free and easy fashion which is common enough at Summer resorts, began to talk." Although the writer discerned the intentions of this would-be clerk, "curiosity" won out over "scruples": "I accompanied my gentlemen to their private parlors, heard the doors locked behind me, and found myself suddenly seated before a rouge-et-noir table."[92] It is no accident that this story included the elements of a classic seduction scene—the charming would-be gentleman, the locked door—for most of the discussion about dangers of fashionable resorts centered not on gambling but on sex.

Columnists and travel writers who spoke of deception, dissipation, and corruption frequently associated these with sexual dangers. An 1865 article warned that "much of the stiffness, staidness and decorum of homes [was] abandoned" at watering places:

> Young men and young women universally keep more of each other's company. There is a certain amount of jostling and forced contiguity which gives free scope to the amorous inclination. Mothers relax the parental discipline, and heavy fathers dip into sports and conversation which at home would be impossible. Scandal is so common as to lose its sting.

According to this correspondent, it was not innocent young lovers but "fortune-hunting Misses of advanced years" and "old bachelors whose accumulated dissipations have made them serious, selfish and carnal" who prowled the piazzas of fashionable resort hotels.[93]

Observers pictured women as both perpetrators and victims. Popular belief held that watering places were crawling with adventurers ready to prey upon unsuspecting women. The *New York Times* in 1856 related the story of a woman who had come to Saratoga twenty years earlier "rich and beautiful" and found there plenty of "wooers for beauty and money." The article explained that "then as now" such women were "perhaps all too easily won." This particular lady "listened to the flattering words of him who pretended to love her, and persevered in his suit till he had obtained her hand." As the reader might guess, things turned out badly. Her family disowned her, then her ne'er-do-well husband spent her money, failed in business, "and having never loved her could not longer conceal his falsehood, hated her, left her and slandered her, and ever since she has lived alone, secluded from the world, with her two children, still unforgiven by her friends, and almost forgotten." The article made its didactic purpose explicit: "We tell the story for the benefit of the fair girl who sits almost every day in the same place and listens to the words which spread over her face a glow like the dawn of a Summer morning."[94]

Many seemed equally worried about the dangers awaiting men. At a place like Saratoga, an unsuspecting young man, listening innocently to the afternoon band playing on the piazza, might "take his seat beside that female spider, so tickled and flattered that the air seems full of happiness; the music seems overwhelming, and the young lady herself an angel of Paradise." Lurking nearby, however, "the future mother-in-law . . . smiles an approbation, at her daughter, and grins horribly a ghastly look of friendship at the victim."[95] Mothers of marriageable daughters came in for special criticism. An 1885 correspondent from Long Branch held that the "purring of these old cats around eligible young men reminds one of the purring of the real animal around a saucer of milk. They are so hungry for young men with good incomes." He admitted that the daughters "are not always so bad. . . . There are prizes among the girls. . . . But it is a hard thing for the young men to discover the girls, hidden as they are under the shadows of their abominable old mothers."[96]

The seamy underside of watering place life captured the attention of many who wrote about fashionable resorts. An article in the *New York Daily Tribune* in 1865 noted that a first glance at Saratoga might make the observer forget "that there is such a thing as pain, suffering, or sorrow, or sighing in the world." A closer look, however, would reveal that "the demon of human wretchedness is here in strange garb. It appears along with the broken-down constitutions, the decaying charms and faculties, the plotting politicians, the sportsmen, the desperate match-seekers and match-makers of either sex who make this their rallying point." The article described the balls and hops that occurred nightly and made it clear that sexual immorality went hand in hand with watering-place life. "Next comes the bold-looking and robust Mrs. Cleopatra Minque, who exults in a magnificent bust and shoulders. She is a fine form and elaborately dressed. Who would imagine that she was forty-one this month? . . . on the arm of a well-known railroad conductor from a lake city. Both are married, and both are flirting without the knowledge of their families, while the petition for divorce has not yet been filed from either."[97] A correspondent writing from Cape May in 1875 observed "with pitying amusement the efforts of thin Miss Virginal to appear easy and dégagée and flirt with a mere boy from college, she being a mature maiden that will never see thirty again."[98] The frequent derision of older women may have masked fears that female maturity brought with it not only experience but certain sorts of power.

According to the popular press, fashionable resorts presented would-be vacationers with an array of potential dangers. These were places where pretense and deception reigned, where opportunities for dissipation tempted, and where sexual immorality lurked. For much of the nineteenth century Americans associated such behavior with the corruption, idleness, and vice of a wealthy aristocracy—the culture they had allegedly rejected when the colonies separated from England. Republican thought held that virtuous women and hardworking men formed the backbone of the republic and allowed for the flourishing of democratic institutions.[99]

But by the last half of the nineteenth century the growth of fashionable

resorts was creating places where middle-class people could not only witness but enjoy the pleasures of wasteful idleness. Bad enough when such
dissipation remained confined within a small, wealthy elite—how much
worse when it threatened to corrupt the middle class. The public discussion
about these resorts may well have reflected fears that the idleness and
immorality of a dissolute aristocracy would infect the middle class and possibly undermine the democracy. A correspondent from the *Chicago Tribune*
explained that the "charms" of Watch Hill, a small resort on the Rhode
Island shore, included more than cool weather, reasonable prices, and good
surf. Visitors to Watch Hill would find "no exactions in the way of fashion
or dress; no gossip; . . . no liquors retailed anywhere within four miles; . . .
family company, with no room nor toleration for snots." Significantly, the
writer went on to describe Watch Hill as "a *little republic*, without vices, and
yet without provincialism."[100]

The press offered various suggestions for circumventing many of the hazards of summer watering places. It was possible, many journalists maintained, to visit a fashionable resort without being seduced by the various
temptations. Vacationers needed to steer clear of fashionable society and
enjoy the innocent pleasures of air, water, and respectable company. T. A.
Richards assured readers of *Knickerbocker* magazine in 1859 that a visit to
Saratoga would prove beneficial if they arrived there "with souls of their
own, imbued with a love for the pure delights of nature and of country life."
For such visitors "the fashionable world may be easily left on one side."[101]
A correspondent writing from Newport in 1865 admitted: "Newport is a
fashionable watering-place, it is true." But, he continued, "it is also a place
of resort for a great many plain, sensible people, who come here for the
bathing, the cool breezes, the invigorating salt air." Those visitors who
chose to stay at some of the "large comfortable houses" on the "Point"
rather than on "the fashionable thoroughfares" would find themselves "free
from all restraints in the way of fashion, or any necessity of a grand toilet,
and [at] prices less than half hotel charges."[102]

Even better, however, would be to choose a vacation place that was not
fashionable—a place like the "little republic" of Watch Hill. The American
press contrasted the dangers of fashionable watering places with the advantages of not fashionable resorts. Indeed, just as "fashionable" could be read
as an epithet (although sometimes an attractive epithet), "not fashionable"
became, in many accounts, a term of praise.

Potential vacationers, for example, learned that at a quiet, out-of-the-way
place like Montvale Springs in East Tennessee they would find neither
"sharpers," "dudes," nor "coquettes."[103] Similarly, an article on Lake Mahopac, a small resort in Putnam County, New York, about fifty miles from
New York City, assured the reading public in July of 1870 that "all the

patrons are, indeed, of the best classes of society, but the rules of Fashion are relaxed, and the people are prone rather to sensible enjoyment than to unvarying observance of the rules." This columnist felt that the absence of the railroad had, thus far, kept Lake Mahopac safe from "the rabble of the fashionable world."[104]

Bolton on Lake George won praise in 1865 for being "delightfully free from the fashionable style or restraint, where you can row, or fish, or walk, and eat and sleep sans ceremonie."[105] Fifteen years later Lake George still held the reputation of being not fashionable. Even though the nearby Fort William Henry Hotel could, by then, house 1,000 guests "comfortably and [had] all the appointments of a first-class resort," journalists continued to extol Lake George for resisting the dictates of fashion: "The visitors to Lake George dress quietly. Even at Caldwell, the fashionable end of the lake, flannel or light airy costumes are the rule among the ladies, silks and satins making their appearance only in the evening or at the hops and receptions." Further down the lake, however, "cigars and cigarettes are boldly displaced by pipes, and the women run and row merrily about in the loosest and least ornamented of garments. We go to bed early and rise before the sun."[106] Just as women's clothes marked a resort as fashionable, so too did what the women wore help, according to the press, create a more beneficial, benevolent environment.

At resorts that were not fashionable one could reputedly reap the rewards that vacations were supposed to provide—health, renewal, relaxation. Oscar Shafter, a well-known California lawyer, traveled with his wife to Lake Tahoe in June of 1864. He described in his diary how "the hotel here is well filled with tourists and successful miners from Virginia City." Shafter specifically observed that "unlike most places of fashionable resort," the women who visited Tahoe "don't bring their fashions with them, which adds very much to their own comfort and that of their husbands." He also noted the beauty of the place and how, after their stay there, they expected to "return with renovated health and spirits to our accustomed labors and duties."[107]

Of course, one could never be absolutely certain. Writers often mentioned the spectrum of people who frequented American watering places. Saratoga, an article in a popular magazine reported in 1871, was populated by

bad men in plenty as well as good; the threadbare broadcloth of the jaded clergyman, who is nervously pursuing the phantom of his lost health, rubs against the velveteen of the hook-nosed professional gambler, who is tranquilly hunting for subjects upon whom to practice his devilish arts; bold French adventurers, whose cheeks have forgotten how to blush except at the bidding of the rouge-pot, sit beside pure young virgins who scarcely know the

vices by their names; and the swindler and confidence man exchange newspapers with the honorable merchant whose long business life has never felt
the touch of dishonor.[108]

Just as one could find threadbare clergymen, pure young virgins, and honorable merchants at fashionable watering places, so too might one encounter
less wholesome characters even at little known, not fashionable resorts. One
correspondent maintained that the guests at Greenwood Lake, a small vacation spot in the southern part of Orange County, New York, ran the gamut
from "few who seek enjoyment and health, and find both" to the "young
ladies who never appear out of doors until 4 o'clock in the afternoon, and
then in a most elaborate toilet." The writer also observed among the guests
"those young gentlemen who spend the most of their days in the billiard or
bar rooms—all flattering themselves that they are gaining health the most
robust" as well as "the maneuvering mamma with her tribe of marriageable
daughters [and] the young 'catches' just coming into capillary bloom." The
resort attracted, as well, "the traveled tourist, who has been everywhere; the
heiress and the adventurer . . . and every fortnight papa runs up from the
hot, dusty City, gets a whiff of fresh air, and returns like a broker to his
gold."[109]

Throughout the last half of the nineteenth century coverage of fashionable resorts appeared regularly in the popular press, with newspapers and
magazines characterizing such places as both attractive and dangerous.
Moreover, the discussion about resorts changed little until the early 1900s,
when warnings about the moral hazards of resort life diminished.[110] But for
most of the century the appeal of leisure and recreation coexisted with the
risks of dissipation and pretense.

The fact that these were environments in which women and men recre-
ated together heightened both the attractions and the dangers. The press
seemed to take a lighthearted look at women's participation in a wide range
of sports, games, and physical amusements. Few articles criticized women's
decisions, for example, to swim in the ocean, hike in the mountains, attend
the race track, or even enjoy a game of billiards. Perhaps such activities
seemed benign when compared to the other possibilities that resort life presented. Descriptions of women's parading themselves for the public gaze
and using fashion to lure potential mates, for example, took on a much
more sinister tone. Columnists seemed to decry the highly sexualized environment of fashionable resorts even as they lamented that the absence of
men sometimes limited possibilities for flirting and courting.

Some of this ambivalence no doubt reflected a larger uncertainty about
leisure and vacationing in general. Americans were just beginning to con-
cede the value of amusements, and many no doubt remained fearful of the

potentially negative consequences of extended leisure.[111] Resort life seemed to encourage people to behave in what historian John Stilgoe has described as "marginal behavior."[112] While Stilgoe maintains that coastal environments, specifically, fostered such conduct, the discussion in the popular press suggests a generalized apprehension about resorts in any location — seashore, lakeside, mountains, or springs. Places where recreation and play were the major focus, these articles implied, encouraged unsavory sorts of behavior. People removed too long from their daily work and routine might learn bad habits and fall prey to temptations of laziness, drink, sex, or gambling. For a middle class that defined itself against such vices and associated the numerous sins of idleness with the vicious poor or the idle rich, resorts could present a serious threat.

The gendered nature of this discussion, however, suggests that fashionable resorts incited misgivings about more than just leisure itself. Summer resorts occupied a sort of hybrid space in late nineteenth-century America, both public and domestic, anonymous and intimate. On the one hand resorts were crowded and open, often thronged with strangers from all parts of the country. On the other, they sometimes served as summer homes, places where women remained ensconced for extended periods. The focus on sexual danger and dissipation within the popular press may well have reflected cultural concerns about how to reorder middle-class gender relations in such environments.

As important, at many resorts women not only were in the majority, but wrote the social rules and set the tone. Such women presided over a sort of public heterosociality not usually associated with middle-class Victorians. Historian Kathy Peiss has suggested that young working-class women helped to create a heterosocial culture in turn-of-the-century cities, prodding American society from a Victorian past into a more modern future.[113] While the balls and piazzas of fashionable resorts differed dramatically from the working-class dance halls and clubs of New York or Chicago, they offered middle-class men and women venues in which to meet, socialize, and court. At fashionable resorts the social disguises of polite society — manners and dress — facilitated the mingling of middle-class strangers, with potentially dangerous consequences.[114] It seems not accidental, for example, that Kate Chopin chose to make a summer resort the site where Edna Pontellier, the tragic heroine of *The Awakening*, not only began "to realize her position in the universe as a human being" but to contemplate an adulterous love.[115]

The discussion of fashionableness that permeated the popular press rested on two assumptions: that women exerted considerable influence at such resorts and that these may be potentially dangerous places at which to vacation. The second proposition grew, in part, from the first. The associa-

tion between women and danger did not, of course, originate in the late
nineteenth-century debate over recreation and vacations. It dates, at least,
from the alleged controversy over an apple. But the negative image of fashionable resorts that pervaded the press stemmed, in part, from the fact that
women were perceived to be exercising undue autonomy there. Female
influence at fashionable resorts became a trope for the dangers of excess,
deception, and dissipation that might result as Americans took vacations
and embraced leisure and recreation.

Of course, the line between fashionable and not fashionable was not always
clear and easily demarcated. Those who wanted to be absolutely safe either
had to design a vacation that did not involve a stay at a resort or to choose
one of the resorts guaranteed to protect its residents from the dangers that
late nineteenth-century Americans found inherent in leisure and recreation.

✑ 4 ✑

"No late hours, no headache in the morning..."

─────•◆•─────

SELF-IMPROVEMENT VACATIONS

In August of 1883 Eva Moll, a young school teacher from Ohio, wrote in her diary: "I so much desire to go to Chautauqua. . . . Could that dream be realized I would consider it the happiest event of my life."[1] Chautauqua, located in western New York state, became a favorite vacation spot for thousands of Americans in the years after 1874. What attracted Eva Moll to Chautauqua was not merely its promise of amusement and relaxation, but also its extensive educational offerings. Chautauqua was one of numerous places where a vacationer could combine recreation with self-improvement.

Throughout the last half of the nineteenth century both religious and secular institutions took shape that provided the middle-class vacationing public with alternatives to regular summer resorts. Some began as Protestant (predominantly Methodist) camp meetings and grew to be religious resorts where, at a minimum, a vacationer would be protected from some of the potential dangers associated with resort life. Others, with more explicit educational goals, became institutions where middle-class people could both enjoy themselves and obtain formal instruction or training.

Both sorts of resorts served similar functions. They broadened the vacationing clientele and diversified the resort experiences. Most importantly, vacationers at these self-improvement resorts could, even while at leisure, reaffirm their commitment to the important middle-class values of sobriety and discipline. Many of these sites provided middle-class men and women an opportunity to combine work with play and thus to use their vacations productively. Those who vacationed at self-improvement resorts were not merely idle and, as a result, vacationing became a little less risky.

———•◆•———

In the years after 1850 religious camp meetings continued to do what they had been doing since the turn of the nineteenth century—attract those in search of spiritual regeneration. During these decades, however, camp meetings came to serve other purposes as well. They provided a vacation-like environment for people who might have felt constrained, either by financial limitations or religious principles, from visiting a summer resort. Those who attended camp meetings did so to renew their faith, but also to get away from home and to socialize with friends and strangers in a new set-ting. Camp meetings increasingly met the recreational as well as the spiritual needs of their participants.

During the last half of the nineteenth century many camp meetings changed from rough clearings in the woods to permanent institutions. Camp Labor, a Methodist camp meeting near Denville in New Jersey, for example, opened in mid August of 1870. The newspaper reported that the area around the preacher's stand had enough seats to accommodate the two thousand people who visited the grounds that day. Besides the tents for prayer meetings, the organizers had also set up "the most perfect Police arrangements," had contrived to bring "fresh spring water" to the "entire ground from a reservoir which is filled by a steam engine," had concocted a "telegraph and post-offices," and had made sure that "all baggage and tents will be forwarded to the grounds free of expense." Moreover, visitors found "a number of convenient boarding-tents . . . with prices ranging from $1 to $2 per day."[2] Camp Labor had become a small, temporary town.

Similarly, the Methodist camp meeting at Sing Sing, New York, which dated from the late 1830s, was by 1870 undergoing significant improvement to its physical surroundings. A reporter for the *New York Times* noted: "The entire ground has been drained, roads have been laid out, streets and tents have been numbered, the water is now thrown up by a force pump on the summit of the hill, and the entire encampment is lighted with . . . gas light." The newspaper waxed eloquent about the pleasures of a sojourn at Sing Sing—"the cheapness, the comfort, and the real solid enjoyment of this life." A visitor could obtain "excellent board" at the cost of $1 to $1.50 a day, and good beds could be had for as little as .50 a night. Moreover "when a family take a tent or tents and board themselves, they live as cheaply as at home; sleeping and eating as they cannot in the crowded City during the heated term."[3]

The camp meeting at Sing Sing apparently offered more than monetary advantages as a place for summer respite: "No Saratoga airs or discomforts, no bed-bugs or fleas or mosquitoes, no flunkey waiters or surly landlords are there, but love, harmony, and sociability prevails, all are in good humor, happy in body and in soul."[4] Comparing a rather primitive camp meeting like Sing Sing to an established, fashionable resort like Saratoga may seem like a case of apples and oranges. But, for this reporter at least, both were summer vacation places.

Not everybody liked the changes at Sing Sing. Some complained that the religious purpose of the camp meeting had diminished, "that the camp meeting has degenerated into a religious picnic, that the days when, with no floors or carpets, . . . with no melodeons or flowers, they went with no desire for show, or rest, or pleasure, but for real hard work—that those days were the best." And, indeed, things had changed: observers noted that visitors to Sing Sing "now . . . mingle pleasure and recreation with work." Moreover, some families were moving to Sing Sing for the week, but the men, rather than remaining and participating in camp meeting events, were returning to work in the city each day. For them, the camp meeting had become a moderately priced vacation spot within a reasonable commuting distance from the city.[5]

The annual camp meeting at Sing Sing continued to attract crowds, drawing an estimated five thousand people on one day in 1885. While some of these visitors were taking one-day excursions, many planned an extended stay. The number of visitors, in fact, far outstripped the accommodations in the hotels and boarding houses, and those who did not have their own tents "had to be sent away to the village." That year some ethnic groups had even established their own mini-camp meetings at Sing Sing. About four hundred Swedes had erected their own boarding house. They occupied "one corner of the grounds by themselves, and conduct[ed] their services in their native tongue."[6]

The 1885 Sing Sing camp meeting had been, according to the *New York Times*, a splendid success. The measure of success rested not only in the spiritual fervor and the number of participants, but also in the ability of organizers to balance two potentially conflicting purposes of the event. Selling both religion and enjoyment, places like Sing Sing strove to make sure that the latter not overshadow the former. To that end, the organizers, for example, prohibited stores from opening on the Sabbath. But visitors and participants still found opportunities to indulge: "All along the line of the road in the vicinity of the camp there were booths where soda water, sarsa-

parilla, clam chowder, and other refreshments were dispensed, the proprietors reaping a rich harvest, as the stores of the camp were closed all day."
Still, the newspaper reported on the orderliness of the meeting and the
absence of disturbances. "Such a thing as an intoxicated person had not
been seen on the grounds."[7]

Large camp meetings like Sing Sing faced the constant challenge of
maintaining the religious focus of the meeting as crowds, often with other
than spiritual matters on their mind, gathered on the grounds. At the camp
meeting at Fair Point, New York, for example, "thousands of pleasure-seek-
ers, who were bound to have a good time at fifteen cents apiece, came pouring upon the ground" on Sundays. Many of these people apparently "cared
nothing about sermons, exhortations, or prayers" but formed part of a
"good-natured crowd, who had paid for the show and were bound to enjoy
it in their own way."[8]

Some camp meetings were more successful than others at keeping religion in the forefront. The *Indianapolis Freeman*, an African-American newspaper, reported in August of 1891 that Irving Park and Asbury Grove, "the
largest and most famous camp meetings held by colored people in this
country," were currently in progress. The reporter noted that "they are
generally successful financially; spiritually they have for years been dead
failures."[9] Not all African-American camp meetings earned such condem-
nation. Tyler City Camp Meeting in Connecticut drew praise for the quality of the lecturers. Those who mounted the platform spoke about the
improvement of the race and the impediments to progress. Some speakers
used the camp meeting as a forum for promoting the fair election bill then
before the Senate. For African Americans, camp meetings served political
purposes as well as religious and recreational ones.[10]

As camp meetings grew into summer resorts, they often influenced the
character of nearby vacation spots. The Methodist camp meeting on
Martha's Vineyard, for example, first met in 1835 when a small group of
Methodists established a site at what they later called Wesleyan Grove. By
1857 250 tents covered 12 to 15 acres, forming, according to historian Ellen
Weiss, "little neighborhoods." The community continued to expand
throughout the late 1850s, building more permanent structures—wooden
buildings and tents with wooden walls. During the early 1860s cottages
began to replace tents, and by the end of the Civil War Wesleyan Grove was
changing from "a city of tents to . . . a city of cottages nestled under the
trees."[11]

In 1860 the camp meeting was large enough for the leaders to see the
necessity of forming a Martha's Vineyard Camp-Meeting Association, a
body that included church leaders and elected officers who managed the
camp and licensed the tents and cottages. Five years later the association

authorized the purchase of over twenty acres, using $1,300 raised from tent and cottage owners, and in 1868 the Massachusetts legislature incorporated the Martha's Vineyard Camp-Meeting Association.[12]

The newly formed Camp-Meeting Association struggled to preserve a spiritual atmosphere as their community grew. By the mid-1860s the potential for profits in resort communities was attracting astute entrepreneurs to seaside spots. The healthful air and possibilities for sea bathing made Martha's Vineyard appealing to investors. Camp meeting people feared that unwelcome neighbors might settle nearby. Hoping to create a buffer that would protect the camp meeting, organizers discussed buying contiguous land. Before the Camp-Meeting Association could decide, however, six businessmen bought the seventy-five acres abutting Wesleyan Grove and offered one thousand lots for sale.

Leaders of the camp meeting, worried about sharing their space with a summer resort, met with the developers and worked out an agreement that would satisfy both groups. The deeds to property on Oak Bluffs, the new development, could be sold only for family dwellings. Liquor, gambling, manufacturing, and trade were forbidden; restaurants would remain closed on the Sabbath; and steamers would be prohibited from landing at Oak Bluffs's wharfs on Sundays. The camp meeting clearly had an impact on the nature of the contiguous resort. That developers of Oak Bluffs conceded to the demands of their neighbors suggests that they did not see such restrictions as a liability. And they were right. Increasing numbers of middle-class men and women were seeking resort communities in which Christian influences would prevail.[13]

Sing Sing and Oak Bluffs were far from unique. By 1870 many other camp meetings were being turned into permanent camp grounds/resort communities. Among the most famous was Ocean Grove, located six miles south of Long Branch on the New Jersey shore. Founded in 1869 by the Methodist Camp-Meeting Association, Ocean Grove began to lease lots at auction in 1870 for prices that ranged up to $75. Within fifteen years the highest priced ocean-front lots were going for $1,500. But the cost of a stay at Ocean Grove still remained within the range of people of moderate means. For $2.50 a week, paid in advance, a family could rent a tent "with a floor and a small kitchen in the rear." Given that a stay at even a small summer boarding house could cost $5 per person per week, a tent at Ocean Grove offered an economical alternative. By 1879 seven hundred tents housed visitors at Ocean Grove.[14]

Ocean Grove was planned as a "retreat for Christians, where sinful pastimes would not be tolerated for an instant."[15] That meant, first, keeping the Sabbath holy. The community forbad swimming on Sunday. Moreover, the large gates to the city were locked at midnight on Saturday night, keeping bicycles and horses from entering or leaving. The *New York Times* reported in 1895 that "even milkmen are tabooed on the first day of the week, and the hotelkeepers and cottagers tramp across to Asbury Park for their Sunday supply of the lacteal fluid."[16] As late as 1925 Ocean Grove reportedly still put "the lid on securely at midnight each Saturday, and [settled] down to genuine old-fashioned Sunday quiet."[17] Visitors and residents alike had to leave their automobiles at the gates and walk into the town.

Ocean Grove prohibited other activities deemed not consonant with Christian living—dancing, cardplaying, and the sale of liquor. On Saturday nights the slot machines that dispensed candy and chewing gum were emptied "thus removing the temptation to chew gum" on the Sabbath. Cigars and tobacco were "also on the black list." And anyone caught smoking near the auditorium could be arrested. By the end of the century, however, some visitors were apparently observing these rules primarily in the breach. Hotelkeepers would not openly sell cigars and cigarettes, but guests who knew to "drop their nickel or dime in a box" could be rewarded with a smoke. Despite such minor infractions, observers maintained that the twenty thousand people enjoyed the "religious resort in every respect."[18]

Ocean Grove, like Wesleyan Grove on Martha's Vineyard, knew that the neighboring community could have a potentially adverse impact on its special environment. One year after the Camp-Meeting Association purchased Ocean Grove, five hundred acres immediately to the north came on the market. James Bradley, an entrepreneurial Methodist and a member of the association, bought the land and named it Asbury Park, after Francis Asbury, the first American Methodist bishop.[19] Bradley helped to protect Ocean Grove by developing Asbury Park as a "non-secular Summer resort," selling or leasing land only to "people who would observe such restrictions as he saw fit to set." This meant no gambling, no drinking, and no bathing on Sundays.[20] While visitors did not always abide by all the rules, Asbury Park took its cue from its neighbor and established a summer resort that offered refuge from some of the moral hazards of vacationing.[21] By 1889 Asbury Park boasted over thirty thousand summer visitors, nearly two hundred hotels and boarding houses, as well as eight hundred private homes.[22]

Ocean Grove spawned other religious resorts. The Reverend Robert W. Todd, the pastor of St. Paul's Methodist Episcopal (M.E.) Church in Wilmington, Delaware, found himself "very feeble from several weeks of camp meeting service" and decided to visit Ocean Grove for "rest and relaxation." The visit, particularly the "lessons of the sea," left him with renewed health and strength, and he decided to purchase a lot and build his own cottage at Ocean Grove. When the prices proved too steep for his budget, his thoughts turned to the possibility of establishing a "Christian seaside resort" along the Delaware Peninsula. Remembering that "he had heard, some

Avenue of tents, Ocean Grove, New Jersey. Many of the vacationers at Ocean Grove, a Christian resort, lived in tents. (Library of Congess, U.S. Geographic File, LC-Z62-120490.)

Bathing at Ocean Grove, New Jersey, 1904. Ocean Grove allowed swimming (although not on Sundays) but proscribed a number of other "sinful" amusements such as drinking, gambling, cardplaying, and dancing. (Library of Congress, U.S. Geographic File, LC-USZ62-95812.)

years before, of the remarkable Rehoboth Bay," Todd wrote to the Reverend William Warner, pastor of a Methodist Church at Lewes, just a few
miles north of Rehoboth, and asked him to scout out the area for a potential
site. Warner "warmly second[ed]" Todd's idea and brought "the intelligence
[information] that he had *found the place.*" The Preacher's Meeting at Wilmington considered the issue, liked the idea, and authorized a committee of
ministers and laymen to visit the spot. In October of 1872 the committee
bought the land.[23]

The following year the Rehoboth Beach Camp-Meeting Association of
the M.E. Church was incorporated with the purpose of "providing and
maintaining a permanent Camp-meeting Ground and Christian Sea-side
Resort, where everything inconsistent with christian [*sic*] morality, as taught
by the said church, shall be excluded and prohibited." Note that the place
was, from its inception, intended to be both a camp meeting ground *and* a
seaside resort. The organizers must have seen no conflict between making
one place serve both purposes. Apparently experience had shown that,
despite occasional complications, the two could be successfully combined.
This new community had two functions: to "hold annual camp meetings"
and to "provide and maintain" a particular sort of summer resort—one in
which "the discipline of the M.E. Church shall be the standard for the moral
government of the place, and any business, avocation or recreation, inconsistent therewith shall be unlawful."[24]

By the mid-1870s places like Ocean Grove, Oak Bluffs, and Rehoboth
were becoming increasingly widespread. In June of 1875 the *New York Times*
reported: "A tendency has been noted among the Methodists to modify the
character of camp-meetings, and to make them health resorts, governed by
religious influences. It is the object to provide pleasant places for Summer-
ing, where only good influences are exerted." Besides commenting on the
by-then "famous spots" on the East Coast, the article noted the recent opening of "Ocean Grove Retreat" near Monterey on the California coast and
"Lake Bluff" about an hour outside of Chicago on Lake Michigan.[25]

Methodists pioneered and dominated the building of religious resorts.
Both the changing nature of the Methodists's constituency and the unchang-
ing nature of Methodist doctrine no doubt encouraged them to establish
these places. Methodists remained during the last half of the nineteenth century reluctant, compared with some more liberal denominations, to relin-
quish their prohibitions of amusements. In 1872 Methodists still forbade
"intoxicating liquors, dancing, playing at games of chance, attending theaters, horse races, circuses, dancing parties, or patronizing dancing
schools."[26] At the same time, the denomination was also enjoying considerable growth, with about 1.7 million adherents in 1860 and almost 4.5 million in 1900. Not only more people, but different sorts of people, were

becoming Methodists. Once concentrated primarily although never entirely among poor country folks, Methodism was drawing members from the urban middle class—the sorts of people who wanted their religion to appear more polished and their clergy to be better educated.[27] While not wealthy, they were the types of people who managed to spare some money for a short summer vacation. Religious resorts thus fit the needs of Methodism's expanding constituency without violating its traditional doctrines.

Although Methodists controlled most religious resorts, members of other denominations made a few efforts in the same direction.[28] Quakers Albert and Alfred Smiley, twin brothers, opened the Mohonk Mountain House in the Shawangunk Mountains of New York during the 1870s. The Smileys intended to attract an educated, well-placed clientele and to run the hotel "along strictly Quaker lines." That meant no liquor, no cardplaying, no dancing. Carriages could neither leave nor enter on the Sabbath. Moreover, the hotel hosted a ten-minute voluntary prayer service every morning and nondenominational services every Sunday.[29] Despite the restrictions, Mohonk flourished. In fact, many found the regulations one of Mohonk's attractions. A Mrs. Brunot wrote, for example, explaining that it had been "years since we heard of the beauty and Christian character of your home and desired to visit it."[30]

Such an environment could be especially appealing to women vacationing alone. Given the rather questionable reputation that many critics attached to summer resorts, a place like Mohonk stood out for upholding moral standards. Albert G. Hook, probably a clerk for a New York City hardware importer, wanted to find a safe place for his sisters to visit: "Being unable to leave the city myself, my sisters are without an escort, they will however find no trouble I trust in arranging their business with you. Please give them all that is necessary to make them comfortable for which you will find me deeply indebted."[31] By the 1870s many families were looking for summer vacation spots for the wife and children—places to which husbands might commute on the weekends. A resort like Mohonk, situated within a reasonable train ride from New York and safe from the dangers that alcohol, dancing, or cardplaying might represent, offered an ideal alternative.

Throughout the last half of the nineteenth century a variety of religiously inspired resorts began to attract growing numbers of vacationers. Some, particularly those that grew out of camp meetings, helped to open the vacation experience to a broader cross section of the population. The tents, cottages, and boarding houses of campgrounds/resorts offered accommodations that people of modest means could afford.[32] Some observers maintained that such places drew a respectable but not terribly refined or educated crowd. Moses Hoge, a Presbyterian minister from Richmond, was vacationing at Berkeley Springs, West Virginia, in the late summer of 1870. He spent one

day of his vacation on an excursion to a nearby Methodist camp meeting—
a "very picturesque place." Hoge, a tourist rather than a participant at the
camp meeting, was curious about the people and the surroundings. He
found surprisingly comfortable and well-appointed tents inhabited by what
he characterized as "a very primitive population":

> [I]n a few minutes I made friends with the inmates of the tent. I asked one of
> the men if Brother Mullins (the singer) would consider it as a liberty if I would
> ask him to sing for us during the intermission. Yes, the man said, he would
> take it as a very great liberty. But seeing he did not understand the word lib-
> erty, I put the question in a different form & he answered, 'O yes, he would be
> very much pleased if you wd. ask him to sing for you.'[33]

Hoge's account suggests that these summer camp meetings were attracting
not the well-educated middle class, but the uncultivated and unlettered people of moderate means.

But camp meetings may have been drawing from a broader social spectrum than Hoge understood. Benjamin Atkins, for example, was a fifty-year-
old president of the Athens (Tennessee) Female College. Atkins had spent
his entire adult life as an educator at numerous institutions in North Carolina and Tennessee. In 1895 he and his two eldest sons participated in a
summer camp meeting. His diary recorded: "returned from Cane Creek
campgrounds, 12 miles south of Athens, where I spent four days attending
camp meetings. . . . Pleasant time and good meeting." Atkins was neither
primitive nor unlettered. He was, however, a man of moderate means. The
schools with which he had been affiliated had been marginal and his
income had barely been sufficient to cover the expenses of raising and educating a family of five children. Occasional trips to teachers' conferences,
visits to relatives, and the "pleasant time" at the camp meeting were the
closest Atkins came to a vacation.[34] As they lost some of their rough, temporary features and became permanent, established institutions, religious
resorts were able to attract a more settled, genteel clientele. While someone
like Moses Hoge only considered a one-day visit to a camp meeting in 1870,
he might have felt entirely comfortable spending a week's vacation at Oak
Bluffs or Ocean Grove in 1890.[35]

Religious resorts diversified not only the vacationing clientele, but the
resort experience itself. The environment of religious resorts differed significantly from that of many secular summer watering places. Rules prohibiting
alcohol, smoking, dancing, and entertainments on Sunday all served to
restrict recreation and to make a place for religion. The fact that these places
continued to grow and prosper suggests that they filled a definite need.

There were, after all, plenty of other choices for a summer vacation. The last half of the nineteenth century witnessed a virtual explosion of resorts of all types in all regions of the country. Lakesides, mountains, seashore, and country towns sported hotels and boarding houses offering summer accommodations at a range of prices.[36] Pitching a tent at a camp meeting was certainly among the cheapest, but a stay at an established religious resorts could run about the same price as a vacation at a secular resort. Why would people choose such places?

Religious resorts offered middle-class people something not available at most other summer watering places, specifically the absence of temptations that middle-class culture associated with idleness. Resorts—as the popular press made clear—encouraged a range of suspect behavior. People on vacation, temporarily released from the discipline of work, tended to forget their principles and to flirt with the dangers of alcohol, gambling, and sex.[37] Many of the growing numbers of upright middle-class Protestant men and women with the means and the desire to take a vacation appeared wary of the consequences. Religious resorts provided a solution, a way to help keep vacationers on the straight and narrow. The rules and regulations of most such places kept the resorts safe. In addition, religious resorts offered visitors the opportunity to use their vacations in a worthwhile pursuit. Vacationers could renew their faith as they enjoyed fresh air, mountains or seaside, and a respite from work and domestic responsibilities. Middle-class people could rest assured that, at the very minimum, vacationing at a religious resort would do no harm and might even do some good.[38]

———— •◆• ————

While religious resorts primarily focused on preventing immorality, other sorts of self-improvement resorts adopted a more positive approach. During the last half of the nineteenth century numerous resorts took shape that beckoned vacationers to use their leisure in the pursuit of knowledge. The pioneering institution was Chautauqua, where Eva Moll yearned to go.

Founded in 1874 by John Vincent, a Methodist minister, and Lewis Miller, a successful inventor and manufacturer, Chautauqua was originally designed as a place to train and educate Sunday school teachers. Vincent and Miller chose a site on Lake Chautauqua in southwestern New York, at a spot that had previously been used as a Methodist camp meeting. The founders made it clear, however, that this would be no camp meeting. Those who expected exhortations and evangelistic preaching would be disappointed. Vincent and Miller allowed only scheduled speakers to mount the platform and remained firm in their resolve that Chautauqua would not become a revival. They even locked the gates on Sunday to keep religious enthusiasts out.[39] Rather, Chautauqua would be a place where leisure could be put to the purpose of education and self-improvement.

The idea of fashioning productive uses for leisure time did not, of course, begin with Chautauqua. Vincent and Miller were drawing on an American tradition that stretched back to the Puritans, found expression in the maxims of Benjamin Franklin, and manifested considerable strength throughout the early nineteenth century. Americans had been using their leisure in the pursuit of self-improvement since long before most would have contemplated a vacation. When journeymen carpenters of Philadelphia campaigned in 1827 for a ten-hour day, for example, they made their claim on the grounds that "all men have a just right, derived from their creator, to have a sufficient time in each day for the cultivation of their mind and for self-improvement."[40] Sentiments like these helped to fuel a variety of educational and self-improvement organizations in early nineteenth-century America.

The lyceum movement was an important example. Begun in the 1820s in Massachusetts, the lyceum movement initially aimed to bring educational opportunities to mechanics and farmers. One of the early proponents, Josiah Holbrook, believed that a network of lyceums would "do more for the general diffusion of knowledge, and for raising the moral and intellectual taste of our countrymen, than any other expedient which can possibly be devised."[41] The movement spread quickly, feeding off the energy of mutual improvement and literary societies that flourished in the antebellum period. Local groups invited lecturers to come and enlighten them. By the mid-1830s ministers, professors, and politicians were traveling and speaking to substantial crowds in small towns and cities throughout the country.[42]

The desire for learning touched a broad cross section of the population. Historian Joseph Kett reveals that the eighteenth-century literary clubs that were the preserve of an eastern, urban elite had by the 1840s spread geographically and become more diverse socially. Self-improvement societies in as many as 4,000 communities sponsored lectures that reached a wide audience—factory women in Lowell, free blacks in New York, Boston, and Philadelphia, mechanics and merchants in myriad cities and small towns. The growing number of rail lines and the willingness of Americans to spend their leisure time for fruitful rather than frivolous ends helped to support the network of national lyceum lecturers in the 1840s and 1850s.[43]

Public lectures continued to draw large and diverse audiences in the years after the Civil War, although many contemporaries claimed that lyceums had lost their serious intellectual focus and had degenerated into mere entertainment. Some historians have echoed that assessment. But Joseph Kett's recent exhaustive study reveals that "no shortage of serious lecturers beset the lyceum after the Civil War."[44] Middle-class men and women did not lose their taste for self-improvement, but rather persisted in finding ways to make their leisure time productive.

The pursuit did become more problematic in the postbellum years, however, as increasing numbers of commercial amusements tempted people to spend their leisure in what many contemporaries feared were frivolous or morally perilous ways. Ministers and moralists who grappled with the problem of leisure both warned of the numerous dangers that urban commercial pleasures presented and tried to celebrate the benefits of healthful, innocent forms of enjoyment and entertainment. Some continued to rely on the old Puritan distinction between "amusements" (which were bad) and "recreation" (which was good).[45] Which pleasures fell under which category remained something that the clergy, along with other cultural critics, debated throughout the rest of the century. Increasing varieties of commercial entertainment only made the conflict more complicated. As the century progressed, the theater began to lose its moral taint, and sports, both participatory and spectator, became more acceptable and popular.[46] What seemed clear, however, was that connecting entertainments and pleasures with either health or education helped make them safe for God-fearing, respectable men and women.

Chautauqua did just that. And it became immediately and tremendously popular. The first two-week Chautauqua session of 1874 drew five or six hundred "elect students" who traveled from twenty-five states.[47] Within five years the fifteen-day term had been extended to forty-three days and the numbers of participants had spiraled upward.[48] The 1880 annual report of the president of the Pittsburgh, Titusville, and Buffalo Railroad credited visitors to Chautauqua with increasing the company's receipts by 39 percent. The railroad judged that 300,000 people had visited Chautauqua the previous summer.[49] While this estimate may have been high, there is little doubt that Chautauqua was drawing large crowds. By the mid-1880s, according to *The New York Times*, from 60,000 to 100,000 people were making the annual trip to the shores of Lake Chautauqua.[50]

Chautauqua not only increased its number of participants, but spread geographically. Within a decade of Chautauqua's founding Vincent could list more than thirty "chautauquas" across the country, from California to Maryland, from Minnesota to Texas.[51] Indeed, very quickly the name was used not only by the original New York site, but by a number of other educational resorts that modeled themselves after the original. Louisa Roberts, wife of a Philadelphia dentist, recorded in her diary a visit to "Crete, the Chautauqua of Nebraska," in the summer of 1888. There she found grounds that were "beautifully laid out in a fine grove," a pavilion that held four thousand people, and a "platform which itself will accommodate about two hundred."[52] By 1886 the summer campground and resort at Bay View, Michigan, had labeled itself a "Chautauqua Assembly."[53]

In the summer of 1888 Henry W. Grady helped to bring chautauqua to the south. That year, in alliance with some wealthy Georgians, he hatched a plan to build the Piedmont Chautauqua at Salt Springs, twenty miles west of Atlanta. The sixty-five acres would include two hundred lots for summer cottages, three hotels, a restaurant to seat a thousand, and an amphitheater that could hold eight times that number. Grady was determined to make it not only the "handsomest chautauqua grounds in the country," but the "literary center for the South" as well.[54] Although the Piedmont Chautauqua did not survive long, the Florida Chautauqua, begun in the late 1880s, continued for more than three decades, offering a winter self-improvement vacation in the western section of the Florida panhandle.[55] The report of the U.S. Commissioner of Education for 1891 described the curriculum and attendance at as many as thirty-seven summer assemblies and listed another twenty for which no specific information could be obtained.[56] By 1895 novelist Hjalmar Hjorth Boyesen, a frequent lecturer at various chautauquas, noted that the various "'assemblies'—offshoots of Chautauqua" were "scattered broadcast over the continent between the Atlantic and the Pacific."[57]

Who were the people who flocked to these assemblies? Like camp meetings and religious resorts, chautauquas appealed to middle-class people of moderate means. Boyesen described chautauquans as "middle-aged men and women who have left their shops, or stores, or farms in charge of a friend or relative, while they employ their hard-earned vacation in gathering knowledge which is to lift their lives and serve them for thought and discussion during the remainder of the year."[58] School teachers were particularly drawn to chautauquas—not only because of the educational opportunities, but because the price fit their budgets. Tents and small cottages on the grounds of these assemblies provided inexpensive if somewhat primitive lodgings. Inez Harris Robinson remembered spending three summers in rented rooms at Chautauqua in the early 1880s: "Mother had the privilege of cooking in the kitchen and we ate from a pine table set between two beds which served as seats." Rates varied. During the 1870s cottage owners apparently agreed that nobody would charge more than 50¢ per person per night, and consequently hundreds of people found accommodations for as little as $3 per week. There were, however, some reports of landlords breaking the agreement and charging more. By the mid-1880s a cottage room could have cost as much as $6 to $8 per week—still a moderate price. All visitors paid, as well, a $1 per week gate fee that entitled them to attend the events on the grounds.[59] Still, the opportunity remained for those who so chose to pitch their tents at Chautauqua and live almost as cheaply as at home. A vacation at Chautauqua thus cost much less than a stay at a fancy resort, in some cases even less than a visit to a small or unassuming summer retreat.

*Athenaeum Hotel, Chautauqua, New York, c. 1880–1897. While a
Chautauqua vacation could be relatively inexpensive, the Athenaeum Hotel
offered upscale accomodations to those Chautauqua vacationers who could
afford the amenities. (Library of Congress, Detroit Publishing Company
Photograph Collection, LC-D4-4425.)*

But chautauquas appealed to others besides those in search of a moderately priced vacation. Ida Tarbell, whose father was a well-to-do oil pro-
ducer, recalled that her family spent a part of each summer at Chautauqua.
Her autobiography recounted the changes as Chautauqua grew from a
primitive spot dotted with tents to one where cottages "were lathed and
plastered, had wicker chairs on their verandahs, and the residents soon
were taking their meals at the really stately Athenaeum Hotel."[60] As early
as 1878 Chautauqua sported many beautiful cottages, reputed to have cost
over a thousand dollars each, that were adorned with "mansard roof, porti-
coes, balconies, towers, verandas, bay-windows."[61] By 1885 Chautauqua
had opened the Athenaeum Hotel, where some of the niceties were available for those who could afford them. While the Athenaeum was no match
for the grand and pretentious hostelries at a place like Saratoga, it still
charged from $2.00 to $4.50 a day for room and board—prices that equaled

those of the most upscale Gilded Age resorts.[62] Especially as the century progressed, Chautauqua may well have attracted increasing numbers of people from the higher reaches of the middle class.

Whether vacationers could afford only a rented room in a cheap boarding house or the commodious surroundings of the Athenaeum Hotel, the experience of a vacation at a chautauqua helped to reaffirm their commitment to a shared middle-class goal. Those who chose such a vacation could feel united—regardless of their specific economic condition—around their common and quite public effort to put their leisure to productive use.

By the 1890s various groups began organizing their own independent chautauquas, making self-improvement vacations available to an even broader range of people. In 1893 Booker T. Washington established a chautauqua for African Americans at the Tuskegee Institute. There is evidence, as well, of blacks holding chautauquas at a variety of places in the South and Midwest during the 1890s: at a black state school in Normal, Alabama; at Mountain Lake Park in Maryland; at Winona Lake near Warsaw, Indiana.[63] In 1897 the Jewish Chautauqua Society began holding annual summer assemblies at Atlantic City, New Jersey—by then an established resort that catered to a vast array of people, from clerks, salespeople, and school teachers to the very wealthy. Whether the Jewish chautauqua attracted the people of moderate means or those with significant wealth is unclear. But the 1900 Jewish chautauqua apparently occurred at the same time that members of Jewish society were in town for an important charity ball—an event that the *New York Times* reported as the "greatest affair of the season." The timing of the two events may have been coincidental, but it seems likely that the elite guests at the charity ball were also attending the chautauqua. By 1903 there was apparently enough interest in a Jewish chautauqua to establish a "branch assembly" in West Virginia as well.[64]

These numerous institutes and chautauquas established a variety of programs and offered a range of activities. The original Chautauqua clearly created an environment in which visitors could, if they chose, engage in serious study and reap considerable educational benefits. Vincent's and Miller's original plan to open a summer training school for Sunday school teachers quickly mushroomed into a much more ambitious educational project. The two founders, both passionately committed to liberal education, began to add secular and scientific study to the Chautauqua program. Miller, the businessman, understood that an added benefit of broadening the curriculum would be an increase in audience and consequently in revenues. By 1879 a School of Languages at Chautauqua offered Hebrew, Greek, Latin, French, German, and Oriental languages. Soon thereafter Vincent instituted a Teacher's Retreat, an effort to teach advanced pedagogical methods and theories to secular school teachers. By the end of the 1880s the offerings had

*Assembly Hall, Chautauqua, New York, c. 1880–1897. The vast size of the
Assembly Hall reveals the large numbers of Chautauquans who chose to spend
their vacations attending lectures on a range of topics. (Library of Congress,
Detroit Publishing Company Photographic Collection, LC-D4-4427.)*

broadened further with a School of Theology and a College of Liberal
Arts.[65] In 1885 John Vincent explained that the summer meetings included
"lectures on the widest range of topics, from the 'Philosophy of Locke and
Berkeley' to the light and cheery discussion about 'Fools and their Folly.'"[66]
Visitors at the 1887 assembly, for example, might have heard Richard Ely
lecturing on the "American Labor Organization," Professor C.J. Little talking about "George Eliot," and Col. Homer Sprague discussing "Shakespeare as an Author." Lectures occurred at least three or four times
throughout the day and evening.[67]

Eva Moll, the Ohio school teacher, got her wish and traveled with her
sister Lillie to Chautauqua two or three times during the 1880s. While there
she was "so very busy" that she "could not take time" even to write in her
diary: "There was a lesson, lecture or concert for nearly every hour of the
day." The program she attended ran from "tourist lectures" ("Rambles
through the British Isles," "A Knapsack Tour around the World," "Here and
There in London,") to more serious fare (lessons in German, lectures on

psychology, "Chaucer and Shakespeare Compared.") Moll found the experience exhilarating. She recorded in her diary: "Oh Chautauqua is doing a grand work for such as she [her sister Lillie] and I. May the good work continue. God bless the hearts that planned and plan it."[68]

It is not difficult to see the attraction of a place like Chautauqua for someone like Eva Moll. Most Americans found few opportunities for formal education once they reached their mid-teens. While public high schools were making secondary education more available, higher education remained primarily the preserve of the wealthy. A visit to a chautauqua, or a membership in the Chautauqua correspondence school, thus offered one of the means by which those with the desire could continue their education.

Women—whose opportunities for higher education were more limited even than those available to men—were particularly drawn to Chautauqua and its numerous offshoots. Elite women's colleges were opening in the East, and some state universities, along with a small number of private schools, were admitting women in the Midwest, but the numbers of collegiate women remained small.[69] Most women who wanted to expand their education had to rely upon self-study, public lectures, female literary clubs, and chautauquas. Charlotte Perkins Gilman, writing in *The Independent* in 1903, recognized the critical function chautauquas performed for women. Gilman explained that vacations should offer an opportunity for change: Those who used their brains all year should let them rest and spend their vacations exercising muscles; those without regular opportunity for intellectual challenge, however, should employ their vacations exercising their minds. The "ordinary working housewife," for example, did not crave a fishing or camping vacation, but rather wanted "association, information and inspiration, some glimpse at least, if not a share of, the large activities of life." This need explained why such women "flock together in our hundreds of 'Chautauquas' and summer schools of this and that branch of study."[70]

No doubt some chautauquas established more serious curricula than others. In 1891 the Iowa Chautauqua Assembly at Colfax taught classes in Christianity, music, political economy, history, biography, science, literature, art, and ethics. That same year the Connecticut Valley Chautauqua Assembly offered courses only in music, elocution, and Bible teaching. While the offerings at Connecticut were more limited, the courses were supplemented with "single lectures on many subjects."[71] Indeed, following the plan of the original Chautauqua, many assemblies offered their participants the choice of enrolling in a series of classes or casually attending assorted lectures.

Black chautauquas, like their white counterparts, offered a variety of programs. Booker T. Washington's Tuskegee Institute hoped to attract the "many tired ministers and teachers who with their wives want to go away this summer for a few days of rest, recreation, and instruction" but who, in the Jim Crow South, found "no where to go." Washington proposed to solve the problem by turning Tuskegee into a "summer hotel or Chautauqua" for two weeks in August. The program, at a cost of $3 per week, offered "three courses of lectures . . . each day, one in theology, one in teaching, and one in domestic economy for the ladies."[72]

By the early twentieth century African-American chautauquas increasingly reflected the cultural imperatives of the black middle class as it strove to combine individual self-improvement with racial uplift.[73] In July of 1910 the white chautauqua at Owensboro, Kentucky, leased its grounds to blacks for a week. The list of speakers that week included well-known reformers, such as antilynching crusader Ida Wells-Barnett. The six-week Summer School and Chautauqua of the National Religious Training School held in Durham, North Carolina, two years later addressed issues of health, civic improvement, and settlement work, as well as temperance and religious education. The sorts of questions with which participants dealt included: "What is the moral condition of the people of your community? . . . What is the sanitary condition? . . . Is the death rate increasing? . . . Has settlement work been conducted to any extent in your community and with what results?"[74] Black chautauquas, like black camp meetings, served as arenas for discussing community problems and searching for political solutions.

The people—black and white—who attended the institutes and chautauquas that spread throughout the United States were doubtless hoping to expand their intellects and augment their educations. But the quest for self-improvement was not their sole motivation for traveling to a summer assembly. Recreation also counted. Vincent and Miller, founders of the original Chautauqua, knew from the beginning that the success of their program required that Chautauquans enjoy themselves. Indeed, entertainment and recreation were critical parts of their vision. Thus the very earliest years of Chautauqua saw musical concerts, humorous lectures, and displays of fireworks alongside the lectures and classes. An 1875 article in the *New York Times* noted the "mirth and jollity" that accompanied meal time and the absence of "formality or stiffness" that characterized social interaction. People passed their time "between meetings . . . engag[ing] in anything they please. . . . swings, boats, baths, ice-cream gardens."[75] Recreation of all sorts—croquet, swimming, fishing, and boating—remained a prominent feature of a stay on the shores of Lake Chautauqua.[76] The schedule of events often included appearances of college glee clubs, stereopticon exhibits, and concerts.[77] Visitors were encouraged to indulge in such recreation, as long as they refrained from doing so on the Sabbath.[78]

Vincent and Miller realized that educational lectures, while enjoyable in themselves, would not serve as a sufficient form of entertainment. And lecturers themselves soon learned that education at Chautauqua needed to be packaged in a fairly entertaining manner. Novelist Hjalmar Boyesen, who spoke frequently at various chautauquas, knew from experience that participants had little tolerance for a lecturer with the style of "Professor Dryasdust." Boyesen firmly believed that those who attended truly sought knowledge, even though he often observed restless audiences as they "get up and straggle toward the outer benches, whence they silently vanish into the woods." He warned the hapless speaker who chose to read a boring lecture that "half or three-fourths of your audience will have evaporated before you have finished."[79]

The organizers of these assemblies fashioned places where people could enjoy learning. Always insistent that vacations should not be wasted, they still agreed that study should not be burdensome. In 1890 Vincent wrote an article explaining the most efficacious manner of "Going to the Assembly." He admonished potential vacationers not to "make vacations a time of irreverence or of religious indifference" and advised those at the assembly to "take up some one department and do a *little* daily work on it: Normal, Art, English Bible, Pedagogy—some thing—any thing." He also warned: "But be careful not to overtax yourself. Do not go to every thing. Pick out the dishes from a full bill of fare at your hotel and select the meetings you can attend from the crowded Assembly program."[80]

It seems that participants followed this sort of advice. Eva Moll summed up her first trip to Chautauqua this way: "We met many grand people, became acquainted with a few of them, heard some excellent sermons and lectures and music—both instrumental and vocal—saw some beautiful sights—fireworks, illuminated fleet and five magic lantern scenes."[81] While education certainly mattered to Eva Moll, her trip to Chautauqua was about more than study.

Those who organized the numerous educational resorts that spread throughout the country often took pains to emphasize that relaxation and enjoyment were integral parts of the program. The Monteagle Assembly in Tennessee offered "to teachers and intellectual people a place where they [could] spend the heated term of each year, combining study with rest and recreation, in a delightful and inexpensive mountain resort, free from all social dissipation." Monteagle could please all types: "[Those] who seek absolute rest on these mountain heights will be free to take it; those who shall seek only lighter courses will find entertainment; and those who wish thorough instruction will not be disappointed." The description of the Assembly at Island Park, Indiana, read like an advertisement for a summer resort. Visitors would find an island "naturally beautiful, always fanned by cool breezes, with hills and miniature valleys, romantic nooks, a beautiful beach, and a drive partially surrounding it, many fountains and wells, and a plaza surrounded by hotels and offices."[82]

Booker T. Washington's Tuskegee Institute advertised that "the social element will not be overlooked" and that the "bill of fare will be excellent."[83] The Winona Assembly and Summer School, another African-American chautauqua, described itself as a "delightful summer haven" situated on Winona Lake in Indiana and open from mid-May through August. It promised to provide "all the comforts and conveniences of a highly enjoyable sojourn. Ample facilities are at hand for satisfactory entertainment at reasonable rates at the commodious hotel which adjoins the railway station at the entrance to the grounds, in cozy cottages, or in tents as may be preferred." Winona Lake was designed to appeal to people "who may desire to combine devotion, entertainment, and instruction with rest and recreation." Participants could enjoy not only the "prominent lecturers" but the race track, fishing, bathing, and boating as well.[84]

Mixing education and recreation presented some of the same problems as mixing religion and recreation and resulted in some of the same solutions. Alcohol was strictly prohibited at Chautauqua. Most likely the numerous independent chautauquas and assemblies followed the lead of the original Chautauqua and instituted bans against liquor. Those who occasionally arrived on the shores of Lake Chautauqua showing "signs of liquor" were refused entry and "allowed to wilt on the dock in the sun till the next boat comes along and removes them." Some guests apparently continued to ignore the prohibition. One Saturday evening, for example, one of Chautauqua's "strong-handed policemen" discovered "a couple of young men who had brought to Fair Point a large square box filled with bottles of whiskey." The officers quickly dispatched the young men and destroyed the whiskey.[85] But the prohibition may not have been quite as effective as this story suggests. Writing in the *Forum* in 1895, Yale English professor Albert Cook stated that "at no time can one purchase intoxicating liquors on the grounds," but that "fortunately for him who needs alcohol for fuel or medicinal purposes, there is no custom-house inspection of imports."[86] Most Chautauquans probably endorsed and obeyed the rules. Sobriety certainly made it easier to maintain a balance between the educational and recreational goals of Chautauqua.

Prohibition of liquor at Chautauqua stemmed in part from the temperance principles espoused by many Methodists. But it may also have grown from efforts of Vincent and Lewis to create a wholesome and safe vacation environment.[87] Journalist Ida Tarbell recalled that the organizers of Chautauqua ran a tight ship: "high fences with gates through which you could not pass in or out after ten P.M.—never pass without your ticket, and not even with one on Sundays," a ten o'clock curfew, and "watchful guards" to enforce these rules.[88] Inez Harris Robinson's recollection of childhood summers at Chautauqua in the 1870s and 1880s have some of the same flavor. She remembered that one day her mother and a neighbor had left the grounds "to buy fresh food from farmers or pick berries in the meadows," but failed to have their season tickets punched as they returned. "The next time they wanted to go out they were stopped. The punches showed they should be on the outside. They were on the inside. Something heinous here! In spite of all their explanations they were tin-typed and the pictures inserted in their tickets marking them for all who saw the tickets as suspicious characters!"[89]

A police force protected the grounds, making sure people without tickets did not try to slip in, helping to "manage the immense crowds," and watching out for any unsavory or "rough" people who might commit "offenses against the rules of order."[90] An 1891 editorial in Chautauqua's daily summer newspaper thanked the hard-working police for the fact that not one "case of robbery" had marred the resort's twenty-one-year history. Patrolling class as well as geographic boundaries, the police remained "on the lookout for questionable characters."[91]

Those who attended chautauquas often took pains to emphasize how the ambience at these places differed from other summer resorts. Hjalmar Boyesen maintained that at most assemblies "rank, wealth, and competitive rivalries appear to be forgotten, and men and women meet, without affectation or constraint, on a broad basis of human fellowship." Boyesen was making an implicit comparison between chautauquas and other summer resorts—particularly fashionable ones—where, according to observers, affectation and constraint appeared in abundance.[92] Of the many assemblies across the country, Boyesen particularly liked the Bay View Assembly, located at the northern point on Lake Michigan. "It is all very attractive, though very primitive. Plain living and high thinking is the rule, and the Sybarite will do well to stay away."[93] Sybarites might be found in numbers at Saratoga or Newport or Atlantic City or Cape May. But not at chautauquas.

Safe from sybaritic influences, those who chose to visit an educational resort could vacation without fear. At Chautauqua, in the words of Ida Tarbell, "hard-working men and women" would not "have to worry about the children."[94] Tarbell may have been referring primarily to the locked gates and well-patrolled grounds, but she no doubt knew that parents considered other sorts of dangers as well. At a chautauqua, no gambling houses or saloons would lure young boys and no dissipated adventurers would compromise young girls. Vacationers who traveled to an educational resort, however, may well have been concerned not only about their children's safety, but about their own as well. "Chautauqua as a Summer Resort," according to an article in the institution's monthly magazine, differed measurably from other summer vacation places:

> There is a law and order clause in the Chautauqua charter and it is most rigorously insisted upon. Blue uniforms flit in and about its streets and their meaning is simply this: that every body shall have a chance to sleep between eleven o'clock at night and six in the morning, if he wants to; that no profanity, unseemly conduct, or drunken insolence will be tolerated on the grounds; that the street vendor and agent will be allowed to disturb no one; that public meetings must not be interrupted by noise; that the unsophisticated need be in no fear of swindlers; and that an absolutely quiet Sabbath shall be insured.[95]

Chautauqua protected vacationers from the disorder of the world at large. Those who chose to vacation at a chautauqua knew, as well, that they would not be troubled by the problems or temptations that plagued other resorts.

Assembly Point, for example, located on Lake George, became the site of one of the numerous independent assemblies that Chautauqua inspired. The Lake George Assembly, organized in 1888, created a resort at Assembly Point that would fill three goals: "recreation, reason, religion." According to an 1891 description of Lake George, the founders of Assembly Point recognized that "while we are recreatingly rusticating we may also reason reasonably and reveal religion in everyday life." Significantly, this observer felt that the community would "attain its end by encouraging everything that is manly, noble and healthful in sport" as well as by offering enlightening lectures from "interesting men" three times a week and Sunday religious services. Assembly Point would therefore be a place where "congenial families" could "gather in a homelike colony," where "Mrs. Grundy and fashionable follies have small part, and where Mrs. Ostentation and Mrs. Extravagance are altogether absent."[96] Visitors at Assembly Point would be safe from the dangers of fashionableness that lurked at other watering places.

It is no accident that this witness explained the differences between Assembly Point and traditional resorts in gendered terms. Significantly, the dangers all appeared in female guise—Mrs. Grundy, Mrs. Ostentation, and Mrs. Extravagance. Equally significantly, at Assembly Point such dangers were replaced by "manly" sport and the wisdom of "interesting men." Contemporaries apparently understood the gendered nature of various resort experiences. At fashionable resorts unwritten "rules" governed the behavior of guests. And it was women who usually "wrote" such rules: what people would wear; whether the balls and entertainments would succeed or fail; who would be welcomed and who would be shunned. But at chautauquas, where fashionable standards did not prevail, female guests could not wield the same kind of social influence. At these self-improvement resorts it was official bylaws as much as social customs that created the resort culture. The people in charge were the ministers who led the services and the boards of Methodists associations who wrote the rules. All were men. Women certainly profited from the educational benefits of the chautauquas, and some women even lectured from chautauqua platforms. Moreover, the pious matrons and school teachers who chose to visit a chautauqua no doubt appreciated the restrained, moral vacation environment. Still, these self-improvement resorts brought the vacation experience back into the hands of men.

By the turn of the century Chautauqua and its numerous clones were well-established summer institutions attracting large numbers of patrons.[97] Most continued to offer a different sort of vacation experience than did traditional resorts. Alcohol, games of chance, and Sunday arrivals were prohibited and curfews were enforced. Moreover, lectures and classes remained a central part of the program.

Despite these differences, summer assemblies seemed in some ways to be growing more like regular vacation places. The organizers of Chautauqua had always emphasized the importance of maintaining a good balance between mental exertion and amusement. Choosing one or the other would not do. In 1885 the publishers of the daily summer newspaper at Chautauqua held that there were "few, very few we believe, among us, who look upon the lake, the tennis grounds, the coaster, etc. as the object of life here."[98] But as the century neared its end, recreation appeared to play an increasingly important role in the lives of those who attended. Or, at least, the organizers seemed more concerned with promoting Chautauqua's latest recreational facilities and programs. In 1901, for example, the Chautauqua bicycle club was organizing group bike rides as well as a "Knights of the Wheel" tournament for bikers. The same year the School of Physical Education added a department of athletics and offered instruction in baseball, football, and other sports. Two days of the season were set aside for Field Day and Aquatic Day at which visitors could compete in a variety of land and water competitions. Chautauqua had even opened a golf course by 1900.[99]

While education remained available for those who wanted it, no onus attached to those who *instead* chose the lake, the tennis courts, or the roller coaster. Stephen Dale, writing in *Ladies Home Journal* in 1904, explained that "while the more studious ones go off to lectures the more frivolous resort to play. Some go to classes; others to tennis or croquet." Similarly, during the evening there were two "centres of life: The Amphitheater and the Athletic Field." In the former a crowd listened to a lecture on the life of the poet Whittier; in the latter "two baseball teams kept half a dozen thousand people cheering on the packed . . . grandstand."[100] Choosing baseball over Whittier, or croquet over classes, was not a moral failing.

Most striking about descriptions of Chautauqua is the absence, throughout the late nineteenth century, of any discussion of courting or romance. The public dialogue on regular summer resorts, by comparison, was filled with talk of flirtation and warnings of sexual dangers. Chautauqua, firmly controlled by Methodist boards and patrolled by vigilant police, never bore the taint that accompanied the more free-wheeling, fashionable watering places. Not until nearly the end of the century did anyone even hint at the possibilities of such goings-on, and then it was to uphold Chautauqua's reputation for moral rectitude. In 1895 Yale English professor Albert Cook, writing in *The Forum,* jumped to defend Chautauqua against a writer who had "insinuated that the spot is mostly frequented by young people who come to indulge in unbounded opportunities for flirtation." He responded by reminding readers that "even cathedrals are sometimes resorted to for this purpose" and that at Chautauqua there was "as much frankness, honor, and decency in the intercourse of young men and maidens" as anywhere.[101] Still, that someone would even make the accusation suggests that Chautauqua was increasingly coming to resemble other, more traditional, summer vacation spots.

By 1904 Stephen Dale acknowledged in his article for *Ladies Home Journal* that vacationers, indeed, courted at Chautauqua: "Young men and maidens seek their favorite nooks in shady spots; the hammocks and the lounging places on piazzas hold still others." And in the evenings, he hinted, some chose to attend neither the lecture nor the baseball game. "Where are the others? Where you would expect them to be, when the fireflies have hung golden lace along the lake shore, when the air is balmy and the forest paths mysteriously, suggestively romantic?" Dale's discussion of courtship and flirting at Chautauqua differed strikingly from descriptions of romantic interludes at traditional resorts. At Chautauqua, according to Dale, flirtation and romance remained entirely innocent. "Along those paths, down by the lake shore, up in the grove, over on the hillside, on the cottage verandas, . . . curfew rings—but nothing happens. Never Mind. They will come presently, leisurely, two by two, like animals into the ark."[102] The Biblical reference reinforced the sense of purity and sexual innocence. Chautauqua, a reader could infer, presented few dangers—sexual or otherwise.

By the turn of the century chautauquans seemed increasingly comfortable with the recreational part of their experience. The self-improvement component, while certainly still present, appeared to be weakening. In part this may have been due simply to the passage of time. By the turn of the century middle-class Americans had been attending resorts for forty years. The millions of apparently respectable people who vacationed at summer watering places each year were offering convincing evidence of the acceptability of the resort experience. While their long-standing suspicion and distrust of idleness persisted, middle-class people were getting more used to playing. Indeed, by the early twentieth century, the moral taint that once attached to fashionable resorts was disappearing. Chautauquas were able to become more like other resorts partly because other resorts no longer looked quite so bad.

But the specific environment of the chautauquas also made it easier for visitors to become comfortable with recreation and play. Those who chose a chautauqua, after all, had by the very choice designated themselves as moral persons. Nobody who visited a chautauqua intended to spend nights in a drunken stupor and days smoking in the billiard hall or playing cards in a gambling den. Given the guidelines, ground rules, and carefully controlled environment, chautauquans could let up and enjoy themselves. As importantly, chautauquans remained committed to a vacation that combined work with pleasure, even if the latter outstripped the former. Vacationers at a chautauqua were shielded from the sin of idleness. By introducing productive work into their vacations, chautauquans had rendered amusement less dangerous. An 1895 editorial in Chautauqua's summer newspaper summed it up this way: "No late hours, no headache in the morning. Pleasure made sensible, amusement made reasonable."[103]

———— •◆• ————

Religious resorts, Chautauqua, and the numerous independent assemblies played a critical role in easing middle-class men and women into vacationing. At these places one could feel safe: safe from the temptations of alcohol or gambling and safe from unscrupulous or dissolute people who might lurk at other resorts. Perhaps more importantly, self-improvement resorts provided safety from the evil that was still associated with leisure. For throughout the last half of the nineteenth century leisure remained, for some, tinged with its Puritan heritage: Those at leisure were idle and idleness meant trouble. Despite the growing public attention to the benefits of relaxation and recreation, the nineteenth-century middle class continued to privilege work. Work, not play, remained the way to spiritual and material rewards. Leisure time away from work, many believed, ought not to be wasted but should rather be put to purposeful pursuits.

Self-improvement resorts offered the perfect package: one could work and play at the same time, be on vacation and yet not be idle. As places like Chautauqua, Ocean Grove, and Rehoboth Beach were replicated throughout the country, they served to diminish the taint that still clung to leisure even as they offered compelling evidence of middle-class Americans' continuing struggle to relax.

❧ 5 ❧

"a jaunt...
agreeable and instructive"

————— ·◆· —————

THE VACATIONER
as TOURIST

While, in ancient times, the costly privilege of traveling at a creeping rate, in a huge and clumsy vehicle, was limited to a few eastern despots; now, it is within the reach of nearly all classes, to be transported, with tempest speed, from place to place, by a locomotive power that does not tire; and in a vehicle that vies with the parlor in splendor and appliances . . . now, nearly all who wish it, may be wafted across the waters, with almost flying celerity, and surrounded with the gorgeousness of a floating palace.[1]

Jeremiah Harris, a school teacher and farmer living in Virginia, made this observation in July of 1856 upon return from a two-week trip to New York City, Niagara Falls, Philadelphia, Baltimore, and Washington, D.C. Harris' choice for a vacation—a sightseeing trip from one place to another—was becoming increasingly popular during the last half of the nineteenth century. Rather than spend a week at the mountains, springs, or seashore, some vacationers visited natural wonders, historic places, and the numerous cultural attractions of cities. They chose to be tourists.

A word on the word "tourism." Many scholars who have studied tourism have defined it as almost any sort of travel for pleasure.[2] Using this definition, tourists would include those who traveled to Cape May or Atlantic

City for a two-week stay by the seaside as well as those who spent their two weeks traveling from Niagara to Montreal to Quebec to the White Mountains to Boston. These two groups of travelers, however, had very different sorts of experiences. I prefer to distinguish them and to call the latter "tourists." For my purposes, touring was a type of vacation rather than a synonym for vacationing.

The history of tourism, however, cannot be entirely subsumed within the history of vacations. Some people became tourists without being on vacation at all—business travelers, for example, who "did" the sights on the way to or from their destination. Moreover, elite Americans were touring and sightseeing decades before vacationing had become a familiar middle-class experience. As a result, this chapter will have to backtrack a bit, exploring the origins of tourism in the United States in the travels and expeditions of a small group of early nineteenth-century elite men and women. The sorts of places that these "pioneer tourists" visited became the established American tourist attractions—spots that would continue to draw people for at least the next hundred years.

In the decades after 1850 tourism changed in important ways. It expanded dramatically as the touring public came to include a broader cross section of the population. Middle-class people took advantage of a growing tourist infrastructure to travel to natural, historical, and industrial sights. Understanding the growth and significance of tourism in the last half of the nineteenth century requires its consideration within the context of the development of vacationing. The increasing numbers of middle-class Americans who chose to become tourists were making a decision *not* to spend their vacation in some other way. A tourist's goal was usually visiting sights— often as many as possible within a short span of time—rather than relaxing at a lake, seashore, or mountain resort. The meaning with which middle-class Americans invested tourism derived, in part, from the alternatives. Touring offered a vacation not tinged with the frivolity, idleness, or dangers of a resort vacation. Indulging in their own forms of self-improvement, middle-class tourists could feel that they had turned their vacations into useful and productive endeavors.

———————— • ◆ • ————————

Americans began to tour at about the same time that they began to frequent watering places and springs. And for the most part the same sorts of people initially indulged in both kinds of expeditions. During the 1820s, as the infirm and the rich journeyed to the springs in search of health and pleasure, small numbers of Americans began to travel in pursuit of sights. These early pioneer tourists—almost entirely members of the elite—sought both scenery and culture.

Typical was the Quincy family. Susan Quincy, daughter of Josiah Quincy, kept a diary of the journey she shared with her sister, aunts, and an uncle in July of 1820: "My aunts traveled in their carriage with one pair of horses, my uncle in a light wagon which held the luggage, driving himself, and Abby and I took turns to drive with him while the other accompanied the ladies." The most they could cover was about thirty miles a day. Given the dearth and poor quality of public accommodations, they often stopped with friends along the way. The Quincy party, for example, was fortunate in knowing "Mr. Bleecker and Mr. Delevan" who paid them "all the attention in their power." From Albany they continued to Niagara Falls, then on to Ballston, Saratoga, and Lake George. Their trip lasted "exactly two months."[3]

Their class, the nature of their touring experience, and their destinations made the Quincys typical of early nineteenth-century tourists. Only the elite could undertake such a trip, because travel was enormously time-consuming and expensive. Indeed, merely having the time for a long journey served as a badge of elite status, marking such tourists as freed from the daily demands of earning a living. Moreover, a tourist infrastructure of hotels and public conveyances was still in its infancy, forcing early tourists to rely on friends, relatives, or acquaintances for accommodation and assistance. Elite travelers called on a network of people who were connected by blood, business, and friendship. Armed with letters of introduction, many of these early tourists could approach perfect strangers and feel assured of hospitality and guidance.[4]

Those without the Quincy's connections and means could still tour, but found the going harder. A man named David Prale, for example, left a diary of a "Jaunt" he took from New York to Niagara in the company of two friends during the summer of 1821. This group had to use public accommodations for both travel and board—and often found both wanting. Prale discovered Syracuse to be such a "very small place" that he had trouble finding someone to carry them on a stage to the next spot. Sometimes the small party had to hire a private conveyance when a stage was not available. Prale often remarked upon the "very poor accommodations" afforded in small towns. The main goal of the trip, to see Niagara, more than met Prale's expectations. He declared Niagara to be "the most sublime sight I have ever witnessed."[5]

It was no accident that both the Quincy party and the Prale party chose Niagara as their destination. Niagara was among the first of America's tourist attractions.[6] Its early popularity testified, in part, to the influence of British models on early American tourism. By the late eighteenth century British tourists were actively searching for scenery in the Lake District.[7] British travelers and writers not only had discovered the pleasure of scenic touring, but had established the categories with which to view nature. Well-read Americans knew well the concepts of the beautiful, the picturesque, and the sublime that eighteenth-century English philosophers and writers had elaborated. A journey to Niagara offered the perfect way to participate in this Anglo-American aesthetic adventure: no sight could call up the sublime better than Niagara, and no scenery was more picturesque than the Hudson Valley, one of the major routes to Niagara.[8] Moreover, the ability to enjoy and appreciate such romantic scenery served as a mark of status, a means of distinguishing the tourist as a person of breeding and sophistication—a member of the "refined and cultivated" classes.[9]

Americans could look to another British model for touring as well. The Grand Tour of Europe had, for more than two centuries, been a staple of English gentry life. An essential part of the education of elite English youth, the Grand Tour endeavored to turn boys into men. Ideally, it would offer young men just enough exposure to the institutions and culture of other countries to affirm their belief in British superiority.[10] But European touring was not confined just to men or to the young; by the eighteenth century increasing numbers of British women and men were traveling abroad for pleasure. Tourists traveled to European capitals and cities searching for the best examples of foreign culture.[11]

While the new United States did not offer the cultural riches of the old capitals of Europe, American tourists—like their British counterparts—sought historic and artistic as well as natural sights on their journeys. The search for nature and culture on which American tourists embarked, then, had roots in British tradition. But the growth of tourism in the United States also spoke to a desire to create a specifically American culture.

Historian John Sears has analyzed American tourist attractions, explaining that they became ways of "defining America as a place and taking pride in the special features of its landscape." With such sites serving as Americans' "sacred places," tourism operated as a secular form of pilgrimage.[12] Tourism grew, Sears explains, not only from the desire for amusement, but from elite Americans' need to fashion a national identity of which they could be proud. By the mid-nineteenth century, the places that pioneer tourists had identified as attractions—Niagara Falls, Kentucky's Mammoth Cave, the Connecticut and Hudson River valleys, the White Mountains of New Hampshire—performed an important cultural function in the young nation. Tourist attractions helped to confirm America's natural beauty and power, its special relationship to the divine, its technological promise, its moral virtue and compassion, and its progressive role in history.

But at the same time tourism also helped to confirm, for many, a loyalty to a smaller, more local community. Upon return from their travels, many tourists commented on how good it felt to be home again. Some of this, no doubt, stemmed from the comfort of being back in familiar surroundings and the relief at finding loved ones well. But many specifically mentioned that a journey elsewhere had made them realize that home was a better place. Edmund Canby, the son of a prosperous Delaware miller, traveled to New England in the summer of 1823. Upon his return to Wilmington he explained that although on his travels he "had seen many finer places and finer houses," he remained persuaded that "I shall never find a spot so lovely or one I can ever like as well as my sweet native soil."[13] Sidney George, an elite member of Philadelphia society, frequently compared the places he visited to his own city. Philadelphia did not always measure up. "Boston and N. England," for example, evinced "the superior civilization of the Yankees," and he admitted that in New York "everything is on a grander scale." Still, after one of these trips he confided to his diary: "Returned to Philad: As I always do, with the conviction that dull, monotonous & humdrum as it is, it is the most *comfortable* & desirable place for a residence in this country."[14] Tourism certainly offered a common, national experience, but it also reinforced a tension between competing local or sectional loyalties. Even as it helped to construct a national identity, tourism demonstrated the distinctiveness, and in some people's minds the superiority, of the local or regional culture.

The belief that home was better did not, however, necessarily diminish tourists' appreciation of or national pride in the places they visited. Niagara, for example, was something uniquely American—something even Europe could not rival. And many early tourists found that not only the falls themselves but also the scenery along the way prompted patriotic sentiments. In 1821, for example, one of these pioneer tourists described the countryside along the route to Niagara this way: "This beautiful country stimulates my patriotism. . . . I should even venture to put our cheerful dwellings, and fruitful fields, and blooming gardens against the ivy-mantled towers and blasted oaks of older regions, and busy hands and active minds against the 'spectres that sit and sigh' amid their ruins."[15]

Niagara, however, was only one stop along what many American tourists called their "grand tour," a route that took visitors up the Hudson to Albany, across New York to Niagara, into Canada—with visits to Montreal and Quebec—and back through New England, sometimes with a stop at the White Mountains.[16] By the 1830s and 1840s, travel, at least in the Northeast, was a bit easier. Steamboats plied the rivers, roads had improved somewhat, and the Erie Canal, open in 1825, facilitated travel across New York state. A variety of new services made travel less onerous. Hotels, for example, began replacing taverns and inns, and guidebooks appeared to help tourists who did not have well-placed friends or acquaintances to show them the sights.[17]

A woman named Catherine Clarkson, who made the journey in 1833, described it as a "jaunt of pleasure." But such a "jaunt" still required considerable time and effort. The trip from Albany to Buffalo alone took four days. Clarkson commented that the roads were "very good until we reached within 20 miles of Buffalo, when we were jotted [jostled] to our hearts and bodies content, especially over what is called the corduroy road."[18] Diaries of others from these decades tell a similar tale—members of the elite traveling in search of the sublimity of Niagara and the beauty and picturesqueness of the Hudson Valley.[19]

The search for history joined the quest for nature as a goal of early American tourists. Military installations, battlefields, and historic markers quickly became tourist attractions.[20] On his 1823 trip to New England, Edmund Canby enjoyed not only the scenery of the Connecticut valley, but the opportunity to visit historic places. Canby recognized Bunker Hill as a site "associated with some of our earliest and best feelings" and Faneuil Hall as where "some of the earliest and best American oratory was displayed."[21] Indeed, historic spots often stirred powerful emotions, not unsimilar to the responses that natural wonders evoked. Richard Henry Dana's tour of Washington in 1843 elicited strong emotional patriotism. Standing on Capitol Hill and looking out over the vista of the city, he wrote, "My heart stirred within me as I saw the broken surface of the Ancient Dominion, & thought of her great men, her revolutionary history." The visit to Mount Vernon fulfilled all his expectations: "I felt as though I had been carried thro' a grand drama. It was almost unreal. I had been on enchanted ground, filled with the presence of a hero long departed."[22] Touring historic spots offered people like Dana a way to reaffirm their connection to America's past and to validate their belief in America's future.

By the 1830s the search for scenery and culture took tourists south as well. Many people who visited the Virginia springs, for example, went out of their way to see Natural Bridge, even though such a detour sometimes meant extra days of uncomfortable travel along terrible roads. Catherine Clarkson, who made the trip in 1835, noted in her diary that "the road was awful beyond description and 6 miles from the bridge wisely called Purgatory."[23] These sightseeing diversions sometimes consumed more time than the stay at the springs itself. Edmund Canby kept a diary of his "journeys for health, pleasure, or business" during 1833. One such trip took him from his Delaware home south and west to White Sulphur Springs in Virginia. The trip lasted about five weeks, only ten days of which he spent at White Sulphur. Indeed, his diary makes clear that much of the "pleasure" derived from sightseeing along the way. In Baltimore he visited the cathedral with "some fine paintings." In Washington he toured the "Capitol, President's House, patent office, etc. etc." and found "the two former" to be "superb buildings." Small towns also afforded attractions. He saw the University in Charlottesville, Washington College in Lexington, and the U.S. Armory at Harper's Ferry.[24]

The "grand tour" to Niagara and the southern tour of the Virginia springs may have attracted the largest number of early tourists, but by the 1830s some Americans searched less celebrated places for sights that both nature and people had created. Christopher Columbus Baldwin, a lawyer and editor in his thirties who lived in Worcester, Massachusetts, embarked on a variety of trips during the 1830s. One journey took him on a week's venture to the White Mountains and another took him to the beach resort of Nahant—both places that were beginning to attract members of the elite. Baldwin, however, made other pleasure trips to destinations that were neither well-known tourist sights nor elite watering places. In August of 1835 he traveled to Pittsburgh, where he visited iron works, "saw the process of drawing bars of iron," had a tour of the glassworks on the Monongahela River, and then "ascended Coal Mountain" and "saw the process of digging coal."[25] Like his namesake, Christopher Columbus Baldwin was a pioneer of sorts. He was experimenting with a new sort of tourist experience—one that turned everyday American industry and work places into tourist sights.[26]

A journey Mary Moragne took with her brother and a group of nine others in 1840 reveals another tourist mentality. Moragne, a young woman in her twenties, was the daughter of a South Carolina slave-owning family. She and her group of friends traveled around the South Carolina countryside for about a week, apparently without a specific destination. Their goal, rather, was to find enjoyment in touring and seeing. The week's trip brought them to "old antiquated Pendleton . . . a rich looking village" where they visited a female seminary and witnessed the "great female examination" then in progress. They spent one night at a mineral spring and stopped one day to "examine Sloane's Factory, an object of very curious interest to those of us who had never traveled North." From there they journeyed to Table Mountain, which they climbed. Moragne, in retrospect, felt the climb to have been "a foolish plan bye the bye, & one which I would not recommend to delicate young ladies." The hike, "a mile & a half *up hill*" proved "no light Herculean task." They apparently arrived at the top "half-dead with heat, agitation & fatigue." She concluded: "I would rather run the risk of breaking my neck on a sure-footed pony, on the narrowest ridge there, than try it a pied again." Despite her complaints, her words suggest a note of triumph. The trip had included a test of her mettle—a test that she passed.[27]

As Mary Moragne's diary makes clear, touring in the early nineteenth century was something that both men and women did. Moreover, there seemed to be few gender distinctions in the sorts of places visited and the emotions recorded. Men and women often traveled together; both sought natural and cultural sights; both used the aesthetic language of the picturesque and sublime to describe what they had seen; both endured the challenges, hardships, and deprivations of travel in early America. But touring, at least during the first half of the nineteenth century, played a somewhat different role in the lives of men and women. Men seemed more self-conscious than women about using their trips to broaden and educate themselves. By the 1840s many young men, especially, were embarking on short, touring-style vacations that served, in some ways, as vastly scaled down models of the old European Grand Tour.

Isaac Mickle, for example, took numerous "touring vacations," during the 1840s—although he would not have called them that. He was in his late teens and early twenties at the time, living in Philadelphia and reading law. One trip was a week's journey around the nearby countryside, during which he and a group of six friends and relatives enjoyed the scenery, observed what they considered the unusual customs of the Pennsylvania Dutch, and visited a Moravian Church. Another was a two-week excursion to New Haven, Boston, and New York. Along the way he made the acquaintance of a young man of about the same age who was "traveling like me, to see the world." They joined forces, lodging and touring together. The places Mickle and his new friend chose to visit included cemeteries, educational institutions, historic sights and markers, public buildings, and churches. He attended the theater in the evenings and spent a day at the Elysian Fields, an amusement park in Hoboken, where he enjoyed the "ladies and plenty to eat" as well as "a balloon ascension and music." Upon his return he concluded that the $50 he had spent on the trip, a considerable sum at the time, had been well worth it: "So ends a jaunt . . . which was very agreeable and instructive, and to which I can long refer with pleasure and profit."[28]

Mickle's tour was not atypical. Diaries of other young men offer accounts of such trips.[29] Many of these journeys occurred during breaks from school or served as respites during professional apprenticeships. The young men, often bachelors, had few family responsibilities and enough financial resources to enjoy the pleasure and edification of touring. Occasionally these tours served to introduce young men to worlds far removed from the respectable homes in which they had been raised. During visits to large cities some male tourists ventured into shady neighborhoods and disreputable parts of town. Richard Henry Dana—lawyer, writer, antislavery activist and member of one of the "first families of New England"—traveled frequently for health, pleasure, and business. On more than one occasion Dana made it a point to venture into the most vice-ridden parts of a city. The reason, he maintained, was that he was "determined to see the whole of this new chapter in the book of life."[30]

During a visit to New York City in 1843, Dana was struck with "a sudden desire to see that sink of iniquity & filth, the 'Five Points.'" There he observed the abundance of "dancing houses . . . grog shops, oyster cellars & close, obscure & suspicious looking places of every description." Overcome with curiosity, he ventured, "almost before I knew what I was doing," into the home of a prostitute. When the young woman invited him into the bedroom, he hesitated. He had "a strong desire to see the whole of the establishment," but felt vulnerable. Not afraid that he would succumb to her charms, he feared, rather, being robbed of his money and gold watch. Nevertheless, he decided to chance it. Dana discovered the bed room to be as small and shabby as the rest of the establishment, and the bed stead "a wretched truck, & the bed was of straw, judging from the sound it made when the woman sat upon it." Learning that the going rate was fifty cents, he "was astonished at the mere pittance for which she would sell her wretched, worn out, prostituted body." Filled with disgust and pity, he wrote: "I told her at once that I had no object but curiosity in coming into the house, yet gave her the money from fear lest, getting nothing, she might make a difficulty or try to have me plundered."

Her response was intriguing. She, of course, took the money. But she also "expressed no surprise" at Dana's "curiosity or strangeness." Dana concluded: "[P]erhaps they are used to having the visits of person like myself from abroad & who wish to see the inside of such places."[31] Dana's story suggests that raunchy districts of large cities might well, by the 1840s, have become male tourist sights, and not only for visiting prostitutes. Rather, houses of prostitution may have served as tourist attractions—places that drew not only customers, but curious male sightseers as well. The educated young man of the world would know, at least as an observer, about the seedy side of life. Tourism provided one vehicle for this education.

Respectable women, of course, would not have put the Five Points district on their touring agenda. Moreover, most women probably would not, at least during the antebellum period, have so self-consciously invested touring with an educational purpose. Widespread cultural norms determined that women did not require preparation for professional or business life. And unlike their male counterparts, female tourists would usually not have embarked unescorted on a sightseeing trip, but would have accepted the assistance and protection of a husband, parent, or older sibling.[32]

Still, women undoubtedly enjoyed and appreciated the ways in which their travels broadened them, and in at least one instance educational possibilities figured prominently in plans for a woman's tour. Calvin Fletcher, a lawyer, farmer, and state senator took his wife, Sarah, with him on a business trip from their home in Indianapolis to Urbana in 1830. Fletcher specifically hoped the journey would cultivate and "improve" Sarah. He recorded in his diary how he "took great pains to show her Steamboats, Steam engines museams [*sic*] paper mills—Sunday schools—Infant schools high life & low life." He believed that "nothing improves a woman with good common sense more than travel—to put up at some of the best houses & stay at some of the meanest." The experience would teach Sarah, according to Calvin, "how to be agreeable to strangers & to keep a neat house when at home." Sarah recorded the sights she had seen and the places she had stayed: "Tuesday Eve I visited the museum. Thursday I went to see the paper mill & took a ride on the rail road carridge [*sic*]. Fri. I went on a steam boat made me sick."[33] While Sarah apparently derived both pleasure and educational benefit from these new experiences, there is little evidence that she, or other antebellum women, saw such tours as an important part of their training for life. Most, after all, expected their lives to be bounded by the demands of domesticity. As such, few would have described themselves as "traveling . . . to see the world" as had Isaac Mickle.

The diaries of these early tourists reveal the instruction and enjoyment they gained by observing the habits and customs of people they encountered on their travels. By the 1840s slavery was a hot topic, and tourists often commented on the behavior of black inhabitants of different regions. While visiting Boston, Isaac Mickle concluded that "Negroes are inconceivably insolent in this land of hot-headed abolitionism, where some of the whites consider them at least equal 'if not a little more so.'"[34] Richard Henry Dana, by contrast, found the blacks whom he met in Baltimore to be "very civil, & seemed such an innocent, well meaning, good natured, simple race, that I always employed and paid them in preference to the whites." Touring afforded people the opportunity to examine everyday differences in the lives and appearances of people in different regions. Dana observed, for example, that men in Philadelphia and Baltimore spit much more than did those in New England. Thomas Hobbs, who took a three-week tour of New York and New England in 1846, particularly enjoyed seeing "the short sleeves and dresses of the Boston ladies, they have nice little feet, and ankles, and round arms, so they dress so as to show off these parts."[35]

These early American tourists were clear and deliberate about what they were doing. They traveled for pleasure and edification; their goal was to see specific places. Touring was not, in the first half of the nineteenth century, necessarily easy or always safe. But in the years between 1820 and 1850 steamboats, railroads, canals, and better roads began to make touring a feasible if still not uncomplicated venture. Even as many Americans were trailblazing into the West and pushing the Anglo-American frontier deeper into the continent, those who lived in more settled areas of the East were finding it possible to travel for pleasure along some increasingly established routes. By 1850 those touring across New York State to Niagara, into the White

Mountains of New Hampshire, or making the southern circuit of the Virginia Springs began to find their travel facilitated by acceptable public accommodations, reasonable roads, and early rail lines. The major urban centers of the East—Boston, New York, Philadelphia, and Washington, D.C.—had also become important tourists attractions. Pioneer tourists helped to make the spots they visited—whether natural, historic, or cultural—popular and enduring American tourist attraction.

———— •◆• ————

In the second half of the nineteenth century tourism changed in ways that were at once subtle and obvious. Most noticeably, tourism became less the preserve of the elite and increasingly an activity available to people of somewhat more moderate, if still decidedly comfortable, social standing. Some of these less-privileged men and women initially became tourists in a rather unself-conscious way. Jeremiah Harris, for example, was a school teacher and farmer who lived in rural Virginia. In 1856 he lost his newly obtained position as county land assessor because of having made "an injudicious disposition" of his property. Bitterly disappointed, he decided to console himself with a trip to a church convention in Lynchburg. He took advantage of the "privilege of a free ride" on the Virginia Central Railroad to attend the annual stockholders meeting in Richmond, and from there continued west to Staunton, Charlottesville, and Culpeper. Upon returning home, he concluded that the trip not only had "added considerably" to his "very limited stock of information," but had whetted his desire to see "something more of the world." As a result, he planned a touring vacation for the following July that took him to New York City, Niagara, Philadelphia, Baltimore, and Washington.[36]

Jeremiah Harris became a tourist as increasing numbers of the emerging American middle class were beginning to embark on vacations. His experience suggests, however, that while the expansion of touring coincided with the growth of vacationing, not all middle-class tourists were vacationers. Men on business trips did a little sightseeing along the way; women who accompanied their husbands on business trips became tourists while their husbands worked; people on their way to or back from meetings of religious or professional associations learned the pleasures of touring.

In 1863 John Long, for example, was a young Massachusetts lawyer earning $500 a year. His employer sent him on a trip "for the purpose of obtaining, from all the papers in the large cities, claims for collection for advertising." But business did not take all his time. While in Washington, D.C., he visited "all the sights": "I did Treasury, Navy & War Departments. I went to the White House and met Old Abe on the steps. . . . I have been to the top of the Washington monument (unfinished) and have ridden in the horse-cars." When his business took him to Detroit, he stopped on the way home at Niagara Falls, which he described as "the most awesome sight I ever saw, or shall see."[37] Mary Daly, wife of a New York judge, traveled with her husband in 1863 from their home in New York to Boston, where he gave a series of lectures. While there she toured the museum, the library, the law school, the Lyceum, and the Historical Society.[38] William Jacobs, a busy and financially hard-pressed Presbyterian minister in Clinton, South Carolina, attended a religious meeting in Washington, D.C., in 1884. He used this opportunity to become a tourist. Once in Washington he tried to "do my duty as a member of the conference," but he found the temptations of the city too great: "I must confess I have far more interest in the sights of this wonderfully beautiful city. . . . I found beautiful lawns, magnificent buildings, splendid trees and foliage, all just like fairyland."[39] Neither Long, Daly, nor Jacobs were technically "on vacation," but all could have been mistaken for people who were.

Vacation tourism grew during the postbellum years for many of the same reasons that the numbers of resorts and resort-goers expanded—an improved transportation system and a growing middle-class population with the discretionary time and money for short holidays away from home. But it was more than the speed of railroads and the convenience of new hotels that made touring popular. Indeed, the touring infrastructure, at least in part, expanded to serve the needs of the increasing number of people with the desire to tour. The two, in effect, fed each other: more tourists clamored for more facilities and more sights to see, and the owners and operators of new hotels and attractions increasingly promoted tourism.

A specific industry emerged both to meet the needs and increase the size of the touring public. Railroad passenger agents who had once sold rail tickets to travelers were by the late 1870s facing competition from independent travel agents. The two vied for the patronage of potential tourists.[40] A touring vacation, as opposed to one spent relaxing (or improving oneself) in a single spot, required considerably more in the way of logistics and preparation. Travel agents promised to handle the complex problems of coordinating train schedules, finding conveyances, and making arrangements for food and lodging for tourists who intended to visit numerous places in one trip. Thomas Cook had begun to fill these needs for British tourists in the 1840s. In 1865 he came to the United States, surveying the possibilities for bringing British tourists to America and looking over the potential American domestic market. Americans traveling to Europe were already familiar, and for the most part pleased, with the services Cook offered.[41] By the early 1870s some people recognized that American tourists at home needed the same kind of services. An editorial in the *New York Times* that year praised Cook for offering "suitable excursions for people who have not the originality, or the time, or the patience to think them out, and attend to them in person." It ended with this wish: "If we only had an American Cook, how much of the troubles of our tourists would be simplified. The field seems to offer a legitimate opening for American enterprise, and we trust before long to see it filled."[42]

Cook did his best. In 1872 he opened an office on Broadway in New York City and took in a man named Thomas Jenkins to run the American side of the business. Within a year Jenkins had expanded the American operation to include branch offices in Philadelphia, Boston, and Washington, had begun to publish an American edition of the *Excursionist* (the agency's public relations organ), and had experimented with a system of circular notes—forerunners of travelers checks—that could be redeemed at any number of hotels, banks, or ticket agencies within the Cook system.[43]

Throughout the 1870s the number of Cook's American clients swelled and their business spread. But Cook, Son, & Jenkins still had trouble turning a profit. A nasty dispute with Jenkins ultimately ended the partnership. John Cook (the "son" in Thomas Cook & Son) reorganized the American business, substantially increased the number of branch offices, and began to plan tours to the West.

Before long Cook faced competition from American entrepreneurs who also hoped to make money arranging tours for the growing population of domestic vacationers. Enterprising agents often began by making deals with railroads. In 1884 T. J. Lamm, proprietor of Lamm's Tourist Offices in Jacksonville, Florida, and Niagara Falls, New York, proposed an alliance with a New Hampshire railroad to offer "tourist tickets for all Atlantic Coast and New England points." He hoped to capitalize on the "thousands of people who visit the Falls every year who would make Tours if they could get tickets as they want them, and have all tickets not used redeemed."[44] Lamm understood that a visit solely to Niagara differed slightly from "making tours," which included visits to other places along the way. He felt, however, that the group who embarked on the former could be encouraged to participate in the latter.

Two Bostonians recognized the same thing. In 1879 Walter Raymond and Irving Whitcomb established the Raymond and Whitcomb Travel Agency. Both had experience as passenger agents for railroads and recognized the demand that the expanding market in tourists was generating. Raymond and Whitcomb began by arranging tours to the White Mountains and to Washington, D.C., but by 1881 they were becoming engaged in the small, if growing, market for tours to the West.[45]

Tourist agencies, of course, promoted all sorts of travel. They were happy to arrange a trip to a single resort as well as to plan more lengthy and complicated tours. Still, travel agents provided services that particularly fit the needs of those touring through numerous places. As an 1887 promotional pamphlet for Raymond and Whitcomb assured its public: "There need never be anxiety about the morrow, since every requirement has been made a matter of pre-arrangement. The excursionists are expected guests, and their places are held in reserve for them, so that there need be no fear regarding accommodations, and opportunities for sight-seeing under the most advantageous circumstances." Such assistance, the company hoped, would be particularly appealing to women: "Ladies traveling alone should have no hesitation about joining our tourist parties, since they are entirely relieved of the ordinary cares, responsibilities, and annoyances of traveling."[46] According to historian Earl Pomeroy, women, indeed, comprised the majority of many of Raymond and Whitcomb's western tours.[47]

The expansion of touring occurred, in part, because a tourist industry and infrastructure made it more possible and comfortable for both women and men to tour and because increasing numbers of middle-class Americans had both the time and resources to embark on such trips. As tourism grew it changed in subtle but significant ways. Specifically, tourism took on a new and somewhat different meaning in a world where increasing numbers of middle-class Americans were discovering the pleasures and pitfalls of vacationing.

The growth in tourism corresponded with the dramatic increase in other sorts of vacationing—specifically the rise in the numbers of people seeking rest and relaxation at seaside, mountain, or country resorts. As chapter three revealed, the discussion that attended the expansion of summer resorts warned of the dangers that lurked at such places. The idleness of resort life could bring intemperance, dissipation, and moral ruin. But tourists were not idle in the same way as those who spent a week or two at the beach or mountains.

Indeed, touring differed from such vacations in more than the amount of planning and logistics required. Although not at work, people who toured from place to place could persuade themselves that they were engaged in purposeful activity. The pioneer tourists of the early nineteenth century were also, no doubt, aware of the educational, spiritual, or patriotic benefits of their "jaunts." But these tourists were relatively few in number and were, for the most part, members of a fairly select elite. Moreover, many combined touring with an extended stay at a spring or spa. By contrast, tourists in the postbellum years could compare their own "touring vacations"—often short journeys packed full of travel and sightseeing—with the more relaxing vacations of their counterparts who were flocking to beaches, springs, and lakesides. In this context, touring may well have seemed less like play, more like a productive endeavor, and consequently less likely to generate the sorts of dangers that resort vacations allegedly bred.

Louisa Roberts, for example, traveled with her family during the summer of 1883 from her home in Philadelphia to the Put-In-Bay Islands in Lake Erie where her husband attended a dental meeting and the family enjoyed a few days of relaxation. Although the resort at Put-In-Bay was the destination, the purpose of the trip was not frivolous amusement. Mr. Roberts, of course, traveled for business. For Louisa, the touring and sightseeing along the way were clearly paramount. When the steamer on which they traveled made an overnight stop in Detroit, the Roberts party had an opportunity to "look about" and were "anxious to make the most of [their] time." From Detroit they chose to alter their itinerary, making a detour that allowed them to visit Cleveland, the "queen of western cities." There they encountered "memorials of the great naval battle. In the centre of the square a monument has been erected to commemorate the occasion." Louisa Roberts and her party clearly did not think that they had spent their vacation in useless idleness. To the contrary, their tour persuaded her of the importance "such recreations have on the life and character."[48] While less self-conscious about the goals of their tour than Louisa Roberts, other vacationers saw touring as a way to combine relaxation with usefulness. Vacationers on tour often felt that they had reaped a variety of patriotic, cultural, and religious rewards.

In 1854 Catharine Sedgwick and her two brothers joined an excursion party of two or three hundred people on a western tour that included Chicago, the Falls of St. Anthony, and the cities of St. Paul and St. Louis. The group covered 3,740 miles, traveling first by rail and then in five chartered steamboats down the Mississippi. Sedgwick waxed poetic about the glories of the journey. The day spent traveling "over the prairie from St. Paul's to the Falls of St. Anthony, to Minnehaha . . . to Fort Snelling" she characterized as "a day better than most lifetimes." The beauty of the scenery along the Mississippi especially moved her. She found it "like the Rhine . . . and yet how unlike any thing in the Old World! So fresh! so young! such abounding, vigorous vitality!" That the tour prompted frequent favorable comparisons to Europe was not insignificant, for Sedgwick took away from her trip an important understanding of the promise that the West held for America's future. She wrote to her niece:

I would give a great deal to transfer to you the pictures in my mind of Western life, Western cities, illimitable prairies, and those beautiful, untrodden shores of the Upper Mississippi. No American can have an adequate notion of the future destiny of this land, of its unbounded resources, of the unlimited provisions awaiting the coming millions, without seeing—for seeing is believing—the great Valley of the Mississippi, and measuring by that 'the West' beyond.[49]

This tour, Sedgwick felt, was an important means of making an easterner understand not only the potential of the West but the destiny of the nation. Touring continued throughout the last half of the century to serve an important role in the development of American nationalism.

"'The West' beyond" became a more feasible if still quite expensive tourist destination after the completion of the transcontinental railroad in 1869. Round-trip coast-to-coast rail service cost upward of $300 in the 1870s and 1880s.[50] East Coast tourists could travel as far as Colorado, however, for less. Rate wars between the Union Pacific and Kansas Pacific helped to keep fares down, so that travelers could get from New York to Denver (and back) for about $100—still an expensive trip. In June of 1875 the *New York Times* ran an article called "Summer Pleasure Trips" that specifically featured the advantages of Colorado as a tourist attraction. Moreover, the article maintained, tourists (as many as 150 a day in August) no longer had to "[confine] their sight-seeing to Denver and vicinity." The Colorado Central Railroad now made it possible to "strike out and 'do' a greater part of the Territory in a month's time." This reporter touted the dramatic western scenery along the route (the "dashing creek on one side, and the high rocks and precipices, often overhanging the railway, on the other") and the excitement of the trip itself ("the windings and twistings of the train").[51]

Yosemite, discovered by whites only in 1851 when a battalion of soldiers pursued a group of Indians into the Yosemite valley, was already attracting tourists by the mid-1860s. The federal government gave the area to California "for public use, resort, and recreation" in 1864. Artists, writers, and photographers celebrated the beauty of Yosemite in words and pictures, and advertisers used both to sell Yosemite to the touring public. Yosemite, like Niagara Falls, offered an American answer to European claims of superiority. Promoters maintained that Yosemite could match not only the scenery, but the architecture of Europe—its natural formations as beautiful as any gothic cathedral, its waterfalls and cliffs as spectacular as the Alps. By the 1870s and 1880s the wild and exotic landscape of Yellowstone, established as a National Park in 1872, became a stop on the western tour and another way for tourists to be reminded of American splendor.[52]

While the West opened to tourists in the years after 1870, it remained accessible primarily to those with substantial wealth. In 1888 Raymond and Whitcomb advertised three "grand trips" to Yellowstone of twenty-five days' duration each. The price was $275, including all traveling and hotel expenses—about the same cost as a trip to Europe.[53] Even for those already in California, a stage ride from San Francisco to Yosemite cost a steep $80.[54]

Scenic vistas and natural wonders of both the West and the East continued, throughout the postbellum period, to draw tourists. Those who made such tours enjoyed the beauties of the American landscape and reaffirmed

*Seeing New York, New York City, c. 1904. Tourists to cities visited
public buildings, monuments, churches, prisons, cemeteries, and universities.
(Library of Congress, Detroit Publishing Company Photograph Collection,
LC-D4-17555.)*

pride in their nation. As it had in the early part of the century, tourism remained a means for Americans to fashion a national identity of which they could be proud. Similarly, American tourists continued in the late decades of the nineteenth century to visit places that glorified American achievement, industriousness, ingenuity, perseverance, and heroism— places that confirmed for them the distinct and special nature of American culture. Many such attractions they found in cities. Colleges and universities, public buildings, libraries, churches, prisons, asylums, and cemeteries interested the growing number of touring American vacationers.

But the late nineteenth century also brought some new places onto tourist itineraries. Civil War battlefields and memorials, for example, became important stops along tourists' routes. In 1866 John Cook's first group of British tourists to the United States found Civil War battlefields a particularly enjoyable sight. This specific group of tourists seemed to take a macabre interest in the "skulls, arms, legs, etc., all bleaching in the sun" that still littered battlefields around Richmond.[55] Americans, no doubt, visited such places for other, more uplifting reasons. An 1868 Virginia guidebook noted that the attractions of Rockbridge County included not only the county seat "celebrated for its institutions of learning" and the "beautiful surroundings" but the place where "hundreds come to pay their homage to the *two heroes*, the living and the dead—the home of Lee and the tomb of Jackson."[56] As early as 1870, people vacationing in Pennsylvania were making it a point to visit the Gettysburg battlefield. The *New York Times* that year reported that the people at Gettysburg Springs were amusing themselves in a more "rational manner" than people at other resorts. Although indulging in the usual round of "hops, gossips, flirtations, mint juleps, sherry coblers and Katalasine water," visitors to this particular spring were also enjoying "out-door exercise and amusements. Prominent among these [was] that of sight-seeing, and the place visited first of all others, and almost immediately after arrival by every one, [was] the Gettysburg battle-field."[57] A tour to the battlefield, this reporter implied, elevated and improved the experience of vacationers at Gettysburg Springs.

By the mid-1880s guidebooks were regularly directing visitors towards spots associated with or commemorative of the Civil War. A guide published by the Chesapeake and Ohio Railroad identified places of interest in Richmond, "the late capital of the Confederacy," including "Libby Prison and Belle Isle, of war fame; Hollywood Cemetery, where 12,000 Confederate dead repose; the Capitol building, where the Constitution of the Confederacy was framed; the White House, once the home of Jefferson Davis."[58] Tourists to such places were engaging in a very different sort of leisure activity from those who spent a week at the beach. Visiting the spot where thousands of young men had recently died did not exactly constitute escape into a world of idle and trivial amusement.

Touring historic sights and monuments served obvious patriotic functions, reminding those at leisure that their country had bred brave and gallant people. In 1886 the *New England Magazine* ran a story about a fictional family who spent their vacation taking "A Trip Around Cape Ann." Amongst the numerous attractions the family enjoyed was the "old fort which, in the time of the revolutionary war, contained enough plucky men to seize a barge with men and a cannon, which a passing British Man of War sent to besiege them." The cannon, now "all renovated," resided in the town-hall yard where it stood "as a precious relic of American pluck."[59]

People on touring vacations often sought to visit spots where Americans had been courageous, strong, and "plucky" or where famous people had been born or laid to rest. Appleton's 1873 *Handbook of American Travel* for the "Northern and Eastern Tour" described places of interest in towns along various routes. When discussing New Haven, the book called attention not only to Yale College but to the Old Burying Ground, where "many interesting monuments" marked the graves of, among others, Theophilus Eaton (first Governor of New Haven Colony), Roger Sherman (signer of the Declaration of Independence), Timothy Dwight, Noah Webster, and Eli Whitney.[60] Apparently tourists followed such advice. During his 1884 vacation tour Franklin Trexler, a young Pennsylvania lawyer, made it a point to visit Longfellow's birthplace in Portland and his grave at Mt. Auburn Cemetery in Cambridge.[61] Paying homage to the great, or to the places where great things had taken place, was a serious endeavor, something that invested vacationing with purpose and raised it from the realm of mere amusement.

American tourists also visited less lofty places. People on vacation seemed, in fact, particularly interested in touring places where other people were working. Tourist curiosity in work sites dates from the early nineteenth century. Mauch Chunk, a town on the edge of the Pennsylvania coal fields and a major coal transportation center, began to draw tourists during the 1820s.[62] Christopher Baldwin visited an iron works in the 1830s and Mary Moragne stopped at Sloan's Factory a decade later.[63] As tourist attractions, work places served to reinforce Americans' belief in their countrymen's ingenuity and technological expertise, allowing elite early nineteenth-century tourists to take pride in American achievement.[64]

Sociologist Dean MacCannell has studied work sites as tourist sights. MacCannell, who analyzes work displays in turn-of-the-century Paris, holds that such places served to "create the impression in the sightseer of having firsthand experience with society's serious side." MacCannell describes such tourism as "alienated leisure." He maintains that workplaces as tourist attractions "represent a perversion of the aim of leisure: they are a return to the workplace."[65] I suggest that for growing numbers of middle-class tourists "returning to the workplace" while on vacation provided a leisure experience that filled many functions. As well as displaying their pride in American technology and know-how, touring a workplace allowed middle-class vacationers to be connected to work while they were also at play—helping perhaps to elide tensions produced by the idleness of vacationing. At the same time such tourism allowed middle-class tourists to measure the gulf between themselves and those whom they observed at work, marking their difference from the working class even while affirming the centrality of work to middle-class life. Not unlike a stay at Chautauqua, such tourism suggests an attempt to make vacationing less frivolous, to relate leisure to work.

During the postbellum decades Americans on vacation continued to tour places where other Americans worked. Matthew Deady, a West Coast jurist, took a touring vacation with his son in September of 1878. They traveled in a small party that included a few other lawyers and their wives. The trip lasted two weeks and took them to San Francisco, Virginia City, Carson City, Lake Tahoe, and Sacramento. Deady commented in his diary on the scenery, the public buildings, the schools, and his visits with important members of the legal community in the places where they stopped. He also noted that in Virginia City

> we got permission to inspect the mill and descend the Cal mine. We descended to the 1700 ft level and then I walked back on the gallery a long ways and took a handful of the soft mealy ore then being taken out. The Thermometer was 110. I had on a flannel shirt and drawers and perspired as if in a hot bath. We reached the daylight again after an hours absence and had a most delicious tepid shower bath.[66]

In some ways Deady seemed to be "playing" at working while on his vacation. He endured the descent and the heat, "dug" some ore, sweated like the miners, and washed himself when finished with his "labor." His experience, of course, was nothing like that of a real miner—especially his being invited by the owner to refresh himself with some champagne after returning to the surface. It did, however, connect him to the seriousness of work. As inauthentic as his mining adventure was when compared with that of men who labored daily in the mines, Deady might still have felt that he had enjoyed a brief yet important encounter with a very physical, potentially dangerous, and entirely novel experience. While late nineteenth-century Americans were looking for such experiences in a wide variety of places, Deady's occurred as he toured a workplace.[67]

Vacationers like Deady were certainly not at work. But by watching others work, or by observing American industriousness in action, they could keep themselves in touch with the world of work, thereby avoiding the potentially dangerous and corrupting influence of idleness. Viewing work while on vacation served as a surrogate sort of work experience.

Guidebooks from the late nineteenth century routinely recommended that tourists include workplaces in their sightseeing. An 1884 pamphlet describing "Seaside and Mountain Resorts of the Old Dominion" recommended "Places at Richmond worth visiting," including the Tredegar Iron Works as well as the usual round of churches, public buildings, and cemeteries.[68] Workplaces did not have to be industrial sites. That fictional family on its tour of Cape Ann made a stop at Rockport where they "went to the Cove to see something of the extensive fish business carried on there."[69] Appleton's 1888 *General Guide to the United States and Canada* offered a fairly detailed description of interesting places in major cities and along popular tourist routes. In Chicago Appleton recommended, amongst other stops, the Union Stock Yards, where "the vast live-stock trade of the city is trans-

Excursion logging train, Harbor Springs, Michigan, c. 1906. Many tourists chose to include work sites such as logging camps and coal mines on their tours. (Library of Congress, Detroit Publishing Company Photograph Collection, LC-D4-19005.)

acted." The book went on to describe how the yards "comprise 345 acres, of which 146 are in pens, and have 32 miles of drainage, 8 miles of streets and alleys, 2,300 gates and cost $1,675,000. They have capacity for 25,000 cattle, 100,000 hogs, 22,000 sheep, and 1,200 horses." The stockyards apparently sported "a large and handsome brick hotel" to accommodate visitors. The guide also noted that the "Grain Elevators are a very interesting feature, and should be visited, in order to obtain an idea of the manner in which the immense grain-trade of Chicago is carried on."[70]

Vacationers who chose to be tourists, then, could persuade themselves that they had spent their leisure far less frivolously than those who vacationed at the beaches, mountains, or springs. Touring differed from resort vacationing not only in the patriotic or educational rewards it promised, but in the amount of energy it required. People who toured were usually not idle; indeed touring could be strenuous and demanding. Despite the improvements in transportation, touring in the late nineteenth century was

Tourists and guides picnicking in Yellowstone Park, 1903. Touring companies provided assistance to tourists who wanted to visit the national parks. Note that the guides maintained a respectful distance from picnicking tourists. (Library of Congress, Frances Benjamin Johnston Collection, LC-USZ62-100864.)

hardly a relaxing undertaking. Even the elite tourists who could afford one of Raymond and Whitcomb's "grand trips" to Yellowstone faced a fairly grueling itinerary. Rarely did the group spend more than one night, sequentially, in the same place and only on Sundays was neither touring, nor travel, planned. The itinerary for the eleventh day, for example, began with a 2:00 A.M. arrival at Livingston, Montana. Raymond & Whitcomb assured its clients, however, that they could "remain on the sleeping-cars undisturbed until morning." After breakfast they would depart at 8:30 via a different rail line that would bring them three hours later to Cinnabar, from where they would climb on a stage for the seventy-five-minute trip to Mammoth Hot Springs Hotel. The entire next day, beginning at 8 A.M., would be spent touring the park via stage, which would deposit them at a different hotel at 6:30 that evening.[71] Viewing the beauties and wonders of the American West, while certainly a form of leisure, could often be a taxing endeavor. Although many tourists traveled in beautifully appointed Pullman cars, they still could not avoid the heat and dust of the desert and the inevitable discomfort that accompanied getting around Yellowstone or down into the Yosemite valley.[72]

Even less elaborate tours could require considerable exertion. Unlike the more leisurely (if still demanding) touring of the antebellum elite, late nineteenth-century tourists were often trying to cram as much as possible into a short trip. Allentown lawyer Frank Trexler took a ten-day touring vacation in early autumn of 1884 in the company of a few friends. Trexler's account suggests that he and his friends tried desperately not to squander their time. They traveled first to Watkins Glen, then across Seneca Lake to Geneva, and from there to Rochester, Niagara, Toronto, Montreal, Quebec, Portland, Boston, New York, and home. Covering that distance in ten days kept the group constantly on the go. They spent nearly every day both traveling and sightseeing. They examined both nature and culture, as they visited the falls at Niagara and at Montmorency, the Dime Museum in Rochester, the Church of Notre Dame in Montreal, the Old South Church, the Public Garden, Faneuil Hall, and the Old State House in Boston, and the university, museums, and Mt. Auburn Cemetery in Cambridge. Only in Boston did they spend as many as two nights; on the remainder of the trip they arrived in a place one day and left after sightseeing the next.[73]

Unlike elite antebellum tourists, who had little choice but to travel more slowly and who often had unlimited time and money to spend, many tourists during the last half of the century seemed to have only enough time for a short vacation. Consequently, they increasingly tried to fit their tours into a one or two-week span. There was an urgency to their experience that suggests they did not want to waste a minute. And as opposed to postbellum resort vacationers, who often wrote of the relaxation and even tedium of a summer watering place, touring vacationers were not taking it easy.

Those who chose touring vacations were primarily people at the higher end of the middle class. A clerk or school teacher could manage to spend a frugal week at the beach, or boarding in a country farm house, for anywhere from $5 to $15 for room and board. A vacationer looking for more commodious surroundings and some amenities could find them for $17 to $20 a week at a place like Mohonk.[74] These vacationers also, of course, needed to pay the cost of round-trip transportation, which varied depending upon how far one chose to travel. But for large numbers of late nineteenth-century Americans the expanding network of railroads put numerous places within a $5 train trip.[75] Thus, $10 to $30 could buy a middle-class person a week's vacation at some kind of summer resort. By contrast, a Raymond and Whitcomb's six-day trip from Boston to Niagara Falls and Saratoga cost $40, while their twelve-day tour to Mauch Chunk, Watkins Glen, Niagara Falls, Alexandria Bay, Montreal, and Lake Memphramagog in northern Vermont went for $70 per person.[76] Raymond and Whitcomb offered first-class travel and accommodations, and a thrifty tourist might have been able to manage for less. But rail fares alone for such a trip ran anywhere from $30 to $35.[77] Adding the cost of hotels, transfers, and meals would have certainly made for a more expensive vacation than a sedentary week at a moderately priced resort.

There was, however, a way to reap the benefits of a touring vacation without paying for an expensive and lengthy tour: attending a world's fair. From the Centennial Exhibition in Philadelphia in 1876 to San Diego's Panama–California International Exposition in 1916, around 100 million people visited the twelve international expositions held in the United States. Almost 10 million people, nearly one fifth of the U.S. population, attended the Philadelphia Centennial Exposition, and the Columbian World's Fair in Chicago in 1893 recorded 27 million paid admissions.[78]

Recent scholarship has revealed the various cultural functions and meanings of these fairs in American life. Robert Rydell has persuasively argued that they served not only to celebrate but to inculcate a belief in American political institutions, capitalist economic progress, and white racial superiority. For Rydell, world's fairs served to reinforce the hegemonic control of the class of people who initiated, organized, and mounted them. The millions of people who visited the fairs were offered "an opportunity to reaffirm their collective national identity in an updated synthesis of progress and white supremacy."[79] More recently, James Gilbert has studied the "contradictions and diversities" of the 1893 Chicago world's fair, recognizing within them a "metaphor for the city itself." Gilbert sees the organizers of the fair as attempting to balance popular culture and high culture, integrating the former while assuring the supremacy of the latter in their vision of the American city.[80]

World's fairs served, as well, as the destination of many vacationers. A trip to an exposition resembled a touring vacation, except that the former required traveling only to one location. In fact, these fairs served as compact touring experiences. Visitors could see many of the sorts of things that they might have encountered on much longer, more extensive, and more costly tours—the grandeur of public buildings, the examples of American technology and know-how, the beauty of art, and the wonders of science. Like a touring vacation, a trip to a world's fair helped to remind vacationers of America's history, achievements, and progress.

Diaries of people who visited fairs read much like those of people who went on tours. Franklin H. Williams, for example, was a Massachusetts tobacco farmer who rarely could find the time or the money for a vacation. Nevertheless, in October of 1876 he set out on a trip to the Centennial Exposition in Philadelphia and Washington, D.C. He and his wife traveled with their minister and another couple, "young Dr. Trow & wife." In Philadelphia they "stoped [*sic*] with Mrs. Attington" at the cost of $1.50 a day. He described his trip this way:

> We went to Centenial Grounds. Visited Art Galery first. Got tired in two hours. was a wonderful collection of pictures and Statuary, also the Annex. Next visited the Horticultural Building is beautiful. Next we went to Agricultural Hall a monster. Spent Sunday & Monday in Washington D.C. Tuesday returned to Phil. spent two days more on Centenial Grounds. Was gone from home 9 days. It was a good trip. The best I ever took because the best opportunity to learn and get information [*sic*].[81]

David Kellogg, a physician from Plattsburgh, New York, visited the 1893 Chicago fair in the company of his adult son. His first day's visit he found "simply tremendous, great beyond comprehension." He was, however, "thoroughly tired out" by one day's visit and would have returned home, had he not feared what others might say: "It would not do to have it said that I stayed so short a time." And, in the end, he "enjoyed, intensely, the anthropological building and the States buildings and the forestry building and above all the fine, massive billows that, during a storm, rolled in over Lake Michigan."[82] Marian Lawrence Peabody, the daughter of an aristocratic Boston family, visited the Chicago Exposition and described what she did and saw this way: "We went on to the Mining Building and saw Negroes washing, cutting and polishing diamonds, and on further to the Machinery Building. Everything that can be done by machinery is shown in this building and that is all I can say about it—it is so vast."[83]

Visitors could "travel" to different states within the confines of the expositions, since many states mounted their own exhibitions in separate buildings.[84] Those who attended the fairs viewed displays that reflected the history, architecture, and culture of the respective states. These state buildings offered information about and examples of the sorts of things a tourist might have encountered—products manufactured in the state, famous people whom the state had produced, the cities and schools of which it boasted.[85]

What a visitor to a world's fair could not encounter were the scenic vistas and natural wonders of the American landscape—highpoints on most tourists' journeys. But for many, the fair became a sight in itself, making its own landscape and producing its own wonders. The size of buildings, for example, recalled the vastness of natural sights. Guidebooks always noted the dimensions of the buildings—not unlike the guidebooks that recorded the height of Niagara Falls or the expanse of Natural Bridge. The Main Building at the Philadelphia Centennial, for example, was the largest wood, iron, and glass structure in the world. It ran 1880 feet long and 464 feet wide and covered 21½ acres of interior space.[86] Many visitors responded to the vastness of the buildings and the layout of the grounds with an awe and wonder reminiscent of tourists' responses to natural landscapes and vistas. Isabelle Maud Rittenhouse, for example, daughter of a Chicago grain merchant, described the Chicago fair: "Oh the nights on the cool lagoons, gondolas gliding by us, water splashing & dimpling, thousands of lights outlining the beautiful buildings, the great fountains playing, their fairy-like tints reflected in the lagoons."[87] Charles G. Dawes admitted that he had "desecrated the Sabbath" by attending the fairgrounds in Chicago. He called the fair "the most stupendous exhibition the World has ever seen—and possibly will ever see." Like many who visited Niagara or Yosemite, he found words insufficient to portray what he had witnessed: "To attempt to describe it is useless. The eye is almost bewildered when it seeks detail."[88] Those who stopped to contemplate the gigantic Corliss engine at the 1876 Philadelphia fair might well have felt a kind of awe similar to that experienced at Niagara, the former offering evidence of the power of man while the latter suggested the power of the divine.[89]

As *world's* fairs, these expositions promised more than a tour of the United States. People who could never have hoped to travel abroad experienced a small taste of foreign culture as well. The arts department at the Philadelphia Centennial housed "works of all the leading artists of the world."[90] Foreign governments erected their own buildings with much the same purpose as did the individual states. The famous Midway at the Chicago Exposition contained, amongst numerous other attractions, Cairo Street—designed to make tourists feel that they were strolling down a typical north African street. The Midway was designed not only to acquaint tourists with the exoticness of other cultures but to assure them of the racial superiority of the white, Anglo-Saxon world.[91] Guidebooks to the fair promised that, after visiting the Midway, one would feel "indeed that he has returned from making a trip around the world."[92]

Guidebooks warned, as well, that a visit to an exposition required the same sort of planning as other sorts of tourist ventures. The official guide to the Philadelphia Centennial of 1876 cautioned the visitor "to acquaint himself with the characteristics and extent of the Exhibition and city" and to "determine the general features of his programme before leaving home."[93] The Rand McNally Guide to Chicago's Columbian Exposition entitled *A Week at the Fair* offered a detailed itinerary of what to see on each of the six days for a complete and successful tour of the fair.[94]

Thus for the price and convenience of a trip to one place, a vacationer could, in fact, become a "tourist" not only throughout the country, but throughout the world. Visitors to expositions and world's fairs could see an array of monuments, products, and artifacts that might otherwise have required an extensive and time-consuming trip. And while a visit to an exposition was not inexpensive, it cost far less than traveling to the many states and foreign countries represented at the fair. The official Visitor's Guide to the Philadelphia Centennial Exhibition listed the cost of rooms in large hotels (fifty guests or more) ranging from $2.00 to $5.00 per day, but as Franklin Williams's diary revealed, lodging could be had for less.[95] For the World's Columbian Exposition in Chicago, hotel rooms "in proximity to the World's Fair grounds" went for between $1.00 and $6.00 per day, with more than half in the $1.00 to $2.50 range.[96] Cost of transportation to a world's fair depended, of course, on where the vacationer originated, but railroads ran excursions that helped keep the cost down.[97] Admission to the fair added $.50 per day (half price for children), plus the cost of various entertainments, foods, and amusements. A careful and very frugal visitor could enjoy the benefits of a week's visit to a world's fair for about $25 — more than the cost of a week's vacation at a comfortable summer resort but still less than the $40 Raymond and Whitcomb charged for their tour through Niagara, Saratoga, and upstate New York.[98] And those willing to cram their visit into fewer days could "tour" for even less. Of course, visiting the fairs in style cost more. Tourist agencies and railroads offered upscale one-week tours from eastern cities to the Chicago fair for $100 per person, a price that included first-class lodging, travel, and admission to the fair grounds.[99]

While even the more reasonable prices would have put the fairs out of the reach of most working-class people, people at either end of the middle class would have found at least a short trip to a world's fair within the range of possibility. The *Indianapolis Freeman*, one of the largest African-American newspapers, ran frequent advertisements for rail excursions to the Chicago Exposition of 1893 and the Louisiana Purchase Exposition in St. Louis in 1904. The Pennsylvania Railroad, for example, offered rates of $7 round-trip from Louisville to Chicago, with the ticket good for ten days.[100]

African Americans participated in the touring experience that world's fairs offered, but often faced discriminatory treatment. The Atlanta Cotton States and International Exposition of 1895, for example, allowed African Americans to enter all the fair's public buildings but prohibited them from buying food or drink anywhere but in the Negro building. Regulations of the fair also mandated strictly segregated audiences at all public performances and events. For many blacks, this exposition became a symbol of the deterioration of American race relations. At the fair's opening day celebration Booker T. Washington enunciated what came to be known as the "Atlanta Compromise," advising blacks to renounce social and political equality for economic opportunity.[101]

African Americans faced problems at other fairs as well. In 1904 agents established an information bureau at the St. Louis Fair catering specifically to black visitors. An ad promised to "locate you in a pleasant home or hotel." This promise, however, may not have materialized. In June of 1904 a front-page story in the *Indianapolis Freeman* told of rumors of discrimination and fears that "the situation at St. Louis is not all that a self respecting colored person would desire." According to this article, the St. Louis fair compared most unfavorably to Chicago's exposition a decade earlier:

> The Negro who visits the World's Fair of 1904 expecting to find the wide open door greeting him everywhere and a glad voice saying: 'Come all ye who have the price,' as was the case at Chicago in 1893, will most assuredly be doomed to disappointment.

The difference stemmed, this reporter felt, from St. Louis being a "typical southern city."[102]

Notwithstanding the special problems it presented to African-American tourists, a visit to a world's fair offered many of the benefits of a touring vacation. For whites and blacks alike, it brought the possibility of tourism more easily within the financial reach of a broader cross section of the middle class. A trip to a world's fair instructed, broadened, inspired, and entertained. Like other tourists, those who visited the fairs could return home persuaded that their vacation had been a useful and productive endeavor.

———— •◆• ————

Tourists have a pretty bad reputation. Call to mind, for example, the stock caricature of the camera-toting, Bermuda-short-clad, noisy tourist. Daniel Boorstin's classic account of the modern American tourist as someone who "fills his experience with pseudo-events" and who believes "that he can have a lifetime of adventure in two weeks and all the thrills of risking his life without any real risk at all" has put a scholarly imprimatur on this familiar cultural stereotype.[103] Tourists, both popular and scholarly wisdom contend, are vulgar, superficial, provincial, gullible, and entirely lacking in taste or sophistication.

While the specific image has changed somewhat, this essentially negative view of tourists grew up almost as quickly as did tourism itself. By the last half of the nineteenth century writers and cultural critics were offering parodies of tourists and noting the inauthentic quality of tourist attractions. Even worse, many thought, tourists brought with them a commercial infrastructure that altered or even destroyed the places they were visiting.[104]

Doubtless much nineteenth-century tourism was superficial, and most tourists acquired a less than profound understanding of the places they visited. But before damning tourists, it is important to ask what they might have been doing instead. Tourism may appear to be a shallow and mind-numbing enterprise, but compared to what? Staying at home and following the routine of everyday life did not necessarily provide opportunities for individual growth and development. Moreover, the increasing numbers of middle-class Americans who became tourists did so in a world where vacationing was becoming more prevalent and where many vacationers were indulging in behavior that seemed not only frivolous, but fraught with potential moral danger.

Tourists, on the other hand, were busy vacationers, people with a purpose. They left home not only to enjoy recreation and amusement but to add to their stock of knowledge, experience, and information. Rather than idling away time at a resort, drinking juleps and flirting with strangers, a tourist could feel engaged in constructive activity. Nineteenth-century tourists could persuade themselves that their precious leisure had been spent seeking out and experiencing, first hand, the best that their country offered—its natural beauty, its technological and industrial mastery, and its cultural and historical artifacts. Many of these places were no doubt manufactured attractions, created or promoted by shrewd entrepreneurs and staged specifically for the benefit of tourists. But to many vacationers, the quest for them still seemed, and indeed probably was, more substantial and more worthwhile than a week at the beach.

❧ 6 ❧

"Unfashionable, but for once happy!"

---•◆•---

CAMPING
VACATIONS

In the summer of 1878 *Scribner's* magazine ran a story called "Camping-out at Rudder Grange." It told of a man who had decided to spend his two-week vacation relaxing at home until his doctor advised him differently: "[D]o nothing of the kind. You have been working too hard; your face shows it. You need rest and change. . . . Get a good tent and an outfit, be off to the woods, and forget all about business and domestic matters for a few weeks."[1] During the last quarter of the nineteenth century potential middle-class vacationers not only would have read such advice in their magazines and newspapers, but might have heard it from their doctors and ministers as well. And apparently many listened, because these years witnessed the emergence of camping as an increasingly prevalent form of vacationing.

The growing popularity of camping stemmed, in part, from an appeal that the wilderness in general held for American people by the last half of the nineteenth century. The rehabilitation of nature that romantic artists and writers had begun in the early nineteenth century proceeded in the years after the Civil War as photographers, painters, and journalists continued to celebrate not only the beauties of the East, but the newly discovered wonders of the West. Pictures and essays depicting Yosemite, Yellowstone, and the Rocky Mountains brought an appreciation of nature and the wild to easterners who had neither the time nor resources to venture so far. American scenery became a source of national pride, a means of countering European claims of cultural superiority. As a result, the suspicion and dread with which many people had approached nature in the early nineteenth century was replaced with a rising interest in and appreciation for the out-of-doors. By the time Frederick Jackson Turner announced that the frontier was closed, Americans were looking more fondly on what had once been seen as only an obstacle to be overcome and an area to be conquered. Contact with primitive nature seemed to offer an increasingly urban society the strength, health, and vigor that teeming cities threatened to sap.[2]

As early as the 1850s some members of the elite began tramping off into the wilderness for rest and recreation, sometimes taking with them an entourage of friends, family, servants, guides, and equipment. But not until the last quarter of the century would middle-class people also experiment with a variety of types of camping—some solitary and physically rigorous, others communal and less demanding. Camping seemed to fit perfectly the needs of a growing vacationing public. It promised health, rest, and enjoyment—all for a moderate price. While much less self-consciously a time for intellectual self-improvement than a vacation at a chautauqua or even a touring vacation, camping nevertheless offered the spiritual benefits that allegedly came from close contact with nature and the physical benefits that accrued from fresh air and healthful outdoor living. Moreover, campers in remote woods or forests remained distant from the temptations and perils of fashionable resorts. And, most importantly, camping required enough effort to keep vacationers safe from the potential dangers of idleness.

Middle-class and elite urbanites began to discover the pleasures of camping during the last half of the century, but they were neither the first nor the only ones to enjoy them. Escaping into the woods or forests—usually to hunt—had long been a familiar pastime in the lives of a wide variety of rural men. Well-to-do planters, small landholders, and poor tenant farmers all shared and often relished the pleasures of a hunting expedition, even if they frequently sought different prey and engaged in different hunting rituals. Some hunted purely for sport; others hoped to fill their dinner tables. Hunting expeditions could last a number of hours, or a number of days.[3]

The camping vacations of the middle and upper class with which this chapter deals differed from the hunting ventures of rural people. Most obviously, health and recreation rather than bagging game were the primary goals of the venture. Campers sometimes hunted, but hunting was not what propelled them into the wild. Vacationing campers—often urban people—had a completely different relationship to and conception of the wilderness than did rural hunters. As importantly, while hunting was and remained primarily a male event, camping often engaged women as well. Women's presence helped to domesticate the camping experience, but, perhaps because of its association with hunting, camping retained a male aura throughout the last half of the nineteenth century.

———— • ◆ • ————

The earliest American "campers" were not on vacation. Pioneers who settled the West and travelers who voyaged through sparsely inhabited areas camped not for recreation but out of necessity. The wilderness, for most such people, held little charm. It represented hardship, strenuous labor, and danger—a place to be traversed, subdued, and settled. Indeed, as historian Roderick Nash has explained, in the early decades of the nineteenth century most Americans were either still engaged in or close enough to the pioneer experience to maintain a decidedly negative, even hostile view of the wild. Given the choice, most travelers would have opted for an inn or a farmhouse and a bed rather than a night under the stars and a meal cooked over a campfire.[4]

But the relationship with nature had, by the second quarter of the nineteenth century, grown more complex than the simple need to tame or conquer. Even as many people continued to face the trials and difficulties of the frontier, others discovered that nature and the out-of-doors held decided benefits. Romantic writers and artists, following the British model, found beauty and sublimity in American scenery. Transcendentalists discovered in nature a better understanding of the divine plan. As residents of increasingly congested cities began to yearn for the salutary influence of open space and natural landscapes, planners and businessmen responded first with the development of scenic, rural cemeteries and later with city parks.[5]

By midcentury a small number of northeastern urban dwellers, hoping to experience nature more closely, were *choosing* to make forays into the woods and forests. Writers, intellectuals, artists, philosophers—people who no longer had to face the hardship of the frontier—found themselves drawn to the outdoors. A small number of privileged urban inhabitants, comfortably sheltered from the most unpleasant aspects of nature, could afford to see a more beneficent side to the wilderness. Released from the settler's burden of crossing formidable mountains and traversing dense forests, these early campers eagerly fashioned an outdoor experience and a conception of the wilderness distinct from that of their pioneering contemporaries. Influenced by romantic literature's glorification of nature and solitude, those who tramped into and camped within the Maine woods or the Adirondack forests at midcentury sought beauty, divinity, and health.[6]

Take, for example, Thomas Wentworth Higginson—reformer, minister, and well-placed member of Boston society. In September of 1855, less than a decade after numerous families had embarked on that long and arduous "camping trip" known as the Oregon Trail, Higginson accompanied a group of like-minded and similarly well-placed men and women on a recreational camping trip to Mount Katahdin in Maine. The trip required considerable physical exertion, yet Higginson seemed to revel in it: "Yesterday we walked about nine miles, seven harder ones today; seven more tomorrow bring us to our highest camp halfway up at the foot of a slide. . . . I cannot say how glorious this mountain is." But not all his time was spent so strenuously. Higginson's diary also recorded the more relaxed moments: "Three figures stand catching fish rapidly . . . ; a few are sitting on a stone to watch them. Three are writing. Mr. Battles is dressing fish, and Martha and Mr. Brown are helping our guides in picking hemlock boughs and piling our soft broad couches in tents. We have all had such a happy afternoon; the freedom of the woods descends deeper and deeper into us; all obstacles have vanished, and everything is easier than we expected." An enthusiastic advocate of women's rights, Higginson saw no reason to exclude women, writing, "It only seems absurd that strong and active women should go anywhere else."[7]

Higginson and his entourage were not the only elite northeasterners who sought recreational pleasures in the woods. In 1858 William Stillman, an artist and a journalist, took a group of ten friends on a trip deep into the Adirondacks. The group included the cream of Boston intellectual society: Ralph Waldo Emerson, Louis Agassiz, James Russell Lowell, John Holmes (brother of Oliver Wendell Holmes), and five other writers, scientists, and philosophers.[8] Although Stillman had devoted his previous ventures into the woods to painting and spiritual reflection, the goal of this trip was primarily recreation. Reflecting on the experience from the distance of almost half a century, Stillman remembered: "In the main, our occupations were those of a vacation, to kill time and escape from the daily groove." They spent the days exploring the region—hunting, fishing, and paddling on the lake. Still, some of the participants put the time to productive use. The scientists examined plant and animal life; Stillman did some painting; Emerson wrote a poem.[9]

Members of camping expeditions like Higginson's and Stillman's sought the pleasures of nature but not necessarily the difficult labor that such an undertaking required. Both parties brought guides to shoulder some of the burdens that accompanied such a venture. The Stillman expedition, for example, consisted of not only the ten "guests" but also eight guides. And while nobody, apparently, expected to be pampered, the guides no doubt helped to set up camp, find and prepare food, and carry provisions.[10]

Higginson, Stillman, and their friends represented a small, elite avant-garde of writers, ministers, and intellectuals who created a rationale for and an example of a rewarding, recreational camping experience. It was, however, William H. H. Murray, minister of the prestigious Park Street Church in Boston, who succeeded in advertising and publicizing the pleasures of wilderness camping to a larger audience. Murray, an enthusiastic sportsman, fervently believed that a stay in the out-of-doors could solve the mental, physical, and social problems plaguing urban dwellers.[11] In 1869 Murray published a book called *Adventures in the Wilderness; or, Camp-Life in the Adirondacks* in which he recounted the glories and delights of a camping experience in the Adirondacks. Murray maintained that a visit to the Adirondack woods not only offered a feast of magnificent scenery, but served as well "to restore impaired health." He recommended the trip "to such as are afflicted with that dire parent of ills, dyspepsia, or have lurking in their system consumptive tendencies." Murray recounted the story of a young man, dying of consumption and so weak that he had to be carried into the woods, who emerged five months later, sixty-five pound heavier, "bronzed as an Indian, and as hearty."[12]

The Adirondacks offered not only health, but sport. Murray promised enough game and fish "to satisfy any reasonable expectation" of the sportsmen.[13] Moreover, a trip to the Adirondacks, according to Murray, offered a perfect recreational outdoor venture because it did not demand too much effort. Where camping in Maine, for example, required miles of "tramping," a visitor to the North Woods of the Adirondacks could make use of the "marvelous water-communication" and "do all your sporting from your boat":

> If you wish to go one or ten miles for a 'fish,' your guide paddles you to the spot and serves you while you handle the rod. This takes from recreation every trace of toil. You have all the excitement of sporting, without any attending physical weariness. And what a luxury it is to course along the shores of these secluded lakes, or glide down the winding reaches of these rivers, overhung by the outlying pines, and fringed with water-lilies, mingling their fragrance with the odors of cedar and balsam! To me this is better than *tramping.* I have sported a month at a time, without walking as many miles as there are weeks in the month.[14]

It was, Murray felt, this feature of the trip that made camping in the Adirondacks "so easy and delightful to ladies." Like Higginson, he advocated including women in camping parties, and his book offered particular advice on what women should bring and wear, suggesting "a pair of buckskin gloves," "thick balmoral boots, with rubbers," and a "short walking-dress, with Turkish drawers fastened with a band tightly at the ankle." In fact, he concluded, "it is safe to so say, that, of all who go into the woods, none enjoy the experiences more than ladies, and certain it is that none are more benefited by it."[15]

Critical to the success of such camping experiences was the presence of guides. While neither Higginson nor Stillman had detailed the specific duties of a guide, Murray's book designated seven pages to the subject, maintaining that "this is the most important of all considerations to one about to visit the wilderness." Murray's language suggests that early campers considered guides in much the same way as many middle-class men and women regarded servants. Murray warned, for example, that "an ignorant, lazy, low-bred guide is a nuisance in camp and useless everywhere else." By contrast, "a skillful, active, well-mannered guide . . . is a joy and consolation, a source of constant pleasure to the whole party." The choice of the wrong guide could prove disastrous: "With an ignorant guide you will starve; . . . with a low-bred fellow you can have no comfort." Most telling, perhaps, was Murray's claim that "a good guide, like a good wife, is indispensable to one's success, pleasure, and peace."[16] Those who pioneered the camping experience intended to avoid the danger, strenuous labor, and privation that real pioneers encountered. The presence of guides helped to bring "roughing it" into the realm of recreation.

Murray offered encouragement, motivation, and advice in order to persuade less adventurous folks to attempt camping trips. In an August 1869 letter to the *New York Tribune*, he explained that not only "the artist, and the lover of nature in her grandest aspects, but the business man and the professional man, weary and jaded by months and years of over-work" could find "rest and recuperation for body and mind" within the "recesses" of the woods.[17] Camping, Murray maintained, would deliver results that other sorts of vacations only promised. Overworked men—especially those who lived in cities—needed time away from home in order to renew themselves. Murray contended that, given the proper planning and assistance, a camping experience could not only achieve that goal, but also would be an enjoyable and reasonable recreational venture.

Murray's was not the only voice advocating the therapeutic benefits of a recreational trip to the wild. An 1870 editorial in the *New York Times* explained that "tens of thousands of our overworked men and exhausted women" needed to get away during the summer: "What people need, who have overstrained the nervous system, is open air and an entire change of scene, occupations and movement." The writer chose a European cruise as the ideal cure, but recognized that such a venture remained out of most people's reach. Instead, he recommended a trip to some remote place—one accessible only by wagon or coach rather than rail. The article suggested the mountain region around Lake Placid, where visitors could stay in farmhouses or little inns, and the "lake regions" around the Saranacs, "where the parties live in camp and depend upon gun and rod for their best supplies." The editorialist concluded that the "atmosphere of this whole region, and the rough out-door life and entire change from civilized habits, make it a perfect sanitarium for our worn-out city workers."[18]

Throughout the last three decades of the century magazines and newspapers reported on the restorative possibilities of camping. Potential health benefits allegedly derived, in part, from the uninterrupted contact with fresh air. In 1880 *Harper's* magazine printed an article by a newspaper reporter who, at death's door and nearly wasted away from consumption, followed his doctor's advice and journeyed to the Adirondacks in search of health. An eighteen-month stay in the wilderness cured him: "For a year and a half the wasted lungs have fed upon this pure air, and upon nothing else. . . . Nature has been patching up the delicate tissues, healing the tubercular formations, ridding the system of fever, checking the cough, putting flesh on the wasted body, and strengthening the flabby muscles."[19] Clearly this was not a vacation, but a desperate attempt to regain health. Still, readers would easily have understood that the fresh pure Adirondack air would benefit even those who chose a shorter stay. And if the poor consumptive could endure life in the outdoors, healthy people might have felt assured of their own abilities to withstand whatever rigors a camping vacation demanded.

Besides the fresh air, campers also enjoyed the advantages of isolation and quiet. By late in the century medical opinion increasingly held that urban dwellers were suffering from nervous diseases brought on by too much civilization.[20] The popular press echoed such concerns in articles that advocated camping as the perfect solution. *Cosmopolitan,* for example, ran an article in 1896 called "A Summer Outing on Northwestern Waters." The author castigated those "fagged out" businessmen who stayed "in close touch with the telegraph, telephone and locomotive" during their few weeks off from work. The three businessmen in question, having "just pulled through a commercial cataclysm," were instructed by the doctor to spend "a whole summer in the Rocky mountains, where outdoor life was compulsory and isolation complete." The men relished the idea but realized that their wives might not prove so eager. "However," they found, "in such a cause they [the women] were enthusiastically ready for anything—even to cooking over a camp fire and sleeping on the ground."[21]

There is no way of knowing exactly how many heeded such advice, but people's interests were clearly piqued. Murray's book sold wildly and apparently set off a stampede of visitors. Many, unfortunately, found their experiences in the wilderness considerably less satisfying than they had anticipated. By the summer of 1870 the press reported stories of the mishaps and misadventures of "Murray's Fools."[22] In part to counter such bad publicity and to help restore his credibility, Murray took to the lyceum circuit, lecturing about "the Adirondack life and experience in the woods." Over a period of three years he spoke more than five hundred times to as many as half a million people throughout New England. He recalled that after finishing a speech he was often besieged by many who, intending to visit the woods the following season, sought "practical information and advice."[23]

While the number of campers no doubt grew, those who joined the "Murray Rush" probably represented a select group of people who could afford the rather steep price of playing at being primitive.[24] Camping, at least in the "comfortable style" recommended by Murray, was not an inexpensive undertaking. Murray offered the following summary of "What It Costs": "Guide-hire $2.50 per day; board for self and guide while in the woods, $2.00 each per week; miscellanies (here is where the ten-dollar greenbacks come in), $25.00." Two campers could share one guide, "making it only $1.25 per day," but Murray did "not advise one to do this." Add the cost of getting there, a $50 round-trip from either Boston or New York, and Murray concluded it was "safe to say that one hundred and twenty-five dollars will pay all the expenses of a trip of a month's duration in the wilderness." But, he justified, "no other excursion" would "return such per cent in health, pleasure, and profit" for "such a small sum of money."[25] Maybe so, but at those prices a month of camping in the Adirondacks cost more than a stay at Mohonk Mountain House and only a little less than booking a single room at the Grand Union Hotel in Saratoga.[26] Murray undoubtedly helped to broaden interest in outdoor experiences beyond a select group of artists and intellectuals, but he was pitching his appeal to those who could spare a month in the summer and who assumed that guides or servants would be part of the adventure.

Throughout the end of the century wealthy people continued to enjoy a variety of elite, servant-equipped, and sometimes extravagant camping experiences. The Adirondacks, in fact, became renowned for luxurious camping. The Anson Phelps Stokes campground at St. Regis Lake, for example, cost $75,000 to build and was rented to a family for $10,000 for the 1890 season.[27] As one writer explained, "Adirondack camp does not mean a canvas tent or a bark wigwam, but a permanent summer home where fortunate owners assemble for several weeks each year and live in perfect comfort and luxury, though in the heart of the woods, with no very near neighbors, no roads, and no danger of intrusion."[28] This was clearly camping in name only. Such "camps" provided the isolation and remoteness of a real camping experience, but eliminated any trace of "roughing it."

By the 1870s middle-class men and women also began to experiment with outdoor vacations. One such indication was the increasing frequency with which articles about camping appeared in magazines and newspapers. From *Harper's* and *Scribner's* to *Catholic World* and the *New York Times*, jour-

nalists and storytellers began to introduce readers to the pleasures and benefits of camping. While no census taker counted the number of campers, the
prevalence of these stories and articles suggests that camping appealed to an
expanding number and variety of people. The popular press revealed that
during the last three decades of the century camping encompassed an array
of experiences—some solitary, others communal; some entirely outdoors,
others under shelters; some primitive, others luxurious. Diversity enough to
appeal to a range of potential vacationers.

Stories in magazines sometimes portrayed campers seeking a solitary
experience in nature. The protagonists, almost always male, usually ventured into the wilderness either alone, in the company of a fellow adventurer, or with a guide. Such campers caught and prepared fish and game,
marvelled at scenery, and enjoyed renewal and recreation. John Todd, a
Yale-educated minister, apparently got his first taste of the wild when two
professors invited him on an excursion into the Adirondacks. According to
his biographer, "from that time he went regularly every summer, for more
than twenty years, into these wilds, and spent from four to six weeks in
hunting, fishing, resting, and enjoying the beautiful scenery. As it was
impossible for him to maintain any communication with the outside world,
he heard nothing from his family or parish to worry him, and so could
throw off all care." When the Adirondacks began to become too crowded
with "excursionists," Todd retreated "to the more distant but lonely forests
of Maine or Canada," taking with him an "Indian or woodsman to do the
hard work."[29]

While such solitary campers probably remained few in number, during
the last three decades of the nineteenth century more vacationers began to
experiment with communal forms of camping. Families or groups of friends
found a camping vacation not only feasible, but enjoyable and beneficial.
The young Theodore Roosevelt, for example, took a trip with his family in
1871 into the Adirondacks and from there into the White Mountains.[30]
While in the Adirondacks they used Paul Smith's hotel—the most famous of
the early Adirondack hostelries—as their base and took camping trips into
the woods. Many campers apparently combined camping with stays in
hotels, boarding houses, or established "camps" that began to dot the
Adirondacks. An 1875 article in the *New York Times* described campers in the
Adirondacks who spend their days alternating "between the innumerable
camps on the mountain sides and along the streams and by the banks of the
lakes, where they sleep on spruce boughs, and look up at the stars if they
wake during the night."[31] Some camps, often built by guides, included huts
or sheds "built of logs and securely roofed with birch bark" that provided,
according to one camper, "quite a comfortable bed."[32] Other campers
apparently made use of small villages nestled in the Adirondacks that served

*Breakfast in Camp, West Branch, Penobscot, Maine, 5 September 1885.
Camping grew in popularity during the last quarter of the nineteenth century.
Both women and men participated in camping vacations. (Library of
Congress, Joseph J. Kirkbridge Collection, LC-USZ62-34544.)*

as "very acceptable head-quarters for the tourist, and relieve[d] him from the necessity of living in camp; though in pleasant weather, at least, he [might] find that mode of life more comfortable."[33]

By 1875 John Bachelder's *Popular Resorts, and How to Reach Them* included a five-page section on "camping out." Bachelder described a variety of sorts of camping experiences. Some people were provisioning a "good roomy covered wagon" and using it to set up "camp for a few days on the banks of some beautiful stream or lake." A few very adventurous types were indulging in "another species of camping-out"—exploring the wild and uninhabited parts of the West. Bachelder had also witnessed larger numbers of people organizing "camping-out parties" during the 1874 season at various summer resorts: "On the shores . . . of Lake Winnipesaukee several parties encamped for the season; and both there and at Lake George they remained until the autumn frost had tinged the foliage. And so at numerous other pleasant localities, and along the routes leading to them, parties were seen who had chosen this mode of recreation."[34] Bachelder and others gave advice on the equipment, clothes, and attitudes necessary for a successful camping experience.[35]

From the very earliest ventures, these groups of vacationing campers included women. While camping of the solitary sort might have been a male experience, members of both sexes braved the wilderness in groups. Women, for example, formed part of the Roosevelt family camping trip in 1871. Twelve-year old Theodore recorded in his diary: "We went back to Paul Smith's today. . . . We found that the Ladies too had camped out for a night."[36]

Many of the camping stories and articles that appeared in popular magazines and newspapers told of female as well as male campers. Central to T. Addison Richards's tale, "A Forest Story," for example, was the role and presence of women in the camping experience. Published in *Harper's*, the story related the adventures of a pair of young men who traveled into the Adirondack woods for a camping and hunting adventure. The two male campers believed that "[s]uch a life . . . is not exactly the thing for women," but their guide disagreed: "'Stuff!' . . . 'They [women] come here safely enough sometimes, and I often wonder we don't see many more of them. If they take care of themselves and don't lose the trail they get along well enough. And it's just the sort of thing they'd like, if they only knew it; for the women has got more grit than the men, after all, when you put them in your trumps." The two men soon learned that the guide was correct, as they happened upon and joined another party of campers, consisting of "three ladies and their maids, and three gentlemen besides two guides."

The storyteller seemed to be suggesting that camping would offer women a chance to cross gender boundaries and take part in men's world. Not unlike resort vacations, camping exposed women to a variety of sports usually reserved for men. The women in the story, for example, fished for trout, trolled for pickerel, "assist[ed] at a deer hunt," and successfully climbed Mount Marcy. Richardson, the author, applauded the enthusiasm, willingness, and skill of the female sportsmen. But fear not, gentle reader, these women were neither de-sexed nor de-classed by the experience. The ladies in the story had all brought their maids, thus assuring that they would be relieved of any labor inappropriate for women of their class. And despite participation of the women in various forms of outdoor recreation, the most skillful fisherwomen and hunters in this story were the maids rather than the ladies. Even as the women—both ladies and their maids—engaged in masculine pastimes, their presence seemed to domesticate the camping experience rather than to de-feminize the women campers. A subplot of the story involved a budding romance between one of the lady's maids and the trusted male guide—a romance that the ladies and gentlemen of the party not only condoned but promoted. The story ended with the lovers deciding to marry.[37]

By the late 1870s camping vacations were capturing the interest of people across the country. George Whitwell Parsons, a young bank clerk in San Francisco, passed a week's vacation along the Pacific shore in 1879. He

Mr. Wilson, Miss Grant, and Miss Townsend on Moosehead, [Maine], c. 1884–1891. Female campers participated in a range of outdoor activities. (Library of Congress, Joseph J. Kirkbridge Collection, LC-USZ62-29817.)

Miss Cox, Miss Towsend, Mrs. Towland, and Mrs. Philla, first Falls of the Location River, Maine, c. 1884–1891. Female campers sometimes brought the entertainment of the parlor— in this case card games— into the camping experience. (Library of Congress, Joseph J. Kirkbridge Collection, LC-USZ62-25358.)

spent one afternoon at Loquel Beach and remarked in his diary: "Numbers camped here. Quite the thing to do."[38] A *New York Times* article about the mountains of Pennsylvania described how "the custom of camping out on the secluded borders of the many charming lakes . . . has recently been growing in great favor with those residing in the inland cities." Residents of Scranton and neighboring towns were making their way to places like Lake Paupack in the Moosic Mountains: "Sometimes parties who pitch their tents by one of these mountain lakelets continue in camp as long as two weeks, where the delights of gypsy life are fully realized and the cares of business forgotten."[39]

Some people advocated camping on their own property, or within the vicinity of their homes, by moving the family outdoors for a two-week holiday.[40] The diary of Benjamin Hart Dally, a young railway clerk, described the "camp" that his future father-in-law, A. G. Rose, an insurance underwriter, established for his family in the summer of 1888. Rose built "Camp Harrison," on a lake about twenty-five or thirty miles, or an hour's train ride, from Milwaukee. Leasing a plot of land from a farmer, Rose first built a one-room cottage for his wife, who did not welcome the idea of sleeping in a tent. He then put up a sleeping tent for the children, tents to serve as kitchen and dining room, and, of course, a tent for the maid. The Rose family apparently had trouble persuading the maid to join them. Dally remembered that "it was very hard to get a maid—evenings too lonesome for them." The family, however, found little trouble supplying their other needs. The farmer furnished milk, eggs, and chickens and every Friday evening Rose arrived, bringing with him a load of groceries, to spend the weekend camping with his family.[41]

This "domestic" camping experience differed dramatically from what a camper in the national parks might have experienced. As early as 1864 Congress had set aside forty acres of land for "public use, resort and recreation" in the Yosemite Valley and around the Mariposa Grove of the Sierra redwoods. Eight years later President Grant signed a bill that designated a much larger tract of land in Wyoming to be "set apart as a public park or pleasuring ground for the benefit and enjoyment of the people." In 1872 Yellowstone was still largely inaccessible, and only the most adventuresome sorts—primarily scientists, explorers, artists, and photographers—would have braved such a journey. The completion of the Northern Pacific Railroad and its connection to the Yellowstone in 1883 made the trip somewhat easier.[42] But by the early 1880s a few daring women and men were taking recreational camping trips into Yellowstone.

In 1882 Mary Bradshaw Richards and her husband Jesse journeyed from New York to Yellowstone. Both in their fifties at the time, they no doubt had considerable financial means.[43] The Richards traveled by train to Salt Lake and then via the Utah and Northern Railroad to Beaver Canyon, where their outdoor adventure began. The trip into Yellowstone required a prodigious amount of equipment and supplies: "Our outfit (two persons) consisted of a wall tent, blankets, buffalo skins, axe, hatchet, nails, ropes, hammer and wheel grease; flour, sugar, lard, ham, eggs packed in oats, canned meats, fruits and jellies; a long tailed frying pan, bake kettle, coffee pot, tin plates, cups and spoons, knives and forks." Essential, as well, were the two horses, the wagon, and, of course, the two guides—"a capital driver, an accomplished cook." The assistance of the "boys," as Mary Richards referred to them, relieved the Richards of many of the onerous chores associated with camping. Ernest, the driver, and Peter, the cook, not only drove the wagon and cooked the food, but apparently did the laundry and prepared the camp sites.[44] The Richards paid handsomely for this camping adventure. The entire outfit (horses, wagon, guides, supplies, and equipment) cost a whopping $18 a day, an amount that would have bought one person a *week's* vacation at a very nice mountain or seaside resort.

Yellowstone in the early 1880s was not yet a mecca for campers, but enough people camped there to leave their mark on the landscape. Richards reported seeing "blackened logs, tin cans, and bits of pasteboard, or paper lying about," all of which "told the tale of former and recent campers."[45] Trash aside, the sights, sounds, smells, and colors of Yellowstone moved Mary Richards: the splendor of Yellowstone Canyon, "unlike anything or place we have seen on either continent"; the "dirty, bad-smelling mud, stones and tree stumps, all boiling like mad, together" of the Great Mud Volcano; and the "pure, exhilarating atmosphere, . . . savage solitude, . . . scenery of varied, inexhaustible beauty" of Yellowstone Lake. The Richards spent their time hiking up and down the hills and canyons and making their way along the often unwelcoming terrain of Yellowstone. At the end of the journey Mary Richards expressed her "genuine regret" at leaving.[46]

By the late 1880s a few hotels offered services to visitors in the park, but many tourists continued to camp.[47] In September of 1887 a man named Webner (first name unknown) spent nine days camping with a friend in Yellowstone. Unlike the Richards, this party of two took neither cook nor driver. Rather, they traveled on horseback, pitched tents, braved cold and snow, caught trout (some of it too wormy to eat), cooked some of their meals in the boiling pools that dotted Yellowstone's landscape, and visited the geysers and springs for which Yellowstone was becoming famous. While Webner and his friend were definitely "roughing it," traveling without the assistance of guides or servants, even their experience was not entirely a wilderness one. Some nights they camped within two hundred yards of one of the hotels and took advantage of the amenities it afforded, walking there to write and post letters or have a smoke.[48]

Both the Richards and Mr. Webner enjoyed an experience that differed significantly from the Rose family of Milwaukee. While they all entailed living outdoors, little else connected the adventure of a stay in Yellowstone to the calm, domesticated summer "camp" of the Roses. By the 1880s a camping vacation included a wide range of possibilities. Some brought people into the wilderness, others deposited them on nearby farmland. Some cost a lot, others much less.

Although the wealthy often continued to camp in style, members of the middle class began to appreciate the possible financial advantages of a camping vacation. A few people—William James among them—had recognized the economical potential of a camping vacation by the early 1870s. James, writing in *The Nation* in 1873, noticed that vacationing was "becoming more and more common"—a trend that he heartily applauded: "Twenty-five years ago, clerks and young employees hardly ever expected a holiday. . . . Now a fortnight of freedom in the year is getting to be regularly understood as a part of their contract." James also remarked, with pleasure, on "the constant increase, in the Northeastern States at least, of the practice of camping out." Such a vacation appealed particularly, he expected, to "artisans . . . who could afford to take the time" but could not "afford to pay for their board in addition. For such, if they be of an active and 'handy' turn, camping out on the shore, or on some mountain side, would seem to be just the thing."[49] James understood that camping held the potential for making vacationing a viable possibility for people of moderate means.

Over the next two decades others began suggesting camping as a less expensive vacation alternative. Those who slept outdoors, after all, did not have to pay hotel proprietors or boarding house keepers. An 1895 issue of the *Boston and Maine Courier*, a railroad promotional magazine, discussed "New England Fishing Resorts" where "people who do not care to spend their money at hotels, can live just as comfortably and much cheaper by camping out." The article explained how: "A guide, who is also a cook, with full camping outfit, can be hired almost anywhere for $3 a day. . . . It is possible to live better, for fifty cents a day for food, for man and guide, than at many of the cheaper hotels."[50] Nor did the railroad think only "man and guide" were suited for such ventures. The same issue offered an article called "Camping Out for Women," demonstrating how, with the help of "a good guide," camping could "be made comfortable and enjoyable" for members of the female sex. At the rate of $3 a day, a guide would provide "the entire camp outfit" as well as a canoe large enough for "two persons and the baggage."[51]

Three dollars a day was still not an inexpensive vacation. But those willing to share or forgo a guide and to eat what they caught or killed could reduce their costs considerably. Nineteenth-century middle-class campers opted for a range of experiences. Some chose to "rough it" and save some money, others required a more comfortable and thus more expensive outdoor adventure. In 1891 S.R. Stoddard described Lake George "teem[ing] with nomadic life in all its varied forms . . . white tents gleam[ing] along the dark-green foliage." He maintained that "in the course of the season a thousand people taste the pleasures and overcome the difficulties of actual camp life at Lake George."[52] But Stoddard, who preferred camping under shelter, suggested that, in fact, living outdoors was not all it was cracked up to be. He recommended, instead, "fishing boxes or shanties, more or less rough in construction, some made simply of rough boards, with bunks for sleeping in, and with chairs, tables, stoves, etc." "Campers" could hire these for between $12 and $30 a week, "including the use of a boat or two and in many cases a well-filled ice house."[53] Depending on how many people shared the space, such a venture could fit the pocket books of many middle-class vacationers.

Other recommendations for economical camping advised larger groups of people—as many as twenty or twenty-five—to pool their resources and share expenses. Writing for *New England Magazine*, Isabel Barrows recommended the following plan:

> A family of twenty or twenty-five is not too large. Twenty dollars will buy a tent with fly, poles and pins, ten by twelve feet square, with high walls. Five dollars more will lay a planed floor, which can be left to bleach in the winter's snows, while the tent is swung safe in the cabin aloft. Ten such tents would shelter the family of twenty luxuriously, and the expense, like all the other expenses, could be divided. They will serve ten summers at least, and can be easily taken from place to place if the families desire to break up or to change their camping place.[54]

The authors of a 1902 article called "The People at Play" described meeting two female teachers from San Francisco who were camping in Yosemite Park. The women were "taking an independent outing by themselves . . . in the forest."[55] Unlike Mary Richards in Yellowstone twenty years earlier, these women brought neither cook nor driver, no doubt sparing considerable expense. They also revealed that, by the turn of the century, some women felt comfortable embarking on a camping venture without the assistance of men.

By the end of the century vacationers seemed to be taking advantage, as well, of more institutionalized and organized forms of camping. Permanent camps were sprouting up in the forests of the Northeast. An 1890 article in the *New York Times* described the numerous camps in the Adirondacks "arranged in various degrees of comfort and luxury." Those who so desired could live "simply indeed, . . . sleeping on the ground and living on food cooked over an open fire." Once the novelty of roughing it had worn off, however, many campers apparently hoped for more amenities and fewer inconveniences—"a floor for the tent, a cooking stove, a dining tent."[56]

Maine boasted numerous "sporting camps" that provided guides, tents, and all necessary provisions. A typical camp would include a cook house, log cabins, and toilets. Promoters insisted that guests could enjoy fishing, hunting, evenings around the camp fires, and rainy days in cozy cabins. Those who desired could take "tenting" trips away from camp. One group of vacationers "arranged it so that one of the central camps was our head-quarters, and from that we made side trips, with tents, so that we saw 'new country' practically every day, and yet had the more substantial log cabin within reach if unfavorable weather made tenting less desirable." Such campers continued to insist that this was an ideal experience for both women and men. A woman who was "properly equipped for such a outing" need fear neither "hardships" nor "privations." "When tenting the ladies can have their own tent and the guide will always see that there is hot water and a separate fire at their disposal, if desired."[57]

Institutionalized forms of camping grew up not only in the forests of the East, but in the West as well. Some campers organized themselves into "cooperative parties or clubs" with the goal of pursuing "life in the open." Club camps dotted the land adjoining the Gunnison River in Colorado, for example. Members enjoyed the excellent trout fishing and the "pic-turesque" scenery.[58]

People who chose a camping vacation could feel that they had reaped numerous benefits: the health that came from all that fresh air; the spiritual peace that derived from associating with nature; the isolation from cares and worries that life in the woods guaranteed. But the benefit of camping also stemmed from what people chose *not* to do instead. Those who pro-moted and discussed camping, and those who chose to become campers, did so knowing what other sorts of possibilities beckoned potential vaca-tioners. Indeed, camping appeared especially salutary and beneficial when compared to some of the alternatives—specifically resort vacations. Before John Todd discovered the pleasures of a summer in the Adirondacks, for example, he had taken a "trip with his family in his own carriage, a short stay on a farm or in the crowd at Saratoga." He found, however, that "he returned to his tasks little refreshed."[59] An 1890 article in *Scribner's Magazine* advised those who wanted the full benefit of a vacation to put themselves "beyond the vexatious comforts of hotels" and give themselves "wholly in trust to nature and the elements."[60]

Advocates of camping touted not only its physical advantages over resort vacationing but its moral value as well. Americans could point to a long tradition that found nature itself as a source of moral uplift.[61] Efforts to build city parks in the late nineteenth century, for example, spoke to the belief that a dose of nature would improve the moral character of city folks.[62] How much more beneficial, then, might a camping trip into the woods prove? An 1875 *New York Times* article on the Adirondacks praised "Old Phelps," a camper's guide, as "simple, honest, truthful, generous, public spirited, reverential, religious, . . . a man of strict integrity." His virtues apparently stemmed from his close connection to nature, and campers guided by him would no doubt benefit from exposure to his numerous good qualities. The same page of the paper reported on "Bathing at Cape May," and readers might well have been struck by the difference between the two articles. While campers guided by Old Phelps were imbibing his integrity and simplicity, the bathers at Cape May that season were busy flirting and gossiping: "The women who bathe here have the same satisfaction that they have in church—they see and they can be seen."[63]

Camping, promoters claimed, offered an antidote to the pitfalls and ills of vacationing at fashionable resorts. In 1873 William James described coming upon a family camping on the shore in Massachusetts: "No one stirred as we came up and held parley, and, in fact, the pretty young lady with the switch of hair seemed too unconscious, and too beautiful even, to raise her half-closed eyelids and examine who we were. *Unfashionable,* but for once happy!"[64] Place this same beautiful young woman at a fashionable watering place, James seemed to imply, and she might well have been primped and ready for flirtatious or unsavory encounters. But camping by the stream rendered her wholesome and content.

Numerous articles on camping made the comparison with hotel vacationing more explicit. An 1881 article in *Harpers* entitled "Adirondack Days" noted how "people who travel through that beautiful mountain land are unhappy and discontented, or find their chief pleasures in the comforts and amusements of the large hotels which have sprung up through the region." But campers who loved "the rough hills and spreading forests for their own sake" found instead "unfailing gladness from the cares of the world and noisy whirl of cities." Such an experience not only brought health to the body but restored "the jaded mind."[65] *Scribner's Magazine* held that campers in the "Lake Country of New England" would learn "how simple, elemental, and healthful human existence may become . . . in the summer season." Women, too, the article maintained, would find a camping vacation to their liking: "Ladies venture on this out-of-door life with entire safety, and none enjoy more than they this perfect escape from conventionality, and restful return to nature and simplicity." Besides being spared the artifice of "conventionality," female campers would be safe from those "special invitations to colds . . . which the drafts and sudden alternations of temperature bring to summer visitors in hotel corridors and on windy piazzas."[66] It is, of course, hard to imagine how sleeping in a tent would offer more protection from the elements than even the draftiest summer hotel. Perhaps the author worried more about the resort's impact on women's moral rather than physical health.

The alleged benefits of camping extended even to those who were campers in name only. The prominent and extremely wealthy people who inhabited the luxurious "camps" of the Adirondacks, could apparently be found "living a most informal existence, wearing stout, simple clothing, blazing trails through the forest, fishing, paddling, . . . and enjoying the refreshment of the woods." Visitors there would encounter "no 'dressing up," no "evening gowns" or "dress coats." Rather, "walking skirts and tennis flannels and knickerbockers are the order of the day—and evening as well."[67] Compare this description to the columns of newspaper ink describing the sartorial excess—specifically the women's toilettes—at popular watering places. Those who touted camping, even the sort of luxurious camps that dotted the Adirondacks, saw its advantages in the context of the problems of vacationing at a fashionable resort.

Those vacationers stuck at resort hotels could, with a little ingenuity, look to another alternative—the "holiday in a vacation." Henry Van Dyke described "a good little summer resort" where "the boy and I were pegging away at our vacation" in 1907:

> There were dinner parties, and tea parties, and garden parties, and sea parties, and luncheon parties, masculine and feminine, and a horse-show at Bar Harbor, and a gymkhana at North East, and dances at all the Harbors, where Minerva met Terpsichore on a friendly footing while Socrates sat out on the veranda with Midas discussing the great automobile question over their cigars.

Vacations dominated by dinner parties, tea parties, garden parties, and dances—even those that allowed men to escape to the veranda with cigars—were clearly orchestrated and planned by women. Despite such a "vastly entertaining and well ordered" experience, Van Dyke and his son began to yearn for a "few 'days off.'" Camping was the answer. The two men packed up their camping gear, made "peace with the family, . . . and set out to find freedom and a little fishing in the region around Lake Nicatous."[68] Camping supplied a masculine remedy for the feminized resort vacation.

Camping thus became one of the means of avoiding the pitfalls and hazards associated with resort vacationing. It offered healthful contact with nature and removed many of the temptations that lurked at fancy spas, seaside resorts, and watering places. Camping provided a manly alternative to stuffy, female-dominated hotels and watering places. Although women certainly camped, a camping vacation required that they cede control to men. Fashion could not hold sway. Comfortable, practical apparel was a necessity. Campers could avoid the artifice and dangers of resort vacationing, substituting plain clothes and the wholesomeness of nature for elaborate attire and attention to etiquette.

But camping was not foolproof. Leisure itself presented risks that even campers might not be able to avoid. In July of 1885 the *New York Times* ran an article called "How to Enjoy Camp Life." The reporter noted the increasing numbers of "city people, especially young men," who had been camping out in the woods, claiming that they had hoped for a healthful, restorative week of fishing and hunting. What many really wanted, however, was an outdoor debauch. A guide for one group of "five young New York business men" contended that although the campers' "outfit included the finest of fishing tackle and guns, . . . not a rod was jointed, . . . not a gun taken out of its case" for the entire week. What the campers enjoyed was "a week's 'racket,'" and they each, as a result, "returned to New-York fagged out, enervated and ill." Perhaps the all-male composition of this camping expedition made it particularly vulnerable to dissipation. The persistence with which advocates of camping encouraged women to participate might have been a subtle effort to domesticate the camping experience and to make sure that male campers did not behave too wildly while in the wild. Ideally, camping would avoid the problems of fashionable "female" resorts without falling prey to the potential dangers associated with exclusively male entertainment. The article ended with this piece of advice: "The bottle should be touched sparingly in camp."[69]

While camping did not guarantee a wholesome vacation, it certainly presented fewer dangers than resort vacationing. Indeed, camping afforded one of the surest ways to guard against the potential hazards of leisure: it furnished the opportunity, indeed sometimes even the necessity, of combining vacations and work. In 1881 a Dartmouth student named Ernest Balch established a camp for boys called Camp Chocorua. Its purpose was to offer rich boys an alternative to the lazy life of a summer hotel. At this island "work camp" the boys not only did their own chores, but used the opportunity to learn the skills of business management. Historian Peter Schmitt has explained how "youthful construction companies . . . bid for carpentry work, the 'Goodwill Contract Company' handled camp laundry, and the 'Soda-Water Trust' provided for refreshments."[70]

Camping offered adults as well as children the work that many believed was a critical part of any vacation. Advocates of camping often walked a fine line, balancing an emphasis on work with the idea that camping was pleasurable, relaxing, entertaining, and safe. Given the help of the all-important guide, they argued, camping required few hardships and little effort. Even women could do it. The emphasis on the ease and leisure of camping especially characterized the earliest advocates and promoters—those who in the 1860s and early 1870s were trying to convince a doubtful public that the wilderness held more than toil and danger. Recall William Murray's promise that a trip to the Adirondacks would "take from recreation every trace of toil."[71]

But by the late decades of the century, as vacationing and its attendant problems began to occupy the time and attention of middle-class Americans, the promoters of camping modified their message somewhat, emphasizing the enjoyment a vacationer received from doing the work that camping required. An 1881 description in *Harper's* of the Adirondacks described the considerable amount of gear that accompanied campers on a three-week trip: "[T]he great trunk, with our tents and blankets and the dishes and all the paraphanalia of camp" would be under the care of Rueb, the "faithful guide." While Rueb, no doubt, was responsible for much of the labor, the writer maintained that the work of camping in fact constituted one of its greatest pleasures: "There is a sense of freedom and freshness in every hour; the wretched cares and complications of our artificial existence, the strifes and rivalries and hypocrisies of society, are far away and forgotten; we possess ourselves in quietness; a round of simple, natural toil fills up each day." Of course, the "simple, natural toil" did not take all the campers' time. The labor of Rueb still allowed vacationers to find "a shady place, amuse [themselves] with a book, . . . or lie and dream, letting [their] thought[s] wander lazily along the curving shores and among the drifting clouds."[72]

In an attempt to persuade its readers of the delight of camping in Pennsylvania, an article in the *New York Times* began by asserting that "persons accustomed to the glare of fashionable enjoyments would, doubtless, think pleasure impossible in such a place." Camping, the author suggested, would offer different diversions from fancy resorts. In fact, much of the satisfaction of camping, the reader learned, derived from the work associated with it: "There was a regular programme. The first duties of the day were to provide the bill of fare." Nothing so strenuous as planting or harvesting, but "a three miles ride through the woods" to a nearby farm "where fruit, fresh eggs, butter, and Spring chickens were purchased at prices astonishingly low." All members of the camp, "ladies included," took turns performing "this duty." Those relieved from "marketing" took on other tasks—gathering berries or fishing for pickerel. Having supplied the day's provisions, the campers were free to enjoy their leisure. They gathered flowers, read, hiked, and savored the scenery. Work clearly played an important part in the camping experience, though it did not need to be any too strenuous.

Ladies could even "nominate some 'slave' who should guide the horse among the trees and carry miscellaneous bundles from the farmhouse."[73] Camping provided a means of connecting work to vacationing, thereby helping to reduce potential dangers associated with extended periods of leisure.

Indeed, for some the chief benefit of camping came from the labor it required. The three "fagged out" businessmen who followed doctor's orders and decided to take their wives camping in the Rocky Mountains in 1896 found that much of their "therapy" derived from the work of camping. First the male campers labored to build a "huge stove (dubbed the 'smelting works') from stone and scraps of heavy tin obtained from empty cans." The writer described the enormous pleasure of the experience—even for three men who had suffered not only recent business reversals but "years of strain such as few middle-aged Americans live through." What they needed, apparently, was not just relaxation, but a way to combine physical labor— something absent from their everyday, middle-class lives—with outdoor recreation. Only men who spent their days doing "brain work" could turn to manual labor for therapy or enjoyment. According to the author, "the novelty of all these little tasks made the experience an unending picnic." The work of maintaining the camp engaged much but not all of their leisure: "Such time as could be spared from camp duties was pretty evenly divided between reading, whist, boating, fishing or hunting. The days seemed all too short."[74] Whether the story was apocryphal or real, the message was clear: work was essential to a successful vacation.

————— •◆• —————

Camping thus offered many middle-class vacationers a host of benefits— financial, physical, moral. Not only could they exchange the sybaritic influences of resorts for the beauty and purity of nature, they could also avoid potentially dangerous consequences of leisure by the "work" that camping required. There is little doubt, however, that camping served other important functions. In the early twentieth century a small number of forward-looking businessmen, politicians, and journalists began to question whether or not the benefits of regular vacations should be limited to middle-class people. Workers and their families, some began to argue, could profit from the advantages of yearly summer vacations. But not just any sort of vacation would do. Camping would be critically important in the process of making vacations part of the lives of working-class Americans.

Into the Twentieth Century

In September of 1912 Rufus Fearing Dawes, the only son of banker and financier Charles G. Dawes, drowned while on vacation in Lake Geneva, Wisconsin. Charles Dawes, reflecting on the horror and anguish of his son's death, described the scene in his diary.

> There, by the light of lanterns, we saw him, our darling, our first born, our only son. For two hours we stood there by him as they worked over him with the pulmotor and then they told us that all was over. . . . There in the night— even then—my heart was full of pride for my boy, and I told those who had worked so hard to restore him, of his noble, useful life,—*that he was not an idler—that this was the only two weeks of his vacation that he was giving up to recreation, that the rest of it had been devoted of his own volition to honest work.*

Dawes seemed compelled to explain to the men who had tried to save his son—"most of whom were laborers"—that, despite wealth and family connections, Rufus too had been a "laborer." The vacation on which his son had died, Dawes protested, had been an unusual episode in the young man's short life. In a written tribute to Rufus, Charles Dawes took pains to describe in some detail the numerous demanding and physically rigorous jobs at which the young Dawes had worked during his vacations from Princeton. Productive labor rather than recreation or leisure had been the goal of those breaks from study.[1] Charles Dawes's pain at the loss of his son seemed heightened because Rufus had died vacationing.

Charles Dawes's sad memorial to his son suggests that nineteenth-century middle-class suspicions about leisure and vacationing persisted into the twentieth century. This distrust remained even as the numbers of vacationers spiraled and despite the enormous growth, popularity, and increasing respectability of a variety of forms of commercial amusements and recreation. By the end of World War I respectable city dwellers were beginning to dance at cabarets and night clubs, pay visits to amusement parks, and enjoy the movies[2] Such entertainments were also finding their way to small towns in the Midwest and to rural areas of the South.[3]

The public discussion about vacationing in some ways reflected this more tolerant attitude toward leisure. While the press had in the nineteenth century focused considerable attention on the moral hazards of resort life, those fears diminished significantly during the early twentieth century. But, at the same time, suspicions about vacationing persisted. The pages of mass market magazines and the policies of many American businesses revealed continuing concern over the consequences of extended periods of idleness.

These enduring doubts about vacations paralleled, not uncoincidentally, the growing presence of workers, immigrants, and African Americans among the vacationing public. Through the end of the nineteenth century vacations had remained primarily the preserve of the middle class and the well-to-do. The early decades of the twentieth century, however, saw the comfortable classes beginning to lose their near monopoly on the privilege. By the end of the 1930s vacationing was well on its way to becoming a mass phenomenon. While certainly not everyone vacationed every year, between 1900 and 1940 growing numbers of people along the social spectrum came to harbor the reasonable expectation of enjoying the benefits of at least an occasional short summer vacation. Indeed, one of the most important changes in the history of vacations from the nineteenth to the twentieth century was its transformation from a largely white middle-class experience to a custom shared by a wide range of the American public.

How and why this transformation occurred is the subject of the remainder of this book. My exploration of the early decades of the twentieth century will be selective rather than comprehensive. The numbers of vacationers and vacationing places mushroomed during these years. While the forms of vacationing invented during the nineteenth century—resort-going, touring, self-improvement vacations, and camping—persisted, the crowds of vacationers fashioned a multitude of creative variations. At the same time a growing vacation industry sought to entice more people to indulge in the pleasures of time spent away from home. So entrenched had vacationing become in American life, that even the hardships of the 1930s did little to diminish the interest or enthusiasm of Americans for their vacations.

My object here is to investigate a small part of the history of vacations during the first four decades of the twentieth century—specifically to examine how a once middle-class custom came to be enjoyed by a broad cross section of the population. How did the white working-class come to be included in the vacationing public? In what ways did their vacation experiences, as well as those of growing numbers immigrants and middle-class African Americans, differ from or resemble the vacation patterns of the white middle class? How, if at all, did the public discussion and cultural attitudes about vacations and leisure change as the vacationing public broadened and as the depression brought economic hardship and insecurity to millions of American families?

∂ 7 ∾

"Vacations do not appeal to them..."

—•◆•—

EXTENDING VACATIONS to the WORKING CLASS

In 1892 Philip G. Hubert Jr., writing for *Century Magazine*, proposed an elaborate, if entirely impractical, scheme for extending vacations to members of the working class. He suggested that poor tenement dwellers "give up their few rooms, store their goods at small expense" and thereby "save enough on the rent to pay for their food during the weeks away." Families could move to the south shore of Long Island or into New Jersey where they could pitch tents and live more healthfully and just as cheaply. Hubert estimated that even the "typical family of slop-shop clothing-makers," including two working parents and four children, could camp out for ten weeks "at an average weekly expense of not more than $5." He did admit some disadvantages to his proposal: "There would be rainy days and the various unpleasant features and hardships of camping out. There would be no corner liquor-store for the man, nor corner gossip for the women. The daily toil might be even a trifle harder, owing to lack of conveniences. Meat would be difficult to get and to keep." Still, the advantages, he felt, would far outweigh such minor liabilities.

In fact, Felix Adler's Society for Ethical Culture tried a similar experiment some years earlier. Adler "subscribed enough money to build a dozen comfortable cottages in a pleasant spot" on Long Island and then "induced some poor families of Polish Jews who worked on cheap clothing to make the experiment of living there." The effort failed miserably. Apparently the people, "especially the women, wanted to get back to the city; they complained that it was lonely. They wanted society—the noise and squabbles, the fights, the dirt, and the crowds of the tenements." Hubert concluded that such an experiment could succeed only if reformers began with the children, teaching the young people the values of "fresh air and quiet." Hubert proposed a "Camping-Out Society" that would "tell poor people where and how they might camp out, the advantages and disadvantages of the life, its cost, its ways and means." And the advantages would be manifold: "There would be clear, cool air for the little ones. . . . The children could run barefoot on the beach, could bathe in the surf and play in the sand; and what more, after all, can the millionaire give his children during these hot weeks?"[1]

Not surprisingly, Hubert did not consider the possibility that these poor slop-clothing workers be offered vacations with pay. He believed that employers would gladly give their employees time off during the slow summer months "provided salaries stopped during those ten weeks." That most poor families lived hand to mouth and would never be able to afford even this much of a vacation, Hubert saw as a potential benefit. New Yorkers need not fear that Long Island would be overrun with poor city dwellers, since only those "with at least a few dollars" could entertain the idea.[2] The outlandish nature of Hubert's plan suggests how little serious consideration anyone gave to the notion of making vacations feasible for working-class families in the 1890s.

But over the next few decades a variety of voices—those of reformers, businessmen, social scientists, and journalists—began to engage in a serious discussion about extending vacations to the working class. The debate began around the turn of the century as some Progressive reformers turned their attention to the problem of vacations for poor children, mothers, and working women. Beginning in the 1910s and continuing throughout the 1920s, social scientists and a minority of forward-looking businessmen joined reformers in exploring the question of vacations for working-class men as well. Persuaded that vacations for workers could make good business sense, a small number of progressive American companies began during the 1920s to institute paid vacation plans. Although it was not until the last half of the 1930s that a majority of working-class people enjoyed the privilege of paid vacations, during the early decades of the twentieth century, middle-class reformers, social critics, and businessmen helped to fashion a rationale for mass vacationing.

The nineteenth century had afforded few members of the working class the opportunity for a vacation. Many had, of course, considerable experience with time away from work. Periodic unemployment, some of it seasonal, plagued poor people, necessitating a variety of strategies to stave off disaster. Some of these resembled leisure pursuits. Fishing and hunting, for example, had long been a way of combining recreation with food gathering for rural people.[3] Working-class residents of cities or small towns may similarly have ventured to the rivers or woods of the nearby countryside to fish or hunt during layoffs. Such excursions furnished enjoyment for hunters and fishermen—usually men—while supplying food for families.

Toward the end of the century some working-class people found other means to eke pleasure out of unemployment. Writing for *Century Magazine* in 1891 Edward Hungerford described a "rambling house of cheap construction" that he encountered in western Vermont. The house offered "only mean accommodations and coarse fare," but the "kindly" owners took in summer boarders:

> During a portion of the hot season all available space had been packed with factory hands. Released for a time by a shut-down, they had rushed hither for rest, under what would have seemed to most of us hard conditions. I doubt not they had a good time, lounging by the water, breathing the fresh air, flirting and courting, and at last going back to their work refreshed.[4]

While a small number of laid-off factory hands may have been making their way to cheap summer boarding houses in the 1890s, for most workers, unemployment could hardly have been labeled a vacation. Members of the working class lacked the financial resources to turn such time into extended periods of recreation or amusement. The vast majority of working-class people took their leisure, rather, in shorter bursts. Congregating on stoops or street corners or spending a Sunday afternoon at a park provided many with an opportunity for socializing and entertainment. Men found amusement in saloons, fraternal lodges, and clubs. Gambling, prizefighting, boxing, wrestling, and cockfighting captured the attention of urban working-class men and the scorn of pious reformers and middle-class moralists. Some men played more innocent sorts of sport, such as baseball; and in some cities large audiences of working-class men attended theaters. By the early twentieth century the movies were offering a cheap source of entertainment to women and men alike. On national holidays—particularly the Fourth of July—whole families enjoyed picnics and parades. Young working-class women and men who lived in large cities spent much of their leisure in dance halls, social clubs, and on the streets.[5]

Working-class people also enjoyed themselves on one-day excursions to picnic grounds, amusement parks, and beaches. Coney Island in New York, Revere Beach outside of Boston, and Dream City in the east end of Pittsburgh, for example, received a mass of working-class patrons.[6] The *New York Times* reported that sixty thousand people crowded the beach at Rockaway, Long Island, on one Sunday in July of 1885. It was not an entirely genteel or quiet crowd. "Pickpockets and 'rounders' from the lower wards of the city" roamed through the throng, stealing watches, pocketbooks, and parasols. Thousands of pleasure seekers also traveled to Starin's Glen Island on the same day and "enjoyed the day thoroughly." The multitude was so great that "two extra boats were required to bring the visitors back to New-York."[7]

Reformers sometimes organized these outings, hoping to offer fresh air and recreation to children from the sweltering tenements of the city.[8] During the summer of 1890 the New York Association for Improving the Condition of the Poor sponsored at least nineteen excursions, some including as many as eleven hundred people. An estimated total of ten thousand "parents and children" had, by summer's end, enjoyed these "well-managed and deservedly-popular 'ocean parties.'" The newspaper lavishly praised such efforts: "Many of the children who seemed tired and listless when they left the pier returned in the evening bright and cheerful, and they all wanted to be sent again." The society sponsored, as well, a separate event for "the poor colored people of the city who have been found deserving and in need of a day's outing by the sea." It, too, promised to be "quite a large party."[9]

Social reformers soon realized that if one day in the country or by the seashore was good, a week was better, but only for women and children.[10] By 1885 the Children's Aid Society of New York had opened a summer home for tenement children at Bath on Long Island that welcomed "some four thousand of the poor little wasted population from the crowded tenements." The newspaper reported that "for a week they are permitted to enjoy the fresh sea breezes, the bathing, outdoor life, and good country fare afforded by this charity, and, it need not be said, return to their homes refreshed and happy." The society also ran a sanitarium for sick children and their mothers on the west end of Coney Island, where the children enjoyed the pure air and the mothers were taught the "science of caring for children." According to reporters, "the few days in the Health Home not only bring back the babe to life, but send the mother away with a new idea of her duties toward her family."[11] Charitable groups occasionally placed children in individual country homes, but housed most together in groups, some as large as two or three hundred, at summer resorts/institutions.[12]

Newspaper coverage of these efforts not only commended the organizers, but frequently made a pitch to readers for financial support. Entitling such articles "Waifs at Bath Beach" and "Fresh Air for Little Ones," reporters pointedly contrasted the experience of fortunate middle-class vacationers with poor tenement-dwelling children: "The many thousands in New-York who . . . are scattered abroad among the mountains and by the sea, must feel most of all in the Summer time the painful contrast between the lot of their children and that of the children of the poor . . . shut up in hot tenements and steaming, filthy lanes and alleys."[13] Guilt may have proven an effective fund-raising technique for an audience of middle-class vacationers already somewhat uneasy about the pleasures they themselves were enjoying.

Some of these summer youth programs clearly hoped to do more than offer poor children the chance for a good time and a breath of fresh air. The three hundred children staying at the summer home of the Children's Aid Society at Bath Beach in June of 1895, for example, demonstrated to visitors the impact of their "vacation." The children marched in to dinner, "some keeping step very well and others not at all to the march that was being played upon the piano. The blessing was asked, and every little child, with clasped hands, eyes tightly closed, and looking something between little imps and angels, gave thanks for the food before them, and asked to be made good children."[14]

Those who harbored doubts about the benefits of leisure might have been assured by the knowledge that many of these poor children were absorbing important lessons while on vacation. Gad's Hill encampment, run by a Chicago settlement house and situated on a "high bluff overlooking Lake Michigan," stressed "cooperation"—meaning "the girls helping in the domestic duties, and the boys in the care of the grounds and the work of the garden." In 1904 Gad's Hill also introduced a vacation school, where the children learned "sewing, basket weaving, nature study, water color and charcoal drawing."[15] Camps like Gad's Hill were not only teaching industrious work habits, they were also imparting a message about leisure and recreation: vacations for working-class people could be used productively rather than simply for relaxation, idleness, or worse. Reformers may well have hoped that these camps, in teaching working-class youths the pleasures of a "self-improvement" vacation, would help inculcate middle-class values.

Working-class mothers also benefited from efforts to bring the pleasures of the country or seaside to the deserving poor. Reformers and religious groups helped to move poor mothers and their children out of the hot city for a short period during the summer. Organizers of these efforts had a variety of objectives—to give poor mothers a well-deserved respite, to encour-

age religious observance, and to offer instruction in proper mothering. At
Camp Goodwill, located on the campus of Northwestern University outside
of Chicago, "religious services [were] arranged" for tenement mothers.
Guests were, apparently, "left entirely free to attend or not as they [might]
choose." While organizers did not mandate church attendance, they did
plan a morning kindergarten for the children at which time "the mothers
gather[ed] for a friendly talk given by some lady on topics relating to family
life, housekeeping and hygiene."[16]

An array of organizations—both secular and religious—continued
throughout the early twentieth century to send children of various ages,
sometimes accompanied by their mothers, to the country and the seashore.
Such efforts reflected the generalized interest in reform that characterized
the Progressive Era and drew upon the same, mixed motives of other Progressive reformers—a genuine desire to help the less fortunate, combined
with an equally genuine belief in the wisdom of teaching working-class, ethnic people to adopt the culture and behavioral norms of the native-born,
white middle class.[17] Settlement houses, churches, newspapers, wealthy
philanthropists, and various charitable groups all worked to establish fresh
air funds for poor women and children—many of them immigrants—who
lived in hot crowded tenements. By 1900 seventeen cities had fresh air relief
programs that reached large numbers of children.[18] A 1906 report revealed
that not only New York and Chicago, but places like Buffalo, Indianapolis,
Washington, and Cleveland had established "well-ordered and efficient
summer outing plan[s]."[19]

Inspired by similar motives as those concerned with mothers and children, other reformers began to focus on the vacation needs of working
women. As early as 1880 the YWCA ran what it called the Seashore Cottage in Atlanticville, on the New Jersey shore, which a reporter for the *New
York Times* described as an "excellent institution, giving store-girls and fac-
tory-girls a chance to visit the seashore, that they could not otherwise
enjoy." The women were "allowed to stay two weeks at a time, at very low
prices" and were "well taken care of." Just how well became evident to the
reporter who, attempting to "get in under pretense of making inquiries,"
was "driven away by a large dog."[20]

By the early twentieth century a variety of groups had become interested
in vacations for working women. They included the sort of reformers—
often upper middle-class, well-educated women—who had been con-
fronting problems of women's wages, hours, and working conditions. Such
reformers subscribed to the belief that female workers were more delicate
and frail than their male counterparts and that, as potential mothers, they
needed and deserved special provisions, protection, and services.[21]

Gertrude Beeks, for example, had been a prominent Chicago social reformer, a friend of Jane Addams, and an active participant in local reform organizations and settlements. International Harvester Company hired her in 1901 to watch out for the welfare of its female employees. In this capacity Beeks organized a summer camp and upgraded the dressing rooms for Harvester's women workers. An argument with a plant supervisor eventually led to her resignation, but Beeks pursued her interest in improving the lives of working women by becoming head of the Women's Welfare Department of the National Civic Federation (NCF).[22] Under NCF auspices, Beeks explored the issue of vacations for working women, writing letters to various companies inquiring about vacation policies for their female employees.[23]

The NCF was not the only organization concerned about vacations for working women. In 1900 a group of New York City women who "devote[d] their time to the condition of the poor of the tenements" tried to place working women in suitable suburban and country houses for short stays during the summer.[24] Eight years later a group called the Committee on Amusements and Vacations Resources of Working Girls in New York began to investigate the conditions at summer boarding places. They were horrified at what they found. In one boarding house "which had been recommended as 'highly desirable,' the beds, in the off season, were used as incubators, and the mattresses were nests." In another, weekly prizefights entertained the guests. In a third the investigators discovered that diphtheria had developed "and no sanitary precautions had been taken to protect the prospective guests from contagion." And in many, they realized, "liquors were sold surreptitiously."[25] In response to such problems, the Women's Welfare Department of the NCF established a Vacation Bureau and a Committee on Vacation Resources, chaired by Gertrude Robinson Smith, that investigated and publicized the names of respectable, inexpensive country boarding houses and lobbied various companies about the importance of paid vacations for female employees.[26]

Many wage-earning women found themselves with time off when factories closed during the slow summer season. But even the inexpensive boarding houses that Smith's vacation committee recommended remained out of reach for women on these "vacations." While NCF welfare workers continued to urge employers to offer vacations with pay, they also encouraged employees to save money over the course of the year for their own vacations.

In 1913 Smith set up the Vacation Savings Fund—a sort of a bank that would hold workers' weekly contributions. With the help of Anne Morgan (daughter of the late J.P.), Smith collected over $50,000 from ten thousand female workers. Depositors earned no interest on their money. The interest went, instead, to cover the costs of the committee—specifically the salaries and traveling expenses of investigators who researched and publicized the names of appropriate summer boarding houses. Apparently as many as four thousand women took vacations with the money they had saved over the course of the year.[27]

Rather than helping to find appropriate vacation places, other reformers tried instead to create those places. In 1909 *Survey* magazine did a study of "organized efforts to provide the working girls of New York City with a summer vacation." The results revealed that churches, department stores, vacation societies, clubs, and settlements all were engaged in establishing vacation homes for working women. One of the most extensive programs came from the Working Girls' Vacation Society. It operated eight vacation houses in 1908, charging patrons $3 to $4 a week but waiving the fee for those who could not afford the price. Working women, aged fourteen to twenty-six, primarily factory workers, saleswomen, teachers, dressmakers, and stenographers, attended.[28] A year later the society acquired its tenth house on a twenty-acre tract of land in Hadlyme, Connecticut. The new property came "with a small endowment," two cottages, a barn, two carriages, and "nearly all the furniture, table and bed linens necessary." The twin cottages could accommodate twenty-two working women—"the tired army of wage-earners, who can, by a little help, secure two weeks during the summer for vacation." With an endowment that covered only part of the expenses, however, the camp made frequent appeals for donations.[29]

Reformers in other cities undertook similar efforts. In Cleveland, for example, the Cooperative Employment Bureau, a joint venture of the local Consumer's League, the YWCA, and other reform groups, tackled the problem of sending "working girls" on vacation by asking people in suburban and country homes to board these people "at a very low rate" and by establishing a camp within commuting distance of the city.[30] The New York Society of Ethical Culture sponsored a rather unusual summer retreat in Mountainville, New York, called Camp Moodna. The camp was comprised of "twenty of the old horse cars which were formerly in use on the Avenue A line of New York City." The cars had been placed "in a long line facing the rippling Moodna Creek and on the border of a fringe of woods." Sixteen sleeping cars, two dining cars, a library car ("filled with good, wholesome books and current magazines"), and a kitchen car graced the property. Guests could also enjoy a tennis court and a dance platform, music from a large phonograph, and a swimming pool. Campers paid $3.50 per week. Two other camps nearby allowed for "an exchange of visits . . . nightly."[31]

While most vacation places for working women originated in the efforts of charitable, reform, or religious groups, a few came from the corporate sector. Two New York department stores, Bloomingdale's and Siegel & Cooper, ran vacation houses at the seashore. The former could accommodate from three hundred to four hundred in a season, while the latter held as many as seven hundred. Both offered the places free to female employees for a week, and both houses were apparently popular, remaining full for the entire summer. At Siegel & Cooper's Cottage at Long Branch, the women made their beds and were "trained in the standards of living."[32] By 1905 this cottage had been in operation for seven years and was, according to an article in the *New York Times,* "not a charity of the company, but . . . owned by the Employes' Association." The newspaper reported a variety of entertainments planned for the "girls" that season: a coaching party "along the beautiful Rumson Road," a "trolley ride to Asbury Park," an outing "in launches on Pleasure Bay," an evening excursion to a "big ice cream resort," and "a theatre party at the Pleasure Bay Opera House."[33]

By the 1910s a few other companies instituted a variety of summer programs for their female employees. Boott Mills of Lowell, Massachusetts, opened a vacation cottage in 1909 at a lake six miles and a nickel street car ride from the factory. The camp, available only to female employees, housed some who chose to "go out there to sleep at night on the open porch, returning to work each day." Others used it on weekends or for "outings of one week." The camp could afford to charge only $1.50 per week—an extremely low rate—because the wife of the mill owner, Mrs. Flather, paid for the rent of the cottage and because the camp hired as little help as possible. Instead the work was "systematized . . . so that one group of girls would wash dishes, another group make beds, another group clear the table, another group burn up the paper tablecloth and paper napkins, etc.etc." But economy proved only one motive. Gertrude Beeks of the NCF explained that "this has been done partly to instruct the girls in home economics."[34]

Despite all these efforts, only a tiny minority of "working girls" were able to take vacations. A 1909 survey of the facilities in and around New York concluded that the vacation accommodations for wage-earning women were decidedly inadequate. New York City housed more than 360,000 female wage earners; the various settlements, charities, clubs, and churches brought vacations to only 6,874 of them.[35] The Siegel & Cooper Company employed 4,000 people but its vacation cottage could never accommodate more than 800 a season. The cottage had served in lieu of a company policy of paid vacations for its workers. When the company changed its policy and instituted vacations with pay in 1912, the employees voted to close the cottage.[36]

Reformers warned that the lack of healthful vacations for working women boded ill: "There being so few week-end resources, the public amusement places with their doubtful attractions are all that is left."[37] Those reformers who supported and promoted vacations doubtless hoped to improve the health and increase the pleasures of the women they served.

They also knew well, however, what other temptations lured young working women. Left to their own devices, many young women enjoyed their
leisure in what middle-class moralists feared to be the unsavory environment of the city street, dance halls, clubs, and amusements parks. Many
reformers feared that such urban amusement brought young women exposure to and opportunities for sexual experimentation and corruption.[38]

It is, unfortunately, difficult to recover the voices of the working women
who were the guests at these various vacation places. Most existing reports
come from the reformers or the press, and both touted the success of such
ventures. These articles invariably point to the happy and appreciative
female vacationers enjoying themselves amid the cool breezes, sunshine,
and welcoming environment. An article by Annie Beard in *World To-Day*,
for example, related the extreme gratitude and good fellowship of the
impoverished mothers who attended these summer camps. One mother, "a
Bohemian Catholic [with] five children" hesitated, Beard explained, about
attending "because if she is away her 'man won't bring his envelope and the
rent is due' or [because] she may lose her 'places to wash.'" In response, a
"truly generous" Bohemian Jew offered "one half the amount needed for
rent" while a Bohemian Protestant donated the other half. Another woman,
according to Beard, summed up the feelings of most guests with these
words: "It is like heaven to be here. If I never have another vacation I shall
always remember this one. Why I haven't done a thing since I came up
here, except mind my own children and wash out a few little things for
myself.'"

Beard maintained that the experiences at camps not only furnished
women with well-needed rest and enjoyment, but also engendered a new
outlook on class relations. One camper had arrived believing "rich people
cared nothing for poor ones. I've found them willing to cut me down to the
last penny about my washing." Her stay at the camp persuaded her, however, that "these women just seem to be happy in looking after us. I am
never going to think so hard of rich people again." Always looking for
donations, Beard informed her readers that "far more than a mere temporary rest and physical benefit are given to these women and children." The
possibility of easing class tensions, she implied, should certainly be "worthy
of a larger sustenance than it receives."[39]

Perhaps Beard's desire to raise money for these summer camps encouraged her to put words into the mouths of imaginary, impoverished mothers.
Or, perhaps, these camp experiences did alter wage-earning women's views
of their tight-fisted employers. In either case, working women and poor
mothers appreciated the facilities made available to them by charitable and
philanthropic groups. The large numbers of women who took advantage of
these various summer resorts and camps testifies to their popularity. A

cheap place to stay in the countryside or by the seashore—even if not per-fect—no doubt beat a week in the sweltering city.

Rose Cohen, a seventeen-year-old Jewish immigrant, remembered her experiences at White Birch Farm, a home for "needy city children" financed by a wealthy and philanthropic doctor. Most of the guests were between the ages of seven and twelve and came in groups of sixteen for a two-week stay. Cohen, recovering from a serious illness, spent the whole summer, although not entirely as a vacationer. She acted as one of two young assistants to Miss Farley, the kind and efficient nurse who ran the place. The house also employed "two coloured women" who performed most of the domestic chores, leaving Cohen to help supervise the children. Not used to the coun-try, Cohen at first felt uneasy: "There was the great quiet. The fields lay so still. Yet life seemed to be teeming and the air was filled with silent voices." While she quickly grew accustomed to her new environment, she never took its pleasures for granted. "In the house too," she explained, "it seemed as if I were living in a fairy tale. . . . There was nothing of the 'institution' about this place and I soon recovered my spirits as well as my health. My face became brown and rosy. The sun bleached my hair, and again I began to find pleasure in whatever work I did." White Birch Farm also exposed Cohen to the kinds of lessons that many reformers hoped young visitors would imbibe: "I saw here modern, orderly, systematic housekeeping. There was time for everything, room for everything, money for everything that was necessary." In retrospect Cohen understood what at the time had been less apparent to her: "The thought did not come to me that all this was possible because there was means. I only saw the facts."[40]

While Rose Cohen relished her experiences, other working women felt differently. Full houses did not necessarily mean enthusiastic guests. Some evidence suggests that, given the money, working-class women would have preferred to fashion their own vacations. An article in *Munsey Magazine* admitted that many of the vacation homes run by churches, settlement houses, and charitable organizations were "unpopular because of the restrictions imposed on the inmates." The women who vacationed at these places "had to live by rigid rule; there was no freedom of action." One saleswoman told an investigator: "Why, you can't even look at a man if you go there! I do not want to be bound to go to prayers twice a day." The arti-cle concluded that self-supporting women "who toiled so hard for the greater part of the year" wanted "a chance to get away from irksome routine of shop and shelf" and "to feel absolutely free to rest or to seek innocent amusement."[41] Reformer Belle Israels, who formed and led the Committee on Public Amusements and Vacations for Working Girls, understood that most working girls disliked performing chores and objected to the rules that charitably run vacation houses imposed, especially the prohibitions on socializing with "fellows" in the evening.[42] The decision of the workers at Siegel & Cooper to close the company cottage once they began receiving paid vacations may speak, similarly, to what had been a less-than-enthusiastic if still plentiful clientele.

Company vacation cottages—like other forms of welfare capitalism—extended the employers' power and authority to non-work time, something female guests certainly understood. Those vacationing at camps run by charitable or reform organizations had to deal with rules and policies that well-meaning middle-class people laid down. Absent other alternatives, working-class women willingly, indeed gladly, went. But given the choice, many probably preferred not to spend their short, precious time off from work doing cooperative chores at vacation camps or being "trained in the standards of living" at a company cottage.

————— •◆• —————

Adult male workers remain glaringly absent as objects of these early vacation plans. Believing that poor women and children needed and deserved special assistance, and chastened perhaps by unsuccessful efforts to pass protective labor legislation for men, early twentieth-century reformers made few attempts to implement vacations for male workers.[43] The first tentative efforts to provide vacations for working-class men came, rather, from the progressive employers who were beginning to take an interest in "welfare work."

The earliest corporate welfare policies, begun around the turn of the century, were efforts to reduce labor problems and increase workers' productivity by focusing attention on the non-work life of employees. As historian Sanford Jacoby has explained, such programs were "rooted in the belief that the worker himself—the intemperate, slothful worker or the ignorant immigrant, prey to radical nostrums—was directly responsible for labor unrest, social tension, and the decline of the work ethic." The answer, some employers felt, was to "recast the worker in a middle-class mold: uplifting him, bettering him, and making his family life more wholesome." A handful of companies experimented in these early years with endeavors as varied as company outings, citizenship programs, and thrift clubs in efforts to turn their employees into better and more pliant workers.[44]

The National Cash Register Company (NCR) of Dayton, Ohio, pioneered in welfare work. John Patterson, the president, described how he came to understand that improving the lives of his workers would ultimately serve the financial interests of his company: "We had made up a group of cash registers to sell in England. It was our first large export, and of course the adding mechanism had to be somewhat changed to calculate in pounds, shilling, and pence. We expected every one of them to be a splendid advertisement." Instead, "every register" came back "because of faulty workmanship"—a $50,000 mistake that resulted, he learned, from the dispirited attitude of his workers. Patterson realized that "we simply had to make that place decent to work in or go out of business." He claimed to have listened to his employees and responded to each of their demands—a cleaner workplace, lockers for all workers, shower baths twice a week on "the company's time," higher wages, and ultimately a new bright and airy factory.[45] NCR's welfare activities concentrated as well on areas not related to the immediate work environment, including medical services, a library, a theater, an employee clubhouse, and choral society.[46]

Patterson also decided, as early as 1902, to close the factory for a two-week "vacation" each summer. During the shutdown neither hourly nor piece rate workers earned wages.[47] Unwilling to pay its factory workers during the yearly vacation, NCR still took a keen interest in how employees spent their time off from work. In 1904 the company helped to finance a trip for two thousand NCR employees—about one third of the work force—to the World's Fair in St. Louis. NCR workers filled four special trains with the employees who attended the fair on "N.C.R. Day." The president of the company delivered an address that "gave praise to the factory" and "paid a high tribute to the officials of the company which had undertaken such a novel experiment in welfare work." The article concluded that the trip gave the NCR employees an "opportunity for a week's study in the world's greatest school."[48]

What prompted NCR's generosity is unclear. Employers, reformers, and civic leaders had, throughout the nineteenth century, expressed concern over how workers spent their leisure time. Many had attempted to limit and control excessive or unruly forms of working-class recreation and to teach workers to enjoy more refined sorts of amusements.[49] In this vein NCR might have brought its workers to St. Louis to instruct them in the productive uses of leisure time. Or the company might have wanted many employees on hand to serve as living examples of the successful, innovative welfare work of NCR.[50]

NCR's interest in its workers' vacations made it unusual for an early twentieth-century company. The vast majority of businessmen opposed the idea of vacations for production workers, as a 1910 article from the Sunday magazine section of the *New York Times* made clear. Entitled "How Long Should a Man's Vacation Be?," the article described President Taft's recent speech to a Bar Harbor audience in which he declared that two weeks was not a sufficient vacation. "The American people," Taft proclaimed, "have found out that there is such a thing as exhausting the capital of one's health and constitution, and that two or three months' vacation after the hard and nervous strain to which one is subjected during the Autumn and Spring are necessary in order to enable one to continue his work the next year with that energy and effectiveness which it ought to have." The *Times* decided to ask a group of important business and political men to respond to Taft's proposal of a two to three-month vacation.[51]

Not surprisingly, almost nobody agreed with Taft. Most acknowledged the importance of vacations, but held that a week or two was entirely enough time. Most also agreed that not *all* people either deserved or needed vacations. William Truesdale, president of the Lackawanna Railroad, believed that "vacations of some length" were a "very good thing" for "the man or woman who is under a mental strain during the greater part of the year." Frank Hedley, a vice president of the Interborough Rapid Transit Railroad, concurred: "I am a great believer in vacations and very liberal ones for men who work under a mental strain. . . . But it is different with the man whose work is merely physical effort." For such men, he believed, the "Saturday half holiday and Sunday brings much greater relief than they do to the man who works with his brain." Manual laborers, he explained, did not experience mental strain and thus had "a much better chance . . . to live longer and enjoy good health" than did those men who worked with their brains. Dr. A. Blauvelt of the U.S. Department of Health also recommended vacations of reasonable length (three months were far too much) for brain workers: "So far as the laboring man is concerned, he apparently does not need so much rest—vacation you may term it—as those men and women who use their brain and are under more or less strain during the greater part of the year." Joseph Davis, controller of the American Locomotive Works, concurred that vacations were unwarranted for laborers, for the reason that most of them worked "under an hourly wage agreement" and rarely had "a full year's work." As a result such men frequently had time "off," although at their own expense. Davis believed it would be "extremely difficult" to arrange vacations for such hourly workers. The general consensus held that only brain workers who were under "mental" or "nervous" strain—by definition members of the middle class—deserved or required a paid vacation. And even those few businessmen who might have been inclined to offer the same to manual laborers found the administrative problem of organizing such vacations overwhelming.[52]

While very few companies offered vacations to their factory laborers, during the 1910s a few tentative voices began to engage the question of vacations for such workers.[53] Some of those businessmen who had extended vacations to female workers in the early twentieth century may have realized that vacations, like other forms of corporate welfare, increased worker productivity and thus made good business sense. A 1913 article in *Munsey's* magazine describing the various reform and philanthropic efforts to facilitate working women's vacations alleged:

Behind the vacation savings movement is a far-reaching significance. It is one constructive step toward the elimination of waste. It helps to give the business woman an economic independence, and it tends to establish better relations between employer and employee. For the worker herself it offers an opportunity for relaxation, which gives her a better physical equipment, and this, in turn, makes her a more valuable part of the business machine. In short, she has the chance to recreate herself in the fullest sense of the word, for she learns how to live—how to get more rest and enjoyment, and how to work with a new zest and efficiency.[54]

NCR, which had been closing its plant for two weeks since 1902, had by 1914 recognized the link between vacations and efficient workers: "The human machine, unlike its mechanical namesake, calls for a period of recuperation from the demands made upon it if its efficiency is to be increased." NCR's in-house newspaper encouraged workers to "forget about the daily grind of shop life" so that "on your return to work you will be physically and mentally stronger, and your vacation will have been a profitable one."[55]

As long as labor remained cheap and abundant, companies like NCR remained in the minority. Most employers expressed little interest in implementing either vacations plans or other progressive management policies. World War I, however, altered the American labor market, changing some employers' views on the potential benefits of corporate welfare. As conscription and the end of European immigration reduced the numbers of available employees, companies found themselves facing a seller's labor market. Workers, secure in the knowledge that another job was always available, felt free to arrive late, miss work, and quit with impunity. At the same time labor organizing increased and a series of strikes hit industries throughout the country. Employers responded by giving serious attention to forms of personnel management that would rationalize and bureaucratize formerly arbitrary and haphazard employment policies.[56] Hoping to stabilize their work force and discourage unionization, a few progressive companies began to consider plans to improve the quality of their workers' lives. A small minority of forward-looking welfare capitalists argued that showers, clean washrooms, dining rooms, company picnics, and vacations would increase workers' loyalty, raise productivity, and decrease the appeal of labor unions. Happy workers, they suggested, were more productive workers.[57]

World War I helped to ignite interest in vacation policies not only because it tightened the labor market, but also because it encouraged an examination of the relationships between work, rest, and productivity. Industrial fatigue studies undertaken during the war confirmed that periodic rest could have "a distinctly favorable effect on production." Reducing workers' fatigue contributed to the general health not only of the employees but ultimately of the company as well.[58] Vacations, a small but growing number of businessmen began to assert, might be good for business. A 1916 article in *Current Opinion* explained one rationale behind these early vacation plans: "It is a pretty generally accepted fact that, if you want your motor car to run well, you must keep it oiled and in whack." Some employers, the author maintained, "have come to regard the human factor in the same way."[59] Such arguments, although justifying the initiation of vacation plans, dehumanized workers in the process.

During the 1920s, debate on this issue became more widespread. Social scientists and reformers began to examine the question, and a variety of national magazines ran articles discussing the pros and cons of vacations with pay for factory workers. In August of 1920 *The Survey* magazine ran an article that held that "vacation with pay for factory workers" was "slowly becoming an established practice." The author, a New York City industrial counselor named J. D. Hackett, seemed to be reading the data a bit optimistically. A survey of 624 businesses conducted over the preceding two years had found that while 85 percent gave their office workers paid vacations, only 18 percent furnished the same benefit to factory workers. Even this, the article claimed, represented a significant increase, and one that had occurred only very recently. The majority of businesses still denied industrial workers paid vacations, partly because these workers, unlike clerical employees, earned overtime (at a rate of time and a half) and "thus the employer considers there is no further obligation to be discharged."[60] Public interest in this issue was apparently growing, because the *Literary Digest* published an article the following month summarizing the findings of Hackett's article.[61]

Labor researchers increasingly turned their attention to whether or not workers were, or should be, earning paid vacations. In 1921 the *Monthly Labor Review*, a publication of the U.S. Bureau of Labor Statistics, described a survey conducted by the Chicago Council of the Industrial Relations Association of America. The Council sent a questionnaire to sixty-three firms asking about their companies' vacation policy. Only eleven offered industrial workers vacations with pay, five allowed for vacations without pay, and thirty-six permitted no vacations to people employed on hourly, daily, or piece rates. More interesting than the statistics, however, were the managers' comments on the issue. Those who responded to the questionnaire revealed the range of opinions on both sides of the debate.

Some of those in favor felt vacations were a carrot—a way to extract loyalty and good performance from a workforce. Vacations, the more progressive businessmen began to argue, could reduce labor turnover and improve morale. One manager believed that "a 10-day vacation with pay . . . is worth while if workmanship, attendance, and tardiness are considered in granting leave to employees." Another agreed that vacations should be "contingent upon length of service and regularity of attendance," while a third felt that those employees with an attendance rate of 95 percent or better deserved vacations. Those who endorsed vacations also spoke to the economic return on rested and happy employees. According to one manager, vacations more than made up for their expense "by additional energy put forth by the workers in an effort to show their appreciation." Another claimed that the men "returned refreshed and in better spirits" and that the vacation plan was actually an "economic advantage to the company."

Those opposed to vacations also offered a variety of explanations. Some feared the loss of productivity and profits: "[O]ur plant could not function properly with part of the men away." Others expressed different objections. One manager asserted that "our pieceworkers are all of foreign extraction and wish to work full time. Vacations do not appeal to them." Another maintained that vacations had "no good effect, since they add nothing to [industrial workers'] industry, efficiency, or loyalty, but might have directly the opposite effect." Still another opponent voiced the frequently heard argument that factory workers and office workers in fact received equal compensation because the former received in overtime what the latter garnered from paid vacations. Thus, to award industrial workers paid vacations would overcompensate them in comparison to white-collar workers. One manager simply claimed that employees who worked on hourly or piece rates were not "entitled to vacations."[62]

By the early 1920s not only labor researchers, social scientists, and reformers, but the popular press was beginning to promote vacations for industrial workers. A *Collier's* magazine article, "The Nose and the Grindstone" in July of 1921, made the case for vacations as a reward for hard work and good service. The author, Walter Camp, was a successful clock manufacturer in New Haven, Connecticut. His real claim to fame, however, was as the "innovator, defender, and propagandist" for American football. Camp wrote the rules of the game, coached Yale's team for more than twenty winning seasons, and defended football against those who complained of its brutality.[63] A long-time proponent of sport and play, Camp also saw the importance of vacations—not only for businessmen, but for industrial workers as well:

The man who soldiers through his day in mill or office, who watches the clock, who schemes eternally to do less work for the money he is paid—that man needs no holiday. He needs his walking papers. But the man who works as hard in peace time as he worked under the stimulation of war, who is as jealous of his good name now as he was when physical danger threatened him, deserves many and long hours for play. And he is getting them, more and more, as time goes on. Even the slave-driving type of employer knows the wisdom of this.[64]

Camp was right. Some employers were beginning, slowly, to come around. In 1913 NCR began giving those who had worked twenty years a week's pay during the annual shutdown. By the early 1920s the company had lowered the requirement to ten years.[65] John Patterson, the president of NCR, believed that vacations benefited not only the worker, but ultimately the company as well. Each summer he reminded his workers what he hoped the vacation would accomplish. Typical was his 1922 message in which he expressed the desire that "we can come back renewed in mind and body, qualified to beat the fine records we made during the year in the factory and the field."[66] In 1923 the Pennsylvania Consumer's League surveyed 163 companies and found that 49 of them, including Carter's Ink Company, Goodyear Tire and Rubber, Studebaker, and Lever Brothers, were granting paid vacations to factory workers. Studebaker was pleased with the policy, believing that "the plan of giving vacations has been a real factor in securing the loyalty and cooperation of our men."[67]

During the 1920s businessmen, reformers, and government researchers continued to engage the issue, and more companies began to struggle seriously with the practical problems that vacations for workers presented. Businessmen weighed, for example, whether to shut their plants down for a vacation period or to stagger the vacations of the workers.[68] Since the absence of even a few workers could seriously hamper production, some businesses opted for closing the factory. This was not an altogether altruistic decision. Shutdowns often occurred conveniently during the slack season. Companies could use this time to service, upgrade, or overhaul machinery. Shutdowns also eliminated the need to maintain complicated vacation schedules among workers.[69] Even those employers who did pay their workers during the closing usually paid only those who met certain criteria of service or production. Large numbers of workers often suffered temporary layoffs rather than enjoying vacations.[70]

The vacation plans initiated during the 1920s varied enormously. Many businesses made one year of continuous work the requirement for a week's paid vacation, but some required as long as ten years' service.[71] Others used a graded method, awarding more vacation time to long-term employees.[72] Some firms offered more liberal vacation policies for their female than male employees, usually requiring that women serve fewer years than men before becoming eligible for vacations.[73]

What united many of these vacation policies was the motivation behind them. Those businesses that did implement vacation plans did so primarily in the hopes that vacations for workers would ultimately redound to the benefit of the company. Little wonder that a variety of publications—from *The Outlook* to the *New York Times*—began to portray employers who instituted vacations plans as not just "kindhearted," but rather as shrewd businessmen. People on vacation were not simply relaxing but were "giving new life to industry, storing up energy that [would take them] through the coming winter, no matter how hard it [might] be."[74]

Such a result could only occur, however, if industrial employees used their vacations wisely. Many who endorsed vacations for workers worried about what these employees would do with their vacation time. The contest over control of working-class leisure had been raging since early in the nineteenth century. Antebellum temperance reformers and Sabbatarians, for example, had been motivated not only by religious zeal but also by an effort to keep working-class people sober and industrious during their hours off from work. Over the course of the late nineteenth and early twentieth centuries, reformers, businessmen, and politicians used a variety of techniques to control the way that workers spent their leisure, with varying degrees of success. Some hoped to contain working-class leisure by enforcing blue laws, regulating saloons, and discouraging "excessive" celebrations of various holidays. Others took a more positive approach, trying to make parks and playgrounds accessible to the working class. Parks and playgrounds would serve not only as places of enjoyment for working-class people, but also as locations where middle-class reformers could dictate appropriate forms of working-class recreation. Reformers especially hoped that supervised city playgrounds would help to Americanize and instruct immigrant and working-class children. Other types of organized leisure—boys clubs, company sponsored sports teams—spoke to the same impulse as did playground reform. Whether through regulations controlling working-class space and institutions or through movements aimed at overseeing working-class play, middle-class reformers and business people remained intensely interested in how workers spent their leisure time.[75]

Perhaps more than other forms of amusement, vacations—especially vacations with pay—represented a serious threat not only to middle-class efforts at channeling working-class leisure, but to the ultimate goal of creating an efficient and productive workforce. It seems no surprise, for example, that the earliest efforts to extend vacations to the working class simultaneously attempted to control the vacation environment. Mothers, children, and working women were offered supervised vacation camps and cottages—places where either reformers or representatives of business could oversee the activities and entertainments. While gender conventions of the early twentieth century perhaps made it easier to control women's than men's leisure, many employers nevertheless attempted to channel and direct their male workers' vacation time as well.

The minority of businessmen who were paying for vacation time wanted their workers returning to the job rested and refreshed, not drained and fatigued. To this end, some companies specifically included in their policies provisions that prohibited employees from taking other jobs during the vacation period. Workers who were laid off while the plant closed during the summer had limited resources to devote to self-indulgence. But extended time away from work—with money in their pockets or pocket-books—raised the possibility of a week of dissipation, and a returning work force that was less rather than more productive. J. D. Hackett, an industrial counselor and an advocate of vacations for workers, warned in 1920 that "not all employees spend their vacations as advantageously as possible. The manual worker, unaccustomed to the joy of leisure with pay, just fritters the time away, somewhat unhappy out of his accustomed environment, or uses the time merely to work elsewhere in order to obtain a little extra money." Hackett explained that for vacation policies to succeed, employers needed to take on "yet another obligation, that of educating the worker as to how his leisure time can best be spent." Those considered smart employers were supplying their workers with information "as to what to do, where to go and how much to spend when the vacation time arrives."[76]

Consequently those workers who did have the luxury of paid vacations often heard much advice and exhortation about how they should spend their time. As early as 1915, the in-house newspaper of the National Cash Register Company, *NCR News*, counseled the employees: "Make your vaca-tion a restful one. Overdoing pleasure is like overdoing work. Both lead to utter weariness of mind as well as body. And come back with a smile on your face."[77] Some companies, such as AT&T, offered employees vacation assistance or advice, while others cooperated willingly with reformers to direct workers toward appropriate forms of vacationing.[78] The Playground and Recreation Association of America established a Vacation Service Bureau in New York City in the 1920s to supply "reliable information con-cerning good vacation places to corporations and other business organiza-tions for the use of their employees, with especial emphasis on the need of the average employee with limited funds." Thousands of vacationers, these reformers worried, were "at a loss" when it came to finding a vacation place and were often duped by "misleading" advertisements. The results were "disappointment and disillusionment . . . with all the attendant evils of a badly spent vacation."[79]

Both businessmen and reformers apparently shared a general consensus that vacations spent outdoors—preferably camping—were the most benefi-cial. In 1921 the president of NCR offered "A Vacation Message" informing his employees, "do as you please." The vacation should be "two weeks in which there will be no one to tell you what to do." He then proceeded to tell them what to do: "It is not necessary for you to go a distance on an expensive trip. Go anywhere out in the open. Nowhere in the world is there more beautiful, undulating country than around Dayton."[80] Two years later the company newspaper offered similar advice: "Make yourself 100% efficient by getting out into the open and living the natural life for the next two weeks."[81] When the Upton Manufacturing company began giving "ten days' rest (with pay) every year" to its workers in 1919, it encouraged those workers to spend their vacation camping by sending "to every vacationist's home a camp cooking outfit."[82]

Some employers did more than exhort their workers to find rest and renewal in the out-of-doors. They established camps of their own at which workers could vacation, either cheaply or for free. In 1927 the U.S. Bureau of Labor Statistics described, although it did not name, a number of companies that maintained such vacation facilities. Some companies continued to reserve vacation camps solely for female employees, which, like the nineteenth-century women's vacation houses and camps, often came equipped with a "house mother who has general supervision of the girls." But other companies built facilities that accommodated both men and women. A meat packing company, for example, maintained a summer camp on a three hundred acre tract of land. The company invited female plant employees with one year's service to spend "a week's vacation at the camp at the company's expense." Other employees who spent their vacation there were charged $10. The camp offered boating, swimming, and tennis. The company also employed "a social worker . . . to supervise the recreation."[83] Company-sponsored campgrounds provided exactly the environment that businessmen believed would produce a rested, efficient, more loyal labor force.

Despite considerable public debate about whether and what sorts of vacations industrial workers should have, the numbers of industrial workers enjoying the benefits of paid vacations—while larger than ever before—remained small throughout the 1920s. In 1927 Charles Mills published a comprehensive study comparing vacation policies in the United States and Europe. His data revealed that although some of America's major corporations were beginning to offer their industrial employees paid vacations, only about 5 percent of the total number of wage earners in the United States worked in plants that provided vacation plans.[84] Historian Donna Allen estimated that by 1930 the number of businesses with permanent vacation plans had increased so that as many as 10 percent of wage earners had earned the privilege of a paid vacation. By comparison, four-fifths of salaried employees—meaning white-collar, middle-class workers—were covered by vacation plans.[85]

The small number of companies with vacation plans for wage earners reflected the still prevalent reluctance on the part of most businesses to rationalize their personnel policies and embrace corporate welfare. The flurry of welfare activities precipitated by the tight labor markets of World War I dwindled in the changed economic circumstances of the 1920s. Although the twenties have rightfully been perceived as a decade of general prosperity and low unemployment, sectors of the population—particularly the manufacturing labor force—experienced less favorable conditions. Not only was manufacturing employment "stagnant" during the 1920s, but industrial unemployment rates climbed in the middle years of the decade. The seller's labor market of World War I had turned into a buyer's market. Labor mobility declined, as did unionization rates and strike activity. As a result, employers, more secure in their ability to attract and retain workers, became less willing to implement liberal employment or corporate welfare policies.[86]

Organized labor's lack of interest in the issue of vacations contributed, as well, to the small number of wage earners with access to paid vacation. Other than typographers and firefighters, few American unions initiated national efforts for vacation provisions, and consequently only scattered locals within each industry, representing a minority of organized workers, wrote contracts that included paid vacations. By contrast, trade unions in some European countries had negotiated industry-wide contracts that brought paid vacations to all the wage earners within the industry.[87]

Union interest in leisure for American workers manifested itself not in a struggle for paid vacations but in a movement for shorter hours. Labor had been campaigning for shorter work hours since the nineteenth century and had presented a varied and changing list of arguments. Increased leisure would, labor leaders asserted, improve workers' health and safety, give wage earners time to pursue worthwhile educational or family activities, and ultimately increase employees' efficiency and productivity on the job. Unions also pointed to the importance of shorter hours as an answer to the problem of unemployment. By the last half of the 1920s labor was arguing, as well, that workers simply deserved shorter hours as their "just reward for increased productivity."[88]

Putting its primary effort on behalf of leisure for workers into its crusade for shorter hours, unions remained, with a few exceptions, mostly silent on the question of vacations. In 1927 Daniel J. Tobin, president of the Teamsters, wrote an article for the *American Federationist* about vacations for wage workers. About one fourth of the members of the Teamsters Union enjoyed paid vacations, still too few for Tobin: "[W]e realize that it is not yet time to boast . . . , but at least a sound demonstration of the possibilities has been made and we will not rest until all of our members are getting vacations with pay." He was, as well, gratified that "many employers have admitted making the astounding discovery that the efficiency and morale of their workers has been vastly improved by vacations." Tobin pledged to win vacations for workers through union efforts rather than company welfare policies.[89] William Green, president of the American Federation of Labor, also weighed in, claiming that "vacation benefits the worker physically and mentally and certainly makes for better industrial relations."[90]

Such statements notwithstanding, unions failed to make vacations a major part of their bargaining plan. In part, this stemmed from the fact that organized labor was strongest in industries that suffered from seasonal or cyclical unemployment. The mining, leather, clothing, and textile industries and the building trades accounted for nearly half of union membership. In these industries, as Charles Mills explained, "neither employers nor workers take an interest in additional time off; their concern is rather with how to keep work going for more weeks during the year."[91]

Although the combination of employer resistance and union indifference left the vast majority of American workers without paid vacations, the first three decades of the century did see some progress. Most importantly, a minority of progressive businessmen became convinced that vacations for wage earners could prove financially beneficial for their companies. Articulating a rationale for mass vacations, these employers argued that paid vacations helped to reduce labor turnover, increase efficiency, boost morale, and promote employee loyalty. Many of these forward-looking employers liberalized their employment policies and instituted vacation plans.

As a result, the number of workers with paid vacations, while still small, increased enough to make working-class men and women a decided presence among the vacationing public. Between 1910 and 1930 tens of thousands of industrial workers found themselves able to take part in what had once been an elite and middle-class convention. A 1930 article in *Business Week* announced, for example, that "just 30 of the 30,000 workers in Western Electric Hawthorne plant—second largest American industrial unit—are not getting vacations with pay this year." And the same year the *New York Times* reported that 100,000 workers at Ford's Detroit plant would "receive a vacation with pay in the last two weeks of July."[92] What they did on those vacations is, in part, the subject of the next chapter.

$\mathcal{\infty}$ 8 $\mathcal{\infty}$

Crossing Class and Racial Boundaries

————— •◆• —————

VACATIONING in the EARLY TWENTIETH CENTURY

In August of 1921 Hiram Johnson, U.S. Senator from California, and his wife decided to escape the heat of Washington, D.C., and motor north for a vacation. Quite taken with Atlantic City, they remained for their entire vacation, staying at the Ritz, where they enjoyed "one of the handsomest apartments at a greatly reduced rate (but still a sufficient sum for a U.S. Senator's income)" and found "everything possible for our convenience and comfort." This was, Johnson explained, "the enjoyable part of Atlantic City."

But two miles down the boardwalk was the "other part"—a "vastly different" sort of place. There huge crowds overran boardwalk and beach. But it was not so much the number of vacationers that disquieted the senator, it was who those vacationers were. "On Labor Day," he wrote, "it was estimated that 350,000 people were in Atlantic City. If this estimate was correct, I am perfectly certain that 249,000 of them were the chosen people. Everywhere, and in everything, the Israelite predominate." He even found Jews among the guests at the Ritz, but explained that "they are the sort that we know, the rich, assertive, self-sufficient." Farther down the boardwalk, he discovered hordes of poor, immigrant Jews—"the short, swarthy men, the squatty, dumpy women, and the innumerable daughters, at an early age bursting into overblown maturity." In some parts of Atlantic City, Senator Johnson "felt a stranger almost in a strange land."[1]

By the 1920s a variety of people were becoming vacationers. Many who once could manage only a one-day excursion to an amusement park, beach, or lake were participating in an experience that a few decades earlier had been restricted primarily to the middle class. During the first three decades of the twentieth century middle-class African Americans and both native-born and immigrant members of the working class joined the growing numbers of white middle-class vacationers.[2] Some chose places like Atlantic City, others opted for very different sorts of ventures.

This chapter will examine the experiences that the crowds of American vacationers created for themselves during the early decades of the twentieth century. I hope to locate those places where the vacation experiences of white middle-class people, working-class people, and African Americans converged and where they parted. Did people of different races and classes vacation together or separately and when, if at all, did their vacation experiences mingle or merge?

The question goes beyond an exploration of different patterns of vacationing. It asks, as well, about the cultural impact of a broadly based vacationing public. In the nineteenth century, as we saw, vacationing came to be one of the ways that the middle class identified itself. Did access to vacations—something once restricted to the middle class—help to confer status and privilege on all vacationers? Ultimately, did vacationing serve as a unifying force in early twentieth-century America, or did it reinforce distinctions of class and race? Finally, I hope to suggest the impact of this broadened vacationing public on cultural attitudes towards vacations. Specifically, what happened to the long-standing suspicions of and prescriptions about vacationing as those who were not members of the white, native-born middle class increasingly claimed the privilege as their own?

———— •◆• ————

The first third of the twentieth century witnessed continual growth in the size and diversity of the vacationing public.[3] The increasing ease of travel, especially the creation of an automobile culture, made vacationing more accessible to both the middle and working class, rendering vacations cheaper, easier, and often more enjoyable.[4] The vacation industry became more organized as it promoted, advertised, and fostered its product. American Express introduced its travelers check in 1891 and by 1906 both the *New York Times* and the *New York Herald* had instituted Sunday travel sections.[5] In 1912 New York City held its second annual travel and vacation exhibition where railroads, resorts, chambers of commerce, hotels, and hotel associations all exhibited their "wares" at booths designed to entice potential clients.[6]

The expansion of the vacationing public no doubt was connected, as well, to broader changes in American culture during the early twentieth century. Historians John Higham, T. J. Jackson Lears, John Kasson, and others have chronicled and analyzed a "reorientation of American culture" that occurred around the turn of the century. Americans—particularly members of the middle class—displayed an interest in vigorous physical activity, a longing for "authentic" experience, and a tendency to reject stuffy and confining Victorian norms. Moreover, middle-class men and women who, in the nineteenth century, had been busy producing goods became, in the early twentieth century, increasingly preoccupied with consuming them. These changes fostered an interest in vacationing, even as the growing numbers of vacationers helped to move American culture in the direction that Higham, Lears, Kasson, and others have described.[7]

But the growth of vacationing in the early twentieth century was not solely due to expanding numbers of white middle-class vacationers. What differentiated vacationing in the twentieth century was the participation of working-class men and women, including immigrants and their children, as well as an increasing number of middle-class African Americans.

Working-class men and women fashioned a range of vacation experiences in the early twentieth century. Given that many of the early blue-collar vacationers still earned no paychecks for their weeks off, vacations that required minimal outlay or that saved money—visiting relatives, fishing, and camping—were popular choices. The National Cash Register Company's monthly newspaper, the *NCR News*, frequently reported that an employee had "paid a visit to his old home town," had "spent two weeks in the western part of the state fishing and hunting," had been "with a party of friends . . . camping at Bear Creek," or had gone "to his mother for pies, cakes, etc."[8] Typical was the fellow who hoped to organize a camping party during the vacation: "We want to get a place near town on the Stillwater, where we can take a run down to the Island Park in our canoe, and where we will be close enough to the Y.M.C.A. Athletic Park to play a couple of sets of tennis when we so desire."[9]

Fishing no doubt provided these vacationers with entertainment and sport. But it may have represented more than mere recreation. Fishing probably also served as one way of feeding the family during the time the plant closed "for vacation," or at least offered the possibility of saving on grocery expenses so that limited funds might be put to the cost of an inexpensive, nearby camping vacation.

Visiting relatives, camping, and fishing in nearby waters were the prevalent but not the only sorts of vacationing in which working-class people indulged. Beginning in the late 1910s workers with cars used them to expand their vacationing horizons. The numbers of working-class people who owned automobiles grew dramatically during the 1920s. Not only reduced automobile prices and the availability of credit, but a growing market in used cars made it possible even for members of the working class to purchase cars.[10]

While many workers had few choices but to spend their vacations fishing and camping, those with cars could pursue these activities in a wider geographic area. Toolmaker Charles Jackson, for example, outfitted his "flivver" with "new parts all around" and then drove it to Spring Lake in Michigan.[11] Indeed, the "flivver" became, for some workers, as important a part of their vacation gear as the reel and the tent, frequently, in fact, serving as replacement for the latter.

An automobile expanded not only the geographic range but the variety of these workers' vacations. Cars, for example, made touring a distinct possibility. John Brower "made an auto trip, stopping in Toledo, Detroit, Kalamazoo, Michigan City, Battle Creek, Chicago and back by way of Indianapolis." Leo Geers and his family "covered over 1,000 miles by auto" in their trip around Ohio and reported "a dandy time."[12] No doubt these people still camped along the way, but the focus of such a vacation was the touring and driving as well as the camping.[13]

For some working-class men and women, vacations became sightseeing adventures. In 1920 two employees from NCR's cutter department "went over the road in a Ford, visiting New York City, Philadelphia, Harrisburg, and other eastern cities." Both reported "a very enjoyable trip."[14] In the *NCR News*, R. H. Kuhlman wrote about what he called "An Ideal Vacation"—a motor trip to Washington, D.C. "Steady driving" allowed him to make the nation's capital in about three and a half days, and he found the drive through the mountains "beautiful." He claimed that the trip would be "even more interesting" and doubtless cheaper "if you take a camping outfit and camp along the way." He recommended visiting the usual tourist sights—the Capitol, the Congressional Library, the Pan American Building, the Bureau of Printing, the Smithsonian, the Zoo, the White House, Mt. Vernon—and suggested, as well, a side trip to Baltimore and the Naval Academy in Annapolis. He concluded, "[T]his is about the best two weeks' trip that I know of."[15] Enough NCR workers were apparently taking autotrips by the mid-1920s that *NCR News* began offering advice on safe motoring vacations.[16]

Growing numbers of working-class vacationers began to frequent other sorts of vacation places. Summer communities that offered more than open spaces for camping but considerably less than luxurious resort accommodations took shape during the 1910s and 1920s. A group of employees from

Campers having breakfast, Fayette Lake (?), Idaho, 1918–1920. Cars became an important part of the vacation equipment for campers in the early twentieth century. Working-class people found that cars increased their vacation possibilities. (Library of Congress, Otto M. Jones Collection, J731-232b.)

NCR's toolmaking and model making departments, for example, took their families to Island Park in Hamilton, Indiana, where they found "good accommodation and good eating at the hotel, good fishing, boating, and bathing." Moreover, the price was "within reach of any N.C.R. employee."[17] Primitive cottages situated around various lakes also attracted NCR employees. Joe Greers favored Ackerson Lake, near Jackson, Michigan, where he found "plenty of fish" and where cottages could be "secured for ten to fifteen dollars per week." Greers made sure to tell readers, however, that "this little spot is not a summer resort, no jazz or merry-go-rounds, just one of those beautiful spots that nature blessed Michigan with: a place to get a good work-out at something different than we have an opportunity to do all the year round." Moreover, since cottages often could accommodate from four to eight people and came equipped "with all the necessary furnishings except linens," those willing to share cottages could manage an inexpensive vacation.[18]

Areas in other parts of the country sprouted similar sorts of working-class vacation communities. Libby's Oceanside Camp on the coast of Maine offered camping sites to working-class autotourists while Lake Winnipesaukee in New Hampshire advertised "little rough shacks" at affordable prices. Salisbury Beach, located not far from the Massachusetts mill cities of Lowell and Lawrence, catered to a predominantly working-class clientele and provided vacationers with "fishing-shacks-turned-cottages" as well as a merry-go-round, bumper car rides, and a dance hall.[19] "Tent City" on Coronoda Beach, California, housed rows of vacationing campers who could either rent tents for $3 to $5 a week, or "bring their own tents and camp free."[20]

Most working-class vacationers fashioned inexpensive vacations. Few, for example, could afford the cost of a stay at Mohonk or Newport or Mackinac Island. The numerous camping ventures—both informal camping and fishing expeditions or trips to more formal campgrounds at lakes or seashore—in which large numbers of working-class vacationers indulged kept them out of the haunts of the more comfortable middle class. In fact, working-class campgrounds that encroached too closely on elite or middle-class vacation communities sometimes brought complaints from patrons. On the coast of Maine, for example, the presence of Libby's Oceanside Camp disturbed the residents of the genteel resort community at nearby York Harbor, who took the campground owner to court to keep him from expanding his facility.[21] Autocamping may have initially brought people of different classes together at various campsites. But by the 1920s the free municipal campgrounds where working-class vacationers in their "flivvers" might have rubbed up against middle-class autotrippers were beginning to charge fees in the hopes of excluding those who could not afford the price.[22]

Some sorts of vacationing did bring middle and working-class people together in the same place. The campgrounds of the national parks, for example, attracted both working and middle-class vacationers. Some of the latter no doubt chose to camp, but others had no alternative since the hotels at the national parks could accommodate only a small percentage of the visitors. Of the more than 51,000 tourists to Yellowstone in 1922 only 1,500 slept in hotels.[23] The remaining 49,500 certainly included both working and middle-class vacationers.

Evidence suggests that campers in the national park, regardless of their actual social standing, sometimes believed themselves the object of invidious class distinctions. William Gossel maintained that campers got decidedly short shrift compared to the tourists who could afford to patronize the hotels. In his letter to President Taft, Gossel complained that campers in Yellowstone were forced to "turn aside" to make way for the coaches that

Line-up teams in front of hotel, Yellowstone National Park, Wyoming, 17 March 1913. Most vacationers at Yellowstone camped in the park, but some enjoyed the benefits of the hotels. (Library of Congress, U.S. Geographic File, LC-USZ62-40978.)

brought people to the hotels and had to enter the park through the "unsightly" side road rather than through the "beautiful Roosevelt Arch" through which the hotel coaches passed. Moreover, the campgrounds were "located at a great distance from the points of interest and often in low, damp localities" while the hotels were "situated one-eighth of a mile from the points of interest."[24] Rather than conferring middle-class status on working-class vacationers, camping in the national parks may have diminished some middle-class vacationers' sense of their own social position.

During the early twentieth century a few large resorts offered sites where vacationers might encounter not only people of a different class but of a different race. Atlantic City was a good example. Atlantic City had, since the 1890s, attracted a diverse clientele: working-class visitors (primarily from Philadelphia) on one-day excursions, along with middle-class and elite vacationers who enjoyed the pleasures of a longer stay at one of the numerous hotels.[25] By the 1920s Atlantic City was offering overnight accommodations even to people of limited means. While hotels continued to welcome both the rich and the middle class, cheaper boarding houses catered to socially and ethnically diverse clienteles. One woman, whose husband worked for the Reading Railroad, explained to an interviewer from the Department of Labor that "when she has had some money ready it has all gone for trips to Atlantic City." She and her family spent a week there every summer where they "take rooms and she does the cooking and the stores are not near, so she doesn't find much rest."[26] Occasionally even an NCR employee mentioned a summer visit to Atlantic City. One, for example, reported that he had found there a "good reasonable-priced hotel . . . that is one block from the boardwalk and one block from the Pennsylvania Depot."[27]

Resorts like Atlantic City included not only white working-class and immigrant patrons, but African American vacationers as well. African Americans had been a presence at many resorts throughout the nineteenth century, but primarily as workers. Black men, for example, worked as waiters at elite hotels in places like Saratoga, Atlantic City, and Mackinac Island. As early as the 1890s African Americans were also beginning to open boarding houses and hotels for black vacationers at some well-known resorts.[28] By the turn of the century some of these hotels were substantial establishments that catered to a middle-class black clientele. The Hotel Dale in Atlantic City, for example, accommodated as many as 150 guests, boasted the most up-to-date conveniences and amenities, and attracted vacationers from as far away as Texas.[29]

Black vacationers at these resorts shared many of the experiences of middle-class white vacationers. They swam in the surf, strolled on the beach and boardwalk, attended "hops" and dances, enjoyed afternoon teas and euchre parties, played tennis and croquet.[30] But their vacation experiences could also be circumscribed by restrictions of race. A reporter for the *Baltimore Afro-American* interviewed many of the proprietors along the boardwalk at Atlantic City and learned, for example, "that they do not want our people to enter their places."[31] While such policies focused partly on black hotel and restaurant employees who tried during their free time to enjoy the benefits of the summer resort at which they worked, some animosity was clearly directed at African-American vacationers. In August of 1904, the *New York Times* reported an incident involving Dr. William Crum, the "negro Collector of Customs at Charleston, South Carolina." Crum and his wife were vacationing at Asbury Park, where one day Crum tried "to hire a wheel chair for his wife for a ride on the boardwalk. Proprietor J. L. Schneider refused to order any of his white lads to push the chair, but said that Dr. Crum might have it if he would wheel his wife himself. Dr. Crum refused in a gentlemanly manner and left."[32] When the Reverend Matthew Anderson, the African-American president of the Berean School in Philadelphia, bought

a cottage in Atlantic City, many of Philadelphia's aristocratic families—
amongst them the Biddle family—became "vexed." The cottage was "across
from the Biddles' home." The *Indianapolis Freeman* reported: "Formerly a
Mrs. Burton owned the Anderson cottage. She was ignored by the blue
blood colony, and this, they think, is her revenge. William Wanamaker and
other rich Philadelphians who finance the Berean School are to be asked to
induce the Rev. Mr. Anderson to take his family to some other summer
resort."[33]

Despite such problems, blacks continued to frequent these resorts, building their own hotels, boarding houses, and bathing establishments. Niagara
Falls advertised the Hotel Vancouver where blacks could enjoy "first class"
appointments at the rate of $2 a day.[34] African Americans vacationed in
Newport, Rhode Island, where black-run boarding houses accommodated
them.[35] And in 1911 another Hotel Dale opened, this one at Cape May,
with claims to be "the finest and most complete hostelry in the United
States for the accommodation of our race." The new hotel advertised a
magnificent view "of the harbor and the sea glistening like gems in the sunlight," electric lights throughout, tennis courts and croquet, private bath
houses, suites with baths and long-distance telephone connections, an ele-
gantly furnished dining room, and a "full Abyssinian Orchestra to render
afternoon and evening concerts . . . daily during the entire season."[36]

Although various groups participated in many identical forms of summer
recreation, this did not spell the beginning of socially or racially integrated
vacationing. Rich and poor shared ocean and sand, but they usually
repaired to different cottages, hotels, and boarding houses. While some
immigrants and African Americans opted for a week at Atlantic City or
Cape May or Niagara Falls, others preferred to build and frequent their
own, separate vacation communities. The endemic racism of early twentieth-century America motivated African Americans to create vacation places
where they could enjoy their leisure without threat of racial confrontation.
Rather than visiting a black hotel at a crowded and predominantly white
resort, many chose black resorts or boarding houses that were separated or
distant from white resort areas. By 1908 a resort for African Americans was
growing up at West Baden, Indiana. That year the Jersey European Hotel, a
new facility "for colored people," opened its doors and over the next
decade welcomed black vacationers from places like Memphis, Louisville,
St. Louis, Chicago, Indianapolis, and Des Moines.[37] In 1923 reputed millionaire Thomas W. Wright was spending $70,000 to build a "new Negro
resort" at Shell Island Beach near Wilmington, North Carolina. The *New
Pittsburgh Courier* reported that "all businesses and every concession are to
be handled by members of the race."[38] Three years later another group of
businessmen were working on a resort at Silver Spring Lake in Warren

Vacationers at Highland Beach, c. 1920–1930s. (Highland Beach Historical Collection, Highland Beach, Maryland.)

County, New Jersey, about sixty miles from New York City. They planned a hotel, tavern, casino, tennis courts, swimming pools, "sunken gardens and lovers lanes."[39]

Some of these places succeeded better than others. The resort at West Baden was, by 1916, apparently suffering. A correspondent for the *Indianapolis Freeman* reported that "'We are not doing so well.' There are few at the hotels and very little doing in the way of amusement."[40] Still the early twentieth century witnessed the beginnings of what would become some enduring black resort communities. Oak Bluffs on Martha's Vineyard, Highland Beach on the Chesapeake Bay, Sag Harbor on Long Island, American Beach in Florida, and Idlewild in Michigan all began in these decades and survived to serve generations of vacationing African Americans.[41]

Highland Beach near Annapolis on the Chesapeake Bay attracted its first black families in the 1890s. Frederick Douglass's son, Charles, built a summer cottage there in 1894 as a place for his family to enjoy the summer free from fear of discrimination. Over the next decades friends and relatives of the Douglasses began to buy real estate and build summer homes. Mary Church Terrell and her husband bought a lot in 1896 and built themselves a summer house in 1915. As early as 1902 Charles T. Bowen opened a nine-bedroom cottage that could be used for "taking in guests." The Bowen cottage offered tennis courts and the pleasures of the beach and the bay to a number of illustrious members of the black intelligentsia.[42]

A few African American families—mostly from Boston—bought houses on Martha's Vineyard at the turn of the twentieth century. During the next decades they were joined by other friends who built small cottages or vacationed at one of two deluxe boarding houses in the community of Oak Bluffs. One of the boarding house keepers, Sadie Shearer, had begun operating a laundry service for white summer residents on the Vineyard in the early 1900s. Within a few years she recognized the potential for a black guest house and converted her laundry into Shearer Cottage—adding rooms and a tennis court. By the 1920s Shearer Cottage attracted prominent African Americans from Boston, Philadelphia, and New York.[43]

Idlewild in northern Michigan began in 1915 when the Idlewild Resort Company of Chicago bought twenty-seven hundred acres of land, including Idlewild Lake. Probably the brain child of an enterprising black Chicago real-estate agent, the Idlewild Resort Company published promotional pamphlets and brought prospective buyers—white-collar and professional African Americans, often leaders within their communities—from midwestern cities. Many apparently bought lots and put up small summer cottages, some only "a bit more substantial than tents," where they could enjoy a week or two of summer vacation.[44]

Like blacks, Jews also faced exclusion from many vacation places and often chose to build their own resorts. The history of anti-Semitic resort policies may have begun as early as 1877. That summer Joseph Seligman, the well-known and wealthy Jewish banker, arrived at the Grand Union Hotel in Saratoga to learn that the hotel no longer admitted Jews. Seligman had visited the Grand Union for numerous seasons but the new manager of the hotel, Judge Henry Hilton, had instituted a policy of excluding

Jewish patrons. Despite a blistering letter from Seligman to Hilton that appeared in the newspaper, Hilton held to his policy, saying "notwithstanding Moses and all his descendants" he could still do as he wished with private property.

The Seligman–Hilton affair became a cause célèbre. Seligman's friends boycotted the A.T. Stewart store (which Hilton also managed); Henry Ward Beecher sermonized on behalf of Seligman; Bret Harte wrote a poem about the incident. But Seligman's exclusion from the Grand Union helped to establish a precedent for other hotels.[45] Adirondack resorts began advertising that "Hebrews need not apply," and Melville Dewey made the Lake Placid Club off-limits to Jews. During the 1880s some summer resort owners addressed their advertisement: "To Gentiles."[46]

Whether as a result of the Seligman-Hilton affair or not, by the early twentieth century numerous resorts had instituted anti-Semitic policies. While some wealthy Jews apparently vacationed at places like the Ritz in Atlantic City, many resorts refused to receive them. Mohonk Mountain House, for example, actively discouraged inquiries from potential Jewish guests or from guests with suspicious sounding names. Hotel managers cooperated in informing each other about Jewish patrons who might attempt to crash their resorts. H.C. Philips, secretary to the owner of Mohonk, for example, wrote to the manager of the Chalfonte Hotel in Atlantic City in February of 1916 inquiring about a Mr. H.B. Houseman. Houseman had apparently written from the Chalfonte to inquire about rooms at Mohonk. Philips explained: "From the nature of the application we are just a little bit curious to know how cordially we ought to reply, although from the fact that the gentleman writes from your good house, we are very much inclined to assume that everything is all right." The manager at Mohonk received the assurance he needed, hearing from his counterpart at the Chalfonte that Mr. and Mrs. Houseman "are both active members of the Christian Science Church. We think you would find them desirable guests."[47] Each year an update on the "Hebrew problem" appeared in the house manager's report at Mohonk, usually under the category of "Undesirable Guests." Not all undesirables were Jews. During the war "Germans or pro-German class" also qualified. Typical was the 1917 report:

Hebrews were few. Wm. W. Cohen, a high-class Hebrew, rather insisted on coming, even after learning that he would probably be unwelcome. It took only three days for him to realize his mistake. George Gravenhorst, on whom we took a chance, may be a Hebrew and has a pronounced accent. He and his wife remained a couple of weeks, and his actions were entirely acceptable. A few Jews crept in on over-night parties, but on the whole the Hebrew question gave no trouble.[48]

Jews, particularly those with anglicized names, found it easier than African Americans to evade discriminatory rules and visit gentile resorts. While some no doubt did, the majority probably preferred to vacation at a place where they would feel welcomed.

As a result, Jews—like blacks—established their own resorts, often in the Catskill Mountains of New York where they could attract New York City's large Jewish population. Fleischmann's, one of the earliest, was catering to well-to-do Jews by the 1890s.[49] Novelist Abraham Cahan offered a fictional picture of a place like Fleischmann's in *The Rise of David Levinksy*. Published in 1917, Cahan's novel described the Rigi Kulm House—"the largest and most expensive hostelry in the neighborhood." Populated by families of "cloak-manufacturers, shirt-manufacturers, ladies-waist-manufacturers, cigar-manufacturers, clothiers, furriers, jewelers, leather-goods men, real-estate men, physicians, dentists and lawyers," the Rigi Kulm attracted an affluent crowd—"ablaze with diamonds, painted cheeks, and bright-colored silks." The hotel also received some younger, less wealthy people—"salesmen, stenographers, bookkeepers, librarians"—on a two-week holiday.[50]

By the early decades of the twentieth century working-class Jews were also finding vacation places for themselves, primarily at kosher boarding houses in the Catskills. Motivated primarily by the hope that country air and wholesome dairy products would protect them and their children from the "white plague" of tuberculosis, poor working-class Jews found their way to summer boarding houses in the southern Catskills. These places were hardly elaborate resorts. Called *kochalein* (meaning, in Yiddish, cook alone), they were usually dingy farmhouses for which families paid from $50 to $100 a season for a room and kitchen privileges. Writing for *The Survey* magazine in 1923, N. B. Fagin described a typical *kochalein*: "Fifteen women used one kitchen with one small stove. Forty children lived under one roof, occupying, with their mothers, but fifteen dingy pigeonhole rooms, playing and sunning themselves on one narrow porch. There was incessant noise." Those who came seeking a respite were often sorely disappointed.[51]

Not only were these boarding houses crowded and noisy, some presented significant health threats. As many as 250,000 summer visitors had brought some serious sanitary problems to Ulster and Sullivan counties in New York. The severe overcrowding—sometimes as many as twenty-five to one hundred people crammed into houses built for five or six—made for a not very salubrious environment. Too many boarding house keepers failed to make any effort to upgrade water and sewer systems. By the late 1910s the New York State Department of Health, with the help of the Jewish Agricultural Society, began "a vigorous campaign to clean up 'the mountains.'" They focused on clean water, disposal of human waste, and keeping flies from contaminating food.[52]

Mitchell's House, New York, c. 1926. Kosher boarding houses in the Catskills attracted Jewish patrons who hoped to escape the heat of New York City. The large numbers of people living in close quarters often made for a less-than-restful vacation. (Thanks to Evelyn Distelman for this photograph.)

A very different vacation experience awaited some working-class people—Jews and non-Jews—who had reaped the benefits of union membership. In 1919 Local 25 of the Ladies Waist and Dressmakers' Union of the International Ladies' Garment Workers' Union (ILGWU) purchased what had been the Forest Park Hotel, a resort "for the idle rich," and turned it into Unity House, a vacation place for union members and their families.[53] Located on seven hundred beautiful acres in the Pocono Mountains of Pennsylvania, the facility included twelve spacious houses "grouped about an open square." Guests enjoyed large, light rooms "equipped with electricity, carpets, curtained wardrobes, sanitary beds, immaculate linen, window screens, shades and other articles of comfort too numerous to mention."[54] The main house offered a central recreation area for meetings and dances, a library and reading room, lovely carpets throughout, and a grand piano. The grounds were apparently equally impressive, with "nooks and groves and thickets abounding." Visitors could enjoy a beautiful lake, fifty rowboats and canoes, seventy-five bathing houses, a swimming pool, tennis courts, and acres of trails for hiking.[55]

Forest Park also boasted its own electricity plant, laundry, and "a kitchen so large and sanitary and scientific that one imagines oneself in the 50th century."[56]

This was neither the first nor the only of the Waist and Dressmakers' vacation resorts. Two years earlier a smaller and less elaborate Unity House had opened in the Catskills. By 1922 Villa Anita Garibaldi, the Staten Island summer home of the Italian Dress and Waistmakers' Union, and the Philadelphia Waist and Dressmakers' Unity House in Orville, Pennsylvania, were also receiving guests.[57] But the Unity House at Forest Park remained the largest, most elaborate, and luxurious of these working-class union resorts. Although originally the property of the female members of Local 25, by the mid-1920s the International had assumed control and welcomed visitors from a variety of other unions as well.[58] Vacationers swam, boated, danced, hiked, sang, slept, bowled, played tennis, and wolfed down huge portions of reputedly wonderful food.

Unity House, however, was about more than recreation. It grew out of the educational work that both the International and specific locals were undertaking during the 1910s. New York's Local 25 had by 1915 organized Unity Centers in New York City where union workers could congregate for lectures, shop meetings, language courses, and physical education. Unity House was intended not only as a vacation resort, but as a place to continue the union's educational work and to display and affirm the spirit of unionism.[59] Supporters of Unity House saw in it a way to demonstrate the union's ability to enhance workers' lives and the workers' ability to "own and control a large scale enterprise."[60]

Unity House purportedly had a significant impact on the workers who vacationed there. According to one visitor, the rest, recreation, and good fellowship of Unity House helped to "make the workers less mean, less selfish, more idealistic."[61] Hiking at Unity House, for example, was thought to be different from hiking elsewhere, because there vacationers often hiked in groups, singing and reinforcing bonds of community.[62] Those who vacationed at Unity House allegedly left with a renewed belief in the possibilities of collective efforts. The beauty and pleasures of the estate at Forest Park came to represent "a foretaste of what the workingmen and women of all countries will have some day not only during the summer months but also throughout the year."[63]

Such statements, coming from the pens of Unity House's promoters, may not have reflected the opinions of all vacationers. But it seems clear that many of those who chose Unity House as a vacation destination expected more than a week of frivolity. Vacationers at Unity House certainly indulged in lighthearted amusements. They sang around campfires, enjoyed presentations by Yiddish comedians, watched folk dances performed by members of different ethnic groups, and danced to jazz orchestras—sometimes "until the wee small hours of the morning." Entertainment at Unity House, however, also assumed a more serious nature—readings of dramatic poems, recitations from the works of various playwrights, and concerts by classical musicians.[64]

By the mid-1920s the Unity House program included formal lectures on a variety of topics, some but not all of which related to trade unionism. One visitor reported that "hundreds of our members relaxed on the lawns under the pines overlooking the lake last Tuesday and Wednesday . . . and listened with great interest to two lectures given by Miss Theresa Wolfson." The topics included "women in the labor movement" and "changing morality."[65] During the summer of 1927 the Educational Department offered "several lectures each week on Psychology, Sociology, Economics, Literature, Art, Drama, and affairs of the day."[66]

Unity House, in some ways, resembled Chautauqua. Like the middle-class Methodist-inspired educational resort, Unity House invested leisure with purpose. Indeed, promoters maintained that Unity House served a spiritual as well an educational and recreational mission. It functioned to combine leisure with self-improvement, drawing on a working-class tradition that had since the early nineteenth century sought to limit work hours so that industrial laborers could engage in education and study. Yet, different from Chautauqua, Unity House seemed little concerned with protecting vacationers from the moral temptations of other vacation places. What the Unity House experiment did sustain, however, was the hope that workers would cease to contribute their hard-earned dollars to the coffers of capitalist resort owners.

Workers, both immigrant and native born, thus established a range of vacation alternatives during the early twentieth century. The vast majority either camped, rented inexpensive tents or cottages at a nearby lake or at the seashore, or repaired to some cheap country boarding house. Those with cars could expand their alternatives—either a trip to a less populated and more attractive camping spot or a sightseeing adventure to a city or a national park. Some working-class vacationers opted for trying to find a low-priced hotel or boarding house at a large resort, where they could combine the enjoyment of various commercial amusements with the pleasures of ocean or lake. Others enjoyed a vacation at a union-run resort or camp. Since money determined where and how working-class people vacationed, few shared the same vacation places with elite or middle-class vacationers. Ethnicity complicated the choice for some poor people. Working-class Jews, for example, faced not only financial restrictions, but cultural ones as well.

Some were self-imposed, as many Jews required vacation places that served kosher food. But Jewish vacationers also confronted anti-Semitic policies of growing numbers of gentile resorts.

Race as well as class and ethnicity influenced vacation patterns. Black men and women found their possibilities circumscribed not only by hotels that would not serve them, but by railroads that relegated them to Jim Crow cars. Still, African Americans established their own hotels and boarding houses at major American resorts. The presence of a local black community at many such places—often composed of waiters and other hotel employees—may have made other institutions, such as churches, available for African-American visitors.[67] Despite the always real possibility of racial confrontation, some blacks nevertheless continued to frequent these resorts. Others chose to create their own, separate vacation communities—enclaves where they could relax amongst family and friends.

In general, segregation rather than integration characterized the experience of most early twentieth century vacationers—regardless of race, class, or ethnicity. Vacationing thus operated somewhat differently from other forms of commercial leisure. Historian David Nasaw has examined the socially integrative role of urban public amusements in the early twentieth century. Nasaw suggests that city dwellers whose home and work lives remained segregated by class and ethnicity were nevertheless "beginning to share a common commercial culture and public amusement sites, where social solidarities were emphasized and distinctions muted." Accessible to a broad cross section of the white population (for blacks remained excluded), urban public amusements were, according to Nasaw, where "the city's peoples came together to have a good time in public."[68] Vacationing, in contrast, reinforced rather than diminished social distinctions.

Vacationing did, however, help to create a collective cultural experience that crossed class and racial lines. People of diverse origins joined in the increasingly familiar experience of "being on vacation." This experience was in certain respects more inclusive than that of public urban amusements because it reached not only members of the white working class, but middle-class African Americans as well. The entire American public did not, of course, enjoy a yearly vacation, but a significant and growing cross section of American men and women shared the expectation that they could or should have the privilege. During the early decades of the twentieth century vacationing began to become part of the American mainstream, something in which increasing numbers of people—regardless of class, race, or ethnic origin—participated.

Moreover, people of different races and classes came to share many of the same sorts of vacation experiences and to hear the same cultural messages and instructions about vacationing. Rich and poor alike, for example, strolled the boardwalk at Atlantic City and frolicked in the surf at Cape May, even though the well-off no doubt enjoyed more comfortable accommodations. Middle-class Protestants and working-class union members (many but not all of them Jews) shared the experience of self-improvement vacations at Chautauqua and Unity House respectively. While Unity House vacationers were certainly trying to disrupt rather than promote class harmony, they nevertheless participated in the same sort of cultural experience that many middle-class Protestant vacationers at Chautauqua enjoyed.

An examination of white, middle-class vacation patterns in the early decades of the twentieth century reveals a variety of ways in which people across classes were coming to share similar vacation experiences. Like their African American and working-class counterparts, the white middle class was busy creating and expanding their own homogenous, summer communities. Since the nineteenth century the elite had built summer cottages at a variety of resorts. During the early twentieth century more middle-class vacationers chose to build or buy modest summer vacation places where their families could enjoy domestic rather than hotel life along lakeside or seashore. And while white middle-class men and women had no desire to welcome black, ethnic, or white working-class vacationers into their summer communities, the experience of vacationing in a homogenous summer neighborhood—whether the middle-class African-American community at Oak Bluffs, the white-working class autocamp around Libby's Ocean Camp, or the white middle-class retreat at York Harbor—crossed racial and class lines.

By the early decades of the twentieth century vacationers across the social spectrum were also sharing similar vacation problems. White middle-class vacationers increasingly encountered inconveniences and difficulties similar to those that afflicted their less privileged counterparts. Even as working-class people were coming to participate in what had once been the middle-class experience of vacationing, middle-class vacationers faced situations that heretofore had troubled primarily people with lesser means.

Overcrowding, for example, plagued vacation places from the eastern seashore to the national parks of the West and affected the quality of middle-class vacations—usually for the worse. Max Siepereman of New York City, for example, visited Mt. Rainier National Park in July of 1920 where he found the public toilets at the Paradise Inn in "deplorable condition." Siepereman was not a camper, but somebody who could afford the price of the hotel.[69] The numbers of people visiting national parks not only overtaxed toilet facilities, but sleeping and travel accommodations as well. E. E. Sykes, a wholesale lumber dealer from New Orleans, complained that the Harvey Company, which ran the transportation facilities in Grand Canyon, put him into a seven-year-old Pierce Arrow for a drive around the rim. During the trip the axle broke, the wheel fell off, and only the skill of the driver saved the passengers from injury or death. The Harvey Company responded that they were using anything "which would run on four wheels" to accommodate the large crush of people.[70]

Even more troubling were some of the sleeping arrangements. A.H. Thompson, the pastor of the First Methodist Episcopal Church in Vancouver, described the accommodations at Mt. Rainier as "positively indecent":

> People are placed in separate compartments or bungalow tents, which are separated only by a piece of canvas. No provision is made to separate the sexes. So that it often appears that a girl or girls are on one side, and a strange man on the other. This is an invitation to immorality.

Not only were visitors forced to share their tents with strangers, but the bed coverings were "too narrow to cover two. Some had no blankets at all, and the night freezing cold." As a result, he and his wife "were compelled to lie rigidly in one position all night. If either moved the other was without cover."[71] Middle-class people who could afford comforts were finding themselves forced to accept less than desirable accommodations.

The growing numbers of middle-class vacationers brought problems not only to national parks, but to an array of resorts and vacation communities. Overtaxed dining rooms caused occasional outbreaks of food poisoning. As many as one hundred guests fell sick on one occasion from ptomaine poisoning at the upscale Mohonk Mountain House, the result of spoiled cream pie. Mohonk guests complained throughout the 1910s and 1920s about bed bugs, red ants, roaches, mice, and even rats—problems with which working-class people were all too familiar.[72] If guests at Mohonk with its nearly fifty-year history of catering to the respectable middle and upper middle class encountered such problems, there is little reason to doubt that vacationers at other resorts—both working and middle class—faced similar ones.

Even more serious was the increasing frequency with which even white middle-class vacationers found themselves in places with an unsafe water supply and inadequate sewer and garbage disposal. Rich and poor people alike needed water and toilets. And too many people of whatever social class could overtax primitive sewer systems. As a result, vacation places that were once touted as the cure for illness became, instead, potential breeding grounds for disease. Articles in newspapers and magazines warned of the numerous health problems that threatened vacationers. Water contaminated by sewage and garbage posed the real possibility of typhoid. In 1924 the *American Journal of Public Health* reported that repeated complaints "about nuisances at resort places" had prompted the state of Michigan to investigate. A traveling laboratory visited seventy-two of the state's resorts and found that only 58 percent had a safe water supply, 46 percent offered adequate sewage disposal, and 42 percent discarded garbage in a safe and healthful manner. The report concluded: "High rates are charged and the front porch, lobby and dining room are made as attractive as possible. In sanitary features . . . the place often falls short. The water supply is frequently from a well, poorly situated; toilet plumbing is antiquated and inadequate, while sewage disposal is neglected. Garbage is improperly handled. The kitchen and food storage facilities are dirty."[73] Increasingly both newspapers and magazines warned vacationers that the cities they had just abandoned — often in search of health — may well have provided more healthful environments than the summer resorts to which they had flocked.

The numbers of people who vacationed close to cities found different sorts of health problems. The water and beaches near places like New York were, by the 1920s, foul with urban refuse. Swimmers at Long Island beaches might encounter not only a little extra seaweed or an occasional beer bottle. B.C. Myers wrote a letter to the editor of the *New York Times* complaining about both beach and water pollution at Long Beach on Long Island:

> It is an uncanny feeling to have a dead body of a dog, sheep, chicken or cat roll against one's leg while in the surf, but a more serious blow to one's nerves to get a crack on the head from a bottle in the crest of a wave, and still more painful to cut one's feet, while walking to and from the surf, and this is a daily occurrence in our community.[74]

People at beaches along Long Island, Fire Island, and New Jersey confronted "thousands of bottles, boxes, barrels, broken furniture of every description, . . . [and] a mass of general garbage that smells to heaven."[75]

While nineteenth-century middle-class vacationers certainly faced their share of uncomfortable hotel rooms, dirty dining facilities, and substandard country boarding houses, the growing numbers of vacationers in the early twentieth century may well have exacerbated such problems even at places that had earlier offered relatively satisfactory services. Being middle class did not, necessarily, guarantee a pleasant, hygienic, or successful vacation. The difficulties and disappointment of vacations, like the pleasures, were crossing class lines.

What about the pleasures? Vacationers of all classes enjoyed many of the same diversions: the excitement at leaving home, the adventure of new places and sights, sunny beaches, bracing surf, cool breezes, mountain air. But they also, no doubt, shared some of the less innocent forms of recreation and amusement.

In the late nineteenth century, working-class codes of conduct allowed for considerably more latitude than did those of the middle class. An urban working-class culture of young people enjoyed dance halls and clubs, alcohol, and frequent encounters with members of the opposite sex.[76] While middle-class norms discouraged all such behavior, fashionable summer resorts throughout the late nineteenth century offered places where middle-class people began to let down their hair.[77] Twentieth-century middle-class vacationers not only continued this tradition, but pushed even farther at the boundaries of the acceptable.

Flora Ward, for example, encountered just such vacationers during her stay at Mammoth Hot Springs Hotel in Yellowstone National Park. In July of 1909 she wrote in a letter of complaint: "Last night there was held a drunken carousal of both men and women on the 4th floor of this hotel."[78] The problem of alcohol—whether or not it should be consumed and in what quantities—remained a source of contention for resort owners, hotelkeepers, residents, and guests. Asbury Park, New Jersey, had long been dry—the result, in part, of the efforts of its founder James Bradley and of its contiguity to the Methodist campground at Ocean Grove. But by 1905 hotel owners and cafe proprietors were fighting with residents over whether to allow the sale of liquor. The manager of one of the hotels explained that "Asbury Park has progressed beyond the point of being a backwoods settlement and the people who come here demand the same liberties they enjoy in other places." Even Bradley had altered his once firm opposition to alcohol. Trying to prohibit vacationers from drinking had, apparently, become increasingly difficult, and regulating the sale of alcohol seemed a better solution. "Conditions in Asbury Park have changed," Bradley conceded, "and what was good then is not so good now."[79]

Mohonk Mountain House, known for its rules prohibiting liquor, dancing, card playing, or traffic in or out on the Sabbath, began by the 1910s to encounter problems with the behavior of some guests. Willie Martin, who worked as a telegraph operator at Mohonk in 1912 and 1913, recalled an incident when a Mr. Hoe, a close friend of proprietor (and strict teetotaler) Albert Smiley, arrived for his vacation: "It was early June and rather cool and when Mr. Hoe's top coat was handled, a pint bottle of whiskey fell out of the pocket and broke on the stone floor." Smiley asked his friend: "Robert, what was that bottle that thee had in thy pocket?" Hoe responded: "Albert, that was my cough medicine."[80]

Other visitors at Mohonk were more successful at sneaking contraband liquor into their rooms. The 1917 annual report of the hotel manager described problems with the conduct of some guests: "It was said that a crowd of young men were indulging in vile talk, cigarettes and liquor, in room 427 (Thomas Crawford) and 431 (F. W. Hamilton)." The hotel staff did "a good deal of midnight watching and room investigations" but found "nothing incriminating beyond the discovery in young Crawford's room of some empty liquor bottles."[81] By the 1910s, the management at Mohonk no longer considered empty liquor bottles very serious. Guests at Mohonk engaged in other forbidden activities as well. In 1921 the house manager reported that "card playing in the public rooms happened a few times," and that "dancing was formally reported but once, but happened a few times in the playroom."[82] It was obviously becoming difficult for Mohonk to enforce the rules that had once made it a model Christian resort.

If twentieth-century resort-goers continued to drink, they also continued to gamble. But gambling, which had engaged primarily men in the nineteenth century, had become—at least at some resorts—entertainment for women as well. At Narragansett Pier, Rhode Island, for example, the police raided a "sumptuously furnished gambling den" in August of 1910 where they found "about thirty or thirty-five persons . . . , half of them being women in evening gowns." These were not ladies of the night. The raiders "recognized several women whose presence, if the names were mentioned, would shock the world of society in New York and Philadelphia." The next day numerous "prominent matrons, personally or through emissaries" contacted the constable and "beseeched" him not to "give out their names."[83]

Not all of the women worried about their reputations. One of the prominent matrons caught in the raid, a Mrs. John Hanan, declared that "the whole affair is more or less a joke, and [I] am treating it as such. . . . The Narragansett Club is like any other well-regulated club, like that in Palm Beach, for instance, or in other places where fashionable people gather. . . . I have been all over the country and it's just the same everywhere as it is here. There is no harm in it." Others agreed, explaining that summer vacationers played only "for small stakes, using it as an after-dinner diversion and not for the gain to be had."[84]

Letting down one's hair and burning the candle at both ends had traditionally been associated with leisure pursuits of the working class. These were not cultural standards to which the middle class was supposed to aspire. During the early twentieth century the behavior of middle-class vacationers continued to push norms of respectability in a more permissive direction. And, increasingly, cultural critics seemed to relax their warnings about the moral perils associated with certain forms of vacationing—specifically, resort vacationing. Even as resort-goers continued to drink, gamble, and enjoy the opposite sex (as well as engaging in more innocent forms of sport and play), the warnings about the perils of resort life diminished significantly. Occasional exposes of illegal gambling at Saratoga hit the pages of the *New York Times*, but in general the popular press seemed more worried about various health hazards—germs, mosquitos, sunburn, and contaminated water—than about virtue and propriety. By 1927 etiquette expert Anna Steese Richardson informed readers of *Woman's Home Companion* that it was "now quite the usual thing for a party of girls to go unchaperoned to a summer resort." She advised such "girls" not how to avoid sexual dangers, but how to choose the right resort, how to select the right clothes, and how to master the rules for tipping.[85] As resorts grew in number and popularity, resort vacationing no longer seemed to pose such a serious moral threat. Middle-class vacationers increasingly enjoyed amusements that once would have jeopardized their claims to middle-class status and respectability.

Cross-class sharing of vacation experiences, if not vacation sites, was nowhere more evident than in the growth in popularity of camping among the middle class. As increasing numbers of working-class vacationers turned to camping as their most economically feasible alternative, large numbers of middle-class people embraced camping for other reasons as well. Numerous mass market magazines ran vacation essay contests during the summer months and offered cash prizes and publication for the best vacation articles and essays. Summer issues of magazines like *The Independent, Women's Home Companion, Ladies Home Journal,* and *Colliers* published not only the one or two prize-winning stories, but several others that offered personal accounts of varied sorts of vacations. By far the most frequent were those that described camping vacations. Indeed, readers of mass market magazines might have assumed (incorrectly) that vacationers had rejected resorts or touring vacations and replaced them with an abundant variety of outdoor adventures.

Some of these camping experiences mirrored the ones that nineteenth-century campers had enjoyed, specifically the practice of traveling by rail or horse cart until finding the most opportune spot, pitching camp, and enjoying the beauties of nature and life in the outdoors. Such camps functioned somewhat like summer cottages—only at a fraction of the cost and with more exposure to nature and the elements. Ruth Harger of Abilene, Kansas, for example, described spending her eight-week vacation camping with eleven other people "On a Mountain Shelf" in western Colorado. They pitched three sleeping tents, one cook tent, and "a dining-room 'fly,'" which sheltered [their] long table very well in sunny weather." The cost of this eight-week adventure was "about $32 per person, not including railroad fare." And the group returned home "in good spirits, with vigorous health and in splendid condition."[86]

Throughout the early twentieth century camping came to encompass an increasingly varied range of experiences—some of them different from what nineteenth-century campers had enjoyed. Specifically, middle-class vacationers in the early twentieth century, like their working-class counterparts, engaged in peripatetic forms of camping. During the nineteenth century only the hardiest and most adventuresome of campers had, with the help of guides, traveled through woods and forests, setting up camps each night and continuing to travel the next day. But in the early twentieth century growing numbers of campers expressed an interest in "gypsying"—a less strenuous if still rambling form of camping.

The automobile was partly responsible. Some of the first automobile owners—people with considerable means—found that cars could serve as portable vacation homes.[87] Despite the problems of bad roads and unreliable machines, many vacationers looked to autocamping as a way to simplify their vacation. They also viewed autocamping as a new sort of adventure and as a welcome alternative to the boredom and restraints of Victorian resorts. Keat Hodtyer, a resident of New Brunswick, Canada, for example, wrote to *The Independent* describing his "Vacation in a Portable Lodging House." He explained that the goal of his vacation was "to lead 'the simple life'; to be independent of hotels and boarding houses as much as possible; see interesting parts of the country off the usual track of sightseers; get away when we wanted to from the people and the nerve-racking noise." In an automobile customized for that purpose—windows could be raised and lowered, screens installed against mosquitos, and seats converted to beds—the Hodtyers drove along at their leisure, provisioning themselves by fishing and hunting along the way, buying chickens from an occasional farmer, and stopping for "one substantial meal each day at a restaurant or hotel, if we happened to be near such." For Hodtyer and his wife, "the fashionable seaside and mountain resorts, with their round of social frivolity—just a repetition of city life" held no attraction; rather, for them, autocamping proved "an ideal way to spend a vacation."[88]

Gypsying did not require a car. A horse and wagon could achieve the same end, and did for many campers.[89] Other vacationers used various sorts of boats—canoes, houseboats, canal boats, small motorboats—on their camping ventures. George Walsh, for example, described his "motorboat vacation" for *Country Life in America* in 1910. He and two friends bought a motor boat (costing each of them $65) that they sold for nearly that amount when their two-week vacation was over. They used the boat to get from New York to Lake Hopatong in New Jersey, where they "negotiated with a landowner for camping privileges at $5 a season. This included firewood to be gathered nearby, water from a neighboring well, and such other little odds and ends of things as [they] might pick up." Their vacation afforded them the best of both possible worlds—the pleasures and healthful benefits of being in the outdoors, and the resort-like "attractions" around Lake Hopatong, including "dancing pavilions, music, and merry-go-round thrown in."[90] Mary Melvin of Baltimore recommended a different sort of boating trip. She and her mother spent a "delightful two weeks" camping and boating on the Chesapeake and Ohio Canal during the summer of 1911. Melvin described their vacation as "a pleasant trip with just enough of the rough in it. . . . Cool springs along the way will refresh your thirst, fresh milk and other provisions purchased at the lock-houses will rest you after long tramps, generous hospitality will be repaid to you by the canal people for all your unpatronizing courtesy. You may fish, sleep out of doors and breathe good pure air at all times."[91] Life in the outdoors brought neither fear nor danger. Melvin and her mother apparently felt entirely safe on their vacation.

Other campers relied on their feet. Tramping was perhaps the most strenuous form of camping, requiring campers to carry provisions on their backs. In the nineteenth century this would have been a form of camping that only men would have attempted. But by the 1910s tramping was becoming popular for women and men alike. In 1910 Eva Foye kept a diary describing a tramping and camping trip she and three other women took in Yosemite. They included no men in their party, but escaped some of the heavy carrying by putting their packs on stage coaches that happened by, collecting them at a convenient stop along their route.[92]

Camping afforded these twentieth-century middle-class vacationers a variety of pleasures. Whether rambling or staying put, camping provided release from the problems, boredom, and restraint of hotel or boarding houses. And, as these magazine articles continued to point out, camping was cheap. An economical vacationer could buy a tent for the "price of a week's board at a summer resort, and the tent [would] last many years." Even those who could afford neither tent nor travel money could still find ways to camp—even if it meant just moving outside. People camped in their own back yards, on porch hammocks, on remote quarters of their farm, and even on the roof of "a three-story store."[93]

The large number of camping stories that appeared in mass market magazines reveals more than the popularity of camping vacations. Like the businessmen who encouraged their workers to take camping vacations, the editors who printed camping stories were promoting camping over other sorts of vacations. Camping, these numerous stories counseled, would yield untold advantages. It promised health. Not only would fresh air and sunshine invigorate bodies, but contemplation of nature would refurbish souls and lift spirits.[94] Another important "advantage," the press seemed to suggest, was that camping required work.

The camping stories that filled mass market magazines often detailed the sorts of work in which campers engaged. Camping vacations—regardless of the class of the vacationer—were usually not vacations spent in idleness. Campers needed to find and prepare food, plot routes, set up tents, wash their clothes in the rivers, chop wood, build fires. Twentieth-century middle-class campers sounded much like their nineteenth-century counterparts in

Ladies of an Idaho camping party washing clothes, c. 1918–1920. Camping required work, and some vacationers suggested such work was fun. (Library of Congress, Otto M. Jones Collection, J731-41-b.)

celebrating the "fun" that such work provided. Ruth Harger, who spent eight weeks with eleven other campers in the mountains of western Colorado in 1910, explained: "In our camp each had his day's duties—and no more. . . . It would have astonished some society friends to have seen us, barefooted, cleaning linen at the river—but we played we were French peasants, and what fun it was!"[95] Not only vacations spent out-of-doors, but those that demanded some physical labor, these stories suggested, were optimal ways to maximize enjoyment and health.

Mass market magazines offered an even less subtle endorsement of the advantages of combining work and vacationing. The vacation essay contests that many of these magazines ran received the largest number of stories from people who camped. But stories and essays about work ran a close second. Indeed, according to the letters and articles sent from readers, large numbers of early twentieth-century women and men spent their vacations working.

The sort of work varied. High on the list was the decision to do some sort of agricultural work—picking fruit, haying, maple sugaring, helping on a farm. A young female office worker from Minneapolis, for example, explained in her letter to *Woman's Home Companion* that she had "no money in my pocket . . . and doctor's instructions to spend two months out of doors." So she resigned her office position, took a job picking berries on a farm "in the beautiful region of summer homes and small farms around Lake Minnetonka," and persuaded her sister to join her. The two remained two months, gained twenty pounds, and returned to Minneapolis "brown and strong with fifty dollars clear apiece."[96] Two other sisters, musicians rather than clerks, described a similar sort of "vacation," but they picked apricots rather than berries.[97] And when James H. Hoadley of New York City decided to vacation in March, rather than during the summer, he set out to help with the maple sugaring back at his boyhood home: "There followed such a month of joy and healthfulness in the open woods, gathering sap, cutting wood and keeping up the fires, boiling the sweet liquid to amber syrup, and making some of it into cakes of delicious sugar, as cannot be described."[98]

Although most of these articles and essays came from the pens of middle-class vacationers, some were purportedly written by working-class men and women. One, called "A Factory's Girls' Vacation," not only won first prize in the vacation essay contest of *The Independent*, but was apparently good enough for *The Literary Digest* to reprint a few weeks later. The "factory girl" had only one day, the Fourth of July, for her vacation. Moreover, she could not afford, even for that one day, carfare out of the city. Her roommate suggested that by spending the day picking strawberries they could earn the necessary carfare plus a little extra and enjoy a "vacation" at the same time. Bright and early they boarded the train and by eight o'clock they were picking berries in Mr. T's berry patch: "We worked hard all morning, but work under such circumstances is a pleasure; although we did get somewhat stiff getting up and down so often." At the end of the day they had each earned about a dollar, plus as many berries as they could eat or carry, and returned home "well pleased with the day's vacation."[99]

A similar story won first prize in a *Woman's Home Companion* contest the following year, this time written by a working-class immigrant boy from

Germany, who, on the suggestion of a "lady at the Boy's club," decided to take a vacation picking berries on a farm. His vacation lasted three weeks, not just one day. He, too, complained at first about stiffness from the stooping, "but soon I felt all right." Not only did he earn a dollar a day, but he spent evenings swimming, fishing, or playing ball. He concluded that "work in the country is a vacation. I like it. I can make something of myself instead of bumming around the streets and smoking and going to moving picture shows."[100]

Despite the didactic tone, these working-class narratives differed little from the essays and stories submitted by middle-class vacationers. Take, for example, an article called "A Haying Vacation," sent to *The Independent* by the Reverend Lincoln Long of Martanville, New York. Leaving "a young minister in charge of my church," Long put on "workmen's clothes" and set off "on foot to hunt up a 'job in haying,'" Three weeks' work on a farm earned him not only $26.25, but, more importantly, enormous pleasure and benefit: "I had a fine vacation. Up at four thirty, milk, eat breakfast, grind scythes and . . . mow by hand or with machine, rake, 'bunch up,' 'draw in', 'mow away'—that was the daily program. My nerves were rested, my muscles became hardened, my skin was browned and I was a new man. I came back to my work with vigor and enthusiasm. . . ."[101]

The previous month *Colliers* had run a similar set of stories—also the result of readers' responses to the magazine's request for "the best short account of a vacation experience." The editors claimed that they had received fifteen hundred manuscripts, and first prize went to Frederick Brush for his story called, interestingly, "The Hayin'." Brush returned to the farm where he had been raised and decided to help an old friend who needed extra hands for the haying. The work was hard: "Unused tendons creaked in their slots. Blisters—blisters?—a spot without them became notable." But slowly, "the tide of vitality turned." He rediscovered his "boyish sleep, appetite, and afternoon staying power. . . . I got to look back on the man I had been as a head, a few clinkered organs and a heavy load." But the best part, he maintained, was the spiritual and intellectual rebirth: "Certain problems seemed to solve automatically and life lined out clearly for the coming year. The most effective thinking of years was done on that mowing machine." Farm work, he discovered, was the perfect vacation for city people: "Not always to do hayings or dig ditches, but to do something, preferably productive, with the hands, close alongside of plain men."[102]

The sorts of work in which such vacationers engaged varied considerably. School teachers and clerks took vacations working as waitresses, cooks, baggage boys, and chambermaids at camps, ranches, and summer hotels. The benefits of fresh air, lovely scenery, and fine weather allegedly offered sufficient compensation for the hard work that such a "vacation"

entailed.[103] Other vacationers devised a variety of ingenious ways of combining income-producing labor with vacationing. L. D. Clarke claimed he
was tired of his usual vacation routine—a month at a resort from which he
returned "so grouchy that the entire office force hated to see me coming."
He decided he had no desire "to sit on any shaded veranda for four weeks,
nor catch fish where no fish had ever been." He wanted to travel, but did
not have sufficient funds. The answer was to be a traveling sales representa-
tive for a publishing firm. Although he found the work "somewhat hard at
first," in the end he enjoyed "a fine vacation" that made money rather than
costing money: "It gave me the opportunity . . . to be out of doors, and it
was wonderful, the number of fine people I met. I saw many of the places I
had wanted to see, and next vacation I'm going to do the same thing, in
new fields, and see some more places."[104]

While most of these stories and articles described ways of enjoying vacations by combining them with work, there were some that entirely erased
leisure from the experience. Instead work itself became a vacation, as long
as the work differed from one's usual routine. For example, William C. Wilson, a clerk for a manufacturing firm, decided to spend his two-week vacation from the office working in the mill itself. The work was, he said, "thoroughly strenuous" manual labor, but "everything was so different from the
routine to which I had been accustomed that the work was fun." Hoping to
become acquainted with all aspects of the business, Wilson expected his
vacation to make him a more valuable employee. He concluded that "the
most restful thing in the world, particularly for people who deserve a rest, is
just to tackle a different kind of work." Wilson required none of the com-
pensations that other working vacationers mentioned—time for an occasional swim in the lake, change of location, the possibility of sightseeing in a
new part of the country, meeting and enjoying the company of fellow "working vacationers." For him, work itself had become a vacation. Indeed, this
vacation was, he claimed, "the very best vacation I ever had."[105]

These stories echo a number of similar themes. Work rather than play was
the key to real enjoyment and benefit. True recreation could be found not in
tennis, ocean bathing, bowling, and dancing, but in the performance of hard,
physical, outdoor labor. Moreover, it mattered little whether the vacationer
were male or female, middle or working-class. A vacation spent doing agricultural work would, these stories and essays suggested, bring innumerable
advantages. Working on a farm meant exchanging the city—a potentially
unhealthful place both morally and physically—for the beneficent countryside. Both "haying" stories implied that for middle-class men, such a vacation served as well to reaffirm manliness in the face of occupations that
demanded little in the way of bodily vigor or strength. The minister and the
office worker could prove that they were as strong and able as the farmhand.

For working-class people, these stories posed working vacations as potential tools for advancement and upward mobility. And for all vacationers, time spent doing agricultural labor promised health and pleasures.

The vacation contest stories raise, of course, a number of questions and problems. Were these authentic accounts of people's vacations or were they the fabrications of writers and editors? Probably both. Some were, doubtless, fabrications. The same Frederick Brush who won first prize for his story, "The Hayin'," in 1909 won first prize again the following year for his story about gypsying in a horse and cart.[106] Brush may, of course, have actually taken both these vacations, but he also knew how to write the sort of stories that won first prize. Articles like Brush's clearly bear the stamp of the professional writer—lively prose, engaging humor, didactic conclusion. But even these often differed little in content (although considerably in style) from those straightforward and probably genuine descriptions of readers' vacations.

Do these articles offer evidence of how people spent their vacations or evidence of the cultural message that editors hoped to send to readers? Again, I would suggest both. Editors obviously printed what resonated with their readers. The range and variety of these stories—as well as the frequency with which they appeared in magazines—suggest that people along the social spectrum were familiar with working vacations. That the majority of these stories came from middle-class readers is not suprising, for only people far removed from demands of daily manual labor could have made arduous physical work into a vacation. By the early twentieth century middle-class men and women, like their working-class counterparts, were coming up with imaginative and innovative forms of vacationing. Despite the explosive growth of vacationing throughout the late nineteenth century, the cost of a vacation still could strain a middle-class budget. As a result, some people apparently sought either cheap vacations (hence the large numbers of articles about inexpensive camping vacations) or ingenious ways to combine vacationing with some income-producing work. Since vacationing had by the early twentieth century become almost a cultural imperative for the middle class, some financially strapped middle-class people looked to creative means of paying for a vacation. Those without the necessary funds fashioned "working vacations," which they then claimed to enjoy immensely.

At the same time, these vacation stories offered a powerful cultural directive to readers: vacationers should remain, in some ways, connected to the world of work. The effort to link work and vacationing had throughout the last half of the nineteenth century influenced not only the vacation patterns of the middle class, but their attitudes about vacations. In the twentieth century the nature of the vacationing public began to change, but the lesson remained the same. Middle and working-class vacationers alike became the object of a similar, ambivalent message about both the benefits and the potential pitfalls of time away from work.

Vacations, increasing numbers of people agreed, were a good thing. They brought health, restoration, and spiritual peace. Most importantly, they returned people refreshed and renewed to the workplace. The belief that vacations would produce better workers took on increasing importance in the early twentieth century. It helped both to persuade some progressive businessmen to extend vacations to their factory workers and to calm middle-class trepidations about the risks of extended periods of leisure. As a 1922 article in *Colliers'* put it: "You'll hoe your row better if you stop to rest once in a while." The author quickly, however, offered the following caveat: "Only, of course, it's hard each time just when you first start at it again."[107]

Here was the rub. Vacations, reputed wisdom held, would make better workers.[108] But lingering doubts remained that vacations might, instead, spoil workers. While the stakes may have seemed higher as the vacationing public came to include more working-class people, the message was not class-specific. Indeed, it mattered little from which class the potential vacationer came. A vacation spent camping or haying, rather than relaxing or, worse, debauching, might well have made it a little less difficult for a member of any social class to "start at it again." During these decades middle and working-class vacationers not only began to share many of the same sorts of vacation experiences, they also heard the same warnings about the importance of keeping themselves somehow connected to work.

The history of vacationing in the early twentieth century reveals that, when it came to leisure, ideas changed more slowly than did behavior. As the multitudes began to enjoy an array of vacation pleasures, the public discussion about vacations reflected the persistent and continuing American suspicion of time spent away from work. Searching for ways to accommodate new behavior to traditional values, keepers of the public conscience offered the vacationing public an equivocal message—attempting to reinforce the importance of work in a culture in which the opportunity for and the desire to vacation were becoming widespread.

◌ 9 ◌

"It's worthwhile to get something from your holiday"

VACATIONING DURING the DEPRESSION

The depression would seem an inhospitable climate for vacations. The economy was in a shambles. Millions of Americans were out of work. Many of those lucky enough to keep their jobs saw significant reductions in their hours. From an average fifty-hour work week in 1929, the number dropped to below thirty-five by 1935 as the depression created a crisis of unemployment, overproduction, and underconsumption.[1] People worried not about taking more time off from work, but about finding enough work to guarantee support for themselves and their families.

Given these conditions, a few voices argued for the suspension of anything as frivolous as vacationing. In August of 1931 the *Literary Digest*, for example, ran an article called "Should Ministers Have a Vacation?" Those who answered "no" pointed to the problems caused by the depression— "lack of work, despondency, and all that goes with discouragement of this kind." During such times ministers needed to give their complete attention to parishioners: "Can one imagine Christ taking a vacation in the midst of such despondency and discouragement as we have now?" Others defended the traditional practice of granting ministers a two- to four-week vacation. Pointing to the wide range of important functions beyond "sermon-preaching and hymn-singing" and to the fact that ministers, often "on call day and night," worked even on Sundays, they argued that ministers deserved vacations.[2]

This specific debate notwithstanding, evidence suggests that Americans continued to promote, endorse, and take vacations—despite hard times. Vacationing remained a prevalent and popular American institution throughout the 1930s, experiencing only a temporary decline in the early years of the decade. Moreover, between 1935 and 1940 the privilege of vacations with pay finally was extended to a majority of America's industrial labor force, ironically making the decade of the depression a period when vacationing became more rather than less widespread.

The depression did, however, bring changes—specifically in the public debate about vacations. As work became both scarce and insecure, the public press stopped touting the pleasures of a working vacation. But long-standing cultural anxieties about leisure and vacationing remained, intensified in fact by the abundance of "leisure" that the depression seemed to be producing. No longer able to suggest that people mix vacations with work, cultural critics returned to a familiar nineteenth-century theme—leisure in pursuit of personal growth and self-improvement. In the 1930s, however, self-improvement was updated, secularized, and directed towards a broad cross section of the American public.

————— • ◆ • —————

What happened to vacationing when work became scarce? The 1929 stock market crash and ensuing economic crises brought widespread financial hardship. By 1932 as many as 13 million men and women were estimated to be unemployed.[3] Not surprisingly, many Americans decided to forgo their vacations.

Numerous vacation spots reported a decline in visitors during the early 1930s. Niagara Falls had welcomed more than 3 million people in 1929; by 1932 only 1,444,0000 visited the famous spot.[4] In 1929 a record 260,694 people journeyed to Yellowstone, but the numbers declined in the years that followed. In 1932 park officials allowed the private company that ran the park's hotels to close three of them midway through the summer.[5] The following year fewer than 162,000 people visited the park.[6] Similarly Grand Canyon saw a drop in numbers, from a high of 184,093 in 1929 to 105,475 in 1933.[7]

Smaller resorts also felt the pinch. At Mohonk Mountain House, for example, the total receipts dropped from over $514,000 in 1928 to about $413,000 in 1931. Not only had the numbers declined, but the requirements of Mohonk's guests had changed as well. In 1931 the manager remarked that "no one professed a very decided preference for accommodations with bathroom." Most guests opted instead for the "most moderately priced rooms."[8] The manager believed that the depression had also altered the ethnic profile of Mohonk's clientele. Venting his displeasure at the changes wrought by the economic downturn, he commented that the "only people who were not restricted in money matters this past summer with [the] 'depression in full swing' were Jews and Germans. We had some of each, fortunately or otherwise, with the majority leaning toward German extraction."[9] Mohonk's problems continued throughout the early 1930s. Income from room and board earned the hotel about 18 percent less in 1933 than it had the year before.[10]

Statistics like these tell two stories. They reveal that although many people put their vacations on hold, considerable numbers continued to vacation—even during the most severe economic times. Moreover, many vacation places where attendance fell off in the early years of the depression saw improvement by the middle of the decade. Grand Canyon experienced a steady decline in tourists from 1929 to 1933, but in 1934 the park welcomed 140,220 visitors, a 33 percent rise over the previous year.[11] As many as 4 million people visited the national parks in 1934.[12] During the same year 13 million people stayed long enough in the national forests "to enjoy real recreation." According to one study, these vacationers "occupied summer homes, lodged at hotels and resorts, stayed at camps operated by municipalities and youth service organizations, camped independently at campsites equipped by the Forest Service, and through the use of these living accommodations were able to enjoy the advantages of a vacation in isolated forest areas."[13]

By the summer of 1935 newspapers were optimistically predicting a good year for vacations. In June the *New York Times* reported on the huge numbers of people expected to travel that summer: "Daily the tunnels and bridges and highways leading out of New York City carry increasing numbers of vacationists. Golf clubs rattle in railroad cars; bags and blankets bear down on a myriad [of] automobile fenders, tarpaulins swell over loads of luggage atop thousands of buses." Tourist agencies, bus lines, and automobile clubs were receiving growing numbers of inquiries and bookings, and "experts" predicted "20 per cent as an estimate for the expected total increase in travel."[14]

The experts apparently figured correctly, for in August hotel owners in Atlantic City were "experiencing the busiest Summer since 1929."[15] Niagara Falls, where the number of tourists had hit a low mark in 1932, saw a steady increase in visitors over the next few years. By 1934 2,258,000 tourists stopped at the Falls and forecasters predicted "that sightseers in 1936 will approach the 3,000,000 mark."[16] In 1934 Yellowstone received 260,775 guests, an increase of 61 percent over the previous year and a few more than the 260,697 who had entered the park in 1929.[17] Mohonk also experienced something of a revival. By 1936 house counts were up more than 10 percent and income was up almost 20 percent over 1935.[18]

Conventions continued to meet at resorts during the depression, both facilitating vacations for some people and helping resorts owners keep their balance sheets in the black. The meeting of the Radio Manufacturers' Association in June of 1930, for example, was expected to attract between twenty and thirty thousand people to Atlantic City.[19]

In 1936 *Fortune* magazine conducted a survey asking people if they expected to take a vacation, how long they would stay away, and how far they would travel. Forty-four percent responded that they intended to take no vacation, while another 4 percent remained undecided. That left a little more than half who anticipated some vacation. The largest group (28%) expected to be gone from eight to sixteen days; a smaller number (14%) intended a vacation of a week's duration or less. The survey also discovered that people "not only like to spend their vacations away from home, but they want to get as far away as they have time to go, preferably to another part of the country."[20]

Interestingly, the author seemed surprised at how large a number planned *not* to vacation, finding the 44.6 percent of "vacationless" Americans "the most notable thing about these figures." The article held, however, that the data may have overstated the number of nonvacationers: "[O]f these vacationless 44.6 per cent, more than half are farmers and their wives who have seasonal leisure during which they do a good deal of driving around without calling it vacation." Guessing, moreover, that some of the "vacationless 44.6 per cent" probably "did not know . . . whether their employers would let them off," the author surmised that many "will probably pack off for a week or two sometime during the summer slack." Vacationing had become so integral to American life that the author found it difficult to believe that a large percentage of people remained "vacationless."

A 1937 study by economist Julius Weinberger confirmed the widespread practice of vacationing during the 1930s. Weinberger examined recreational expenditures between 1909 and 1935 and found a persistent increase in Americans' willingness to allocate funds to leisure-time pursuits. Although the money spent on recreation declined from 1929 to 1935, it still represented a sizeable portion of the national economy, "exceed[ing] the value of the products of the entire motor vehicle and rubber tire industries." During the early years of the depression people cut back on their purchase of recreational products (athletic equipment, musical instruments, toys), recreational services (movies, theaters, cabarets, country clubs, athletic clubs), and vacation travel. The latter, however, declined significantly less than other forms of recreation. Automobile operating expenses, which represented the chief

Lee Monument Ball, the Greenbrier, White Sulphur Springs, West Virginia, August 1932. The depression made little impact on the vacation habits of the wealthy. (The Greenbrier, White Sulphur Springs, West Virginia.)

item in vacation expenditure, "fell only slightly during the depression, and made a new high record in 1935—an achievement unequaled by any other major form of recreational expenditure." People did reduce the amount they paid for hotels, meals, gifts, and entertainment during their trips, but continued to take their vacations regardless. In 1929 Americans spent approximately $2.7 billion on vacation travel. The number dropped to $1.7 billion in 1933, but by 1935 had rebounded to $2.3 billion. [21]

Neither the *Fortune* survey nor Weinberger's study revealed which sorts of people vacationed and which did not.[22] Obviously, people with money were least likely to let the depression interrupt or alter their vacation plans. The newspapers, in fact, continued to report on the luncheons, regattas, golf tournaments, and tennis matches of those who could afford vacations at Newport, the Hamptons, Lenox, and Bar Harbor. Depression or not, the wealthy continued to vacation in the style to which they were already well accustomed.[23]

Harold Ickes recorded in his diary one particularly interesting example of elite vacationing. On a visit to the West Coast in the summer of 1934, Ickes spent one night at Bohemian Grove, a camp about seventy-five miles north of San Francisco that served as a vacation spot for wealthy and influential members of the Bohemian Club and their guests. Key business and political figures such as former President Herbert Hoover, Eugene Meyer (publisher of the *Washington Post*), and Arthur Reynolds (past president of Continental-Illinois Bank) vacationed at the fifteen hundred acre site—a beautifully laid out camp ground that included a pond, an open-air theater, and cabins for visitors. According to Ickes, members of the elite club spent three weeks at the Grove every summer, living "in cabins . . . [equipped with] sanitary sewage, hot and cold running water and gas for both lighting and cooking." Guests enjoyed "excellent" food, "a general bar for the camp," and a bar for "each particular subcamp." On the last night of the three-week stay the members not only indulged in "a good deal of drinking" but also performed a play in the outdoor theater. Ickes was particularly impressed with the quality of the acting, costumes, and lighting. "I was told," he confided to his diary, "that the lighting for that one play cost $25,000."[24] The well-to-do obviously did not let the depression affect the quality of their vacations.

Farther down the economic ladder, Winifred Woodley and her family continued during the 1930s to enjoy a variety of sorts of summer holidays. Woodley, wife of a lawyer and mother of two adolescent children, lived in a comfortable middle-class suburb of New York. With the help of a live-in housekeeper, Woodley had time to chauffeur her children, engage in a variety of community affairs, and also spend time working on a novel. In August of 1935 the family rented a remodeled farmhouse in Connecticut, complete with swimming pool, for $50 for the month. Woodley's husband, Hugh, spent his two-week vacation there with his family and commuted on the weekends during the other two weeks. The following summer Winifred and the children spent thirty days in the Catskills (Hugh visiting on weekends) and another thirty in a cottage on the Carolina coast. The place in the Catskills apparently offered little in the way of comfort or convenience. Winifred's diary described the "primitive living": "cooking on an oil stove, drawing water from a well, washing clothes and spreading them on hot grass to dry, bathing in the river, walking to the cross-roads store, reading by an oil lamp until aches and weariness sent me to bed under the rafters." Whether she disliked vacationing under such primitive conditions is unclear. Someone of her status, used to the amenities, might have considered a month of drawing water from the well and bathing in the river a romantic adventure—an opportunity to indulge in simple living. In any case, the time spent in the cottage in Carolina offered a different sort of vacation experience: "blue sky, yellow sand, the music of the surf, all modern conveniences, good food, Southern talk."[25]

Selma Squires, daughter of immigrant Jewish parents, remembered vacationing as a child with her mother for two weeks in a boarding house on the

Connecticut shore. Her father, a small businessman who managed to sustain little economic damage during the depression, joined them on the weekends. Squires recalled the luxury of eating every meal at a kosher restaurant on the beach. Her mother, a woman who rarely ate at restaurants, enjoyed two weeks of beach, ocean, and freedom from preparing meals and cleaning house. Most of the families in the boarding house, however, made use of kitchen privileges—the women shopping for food, labeling it for the refrigerator, and cooking meals for their families.[26] Such women, still responsible for feeding and care of their families, might have felt that they had simply moved their normal work to a different and less commodious place. At the same time the change of location and opportunity to enjoy the surf and the sun may have made these sojourns welcome respites from everyday life.

Nearly a continent away, Ann Marie Low and her brother managed to eke out a different sort of vacation. In 1933 Low was in her early twenties, dividing her time between college and the family's North Dakota farm. Low's father had been a prosperous farmer until 1927, the "last of the 'good years.'" After that, a series of economic problems, hailstorms, and dust wrought havoc, and the family worked desperately hard to keep the farm going. No longer able to afford hired help, her father depended upon the labor of his two daughters, son, and sickly wife. Ann Marie raised chickens and did typing for the superintendent of schools to earn extra money. Winning a scholarship to Jamestown College, she returned home every weekend to work on the farm.

Despite severe economic constraints, Low managed to take a five-day vacation with her brother and a friend in the June of 1933. They did not, needless to say, journey to some posh resort. They piled into the "old Ford" and drove to Bismarck where they toured the sights of the state's capital. The three stayed in a "log tourist cabin near the river." The accommodations offered little in the way of comfort or luxury, but the price—$1—was right. The young women shared the "uncomfortable" bed, and Bud, her brother, slept on the floor. The following day they did a little more sightseeing before leaving for the 150-mile road trip to Medora, where they stayed with an aunt and uncle who owned a hotel. Ann Marie explored both the town and the surrounding area, visiting Little Big Horn and the petrified forest. The entire trip—"the gas, Bismarck motel, breakfast and lunch Tuesday, and a snack for . . . [the last] afternoon"—cost $10. As they headed home, a whole day's drive "at a top speed of 35 miles an hour," Low's thoughts turned to the work that awaited and confided to her diary: "I can't feel any enthusiasm as I think of the all washing, ironing, and baking to be done at home. Haying is starting too."[27]

The pages of *NCR News*, the in-house newspaper of the National Cash

Register Company, reveal that midwestern factory workers, like western farmers, middle-class suburban matrons, and East Coast immigrants, found a variety of ways to take vacations during the depression. The editors of the paper did express some concern about vacationing in hard times. An article in the summer of 1930, for example, encouraged NCR employees to "spend [their] vacation closer to home." Assuming that some workers might be "a trifle embarrassed financially this year," the paper suggested enjoying the rivers and the sunshine right around Columbus: "The water of the Scioto River is just as wet as that in the Potomac, the Ohio, the Mississippi, the Amazon, etc. The grass along its banks is just as green . . . and the same sun shines overhead."[28]

Many NCR workers chose not to follow such advice. While some employees anticipated spending their vacations motoring, camping, and fishing in and around central Ohio, others planned to travel much farther — to Chicago, Atlantic City, Yellowstone, California, New England, and Washington, D.C.[29] One worker described the two weeks spent with his wife, daughter, and uncle in a rented cottage on the upper peninsula of Michigan — a 760-mile trip. The cottage cost them $10 per week, and they enjoyed "wonderful sport with rod and line."[30]

For a significant proportion of the American populace, vacationing had by the 1930s become an important component of an acceptable standard of living.[31] The widespread ownership of cars no doubt allowed many of these depression-era families to continue to enjoy vacations — hard times or not. Ann Low and her brother could never have contemplated their five-day trip, for example, were it not for "the old Ford." According to historian Warren Belasco, "Americans spent almost as much on gas, oil, and other vacation car operating expenses in 1933 as in 1929, $1,102 million and $1,040 million, respectively."[32] The *Fortune* magazine survey confirmed that cars served as the vacation vehicles of choice. Three quarters of vacationers drove, while only 13.6 percent took the train and 5.6 percent chose the bus.[33]

Those who vacationed in cars had a variety of options when it came to lodgings. The cheapest — camping by the side of the road — appealed to many. But during the 1930s numerous autotrippers, while still "budget-minded," sought slightly more in the way of overnight accommodations than a field, farm, or campsite.[34] Both farmers and former campground owners responded quickly to the demand and a new industry — roadside tourist cabins (the forerunners of motels) — emerged. Estimates suggest that the number of tourist cabin–camps had grown from 5,000 in 1927 to between 15,000 and 20,000 by 1935.[35]

Staying in cabins eased many of the burdens of autocamping: vacationers no longer needed to carry camping paraphernalia or to pitch camps

Fishing party at Emerick and Stuart's Camp, vicinity of Boise, Idaho, c. 1920. Although many autotrippers chose roadside tourist cabins, camping remained a popular vacation alternative during the 1930s as it had been in the first two decades of the century. (Library of Congress, Otto M. Jones Collection, LC-J73-4-52.)

nightly. Primitive enough so that the family could still feel as though it was "roughing it," roadside cabins were also inexpensive. A 1935 article in the *New York Times* maintained that prices of cabins varied, ranging from $.50 to $8.00 per night, but that the most popular price was $1.00 per person per night.[36] Moreover, as the number of such places proliferated and competition between them increased, tourists often found themselves in an ideal situation to "haggle for lower prices." Some succeeded in bringing the price down, while others cut their vacation costs by sneaking extra family members in after dark.[37] Many of those who managed a vacation during the 1930s did so only because low gas prices and the availability of inexpensive cabin camps made vacationing cheap.

Whether all members of the family enjoyed autotripping vacations equally is difficult to determine. For women, such trips may in fact have been no vacation at all. Preparing meals on primitive stoves in rustic, crowded roadside cabins, keeping small children entertained on long and dusty car trips, and finding ways to maintain some level of cleanliness could well have been considered work not recreation. Such problems were, of course, not new to the depression. But hard times caused many families to reduce the cost of their vacations. Those who once could have afforded an inexpensive hotel where women found some relief from domestic chores instead spent a week autotripping and either camping by the road or staying at rustic roadside cabin–camps.

Various New Deal initiatives helped to expand the vacationing infrastructure and to stimulate tourism. In July of 1935 the *New York Times* reported on the increasing number of people camping and hiking in New York's "high mountains," "secluded forest," and on the 2½ million acres of the State Forest Preserve. Those who chose such a vacation could enjoy the new facilities available along 600 miles of trail: "There are now 1,800 lean-to shelters for the free use of the public over night. About one-third have been erected by CCC workers."[38] The Civilian Conservation Corps (CCC) had also helped to build new paths for tourists in Mammoth Cave.[39] By the mid-1930s projects constructed with Public Works Administration (PWA) funds were beginning to attract tourists. Describing the various sights that large numbers of summer vacationers were visiting that summer, a reporter for the *New York Times* remarked that "dotting the Southern and Western itineraries are the great PWA projects—Muscle Shoals, Norris, Grand Coulee and Bonneville Dam, the Tennessee Valley development, the great Navajo erosion and reclamation project in Arizona and New Mexico, the incredible Boulder Dam. . . . Each will be a mecca for the traveler, who needs only a glance at a map to see how neatly one or more will fit into nearly almost any trip."[40]

Both statistical and anecdotal evidence thus reveals that vacationing during the depression remained a viable alternative across much of the social spectrum. While those standing in bread lines obviously could not indulge in vacations, people of moderate means could, and did. In fact, the 1930s witnessed the possibility of vacationing expanding to new sectors of the population as policies granting paid vacations to industrial laborers finally reached the majority of wage earners.

During the 1920s businessmen had begun to discuss the issue of paid vacations for factory workers, and a small number of progressive companies had started to implement policies offering vacations with pay to their industrial laborers. The early years of the depression, however, brought a temporary setback for the paid vacation movement. Some employers, faced with a glut of unemployed workers and therefore unconcerned about maintaining the loyalty of their labor force, rescinded their vacation plans. A 1932 study prepared by the Industrial Bureau of the Merchant's Association of New York surveyed 273 firms—including manufacturers, wholesale and retail establishments, banking and investment houses, insurance companies, contractors, and builders. Seventy-four of the companies altered their vacation policies in the hopes of economizing and weathering the financial crisis. The changes, not surprisingly, limited vacationing privileges either by "requiring employees to accept vacations at a fraction of their scheduled salary rates, imposing additional vacations without pay, or requiring that regular vacations be taken without pay." These businesses curtailed the vacations of their hourly workers but usually left the vacations of salaried workers intact.[41]

A 1935 study by the National Industrial Conference Board found similar results. Half of the 274 companies surveyed retained their vacation plans throughout the depression, 87 suspended their policies, 10 discontinued paid vacations, 28 companies initially cancelled vacations for workers but by 1935 had already reinstated them, and 13 companies established new vacation plans between 1932 and 1935. What seems most compelling about these data are not the numbers of workers who lost their vacations, but the numbers who, despite the depression, retained them. Of the 274 companies studied, 177—employing nearly a million workers—had some sort of vacation plan.[42]

This study showed how "firmly established" vacation policies had become, and revealed, as well, an important new trend among American businesses. Not only had "nearly one quarter of the suspended plans" been reinstated by 1935, but "the rate of establishment of new plans was increasing."[43] By the mid-1930s companies were expressing renewed interest in the issue of paid vacations. Numerous major corporations either introduced vacation plans for factory workers or began seriously to consider doing so. In 1936 five large iron and steel companies—"controlling about 60% of the industry's tonnage"—offered paid vacations to hourly wage earners. The steel companies joined corporations such as DuPont, General Foods, Standard Oil, Armour, and Proctor and Gamble in establishing vacation policies. The plans varied. Republic Steel insisted upon an "unbroken service record with the Corporation or Subsidiaries for five years or more preceding May 1, 1936" for an employee to be eligible for one week's paid vacation, while Standard Oil required only "completion of one year" before awarding a week's paid vacation. Some companies established different criteria for male and female employees. At Armour and Company, male employees needed five years' service before qualifying for a week's vacation, while female employees needed only to have worked for three years.[44]

In 1937 the U.S. Bureau of Labor Statistics canvased 90,000 firms and discovered that, despite the temporary setback in the early years of the depression, "the number of plants and wage earners working under paid vacations plans [had] tripled" since 1934. The vast majority (70%) of the companies that offered paid vacations initiated those policies between 1930 and 1937. Despite the continuation of hard economic times, more than 3,300,000 wage earners were by 1937 working with vacation plans.[45]

Why did industry choose this moment to make paid vacations a reality for so many workers? Little encouragement came from government. By 1936 the Department of Labor had established a Committee on Vacations with Pay. Chaired by the State Labor Commissioner from Connecticut, the committee included national legislative representatives from two rail unions, Mary Pidgeon of the Women's Bureau, and Ruth Scandrett of DOL's Division of Labor Standards. In a report to the Third Annual National Conference on Labor Legislation in 1936, the committee shamefully contrasted the absence of a national policy on vacations in the United States to the thirty countries that "have laws under which some groups of workers enjoy the benefits of annual vacations with pay" and recommended that the Secretary of Labor promote such legislation and "draft a bill on vacation with pay for the use of States in furthering such legislation."[46] Despite such suggestions, no such legislation was forthcoming.

The major impetus for extension of paid vacations to wage earners came not from government, but from industry itself. Employers who instituted vacation plans were looking to company interests in an environment of growing union strength and increasing government regulation. In the years following the passage of the National Industrial Recovery Act more companies began to consider instituting personnel and management programs that would co-opt union demands. Such efforts increased in the wake of the Wagner Act and the successful union organizing of the mid-1930s. During the last half of the decade significantly more companies created personnel departments, established bureaucratic hiring and promotion policies, and offered welfare benefits such as pension programs, profit sharing, health insurance, and paid vacations.[47] The latter was, perhaps, one of the most attractive from the company's vantage point. Since rested workers, many experts argued, were more efficient, vacation policies promised benefits for employers in the form of increased worker productivity. But as a result, paid vacations were still initiated selectively. Seasonal industries, or those in which workers changed jobs frequently, for example, rarely established vacation plans. The efficiency boost promised by vacations could occur, employers argued, only when applied to employees who worked continuously. Those companies that instituted paid vacations did so in the hopes that these policies would increase profits by returning a more productive labor force while simultaneously demonstrating "the employer's interest in his workers' welfare." For many employers paid vacations figured as a financially advantageous means of appeasing workers at a time when labor was successfully flexing its muscle.[48]

Historian Donna Allen has persuasively argued that organized labor played an important but indirect role in this process. It is certainly no coincidence that major corporations instituted vacation policies at the same moment when unions were striking and organizing successfully. The steel industry, for example, began to offer workers paid vacations as the Steel Workers' Organizing Committee reached the height of its unionization drive.[49] But union demands did not compel industries to implement paid vacations. In fact, organized labor continued, as it had in the early part of the century, to display little interest in the issue of vacations. Unions were concerned primarily with regularizing work and ending the periods of cyclical unemployment that still plagued workers in many industries. Vacations, they reasoned, made little sense for those who could not be guaranteed a full year's work and a full year's pay.[50] Moreover, workers understood all too well what motivated most employers to establish vacation coverage. Vacation plans were not initiated to reward employees for good service or to promote employee well-being, but to improve workers' productivity. As Allen has explained, "workers were not likely to take paid vacation plans to their hearts" as long as companies initiated such policies primarily to increase profits. Unions preferred to concentrate their efforts on campaigns for guaranteed work, higher wages, shorter hours, and union recognition.[51]

A few high-profile union contracts of the mid-1930s did include vacation provisions. An agreement between Sinclair Oil Company and the International Association of Oil Field, Gas Well, and Refinery Workers, for example, brought paid vacations to fifteen thousand oil workers in 1934, and the Teamsters concluded numerous local agreements that provided vacations for its members.[52] But most vacation plans that appeared in union agreements during this period either originated with management or were already part of existing company policies.[53] The decision to extend vacations to industrial workers came primarily from businesses hoping simultaneously to increase the bottom line while forestalling union organizing.

As a result of these new company policies, fully half of the American industrial workers came to enjoy the privilege of paid vacations during the 1930s. By the eve of World War II vacationing was well on its way to becoming a mass phenomenon.

The arrival of mass vacations did not signal the end of American anxieties about leisure. The long-standing ambivalence about vacationing persisted even as the numbers of vacationers climbed. The depression complicated the issues that a growing consumer culture had been raising since the late nineteenth century and helped to initiate a larger cultural discussion about leisure.

By the early 1930s the traditional balance between work and leisure looked as though it had been fundamentally altered. Where once workers labored long hours to fill the needs of an expanding economy, now America appeared to be producing too much. Production was outstripping demand, companies were laying off workers, and much of the population was cutting back on consumption. As armies of the unemployed found themselves with an excess of unwanted leisure, social scientists, government and political figures, and journalists began to confront a startling new reality: people needed to work less.

Estimates of how much less varied. Organized labor favored a thirty-hour work week. Sharing the work, union leaders had long argued, would end unemployment and offer workers well-deserved leisure as well as economic security.[54] Others suggested even more radical reductions. Writing for *Harper's Magazine* in 1931, Henry Pratt Fairchild maintained: "It is quite a conservative estimate that if all our productive plant were operated [sic] at its maximum efficiency we could turn out more goods than we know how to dispose of wisely with an average working day for all the available labor of not more than four hours."[55] Although some legislators joined labor and pushed for shorter hours, President Roosevelt never felt comfortable with the idea. He preferred to find ways to keep people at work through federally funded public works projects. Work hours declined during the depression, but not as much as some feared or others hoped. Codes established by the National Recovery Administration (NRA) generally set a forty-hour work week, reducing by about one fifth the average number of hours worked during the 1920s. In 1937 the Fair Labor Standards Act made the forty-hour week the norm.[56]

Although opinions diverged on the exact amount of leisure that the future held, few doubted that work time would decline and leisure time would expand. Sociologists, economists, journalists, and educators sprung immediately into action, spilling oceans of ink that addressed the "problem" of the "new leisure."[57] The shift from a culture focused on production and work to one centered around consumption and leisure had been engaging Americans since the late nineteenth century, with some bemoaning the change and others celebrating it.[58] The Great Depression, however, demanded and received a new, more critical examination of work. Labor in the endless pursuit of wealth, many social commentators acknowledged, was not only outdated but potentially dangerous to the welfare of the nation. Most conceded the need to reorder long-standing mandates about the importance of work and production. "Industry and thrift have outlived their pristine usefulness, and ought to be put on part time," wrote one critic.[59] People needed, instead, to learn how to be at leisure.

The problem took on increasing significance because the masses, not only the middle or upper class, now had significant amounts of leisure at their disposal. Supervising such leisure assumed the proportion of a national problem as play became a serious subject, demanding the attention of both scholars and policymakers. In 1933 Grover Whalen, New York City's chairman of the President's Emergency Re-employment Campaign, formed a committee of nationally known educators, lawyers, recreation workers, and journalists to study the issue. Whalen explained why the committee was essential: "With hundreds of thousands of workers all over the United States about to experience a sudden shortening of their working week, due to the NRA, giving them in many cases as high as thirty-five additional hours of leisure, the work of this new committee assumes top rank in importance."[60] Well-known educator Nicholas Murray Butler cautioned that "the hand worker should not only be offered leisure but should be guided toward its interesting and helpful use."[61]

Even though fears of a leisured working class troubled many, the "problem of the new leisure" was not, most critics agreed, confined to any one group on the social spectrum. Both the middle and working class alike, rather, were directed to put leisure to some form of self-improvement. The endorsements of leisure that filled the popular press usually came with qualifiers and warnings—increased leisure did not mean license to indulge in any sort of pleasure. In his 1934 book, *The Challenge of Leisure*, Arthur Pack advocated "the pursuit of constructive leisure," suggesting "activities affording satisfaction to creative impulses." He advised active, participatory forms of recreation rather than passive ones: better, for example, to learn to play golf than to watch a baseball game; to take up painting or sculpture than attend the movies; to participate in an amateur dramatic production than listen to the radio.[62]

Many commentators feared that commercialized pleasures—the movie theater and the football stadium—would consume the ever-growing number of leisure hours. Americans might be content to fill their days with what one writer called "the most trivial kind of satisfaction."[63] An article in *Collier's* cautioned: "The hardest work many of us have to do is to decide what to do when we are not working. We have not learned how to use our leisure pleasantly and profitably."[64] Agreeing with those who found "the mass production of pleasure . . . a dreary thing," Walter Lippmann cautioned that "in seeking to be happy simply by ministering to our appetites we subject ourselves to the cruelest and most ironical disappointments. We may get what we wanted; likely as not we shall not want it when we have it." The answer to the problem, for Lippmann, lay not in collective attempts to reform leisure but in each individual's search for a spiritual "unity and peace"—a way "to absorb this free energy so that it intensifies rather than fights against the order of our being."[65]

In this new, leisure-filled world, children would have to be taught not only how to work, but how to play. Since "the best recreation is that which contributes to the development of the individual," it was necessary "to prepare for leisure . . . in youth." A writer for *Collier's* advised parents to "teach your children how to employ their free time fruitfully as well as to work competently and you will add measurably to their chances of happiness.[66] Similarly, an article in *The Survey* predicted "that the problem of the future will be lessened if attention is focused upon helping youth to form habits in the use of leisure that will carry over into their mature years."[67] Children and adults alike heard advice about pursuing hobbies, taking up avocations, and learning to excel at sports. As the amount of leisure time increased and the population with access to leisure grew, having fun assumed a more serious and important function in American culture.

While those who addressed the problem of the new leisure thought about it primarily in terms of extra hours each day rather than extended periods spent away from work, their ideas both influenced and reflected attitudes about vacations. In fact, the conversation about vacations paralleled the discussion of the new leisure. Recognizing that, despite the reduction in work hours, vacationing continued to be a popular and viable American pastime, newspapers and mass market magazines offered lots of vacation advice. Foremost was the suggestion that readers *not* let the depression render them "vacationless."

Millions of depression-era people who continued to vacation would have been following the recommendations found in their daily newspapers and mass market magazines. Some advised hard-pressed men and women to make the best of a "stay-at-home" vacation by enjoying public parks, municipal swimming pools, community golf courses, and backyard barbecues.[68] Many others offered a variety of suggestions for finding ways to leave home despite the financial problems that beset families and communities.

Given the current economic problems, some argued, vacations had, in fact, become more rather than less important. Writing in *Ladies Home Journal* in 1930, Clara Ingram Johnson asked a question that might have been plaguing many American families: "With every department of the family budget clamoring for cash, should one spend for such an unessential as a vacation?" The answer was clear: "Indeed you should! Let the house go a bit; . . . Save nickels and dimes from food and clothing; get your vacations, and never, never say they are not important. They are."[69] Leon Meadow, the financial editor of *Popular Science Monthly*, believed that since the chaotic condition of the economy had made a mockery of efforts at sound financial decisions, a vacation might be the best investment a prudent person could make: "The man who wants to make an investment right now had best forget the market for the present and turn to something that can directly and indirectly lead to greater profits for him. . . . The best thing he can do is to follow my own plan—an investment I'm so sold on. I'm buying some of it tomorrow when I start on my vacation." Investing in a vacation would yield "rebounding health and a return to calm, clear, normal thinking." The vacationer would arrive home "all set to weather out any depression, to come back to [the] job and [any] investment problem in a better frame of mind."[70] Amidst so much insecurity, investing in yourself seemed a sure thing.

Johnson and Meadows offered such counsel in the early years of the depression. Even as the economic crisis persisted, the popular press continued to endorse vacations, recommending various ways to manage a vacation during hard times. The family car, many felt, provided the ideal vacation vehicle. A 1932 article in *Ladies Home Journal* encouraged women to "pack up your family and go!": "Who said this was a 'stay-at-home year'?" Conditions were, in fact, optimal for a motoring vacation: "With roads and highways better than they have ever been before? With gas and oil at present prices? With every trail and highway dotted with comfortable camps? . . . When you can plan any kind of family motoring vacation to fit any amount of time or any amount of money?" The author advised readers to travel light, start early in the morning, and not try to cover too many miles per day (250 optimally, 400 maximum). Those who craved beautiful scenery, for example, should head west. Vacationers could enjoy Yosemite for "1.50 per day—per night, one should say—in a tent without meals," or for "a few extra shillings, . . . [in] a bungalow." Camping by the side of the road or at one of the numerous municipal or private camps would afford the cheapest vacation. Realizing, however, that for many women vacation was "spelled h-o-t-e-l," the author suggested the "chains of little hotels and tourist homes" throughout the West and South, some of which charged as little as a dollar or two "for the night and breakfast for two."[71]

Eleanor Roosevelt joined the chorus of those recommending various sorts of vacations to depression-era families. In a 1934 column for *Women's Home Companion*, she explained that "many people this year may be in greater doubt than ever before as to what they can afford to do in the way of vacation which will give them a needed rest and change yet conform to the family budget." The first lady passed on other readers' suggestions of successful but inexpensive vacations. One family, for example, traveled only as far as the "nearest state park, where they rented a tent on the shore of the lake," buying their groceries from a nearby farm "at a very modest price." Fishing and swimming in the lake, hiking, lying in the sun, reading, writing, and sleeping furnished relaxation and enjoyment. Roosevelt claimed that "two weeks of this existence will cost you, I am sure, no more than you would spend on living expenses at home." She understood, however, that camping had its hardships: "[Y]ou may find your first day or two a little difficult, [but] when you become accustomed to camp life I am sure you will look back even on the rainy days, when you had to eat under the flap of your tent and devote your time to reading or writing, as a very pleasant memory." Roosevelt fully realized that such suggestions "may be of little use to many people." She addressed an audience that included "primarily . . . those who get two weeks' holiday a year and who need to build up health and resistance in that time to cover the other fifty weeks."[72]

Although the press recommended that people continue to take vacations, the advice had changed in ways that reflected the new and difficult economic conditions. Editors and writers no longer published stories about the pleasures of a vacation spent picking strawberries or haying. During a depression people rarely need to be reminded of the value of work. In the 1930s, when paid labor was scarce, few would have advocated income-earning work as a form of recreation. People who could afford a vacation would likely not have considered taking work away from someone who needed it.

While the 1930s saw few recommendations for a working vacation, most who tackled the topic of vacations agreed that vacations be neither trivial nor worthless. Like the "new leisure," vacations needed to serve a useful purpose. While advocates continued to emphasize the importance of vacations in restoring health and energy, they focused increasingly on using the time for personal growth and self-improvement. "The right vacation often matches you against something hard to do. And when you win, it's a real victory," stated a writer for the *Ladies Home Journal* in 1931. Any number of challenges would do: "Bicycle through a state that's new to you. . . . Learn something you've never had time to take up. Golf with a professional. . . . Organize a group of your friends to spend the vacation rehearsing a play. . . . Camp in a hut high up on a mountain with no soft food or civilized luxuries except what you pack up the trail yourself on your back."[73]

The public press particularly favored vacations put to intellectual and artistic uses. Writing for the *Delineator* in May of 1931, William Lyon Phelps asked why vacationing required people to "check all mental growth?" "Why not, even if we travel abroad, or go into the Canadian woods, or camp in Wyoming, or stay at home, why not continue to enjoy mental activity?"[74] The following month an editorial in *Nature Magazine* similarly asked: "Must the mind also be on vacation?" Agreeing that holidays should remain a matter of personal taste, the writer still maintained that vacations should offer more than recreation and physical renewal. The ideal vacation should "outlast the tan, . . . [and] endure by virtue of some inspiration, some new knowledge, some idea that it has left one with." Those whose vacations exposed them to the beauties of nature should, for example, do more than simply gaze at the scenery. Trips organized by the American Nature Association offered vacationers "a real appreciation of how these scenic glories came about, what treasures of wild life they hold." The editor cautioned: "Holiday hours are too valuable to be wasted, life is too fleeting to let moments of leisure be frittered away. It's worthwhile to get something from your holiday."[75] A 1935 editorial in the *New York Times* advised people to "travel as widely as your means allow." The purpose of such travel, however, should be "to look into things but never merely to look at them."[76]

While many people certainly continued to use their vacations for nothing more edifying than recreation and relaxation, contemporaries commented on the numbers of depression-era vacationers who displayed a lively interest in artistic and intellectual pursuits. In June of 1935 the *New York Times* reported that "summer resorts, to which thousands will be traveling by the end of the coming week, are rapidly changing in character. . . . Their interests are shifting from the purely physical and sporting—outstanding characteristics of ten years ago—and turning toward the cultural and esthetic."[77] Summer resorts, for example, became popular places for the arts. New theaters, some of which originated in the "little theater" movement of the 1910s and 1920s, were by the 1930s finding homes at places that drew summer vacationers.[78] Cape Cod sported a number of these—the Little Theatre at Provincetown, the Beach Theatre at West Falmouth, the Cape Playhouse at Dennis.[79] The *New York Times* reported in June of 1933 that "this season there will be scarcely a resort" from Maine to Virginia "which will not boast its troop of modern troubadours or be within driving distance . . . of one."[80]

Resorts sponsored other sorts of arts as well. The summer of 1935 saw a symphony festival in the Berkshires and members of the Boston Symphony Orchestra giving weekly concerts at Lake Placid. Numerous vacation communities sponsored annual art exhibits and "schools of painting also flourish[ed] in the resorts."[81] These culturally oriented vacation activities and projects reflected a revived interest in the arts that the depression had helped to inaugurate. The federal government's efforts to support unemployed artists resulted in the Federal Arts Project, a program that brought a variety of affordable artistic and cultural events to a depression-era public.[82]

Vacationers displayed interest in intellectual as well as artistic endeavors. Historian Joseph Kett has explored the widespread concern with adult education during the 1930s. According to Kett, Americans "crowded libraries and attended forums in order to understand the roots of the catastrophe."[83] Some of this learning occurred during summer vacations. In July of 1930 the *New York Times Magazine* reported that "of all American Summer resorts, none probably is more widely popular than the classroom." The writer maintained that while "beach, mountains and lake may draw their thousands, . . . it is doubtful whether any of them has a steadier or more rapidly increasing clientele than the university campus."[84] A gross exaggeration, the article nevertheless pointed to an important phenomenon—the growing numbers of adults who chose to spend their vacations in a variety of summer education programs.

The general depression-era discussion of the problems and challenges of the "new leisure" may have influenced the choices of some of these vacationers. Adult summer institutes emerged throughout the country—at Wellesley College in Massachusetts, Vassar College in upstate New York, Lafayette College in Pennsylvania, and the New School for Social Research in New York City.[85] During the summer of 1930 the universities of Iowa and Georgia offered "round tables of public affairs," while Middlebury College in Vermont taught French and Spanish.[86] Those who chose such vacations usually sought neither degrees nor specific work-related skills. As Kett explains, these adults "were motivated far less by job improvement than by eagerness to understand world and national affairs, to work out personal problems, to find new ways to express themselves, and to become socially more acceptable."[87] Students who attended the second annual alumni college at Lafayette College in Pennsylvania could hear lectures on topics as diverse as "The Problems of Industrial Unemployment," "The Comic Spirit in English Drama," and "The Influence of Biology on Modern Thought and Practice."[88]

Self-improvement vacations were of course not new to the 1930s. Chautauqua and its offshoots had since the 1870s been attracting men and women who chose to combine learning and vacationing. The press's attention to cultural events at summer resorts and the increased enrollment at summer institutes during the 1930s spoke to the long-standing American suspicion of idleness set within the specific context of severe economic depression. The suffering of the depression seemed to have added another reason to be wary about vacationing and to have made some vacationers a little more uneasy about the indulgence of time devoted solely to recreation. In July of 1930 the *New York Times* reported, for example, that the mayor had just returned from a six-day vacation spent fishing on Barron Collier's yacht. When a reporter asked if he planned to "take any more vacations this summer," the mayor responded testily: "'No, I don't contemplate any other vacations. Why is it that every one gets excited when I take a few days off like every one of the 120,000,000 people in this country? Why am I not privileged to do that, so long as my official duties are not neglected?'"[89]

Such defensiveness notwithstanding, vacationing not only persisted but increased its hold on the American public during the 1930s. By the end of the decade more Americans than ever before found themselves with time off from work *and* a week's pay in their pockets. At the same time, the public discussion about vacationing continued to reflect a cultural uneasiness with the idea of extended periods devoted solely to leisure or idleness. The depression pushed that discussion in a somewhat different direction. The preoccupation with work that had engaged advocates of vacationing in the early part of the century no longer fit a society in which work was scarce.

But the connection between work and leisure was reshaped rather than discarded during the 1930s. Depression-era Americans continued to receive a message that advised tempering pleasure with productivity. Dr. Walter Eddy, for example, offered a prescription for a successful vacation in the August 1937 issue of *Good Housekeeping.* He recommended trying to "make every hour of the vacation a happy one" and advised readers to "be thoroughly selfish for a few days and consult your own likes and dislikes." Restful sleep was critical to a successful vacation, but achieving that end demanded that the vacationer "get physically and mentally tired, and the best way to do that is to work hard at something that is enjoyable, something that keeps your attention centered on the doing and your mind applauding your efforts."[90] The message was a variation of the one that vacationers had been hearing since the middle of the nineteenth century: take a vacation, relax, and enjoy yourself; but be wary of idleness and try to make your vacation a useful, productive endeavor. The fear of leisure and relaxation—expressed as soon as mid-nineteenth-century middle-class vacationers began traveling to beaches, springs, and mountains—took new forms but endured not only through the 1930s but, I would suggest, until today.

Epilogue

—————◆—————

L ast summer my husband, daughter, and I returned to the family beach house for a two-week vacation. As usual, the number of people staying at the house varied from about a half dozen on quieter week days to as many as eighteen on one very hectic and crowded Saturday night. During our stay we celebrated birthdays for a five-year-old and a ninety-year-old. We also cooked and ate wonderful meals, drank great red wine, went antiquing, took walks along the sea wall, and swam in Long Island Sound. By unanimous consent the beach house contains no television, allowing us to enjoy our evenings with conversation, Scrabble, and books. The important social and cultural work of the family beach house continued as we rehashed old problems, tried to heal old wounds, retold old stories, and remade family ties.

But other sorts of work sometimes intruded. The multitude of vacationers brought with them one laptop computer (I admit, it was mine, but in past years others have brought theirs), one fax machine, and three cellular phones. The FedEx truck arrived almost every day with a package of papers. I recall one specific afternoon when a fax was arriving over the phone line, one person was talking on a cellular phone on the porch, another on a cell phone in the living room, and FedEx was making a delivery. One disgusted relative shook his head and muttered something that sounded like, "whatever happened to vacations?"

Technology has made it too easy to carry our work with us. Indeed, it is getting harder to escape, as pagers and cell phones make their way even onto sailboats and golf courses. Technology, however, does not entirely explain why work intrudes into leisure. We could, after all, choose to leave our cell phones and laptops behind. That many do not speaks to the variety of ways in which leisure and labor remain connected.

For some people, the demands of the job require that they make themselves available even while on vacation. Executives, for example, feel they need to be reached in case of a crisis in the company. Small entrepreneurs contact their offices out of fear that their absence will ruin a potential sale or discourage a new client. Employees in a variety of businesses are being asked to use fax and phones to keep in touch with offices or customers. While for these vacationers work is often an unwelcome intrusion, others clearly choose to bring work with them. Some find work more fun or more rewarding than anything a vacation might offer. Simply put, they like to work. Others may use work as a way of avoiding the family and social demands that a vacation presents.

While work that spills over into leisure was not a problem that our forbears faced, America's contemporary vacation habits nevertheless reveal the legacy of the nineteenth century—particularly its discomfort with and suspicion of leisure. Consider, for example, the relatively limited amount of time that Americans spend vacationing. Up until about ten years ago most companies allowed workers two weeks of paid vacation a year. Employees with more than five years of service sometimes earned an additional week. Recently vacation policies have liberalized somewhat. According to a report in the *Washington Post*, about half of large firms now "start workers at three paid weeks of vacation, with the other half clinging to the old two-week standard."[1] By comparison, most Europeans enjoy between four and six weeks of vacation, and in many countries these provisions are written into law.[2] American vacations are set not by national standards but by company policy or union agreement, and vary from one industry—even one company—to another. Americans thus enjoy their vacations not as a right of citizenship, but at the discretion of their employers.

The legacy remains not only in how much (or how little) Americans vacation, but in the nature of those vacations. Nineteenth-century vacationers could not so easily bring their work with them, but they often fashioned vacations that served as substitutes for work. Troubled by idleness we, like they, continue to find ways to make our vacations worthwhile endeavors. The vacation industry, savvy to customers' needs and desires, has provided a wide range of vacation possibilities that promise to challenge, instruct, condition, or enlighten.

Disney, with its attention to the interests of a broad cross section of the American population, understands full well the continuing appeal of self-improvement vacations. Its aborted plan to build an American history theme park in the Virginia countryside outside of Washington, D.C., testifies to the company's belief that vacationers want to spend their leisure, and their money, learning about America's past. The effort failed because local residents objected, not because Disney was worried about attendance. If Disney has, for now, abandoned that endeavor, it has found other ways to reap profits from Americans' desire for leisure well spent. Epcot, for example, extends the pleasure of Florida's Disney World beyond rides and meetings with Mickey. The visitor can learn about "the latest gadgets, products and advances in technology," become a world traveler through the eleven countries represented at the World Showcase, and "fathom the mysteries of the deep" at an exhibit called the Living Seas.[3]

Two years ago Disney added "The Disney Institute" to its Florida empire. There guests can structure a vacation devoted to personal enrichment. The Institute offers courses in a variety of categories. A course called "Hidden Treasures," for example, promises a "close up look at the art of Mexico, Morocco, Japan, all the countries of Epcot" and a chance to "learn things you've never known about their traditions, their history and their architecture." Other courses offer help with more personal issues. Those who choose the two-hour workshop called "Time Quest" are taught "the basics of planning, prioritizing and setting value-based goals for [their] personal, professional and academic life." The Institute includes workshops in culinary arts, animation, and gardening. Even canoeing is presented as more than just amusement: "You'll be challenged to improve your wildlife watching skills and canoe talents."[4]

These examples could be multiplied numerous times. Elderhostel provides "educational adventures all over the world to adults aged 55." Participants can "study the literature of Jane Austen in the White Mountains of New Hampshire, or travel to Greece to explore the spectacular art and architecture of its ancient civilization, or conduct field research in Belize to save the endangered dolphin population."[5] Outward Bound runs five wilderness schools in the United States where it offers courses "designed to help people develop confidence, compassion, and appreciation for selfless service to others, and a lasting relationship with the natural environment." The overall purpose is more than mere amusement: "The most important lesson you will learn is that you can overcome the limitations that hesitance and fear of failure place on each of us. If you can learn to navigate a sailboat, you can learn to master the tasks that you face every day."[6] A company called IST Cultural Tours offers trips to exotic places led by erudite specialists, while Canyon Ranch promises vacationers that they can not only "experience the great feeling of healthy living" but can "learn how to live that way every day."[7] Both by choice as well as by compulsion, Americans inject work into play.

How many of us have dragged our children (or remember being dragged by our parents) on instructive and culturally enriching vacations? The American tourists who run themselves ragged visiting European museums and churches, the families who journey to Washington, D.C., and tramp through the Smithsonian museums and government buildings, and the vacationers who (even if they leave their laptops at home) try to take at least one serious book with them to the beach are all finding ways to make leisure useful and productive. Certainly not everybody chooses these options, but enough people do to suggest that frivolous amusement and idleness are still suspect among many Americans. Labor and leisure, in some ways at odds with each other, continue to overlap. The tension between work and play with which American culture struggled in the nineteenth century and early twentieth century has taken on some new guises, but flourishes still.

Notes

--------◆--------

List of abbreviations used in notes.

CHSS   Collection of City Historian, Saratoga Springs, New York

CHT   Smith Memorial Library, Chautauqua Institution, Chautauqua, New York

DOL   U.S. Department of Labor, Washington, D.C.

GBR   The Greenbrier, White Sulphur Springs, West Virginia

HSSS   Historical Society of Saratoga Springs, Saratoga Springs, New York

MMH   Mohonk Mountain House Archives, New Paltz, New York

NA   National Archives, Washington, D.C.

NCR   Archives of the National Cash Register Company, Dayton, Ohio

NMAH   National Museum of American History

NYHS   New-York Historical Society, New York, New York

NYPUB   New York Public Library, New York, New York

NYSHA   New York State Historical Association, Cooperstown, New York

NYSL   New York State Library, Albany, New York

SLV   State Library of Virginia, Richmond, Virginia

SSPL   Saratoga Springs Public Library, Saratoga Springs, New York

UVA   Special Collections, Alderman Library, University of Virginia

VHS   Virginia Historical Society, Richmond, Virginia

Introduction

1. See Mary P. Ryan, *The Cradle of the Middle Class: The Family in Oneida County, New York, 1790–1865* (New York: Cambridge University Press, 1981); Stuart Blumin, *The Emergence of the Middle Class: Social Experience in the American City, 1760–1900* (New York: Cambridge University Press, 1989); Olivier Zunz, *Making America Corporate, 1870–1920* (Chicago: University of Chicago Press, 1990); Alfred D. Chandler, Jr., *The Visible Hand: The Managerial Revolution in American Business* (Cambridge, Mass.: Harvard University Press, 1977).

2. Blumin, *Emergence of the Middle Class*; Richard L. Bushman, *The Refinement of America: Persons, Houses, Cities* (New York: Alfred A. Knopf, 1992).

3. See, for example, Roy Rosenzweig, *Eight Hours for What We Will: Workers and Leisure in an Industrial City, 1870–1920* (Cambridge: Cambridge University Press, 1983); Kathy Peiss, *Cheap Amusements: Working Women and Leisure in Turn-of-the-Century New York* (Philadelphia: Temple University Press, 1986); Richard Butsch, ed., *For Fun and Profit: The Transformation of Leisure into Consumption* (Philadelphia: Temple University Press, 1990).

4. There is a huge literature on Puritanism. I have benefited particularly from Stephen Innes's recent insightful book. Stephen Innes, *Creating the Commonwealth: The Economic Culture of Puritan New England* (New York: Norton, 1995), 113 and passim.

5. Innes, *Creating the Commonwealth*, 118, 140, 147–48.

6. Bruce C. Daniels, *Puritans at Play: Leisure and Recreation in Colonial New England* (New York: St. Martin's Press, 1995), ch. 4; Edmund S. Morgan, "Puritan Hostility to the Theatre," *Proceedings of the American Philosophical Society* 110 (October 1966): 341.

7. Daniel T. Rodgers, *The Work Ethic in Industrial America, 1850–1920* (Chicago: University of Chicago Press, 1974), 6.

8. This discussion of republicanism benefits from the work of Gordon S. Wood, *The Radicalism of the American Revolution* (New York: Alfred A. Knopf, 1991).

9. Wood, *Radicalism of the American Revolution*, 278. See also Bushman, *Refinement of America*, ch. 6.

10. Wood, *Radicalism of the American Revolution*, 285; Rodgers, *Work Ethic in Industrial America*, 10–11. Ronald G. Walters, *American Reformers, 1815–1860* (New York: Hill and Wang, 1978), 82–83.

11. Rodgers, *Work Ethic in Industrial America*, xii–xiii, ch. 1.

12. Paul M. Gaston, *The New South Creed: A Study in Southern Mythmaking* (New York: Alfred A. Knopf, 1970), 107–13.

13. Thorstein Veblen, *The Theory of the Leisure Class* (New York: Penguin Books, 1967, first published 1899).

14. Bushman, *Refinement of America*, 219; Rodgers, *Work Ethic in Industrial America*, 10–11.

15. Jeanne Boydston, *Home and Work: Housework, Wages, and the Ideology of Labor in the Early Republic* (New York: Oxford University Press, 1990).

16. There is a large literature on the role and place of middle-class women in the nineteenth century. For a good synthesis see Sara Evan, *Born for Liberty: A History of Women in America* (New York: Free Press, 1989), 130–43.

Chapter 1

1. Elihu Hoyt, Journal of a Tour of Saratoga Springs, 6 August 1827, typescript, HSSS. (Consulted photocopy of this material found in the collection of Field Horne in Saratoga Springs, N.Y.)

2. Carl Bridenbaugh, ed., *Gentleman's Progress: The Itinerarium of Dr. Alexander Hamilton, 1744* (Chapel Hill: University of North Carolina Press, 1948); Barbara G. Carson, "Early American Tourists and the Commercialization of Leisure," in *Of Consuming Interest: The Styles of Life in the Eighteenth Century*, ed. Cary Carson et. al. (Charlottesville: University Press of Virginia, 1994), 373–405.

3. Carson, "Early American Tourists," 383–89.

4. Richard L. Bushman, *The Refinement of American Culture: Persons, Houses, Cities* (New York: Alfred A. Knopf, 1992).

5. Carl Bridenbaugh, "Colonial Newport at a Summer Resort," *Rhode Island Historical Society Collections* 26 (January 1933): 1–23.

6. Carl Bridenbaugh, "Baths and Watering Places of Colonial America," *William and Mary Quarterly* 3 (April 1946): 151–81; Carson, "Early American Tourists," 373–405.

7. Paul P. Bernard, *Rush to the Alps: The Evolution of Vacationing in Switzerland* (New York: Columbia University Press, 1978) 72–75. See also James Walvin, *Beside the Seaside: A Social History of the Popular Seaside Holiday* (London: Penguin Books, 1978).

8. Walvin, *Beside the Seaside*, 14.

9. Bernard, *Rush to the Alps*, 75–76; Walvin, *Beside the Seaside*, 15.

10. Quoted in Bridenbaugh, "Baths and Watering Places," 161.

11. Philip Hone, *The Diary of Philip Hone, 1828–1851*, ed. Allan Nevins (New York: Dodd, Mead & Co, 1936), 74. In the late 1840s and again during the 1850s, George Templeton Strong, another elite New Yorker, planned to take his wife to West Point in the hopes of avoiding the cholera epidemic that threatened the city that summer. George Templeton Strong, *The Diary of George Templeton Strong* (New York: MacMillan, 1952), 2:177.

12. Charles Francis Adams, *Diary of Charles Francis Adams*, ed. Aida DiPace Donald and David Donald (Cambridge, Mass: Harvard University Press, 1968), 4:317.

13. Patricia Click, *The Spirit of the Times: Amusements in Nineteenth-Century Baltimore, Norfolk, & Richmond* (Charlottesville: University Press of Virginia, 1989), ch. 6; Charlene Boyer Lewis, "Ladies and Gentlemen on Display: Planter Society at the Virginia Springs, 1790–1860" (Ph.D. diss., University of Virginia, 1997); Albert Virgil House, ed., *Planter Management and Capitalism in Ante-Bellum Georgia: The Journal of Hugh Fraser Grant, Ricegrower* (New York: Columbia University Press, 1954), 106–7.

14. For a discussion of nineteenth-century medicine see James Bordley III and A. McGehee Harvey, *Two Centuries of American Medicine, 1776–1976* (Philadelphia: W.B. Saunders, 1976); Richard Shryock, *Medicine and Society in America, 1660–1860*

(New York: New York University Press, 1960); William G. Rothstein, *American Physicians in the Nineteenth Century: From Sects to Science* (Baltimore: Johns Hopkins University Press, 1972).

15. See Susan E. Cayleff, *Wash and Be Healed: The Water-Cure Movement and Women's Health* (Philadelphia: Temple University Press, 1987); Harvey Green, *Fit for America: Health, Fitness, Sport and American Society* (Baltimore: Johns Hopkins University Press, 1986); Jane B. Donegan, *"Hydropathic Highway to Health": Women and Water-Cure in Antebellum America* (New York: Greenwood Press, 1986).

16. James Gregory, *A Dissertation on the Influence of a Change of Climate in Curing Diseases*, trans. William P.C. Barton, M.D. (Philadelphia: Thomas Dobson, 1815), 18–19; James B. Clark, *The Influence of Climate in the Prevention and Cure of Chronic Diseases* (London: Thomas and George Underwood, 1829), 8–9. Although Clark was British, he was quoted in American publications—for example, "The Medical Philosophy of Travelling," *United States Democratic Review* 13 (July 1843): 51–70. See also A.P. Buchan, *A Treatise on Sea Bathing* (London: T. Cadell and W. Davies, 1810), Green, *Fit for America*, chs. 3, 4.

17. Robley Dunglison, *On the Influence of Atmosphere and Locality; Change of Air and Climate; Seasons; Food; Clothing; Bathing; . . . etc. etc. on Human Health; Constituting Elements of Hygiene* (Philadelphia: Carey, Lea & Blanchard, 1835), 152. See also Gregory, *Influence of Climate*, 18–19, 21–22, 49.

18. For more on hydropathy see Cayleff, *Wash and Be Healed* and Donegan, *"Hydropathic Highway to Health."*

19. John Bell, *The Mineral and Thermal Springs of the United States and Canada* (Philadelphia: Parry and McMillan, 1855), 17–18. (Bell's book was initially published in 1831, republished in 1850 under the title *A Treatise on Baths* and then published again in 1855 under the title *The Mineral and Thermal Springs of the United States and Canada.*) See also Henry Huntt, *A Visit to the Red Sulphur Spring of Virginia, During the Summer of 1837: With Observations on the Waters* (Boston: Dutton and Wentworth, 1839) 3; also Donegan, *"Hydropathic Highway to Health,"* 5.

20. Thomas Goode, *The Invalid's Guide to the Virginia Hot Springs* (Richmond: P.D. Bernard, 1846), 42–58.

21. See George R. Taylor, *The Transportation Revolution, 1815–1860* (New York: Harper Torchbooks, 1968); Carol Sheriff, *The Artificial River: The Erie Canal and the Paradox of Progress, 1817–1962* (New York: Hill and Wang, 1996).

22. "Letter of a Virginian," *Albany Statesman*, 6 September 1820, typescript, McClellan Collection, SSPL.

23. Mr. and Mrs. Sipple, Travel Diary, 1821, NYHS (Consulted typescript of this material found in the collection of Field Horne in Saratoga Springs, N.Y.)

24. Philip Stansbury, *A Pedestrian Tour* (New York: J.D. Myers and W. Smith, 1822), 1884.

25. Hoyt, Journal, 5 August 1827, HSSS (Consulted photocopy of this material found in the collection of Field Horne in Saratoga Springs, N.Y.) During the 1820s Hot Springs, Arkansas, also began to attract guests, until by the early 1830s as many as 400 visitors a year were coming to Hot Springs. Dee Brown, *The America Spa: Hot Springs, Arkansas* (Little Rock: Rose Publishing Company, 1982), 12–13; Ruth Irene Jones, "Hot Springs: Ante-Bellum Watering Place," *Arkansas Historical Quarterly* 14 (spring 1955): 3–31.

26. Marshall Fishwick, *Springlore in Virginia* (Bowling Green, Ohio: Bowling Green State University Popular Press, 1978); Stan Cohen, *Historic Springs of the Virginias: A Pictorial History* (Charleston, W.Va.: Pictorial Histories, 1981).

27. William Stabler to Cousin Sallie [Sallie Stabler Jordan], "7 mos." 1838, Red Sulphur, Jordon and Stabler Family Papers, VHS.

28. Alain Corbin, *The Lure of the Sea: The Discovery of the Seaside in the Western World 1750–1840* (Cambridge: Polity Press, 1994), 164 and passim. For more on the development of the belief in the health benefits of sea bathing, specifically in England, see Walvin, *Beside the Seaside*, ch. 1.

29. George H. Gibson, ed., "William Brobson's Diary, 1825–1828," *Delaware History* 15 (April 1972): 80; George E. Thomas and Carl Doebley, *Cape May: Queen of the Seaside Resorts* (Philadelphia: Art Alliance Press, 1976), 21 and ch. 4; Jeffery M. Dorwart, *Cape May County, New Jersey: The Making of an American Resort Community* (New Brunswick, N. J.: Rutgers University Press, 1992), ch. 4.

30. M.A. DeWolfe Howe, ed., *The Articulate Sisters: Passages from the Journals and Letters of the Daughters of President Josiah Quincy of Harvard University* (Cambridge, Mass.: Harvard University Press, 1946), 52; Hans Huth, *Nature and the American: Three Centuries of Changing Attitudes* (Lincoln: University of Nebraska Press, 1957), 112–14.

31. Richard O'Connor, *The Golden Summers: An Antic History of Newport* (New York: G. P. Putnam's & Sons, 1974), 17.

32. Jane Cary Randolph to Mrs. Randolph Harrison, 25 August 1829, Salt Sulphur Springs, Harrison Family Papers, VHS.

33. George Evelyn Harrison to Anne Harrison Byrd, [date torn], Warm Springs, Va., Francis Otway Byrd Papers, VHS.

34 Mrs. E.M. Grosvenor to Charlottes & Sarah Holcomb, 5 June 1833, Saratoga Springs, FM11336, NYSL (Consulted photocopy of this material found in the collection of Field Horne in Saratoga Springs, N.Y.)

35. Susan Harrison Blain to Randolph Harrison, 16 September 1841, White Sulphur, Harrison Family Papers, VHS. See also Lewis, "Ladies and Gentlemen on Display," 274–76 for a discussion of the public weighings that went on at some springs.

36. Charles R. Irving to Dearest Wife, 1 August 1834, Red Sulphur Springs, Va., Irving Family Papers, VHS. The diary of Edwin B. Jeffress of Charlotte County recorded his travel to various Virginia Springs during the summer of 1852 in search of health. He visited White Sulphur and Rockbridge Alum before heading towards the Healing Springs, the place he called the "Wonder of the Mountains." There, he had heard, "the poor invalids come to bathe and drink to cure everything, you see every kinds of sores, rheumatism & skin diseases, warts & even a man who had no bone in his neck (I was told) and supported his head by lacing up his neck with tape." He noted that he had faith in the water's power to cure "dyspepsia, Rheumatism, and liver complaints &c. It is also very fine for diseases of the skin." Edwin B. Jeffress, Diary, 1 Aug.–12 Sept., 1852, typescript, VHS.

37. "The Medical Philosophy of Travelling," *United States Democratic Review* 13 (July 1843): 51–70. See also Clark, *Influence of Climate*, 11.

38. Anna Eliza Safford, *A Memoir of Daniel Safford* (Boston: American Tract Society, 1861), 297–99.

39. Rutherford B. Hayes, *Diary and Letters of Rutherford Birchard Hayes*, ed. Charles Richard Williams (Columbus: Ohio State Archeological and Historical Society, 1922), 1:202–18.

40. Almira Hathaway Read, "A Visit to Saratoga: 1826," in Genevieve M. Darden, ed. *New York History* 50 (July 1969): 290. As early as 1821 the diary of Mr. and Mrs. Sipple of Milford, Delaware, described the two handsome hotels in Saratoga where they found "people collected from all the states in the Union some from the

West Indies & some from Europe and these of the gayest sort." Sipple, Travel Diary, NYHS.

41. Jason Russell, Journal, 1839, Quoted in J. Almus Russell, "Say Hello to Yesterday" (Bloomsburg, Pa., 1973), typescript, New Hampshire Historical Society, Concord, NH (Consulted photocopy of this material found in the collection of Field Horne in Saratoga Springs, N.Y.)

42. S. Hoffman to Mrs. S. Hoffman, 6 July 1832, White Sulphur, Samuel Hoffman Papers, Swem Library, College of William and Mary, Williamsburg, Va, (Consulted photocopy of this material found at GBR, White Sulphur Springs, W. Va.)

43. F.W. Gilmer to Dear Brother "Peachy," July 1816, Bedford Springs, Pa., Peachy Ridgway Gilmer Papers, VHS; Charles Latrobe, *The Rambler in North America 1822-1823* (London: R.B. Seeley and W. Burnside, 1836) 2:130; John Pendleton Kennedy, Diary, 26 July 1851, West Virginia Collection, University of West Virginia. (Consulted typescript of this material found at GBR, White Sulphur Springs, W.Va.); Samuel Dawson, "High Life At Saratoga—1837," *American Heritage* 18 (June 1967): 107.

44. Blair Bolling, Diary, Vol. 3, 12 August 1839, 23 August 1839, VHS.

45. Robert McCoskry Graham, Diary, 31 July 1848, 2 August 1848, NYHS (Consulted photocopy of this material found in the collection of Field Horne in Saratoga Springs, N.Y.)

46. See chapter 3 for how norms of decorum would continue to be challenged at resorts during the last half of the century.

47. William Stabler to Sallie (Stabler) Jordan, July 1838, Jordan and Stabler Family Papers, VHS.

48. Hoyt, Journal, August 1827, HSSS (Consulted photocopy of this material found in the collection of Field Horne in Saratoga Springs, N.Y.)

49. Dawson, "High Life At Saratoga," 107.

50. Caroline Gilman, *The Poetry of Travel in the U.S.* (New York: S. Colman, 1838), 85–86.

51. For an excellent analysis of this form of amusement see Lewis, "Ladies and Gentlemen on Display," ch. 5.

52. William Hoyt, Jr. "Journey to the Springs, 1846," *Virginia Magazine of History and Biography* 54 (1946): 127–28.

53. Gibson, "Brobson's Diary," 80.

54. Thirteen years later Edmund Canby described his two weeks at Cape May this way: "Spent our time in riding and walking on the fine beach, bathing, playing nine pins, and lolling about." He did not specify whether women and men bathed together or separately. Carol E. Hoffecker, ed., "The Diaries of Edmund Canby, A Quaker Miller, 1822–1848," *Delaware History* 16 (spring/summer 1975): 203. Jeffery Dorwart maintains that at Cape May in the 1840s men and women bathed at separate times of the day, but he offers no sources to substantiate the claim. Dorwart, *Cape May County, New Jersey*, 70–71.

55. Dawson, "High Life At Saratoga," 107.

56. Emily Wheeler, for example, spent a week at Saratoga in early August of 1839 and began each day by walking to the spring to drink the water. The remainder of the day she filled by taking a walk, occasionally going for a ride, reading, and one morning she "went out shopping." Emily Wheeler, Journal, 1–6 August 1839, NYSHA (Consulted photocopy of this material found in the collection of Field Horne in Saratoga Springs, N.Y.)

57. J.K.S. to Dear Charles, 5 September 1834, Red Sweet Springs, Va., Henry

Carrington Papers, VHS. Tableaux vivants were essentially "paintings" created by living people. Those participating would portray a famous event or historical moment by dressing in costume and striking an appropriate pose.

58. Anonymous Diary, 1825, #10351, NYSL (Consulted photocopy of this material found in the collection of Field Horne in Saratoga Springs, N.Y.)

59. Susan Blain to Mr. Mary Harrison, 24 Aug. 1831, White Sulphur Springs, Va., Harrison Family Papers, VHS. For more on these balls see Lewis, "Ladies and Gentlemen on Display."

60. Achille Murat, *A Moral and Political Sketch of the United States of North America* (London: Effingham Wilson, 1833), 358.

61. J.K.S., 5 September 1834, VHS.

62. For a discussion of working-class sports in the early nineteenth century see Elliott Gorn and Warren Goldstein, *A Brief History of American Sports* (New York: Hill and Wang, 1993), ch. 2. For a discussion of the rough sorts of amusements in which men living in rural parts of the Midwest engaged see John Mack Faragher, *Women and Men on the Overland Trail* (New Haven: Yale University Press, 1979), ch. 5.

63. Read, "A Visit to Saratoga," 294.

64. Gibson, "Brobson's Diary," 83.

65. Lewis, "Ladies and Gentlemen on Display," ch. 5.

66. Howe, *The Articulate Sisters*, 50–63.

67. Catharine M. Sedgwick, *Life and Letters of Catharine M. Sedgwick*, ed. Mary E. Dewey (New York: Harper & Bros., 1871), 217, 234–36, 240.

68. Sidney George Fisher, *A Philadelphia Perspective: The Diary of Sidney George Fisher Covering the Years 1834–71*, ed. Nicholas B. Wainwright (Philadelphia: Historical Society of Pennsylvania, 1967), 55–58, 82–83.

69. Hone, *Diary of Philip Hone*, 45–46, 74. Fanny Appleton Longfellow, daughter of banker, manufacturer, and politician Nathan Appleton and wife of Henry Wadsworth Longfellow, spent summers as a young girl in Newport or the Berkshires. After her marriage she and her husband regularly summered together either at Newport or Nahant. Edward Wagenknecht, ed., *Mrs. Longfellow: Selected Letters and Journals of Fanny Appleton Longfellow (1817–1861)* (New York: Longmans, Green and Co., 1956), 52–54, 92, 139–40, 189–90.

70. Adolphus Sterne, *Hurrah for Texas! The Diary of Adolphus Sterne, 1838–1851*, ed. Archie P. McDonald (Waco, Tex.: Texian Press, 1969).

71. Sally and Pamela Brown, *The Diaries of Sally and Pamela Brown, 1832–1838; Hyde Leslie, 1887, Plymouth Notch, Vermont*, ed. Blanche Brown Bryand and Gertrude Elaine Baker (Springfield, Vt.: William L. Bryand Foundation, 1979).

72. Margaret L. Brown, ed., "John Peters' Diary of 1838–41," *Mississippi Valley Historical Review* 21 (1934–35): 529–42.

73. Hezekiah Prince Jr., *Journals of Hezekiah Prince, Jr. 1822–1828* (New York: Crown Publishers, 1965), 313–14.

74. Charles A. Johnson, *The Frontier Camp Meeting: Religion's Harvest Time* (Dallas: Southern Methodist University Press, 1955), 87, 109, 210, and ch. 11; Dickson D. Bruce, *And They All Sang Hallelujah: Plain-Folk Camp-Meeting Religion, 1800–1845* (Knoxville: University of Tennessee Press, 1974), 54; Bernard A. Weisberger, *They Gathered at the River: The Story of the Great Revivalists and Their Impact Upon Religion in America* (Boston: Little, Brown 1958), 37.

75. See chapter 4.

76. William Warren Sweet, *Methodism in American History* (New York: Abingdon Press, 1953), 160; Johnson, *Frontier Camp Meeting*, 70, 85.

77. Bruce, *And They All Sang Hallelujah*, 70.

78. Robert Eden Peyton to My Dear Friend, 23 August 1822, Peyton Family Papers, VHS.

79. Johnson, *Frontier Camp Meeting*, 91–92.

80. Solon J. Buck, ed., "Selections from the Journal of Lucien C. Boynton, 1835–53," *Proceedings of the American Antiquarian Society* 43 (October 1933): 351.

81. Quoted in Johnson, *Frontier Camp Meeting*, 210.

82. Peyton, 23 August 1822, VHS.

83. Johnson, *Frontier Camp Meeting*, 245.

84. Marryat also remarked: "In one quarter the coloured population had collected themselves; their tents appeared to be better furnished and better supplied with comforts than most of those belonging to the whites." Quoted in Johnson, *Frontier Camp Meeting*, 245–46.

85. Peyton, 23 August 1822, VHS.

86. Charles Francis Adams, for example, began a section of his 1823 diary with this heading: "Journal of Vacation spent in Washington in the winter of my Junior year. . . ." Adams, *Diary of Charles Adams*, 1: 9. See also Charlotte L. Forten, *The Journal of Charlotte L. Forten: A Free Negro in the Slave Era*, ed. Ray Allen Billington (New York: Collier Books, 1961), 56, 76; Elizabeth Curtis, comp., *Letters and Journals of William Edmond Curtis* (New York: Eliz. Curtis, 1926), 144, 150.

87. T. Addison Richards, *Appleton's Illustrated Hand-Book of American Travel* (New York: D. Appleton & Co., 1857), 9–10.

88. Richard Henry Dana Jr., *The Journal of Richard Henry Dana, Jr.*, ed. Robert F. Lucid (Cambridge, Mass.: Harvard University Press, 1968), 2:692, 822. See also Hayes, *Diary and Letters*, 1:418.

89. *New York Times*, 6 July 1855, p. 4.

90. *New York Times*, 21 August 1855, p. 1.

91. M.J. Merwin, "The Wilds of Northern New York," *Putnam's Monthly Magazine* 4 (September 1854): 269–70.

92. "Medical Philosophy of Travelling," 51–70.

93. Edward Everett Hale, "Public Amusements and Public Morality," *Christian Examiner* 62 (July 1857): 52.

94. New York City had more than 515,000 people, Philadelphia had over 340,000. J.D.B. DeBow, *Statistical View of the United States* (New York: Normal Ross Publishing, 1990), 192.

95. Foster Rhea Dulles, *America Learns to Play: A History of Popular Recreation, 1607–1940* (New York: D. Appleton-Century Co., 1940); Gorn and Goldstein, *Brief History of American Sports*.

96. Hale, "Public Amusements and Public Morality," 52.

97. On the role that religion played in the process of secularization see Richard Wightman Fox, "The Discipline of Amusement," in *Inventing Times Square: Commerce and Culture at the Crossroads of the World*, ed. William R. Taylor (New York: Russell Sage Foundation, 1991): 84–86.

98. Quoted in Edmund S. Morgan, "Puritan Hostility to the Theatre," *Proceedings of the American Philosophical Society* 110 (October 1966): 341.

99. "Amusements," *New Englander* 9 (August 1851): 347–48.

100. "Amusements," *New Englander* 26 (July 1867): 400–24.

101. R. Laurence Moore, *Selling God: American Religion in the Marketplace of Culture* (New York: Oxford University Press, 1994), 100–102; Fox, "Discipline of Amusement," 90–91.

102. Isaac Mickle, *A Gentleman of Much Promise: The Diary of Isaac Mickle,*

1837–1845, ed. Philip English Mackey (Philadelphia: University of Pennsylvania Press, 1977): 2:252, 359 and passim.

103. Richard Wightman Fox sees ministers, in fact, playing a critical role in helping to make amusements more acceptable. Ministers, he claims, led the way. Wary of danger or sin, parishioners looked to their moral guardians for advice, and some ministers helped to persuade them that "it was all right to embrace the world." Fox, "The Discipline of Amusement," 85. Laurence Moore suggests that rather than taking the lead, religious figures were forced to modify the traditional Protestant opposition to play. Fearful of losing their flock to the temptations of commercial culture and making themselves irrelevant to an increasingly secular urban population, ministers grudgingly learned "to pronounce the word 'leisure' without a grimace." Moore, *Selling God,* 93 and ch. 4.

104. William Ellery Channing, *The Works of William E. Channing, D.D.* (Boston: American Unitarian Association, 1890), 110–12.

105. Channing, *Works,* 110–12.

106. Channing, *Works,* 110.

107. For the Puritan's distaste for the theater see Morgan, "Puritan Hostility to the Theatre," 340–47; Fox, "Discipline of Amusement," 87.

108. "Amusements," *Christian Examiner* 45 (September 1848): 158, 162, 163.

109. Hale, "Public Amusements and Public Morality," 56.

110. "Amusements," *Christian Examiner,* 168; Hale, "Public Amusements," 47–65; Frederic W. Sawyer, *A Plea for Amusements* (New York: Appleton and Co., 1847).

111. Horace Bushnell, *Work and Play* (New York: Charles Scribner's Sons, 1883), 12–20 (specific quotes come from pages 12, 14, 13 in that order).

112. "Amusements," *New Englander,* 9 (August 1851): 347.

113. Bushnell, *Work and Play,* 17, 18.

114. Quoted in Bushman, *Refinement of America,* 330.

115. Bushman, *Refinement of America,* 323.

116. Daniel T. Rodgers, *The Work Ethic in Industrial America* (Chicago: University of Chicago Press, 1974), 96.

117. Henry Ward Beecher, *Addresses to Young Men* (Philadelphia: Henry Altemus Company, 1895); Rodgers, *Work Ethic in Industrial America,* 12–13; Moore, *Selling God,* 95–96; Fox, "Discipline of Amusement," 87–88.

118. Beecher, *Addresses to Young Men,* 9–10.

119. Beecher, *Addresses to Young Men,* 221–59.

120. As historian William McLoughlin explains, Beecher had become "perforce the philosopher of a new leisure class." William G. McLoughlin, *The Meaning of Henry Ward Beecher: An Essay on the Shifting Values of Mid-Victorian America, 1840–1870* (New York: Alfred A. Knopf, 1970), 101, 111.

121. Rodgers, *Work Ethic in Industrial America,* 97–98.

122. Henry Ward Beecher, *Star Papers: or Experiences of Art and Nature* (New York: J.C. Derby, 1855), 262.

123. Beecher, *Star Papers,* 268.

124. Henry Ward Beecher, *Eyes and Ears* (Boston: Ticknor and Fields, 1862), 41–42.

125. According to historian William McLoughlin, Beecher held that "men could only progress when science gave them the knowledge, and technology the leisure, to pursue new studies which would lead to better means of advancing and perfecting the world and its inhabitants." McLoughlin, *Meaning of Henry Ward Beecher,* 110.

126. Rodgers, *Work Ethic in Industrial America,* 97–98.

127. Edmund Morgan, *American Slavery, American Freedom* (New York: Norton, 1975).

128. See Mechal Sobel, *The World They Made Together: Black and White Values in Eighteenth-Century Virginia* (Princeton: Princeton University Press, 1987), ch. 5.

129. David Bertleson, *The Lazy South* (New York: Oxford University Press, 1967), 180.

130. Bertleson, *Lazy South*, 183.

131. Ted Ownby, *Subduing Satan: Religion, Recreation and Manhood in the Rural South, 1865–1920* (Chapel Hill: University of North Carolina Press, 1990), 12.

132. Thomas Wentworth Higginson, "Saints and Their Bodies," *Atlantic Monthly* 1 (March 1858): 582–95; Thomas Wentworth Higginson, "Gymnastics," *Atlantic Monthly* 7 (March 1861): 283–302.

133. As its branches spread across the country over the next half century, the YMCA became one of the most important institutional expressions of muscular Christianity. Moore, *Selling God*, 112–16; Gorn and Goldstein, *Brief History of American Sports*, 81–97.

134. Read, "A Visit to Saratoga," 290.

135. Lewis, "Ladies and Gentlemen on Display," ch. 6.

136. Read, "A Visit to Saratoga," 283–301.

137. The analogy to P.T. Barnum's "museum" may be useful. Barnum maintained an establishment that, he claimed, would provide morally pure family entertainment. People could enjoy theatrical performances in his "lecture room" (as well as gawking at the 619-pound Canadian giant and the midget Tom Thumb) without feeling that they had transgressed spiritual or moral precepts. See Moore, *Selling God*, 107–8; Dulles, *America Learns to Play*, 120–27; Neil Harris, *Humbug: The Art of P.T. Barnum* (Chicago: University of Chicago Press, 1973).

Chapter 2

1. Louisa Roberts, *A Biographical Sketch of Louisa J. Roberts* (Philadelphia: A. J. Ferris, 1895), 155–57.

2. Margery Davies, *Woman's Place is at the Typewriter: Office Work and Office Workers 1870–1930* (Philadelphia: Temple University Press, 1982); Olivier Zunz, *Making America Corporate, 1870–1920* (Chicago: University of Chicago Press, 1990); Cindy Sondik Aron, *Ladies and Gentlemen of the Civil Service: Middle-Class Workers in Victorian America* (New York: Oxford University Press, 1987); Alfred D. Chandler, Jr., *The Visible Hand: The Managerial Revolution in American Business* (Cambridge, Mass.: Belknap Press, 1977); Stuart Blumin, *The Emergence of the Middle Class: Social Experience in the American City, 1760–1900* (New York: Cambridge University Press, 1989); Mary P. Ryan, *The Cradle of the Middle Class: The Family in Oneida County, New York, 1790–1865* (New York: Cambridge University Press, 1981); Richard L. Bushman, *The Refinement of American Culture: Persons, Houses, Cities* (New York: Alfred A. Knopf, 1992).

3. Bruce A. Kimball, *The "True Professional Ideal" in America: A History* (Cambridge, Mass.: Blackwell, 1992), 256–57.

4. Aron, *Ladies and Gentlemen of the Civil Service*, 84–85.

5. When their salaries were combined with "other earnings" the annual income for men increased to $1,231 and for women to $524. Massachusetts Bureau of Statistics of Labor, *Seventh Annual Report* (Boston, 1876), 3, 214, 215, 216.

6. Blumin, *Emergence of the Middle Class*, 271–74.

7. David B. Tyack, *The One Best System: A History of American Urban Education* (Cambridge, Mass.: Harvard University Press, 1975), 62; Kimball, *"True Professional Ideal,"* 262.

8. Blumin, *Emergence of the Middle Class,* 290.

9. For medical concern with these problems see George M. Beard, *American Nervousness: Its Causes and Consequences* (New York: Putnam, 1881); S. Weir Mitchell, *Wear and Tear, or Hints for the Overworked* (Philadelphia: J.B. Lippincott, 1871).

10. George Whitwell Parsons, *The Private Journal of George Whitwell Parsons* (Phoenix, Ariz.: Arizona Statewide Archival and Records Project, 1939), 15.

11. Daniel T. Rodgers, *The Work Ethic in Industrial America 1850–1920* (Chicago: University of Chicago Press, 1974), 105; Aron, *Ladies and Gentlemen of the Civil Service,* 94.

12. *New York Herald,* 21 August 1847, typescript, CHSS. Others made similar observations. In 1847 Sidney George Fisher, a member of wealthy Philadelphia society, complained that despite its fine hotels and excellent bathing, Cape May suffered from "the vulgarity of the society. It is the great resort of the shopkeeping class, who tho respectable are intensely vulgar." Sidney George Fisher, *A Philadelphia Perspective: The Diary of Sidney George Fisher Covering the Years 1834–1871,* ed. Nicholas B. Wainwright (Philadelphia: Historical Society of Pennsylvania, 1967), 197.

13. *New York Times,* 12 August 1852, p. 2.

14. *New York Times,* 1 August 1855, p. 2.

15. *New York Times,* 1 August 1855, p. 2.

16. Columnist "Minnie Myrtle," who usually wrote from the well-established resorts like Saratoga, for example, advised her readers: "If you are 'wilted with Summer heats' and sick from the smell of gas, and have no country seat of your own, nor a father's farm house to flee to, take your carpet bag in your hand and follow the present writer to the Franconia Mountains, where you will be sure of an exhilarating atmosphere and beautiful sights enough to repay you a thousand times for the time and money which their enjoyment costs." *New York Times,* 15 August 1855, p. 2. Another article suggested that not enough people were taking advantage of the nearby Catskills: "It is a wonder people do not know the Catskills better. . . . Do our busy, overworked dwellers in the hot cities know that six or seven hours of pleasant journeying will bring them here into the very solitudes of nature—to pure mountain air and healthy mountain exercise?" *New York Times,* 10 August 1855, p. 2.

17. "Summer Travels in the South," *Southern Quarterly Review* 18 (September 1850): 24. See also T. Addison Richards, "Landscape of the South," *Harper's New Monthly Magazine* 36 (May 1853): 721–33. Some southerners apparently continued to frequent northern watering places. One newspaper article explained that southern visitors at Saratoga would be remaining longer because of the "prevalence of yellow fever in Southern cities." *New York Daily Times,* 7 September 1854, typescript, CHSS.

18. "Summer Travels in the South," 50, 60. Merchants and planters fled the cholera scare in New Orleans for summer homes or "hotels at the various watering places" including West Pascagoula, Pass Christian, Boloxi, Pensacola, Dernier Isle—all of which the *New York Times* characterized as "fine summer resorts" that were "always filled." *New York Times,* 15 June 1852, p. 1.

19. Randal W. McGavock, *Pen and Sword, The Life and Journals of Randal W. McGavock,* ed. Herschel Gower (Nashville: Tennessee Historical Commission, 1960), 427–28.

20. Charlene Boyer Lewis, "Ladies and Gentlemen on Display: Planter Society at the Virginia Springs, 1790–1860" (Ph.D. diss., University of Virginia, 1997).

21. John F. Stover, *American Railroads* (Chicago: University of Chicago Press, 1997), 134.

22. In the 1870s it cost $15 to ride the train from New York to Chicago. Within ten years the price had dropped to $5. Hugh DeSantis, "The Democratization of Travel: The Travel Agent in History," *Journal of American Culture* 1 (spring 1978): 3.

23. *New York Times,* 8 August 1880, p. 5.

24. Charles E. Funnell, *By the Beautiful Sea: The Rise and High Times of That Great American Resort, Atlantic City* (New Brunwsick, N.J.: Rutgers University Press, 1983), 5.

25. Robert S. Conte, *The History of the Greenbrier: America's Resort* (White Sulphur Springs, W. Va.: The Greenbrier, 1989), 75–76.

26. *New York Times,* 10 June 1870, p. 7.

27. The Red Sweet Springs placed an article in the Richmond *Dispatch* in August of 1870 explaining that "passengers can leave here [Richmond] by the Chesapeake and Ohio train on Wednesday, in the morning or the evening, and reach the springs in time for the ball" that was scheduled to take place on Thursday night. *Richmond Dispatch,* 1 August 1870, p. 1. See also J.E. Cooke, "The White Sulphur Springs," *Harper's New Monthly Magazine,* 57 (August 1878): 337–55; Charles H. Jones, *Appletons' Hand-Book of American Travel: Southern Tour* (New York: D. Appleton and Co., 1874), 90–91.

28. *Blue Ridge Springs,* Botetourt Co., Va., 1874, p. 7, UVA.

29. William Cronon, *Nature's Metropolis: Chicago and the Great West* (New York: Norton, 1991), 382–83.

30. Dee Brown, *The America Spa: Hot Springs, Arkansas* (Little Rock: Rose Publishing Company, 1982), 22–23.

31. For example, in 1882 the Norfolk and Western published *Tourists and Excursionists Guide Book to Summer Homes in the Mountains of Virginia on the Line of the Norfolk and Western Railroad* and in 1887 the Richmond and Allegheny Railroad published *Rates and Routes to the Health and Pleasure Resorts, Summer Homes and Country Farm Houses, Prepared to Take Summer Boarders, on and Reached by the Richmond and Allegheny Railroad,* UVA. The New York, Ontario and Western Railway published a "neat and handy" volume in 1885 that included "no less that fifteen hundred summer hotels, boarding houses, &c. in the Highlands of the Hudson, the Catskills, the Mountains of Central New York and along the valleys of the Delaware Susquehanna, and Chenango Rivers." *New York Times,* 7 June 1885, p. 3.

32. Quoted in Funnell, *By the Beautiful Sea,* 9–11.

33. *New York Times,* 23 August 1865, p. 2.

34. "'May' in June," *Lippincott's Magazine of Popular Literature and Science* 16 (July 1875): 19; *Lake Mohonk Mountain House, 1874,* Annual Booklet, MMH.

35. *New York Times,* 28 July 1865, p. 3

36. *Chicago Tribune,* 26 August 1865, p. 3.

37. *Chicago Tribune,* 21 August 1870, p. 2.

38. *New York Times,* 5 June 1870, p. 6; 1 July 1870, p. 1. By 1885 the *Times* was regularly running long articles describing the wide variety of summer vacation spots in the Erie Region of Pennsylvania, on the coast of New Jersey, in the Allegheny Mountains, in the Adirondacks and Catskills, and along the beaches of Long Island. See, for example, *New York Times,* 7 June 1885, p. 3.

39. F. Mitchell, "Cape Cod," *The Century Magazine* 26 (September 1883): 658.

40. *Richmond Dispatch,* 2 July 1870, p. 1 (suppl.). Jones, *Appletons' Hand-Book . . . the Southern Tour,* 103–8.

41. Felix L. Oswald, "Southern Summer Resorts: First Paper," *Southern Bivouac* 2 (June 1886–May 1887): 123-28; Felix L. Oswald, "Southern Summer Resorts: Lookout Mountain and Caesar's Head," *Southern Bivouac* 2 (June 1886–May 1887): 190–94; Felix L. Oswald, "Southern Summer Resorts: Tallulah and Montvale," *Southern Bivouac* 2 (October 1886): 165–71. See also Frederick Stielow, "Grand Isle, Louisiana, and the 'New' Leisure, 1866–1893," *Louisiana History* 23 (summer 1982): 239–57; Nina Silber, *The Romance of Reunion: Northerners and the South, 1865–1900* (Chapel Hill: University of North Carolina Press, 1993), ch. 3.

42. Orville Hickman Browning, *The Diary of Orville Hickman Browning*, ed. Theodore Calvin Pease and James G. Randall (Springfield, Ill.: Springfield State Historical Library, 1925) 2:276–77, 455.

43. Cronon, *Nature's Metropolis*, 382. *Chicago Tribune*, 6 June 1875, p. 6; 20 June 1875, p. 3. Phil Porter, *View from the Veranda: The History and Architecture of the Summer Cottages on Mackinac Island* (Mackinac Island State Park Commission, 1981); John McCabe, *Grand Hotel: Mackinac Island* (Sault St. Marie, Michigan: The Unicorn Press, 1987). By the 1890s the *Chicago Tribune* was reporting on the summer season at a variety of midwestern lakes, including Spring Lake in Iowa and Grass Lake in Illinois, among others. See *Chicago Tribune*, 2 June 1895, p. 25.

44. Browning, *Diary of Orville Hickman Browning*, 2:326. In 1864 Justice Oscar Lovell Shafter of the California Supreme Court wrote to his sister about a trip he and his wife had taken to Lake Tahoe. "The Hotel here is well filled with tourists and successful miners from Virginia City." Oscar Lovell Shafter, *Life, Diary and Letters of Oscar Lovell Shafter*, ed. Flora Haines Loughead (San Francisco: Blair-Murdock, 1915), 225. Alfred Doten, *The Journals of Alfred Doten, 1849–1903*, ed. Walter Van Tilburg Clark (Reno: University of Nevada Press, 1973), 2: 1171.

45. *Appleton's General Guide to the United States and Canada: Western and Southern States* (New York: D. Appleton and Co., 1888), 447. Matthew Deady, an established lawyer living in Portland, Oregon, with his wife and three children, frequently went with his wife to Clatsop Beach during the 1870s where they stayed at Grimes Hotel and "bathed in the surf." Matthew P. Deady, *Pharisee Among Philistines: The Diary of Judge Matthew P. Deady, 1871–1892*, ed. Malcolm Clark Jr. (Portland: Oregon Historical Society, 1975), 1:133. In 1862 Sam Brannan opened the Hot Springs Hotel in Calistoga in California's Napa Valley. Brannan envisioned Calistoga becoming the "Saratoga of California" and hoped to attract wealthy patrons from San Francisco. Kay Archuleta, *Early Calistoga* (Calistoga: Illumination Press, 1977), 1, 41.

46. J.A. Butler, "Some Western Resorts," *Harper's New Monthly Magazine* 65 (August 1882): 325.

47. "The Summer Exodus," *Century Magazine*, 28 (July 1889): 47–48.

48. Roberts, *Biographical Sketch*, 157.

49. Charles Ellis to Powhatan Ellis, 21 July 1881, Warm Springs, Va., Ellis Powhatan Papers, VHS.

50. Fannie A. Cocke to Dear Sister, 21 July 1881, Warm Springs, Va., Powhatan Ellis Papers, VHS.

51. Fannie A. Cocke to Powhatan Ellis, 1 August 1882, Warm Springs, Va., Ellis Powhatan Papers, VHS.

52. Larry E. Burgess, *Mohonk Its People and Spirit: A History of One Hundred Years of Growth and Service* (New Paltz, N.Y.: Smiley Brothers, 1980), 15–28.

53. Eugene Du Bois to A. K. Smiley, 30 July 1873, New York, MMH.

54. A.N. Luchs to A. K. Smiley, 14 July 1873, New York, MMH.

55. Whether Romceine requested one bed because he and his friend hoped to

save money or share pleasure remains unknown. F.H. Romceine to A.K. Smiley, 8 June 1871, New York, MMH.

56. Walter Leech to Dear Sir, 23 June 1873, New York, MMH.

57. Eliza J. Lee to Mr. Smiley, 17 June 1872, Brooklyn, MMH.

58. Edward A. Casey to Albert Smiley, 12 June 1872, Philadelphia, MMH.

59. *Lake Mohonk Mountain House, 1874*, MMH.

60. *New York Times,* 19 July 1885, p. 4.

61. *Chicago Tribune,* 6 June 1875, p. 6.

62. Deady, *Pharisee Among Philistines,* 1:86–87.

63. Deady, *Pharisee Among Philistines,* 1:259.

64. Deady, *Pharisee Among Philistines,* 1:268. For more on Deady's touring vacation see chapter 5.

65. James. B. Bouck to Mr. Smilie, 26 June 1873, New York, MMH.

66. R. D. Fonda to Albert K. Smiley, 22 July 1872, New York, MMH.

67. *New York Times,* 7 June 1885, p. 3.

68. *New York Times,* 5 June 1870, p. 3.

69. *The Nation* 49 (29 August 1889) 163.

70. J.H. Browne, "The Queen of Aquidneck," *Harper's New Monthly Magazine* 49 (August 1874), 310.

71. Andrew D. White, *The Diaries of Andrew D. White,* ed. Robert Morris Ogden (Ithaca, N.Y.: Cornell University Library, 1959), 177.

72. *Harper's Weekly* (25 July 1874): 628. In 1880 the prices at many of the hotels at Saratoga had increased. The Grand Union was charging as much as $5 a day; Congress Hall and the Clarendon were up to $4 a day, and "smaller hotels" were charging $3. *New York Times,* 22 July 1880, p. 5.

73. Bill for Mr. G.H. Scribner and Wife, Congress Hall, 29 August 1870, SSPL.

74. Frank Graham Jr., *The Adirondack Park: A Political History* (Syracuse, N.Y.: Syracuse University Press, 1984), 35.

75. John McCabe, *Grand Hotel: Mackinac Island* (Sault St. Marie, Mich.: The Unicorn Press, 1987), 41.

76. *Lake Mohonk Mountain House, 1874*, MMH; Albert Smiley, "Lake Mohonk Mountain House: Rates Reduced," 1877, MMH; *Lake Mohonk Mountain House, 1882,* Annual Booklet, MMH.

77. Scott Derks, ed., *The Value of a Dollar: Prices and Incomes in the United States, 1860–1989* (Detroit, Mich.: Gayle Research, 1994), 26, 35, 39.

78. C.C. Kelsey to Sir, 14 July 1871, Brooklyn, MMH.

79. Mrs. Wm. Gilfillan to A. K. Smiley, 16 July [1874], Brooklyn, MMH.

80. Henry M. Haynes to Mr. Smilie, 10 April 1888, Boston, MMH.

81. *New York Times,* 28 June 1885, p. 3. In 1885 places on Long Island ranged from $31 to $35 per week for the most expensive (the Long Beach Hotel, which accommodated 900 people), to $17.50 to $21 for the Osborne House on the Isle of Wight, to $12.50 to $21 at the Pavilion Hotel at Woodsbury, to $8 to $15 per week at the Ocean-Avenue Hotel at Patchogue. *New York Times,* 7 June 1885, p. 3.

82. Nathaniel Beverley Tucker to Powhatan Ellis, 14 August 1887, Bath Co., Va., Ellis Powhatan Papers, VHS; Fannie Cocke to Dear Sister, 21 July 1881, Warm Springs, Virginia, Ellis Powhatan Papers, VHS. Philip. F. Brown, *An Account of Blue Ridge Springs* (New York: Leve & Alden Printing Co., 1885), 2.

83. Doten, *Journals of Alfred Doten,* 2:1202.

84. Deady, *Pharisee Among Philistines,* 197.

85. Norfolk and Western Railroad, *Tourist Excursionists Guide Book to Summmer*

Homes in the Mountains of Virginia on the Lines of the Norfolk and Western Railroad (Philadelphia, 1882), 13, UVA.

86. *Tourists and Excursionists Guidebook,* 15, UVA.

87. *Rockingham Springs, Season 1880,* (Harrisonburg, 1880), UVA.

88. A booklet put out in 1887 by the Richmond and Allegheny Railroad listed 889 summer resorts, country homes, and farmhouses that could be reached on the Richmond and Allegheny Railroad. Fifty five of them charged under $8 a week, numerous ones charging half that much. Many could accommodate only ten or twenty people, a few accommodated only three or four. *Rates and Routes to the Health and Pleasure Resorts . . . Reached by the Richmond and Alleghany Railroad* (Richmond, 1887), 14–5, 18, UVA.

89. *New York Times,* 24 July 1875, p. 4; By the mid-1870s Cape May was becoming known as a place that was "cheap." "The number of excellent second-class hotels here is very great. . . . The number of cheap small hotels and boarding cottages here is so large as to accommodate five sixths of the people who come here." *New York Times,* 18 August 1875, p. 1. According to one newspaper report, in 1885 "board with room" could be had on Martha's Vineyard for as little as $5 a week. *New York Times,* 15 July 1885, p. 5.

90. Frank M. Trexler, *The Diary of Judge Frank M. Trexler,* ed. Edwin R. Baldridge (Allentown, Pa: Lehigh Country Historical Society, 1982), 126, 131–34, 180–81, 231–33.

91. J.M. Winfield, M.D. to A. K. Smiley, 6 April 1882, New York, MMH.

92. Laura Woodward to Mr. Smiley, 13 April 1886, New York, MMH.

93. John C. Beekman, M.D. to Albert K. Smiley, 20 April 1886, New York, MMH.

94. Robert Wiebe, *The Search for Order, 1877–1920* (New York: Hill and Wang, 1967).

95. *New York Times,* 5 August 1865, p. 5; 28 June 1875, p. 5.

96. *New York Times,* 25 July 1880, p. 7.

97. *New York Times,* 23 June 1885, p. 2; 28 June 1885, p. 3.

98. *New York Times,* 18 July 1885, p. 3.

99. *New York Times,* 2 June 1895, p. 28.

100. *New York Times,* 8 July 1885, p. 5; 15 June 1890, p. 10.

101. McCabe, *Grand Hotel,* 72.

102. Benjamin Elberfield Atkins, *Extracts from the Diary of Benjamin Elberfield Atkins: "A Teacher of the Old School,"* comp. Emmet D Atkins and Jas W. Atkins (Gastonia, N.C.: Privately Published, 1947), 44–45.

103. *New York Times,* 18 July 1885, p. 3.

104. Roberts, *Biographical Sketch,* 155, 158.

105. *New York Times,* 9 July 1885, p. 5.

Chapter 3

1. *New York Times,* 1 July 1870, p. 2.

2. Alfred Doten, *The Journals of Alfred Doten 1849–1903,* ed. Walter Van Tilburg Clark (Reno: University of Nevada Press, 1973), 2:1201–3.

3. J.E. Cooke, "White Sulphur Springs," *Harper's New Monthly Magazine* 57 (August 1878): 352.

4. *New York Times,* 1 July 1870, p. 2.

5. T. Addison Richards, "Cape May," *The Knickerbocker* 54 (August 1859): 121. By

1865 Saratoga had ten hotels plus "a score or more" of large boarding houses, some of them containing as many as one hundred rooms. *New York Times,* 9 July 1865, p. 3. The largest of these hotels could hold as many as 1200 people. *The National Era,* 11 August 1859, p. 1 (Consulted photocopy of this material found in the collection of Field Horne in Saratoga Springs, N.Y.)

6. *New York Times,* 10 August 1855, p. 2.

7. Cooke, "White Sulphur Springs," 344–45.

8. See, for example, John Higham, "The Reorientation of American Culture in the 1890s," in *The Origins of Modern Consciousness,* ed. Horace John Weiss (Detroit, Mich.: Wayne State University Press, 1965), 25–48; Foster Rhea Dulles, *A History of Recreation: America Learns to Play,* (New York: Appleton-Century-Crofts, 1965).

9. Elliot Gorn and Warren Goldstein, *A Brief History of American Sports* (New York: Hill and Wang), ch. 3.

10. Sheila M. Rothman, *Woman's Proper Place* (New York: Basic Books, 1978), 26–41; Higham, "Reorientation of American Culture," 31. For more on women and sports see Roberta J. Park, "'Embodied Selves': The Rise and Development of Concern for Physical Education, Active Games and Recreation for American Women, 1776–1865," *Journal of Sports History* 5 (summer 1978): 5–41; Nancy L. Struna, "'Good Wives' and 'Gardeners', Spinners and 'Fearless Riders': Middle- and Upper-Rank Women in the Early American Sporting Culture," in J.A. Mangan and Roberta J. Park, *From 'Fair Sex' to Feminism: Sport and the Socialization of Women in the Industrial and Post-Industrial Eras* (London: Frank Cass and Company, 1987), 235–55.

11. *New York Times,* 9 August 1880, p. 2; 19 August 1880, p. 3. Cottage City, on Martha's Vineyard, hosted a tennis tournament in 1885; see *New York Times,* 18 July 1885, p. 3. For more on tennis at other summer resorts see *New York Times,* 19 July 1885, p. 4; S. R. Stoddard, *Lake George and Lake Champlain* (Glen Falls, N.Y.: Published by the Author, 1891), 10; John McCabe, *Grand Hotel: Mackinac Island* (Sault St. Marie, Michigan: The Unicorn Press, 1987), 55–66.

12. Geo. P.F. Hobson to Mr. Smiley, 25 August, 1894, Brooklyn, MMH; *New York Times,* 18 July 1885, p. 3; 9 August 1885, p. 3. For more on roller skating and bicycling at resorts see *New York Times,* 19 July 1885, p. 4; 2 August 1885, p. 3; 2 June 1895, p. 28. For a description of Americans' fascination with roller skating and bicycling see Dulles, *America Learns to Play,* 192–97.

13. *New York Times,* 29 August 1885, p. 3. One reporter commented: "Nearly every young fellow in town has brought his wheel with him, and tricycling is fast coming into favor with the ladies." (*New York Times,* 18 July 1885, p. 3)

14. *New York Times,* 10 August 1890, p. 10.

15. McCabe, *Grand Hotel,* 66.

16. *The National Era,* 1 September 1859, p. 1 (Consulted photocopy of this material found in the collection of Field Horne in Saratoga Springs, N.Y.)

17. *New York Times,* 24 August 1890, p. 10; 17 July 1895, p. 12. See also Frederick Stielow, "Grand Isle, Lousiana, and the 'New' Leisure, 1866–1893," *Louisiana History* 23 (summer 1982): 250.

18. [Anne Harrison Cocke Mason] to George Mason, 17 August 1887, Yellow Sulphur Springs, Cocke Family Papers, VHS. Fanny Longfellow, elite Bostonian, daughter of Nathan Appleton and wife of Henry Wadsworth Longfellow, wrote in her diary about the time she spent at Newport in the summer of 1852: "After dinner another chat or playing of foot ball on the lawn, even the ladies having taken to tossing it . . . ." Edward Wagenknecht, ed., *Mrs. Longfellow: Selected Letters and Jour-*

nals of Fanny Appleton Longfellow (1817–1861) (New York: Longmans, Green and Co., 1956), 190.

19. *New York Times,* 17 August 1890, p. 10.

20. *New York Times,* 31 August 1890, p. 10.

21. *New York Times,* 21 August 1875, p. 5. At Saratoga in 1865 the newspaper reported on a foot race between two men and a shooting competition in which one man shot an orange off another's head and a cigar out of someone's mouth. But the article revealed that this was not only male fun: "Mrs. Bansom, of New York, is also a capital shot. This lady yesterday hit a penny at ten paces twice in four shots." *New York Times,* 29 July 1865, p. 5.

22. Neither was swimming the only outdoor activity in which she participated: "We went out fishing six times but caught very little. . . . We went sailing in the bay often it was [splendid], especially moon light nights. . . . I played ten pins, & billiards with moderate success." Floride Clemson, *A Rebel Came Home,* ed. Charles M. McGee Jr., and Ernest M. Lander Jr. (Columbia, S.C.: University of South Carolina Press, 1961), 60. Mrs. Deady accompanied her husband Matthew into the surf at Clatsop Beach in the mid-1870s. Matthew P. Deady, *Pharisee Among Philistines: The Diary of Judge Matthew P. Deady, 1871–1892,* ed. Malcolm Clark Jr. (Portland: Oregon Historical Society), 1:196. Ellen Turner wrote in a letter to Dr William Bagby from Cape Island, New Jersey, in Aug. of 1857 describing "How much I enjoyed the bathing I can never tell." Ellen Turner to Dr. Bagby (typescript), 20 August 1857 [Cape Island, New Jersey], George William Bagby Papers, VHS.

23. [Wm. Thomas], "'May' in June," *Lippincott's Magazine of Popular Literature and Science* 16 (July 1865): 20.

24. Felicia Holt, "Promiscuous Bathing," *Ladies Home Journal* (August 1890), 6.

25. John R. Stilgoe, *Alongshore* (New Haven: Yale University Press, 1994), 348.

26. *New York Times,* 23 August 1865, p. 2. In 1880 a reporter noted that the women at Long Branch seemed to need less assistance: "There is a faint scream, a gurgling sound, followed by the roar of the green water as it breaks in foamy masses on the sand. A second later a fair head emerges from the bubbling expanse beyond, the straw hat a little crumpled and awry, and the long black hair floating backward on the waves. Her uncle . . . comes in and tells her that she is the most courageous girl on the beach, and that he couldn't have done it better himself, which she believes until she has seen 20 other young women do the same thing without flinching." *New York Times,* 26 July 1880, p. 5.

27. *New York Times,* 23 August 1885, p. 3.

28. *New York Times,* 20 August 1875, p. 1.

29. *New York Times,* 24 July 1870, p. 5. See also [J.H. Brown], "The Queen of Aquidneck," *Harper's New Monthly Magazine* 49 (August 1874): 312; *New York Times,* 7 July 1875, p. 1.

30. *New York Times,* 15 August 1865, p. 5.

31. Holt, "Promiscuous Bathing," 6.

32. *New York Times,* 15 August 1865, p. 5.

33. *New York Times,* 31 July 1865, p. 1. In *The Lure of the Sea: The Discovery of the Seaside in the Western World 1750–1840* (Cambridge, England: Polity Press, 1994) Alain Corbin offers an excellent analysis of the sexual implications of sea bathing for nineteenth-century European bourgeois women. He explains: "Even more than aristocratic ladies accustomed to the social circuit, bourgeois women trapped in their homes found in the medical prescription [of sea bathing] an unexpected freedom that offered undreamt-of pleasures." Corbin, *Lure of the Sea,* 76–77.

34. Much has been written on Victorian sexuality. For an overview see Estelle Freedman and John D'Emilio, *Intimate Matters: A History of Sexuality in America* (New York: Harper & Row, 1988).

35. *New York Times,* 15 July 1900, p. 15.

36. *New York Times,* 8 August 1875, p. 1.

37. J.R.V. Daniels to My dearest little wife, 8 July 1885, Richmond, Va., Daniels Family Papers, VHS.

38. A reporter writing from Martha's Vineyard in 1885 made special notice of a "pretty girl" from New York who "baths at 11 o'clock prompt every morning. . . . She is always attired in a gorgeous striped costume, with scant skirts, short trousers, and pink silk hose. The dress has completely captivated the crowd of imported dudes who frequent the beach." This particular swimmer, however, remained safe from unwanted attention or nasty gossip, thanks to an "argus-eyed female attendant" who remained "constantly on the watch to arrest any symptoms of flirtation." *New York Times,* 26 July 1885, p. 4.

39. *New York Times,* 15 June 1890, p. 10.

40. See chapter 1.

41. *New York Times,* 23 August 1865, p. 2.

42. *New York Times,* 19 August 1880, p. 3.

43. *New York Times,* 1 July 1900, p. 17.

44. Edwin Bedford Jeffress, Diary (typescript), 7 August 1852, 8 August 1852, 11 August 1852, 1 September 1852, 2 September 1852, VHS.

45. Copy of part of a letter or diary, no name, 27 August 1868, SLV. (Consulted photocopy at GBR).

46. Ned to Caz, 4 August 1881, White Sulphur Springs, GBR. James Daniel wrote to his friend Lewis Gwathney from White Sulphur in August of 1870 listing the names of the "lady friends" who were there and describing the social scene: "It is as gay as possible. The German is danced every night in the ball room, with its bright dresses & brighter faces, is indeed a pretty sight. The dressing is gorgeous & expensive—the undressing—well, pretty high and low." Daniel felt sure that his friend would appreciate the spectacle and that the "massive marble-like shoulder, the full rounded arms & exquisite feet &c here displayed, wd. attract your attention & admiration." J.R.V. Daniel to Lewis Temple Gwathney, 19 August 1860, White Sulpur Springs, Gwathney Family Papers, VHS.

47. Ellen Turner to George W. Bagby, 20 August 1857, Cape Island, N.J., George William Bagby Papers, VHS.

48. Lucy Breckinridge, *Lucy Breckinridge of Grove Hill: The Journal of a Virginia Girl, 1862–1864,* ed. Mary D. Robertson (Kent, Ohio: Kent State University Press, 1979), 119–20.

49. Nelson J. Callahan, ed., *The Diary of Richard L. Burtsell, Priest of New York: The Early Years, 1865–1868* (New York: Arno Press, 1978), 122.

50. Charles Ellis to Powhatan Ellis, 6 August 1876, Warm Springs; Charles Ellis to Powhatan Ellis, 3 June 1887, Warm Springs; Papers of Powhatan Ellis, VHS.

51. Anne Harrison Mason to George Mason, 17 August 1887, Yellow Sulphur Springs, Cocke Family Papers, VHS.

52. Descriptions of the dances were ubiquitous. See, for example, *New York Times,* 7 July 1875, p. 1; Maria Louisa Fontaine to Kate, 10 August 1860, White Sulphur Springs, Meade Family Papers, VHS; Robert E. Lee to Charlotte Haxall, 28 August 1868, White Sulphur Springs, Lee Family Papers, VHS; Moses Hoge to Bessie, 19 August 1870, White Sulphur Springs, Hoge Family Papers, VHS.

53. There is a huge literature on middle-class women's non-domestic activities in the late nineteenth century. For an overview see Sara Evans, *Born for Liberty: A History of Women in America* (New York: Free Press, 1989), ch. 6.

54. Barbara Miller Solomon, *In The Company of Educated Women* (New Haven: Yale University Press, 1985), 50–54.

55. Helen Lefkowitz Horowitz, *Campus Life: Undergraduate Cultures from the End of the Eighteenth Century to the Present* (New York: Alfred A. Knopf, 1987), 195–201.

56. Cindy Sondik Aron, *Ladies and Gentlemen of the Civil Service: Middle-Class Workers in Victorian America* (New York: Oxford University Press, 1987), ch. 7.

57. John F. Kasson, *Rudeness and Civility: Manners in Nineteenth-Century Urban America* (New York: Hill and Wang, 1990), 132–36.

58. For more on the social activities of urban, working-class youths see Kathy Peiss, *Cheap Amusements: Working Women and Leisure in Turn-of-the-Century New York* (Philadelphia: Temple University Press, 1986); Joanne Meyerowitz, *Women Adrift: Independent Wage Earners in Chicago, 1880–1930* (Chicago: University of Chicago Press, 1988).

59. *New York Times,* 23 August 1860, p. 1.

60. *New York Times,* 16 August 1860, p. 1.

61. "Saratoga: The American Baden-Baden," *Every Saturday* 11 (9 September 1871): 261.

62. A correspondent who marvelled in 1875 at how "cleverly" the women at Long Branch adorned themselves for the evening dances lamented that "pretty girls, wearing costly clothes, able to dance gracefully, having wealthy parents, without matrimonial engagements, are compelled to take other girls for partners in waltzes and quadrilles." *New York Times,* 7 July 1875, p. 1. See also Henry James, "Saratoga," *The Nation* 11 (August 11, 1870): 87–89.

63. Mary Randolph Custis Lee to Robert E. Lee Jr., 6 August [1867], White Sulphur Springs, Lee Family Papers, VHS. See also Charles Ellis to Powhatan Ellis, 14 August 1879, Warm Springs and Charles Ellis to Powhatan Ellis, 1 August 1885, Warm Springs, Papers of Powhatan Ellis, VHS.

64. See chapter 2.

65. Stielow, "Grand Isle, Louisiana, and the 'New' Leisure," 252–53.

66. Theodore Ledyard Cuyler, *Recollections of a Long Life: An Autobiography* (New York: The Baker & Taylor Company, 1902), 226.

67. For descriptions of the routine at Saratoga see "First Impressions of Saratoga," *The National Era,* 11 August 1859–11 September 1859 (from photocopy in Field Horne's collection); [T.A. Richards], "Saratoga," *Knickerbocker* 54 (Sept., 1859), pp. 241–56; Ernest Dubergier de Hauranne, *A Frenchman in Lincoln's America,* ed. Ralph Bowen (Chicago: R.R. Donnelley & Sons, 1974), 1:135–37; Charles Richard Weld, *A Vacation Tour in the United States and Canada* (London: Longman, Brown, Green and Longman, 1855).

68. *New York Times,* 4 July 1875, p. 1.

69. *New York Times,* 30 July 1880, p. 3.

70. See, for example, the description of Montvale Springs, a resort in eastern Tennessee. "Southern Summer Resorts," *The Southern Bivouac* 2 (October 1886): 269–71.

71. Browning, *Diary of Orville Hickman Browning,* 2:297, 479. See also diaries of Alf Doten and Matthew Deady for their descriptions of Lake Tahoe and Clatsop Beach. Doten, *Journals of Alfred Doten,* 2:1201–4; Deady, *Pharisee Among Philistines,* 1:132–34, 216–17.

72. See, for example, *Chicago Tribune,* 9 August 1870, p. 2; 11 August 1870, p. 3; 21 August 1870, p. 2, 5 (suppl.); 22 August 1870, p. 3; 28 August 1870, p. 5 (suppl.); 29 August 1870, p. 4; *New York Times,* 8 June 1890, p. 10; 10 August 1890, p. 10.

73. "The Ethics and Aesthetics of Our Summer Resorts," *National Quarterly Review* 19 (1869): 327–28.

74. *New York Times,* 5 July 1880, p. 1.

75. *New York Daily Tribune,* 14 August 1865, p. 1. The *New York Times* ran an article in July of 1875 called "Summer Fashions: The Sex at the Seaside" in which it discussed the "serious matter" of dressing at "fashionable country watering-places." At such spots, it maintained, "the fair sex devotes the larger part of their time to their toilets. First comes the breakfast dress, then the bathing suit, the walking suit, dinner and evening attire, and, in short, changes without limit." (*New York Times,* 25 July 1875, p. 10)

76. *New York Times,* 20 August 1875, p. 1.

77. *The National Era,* 25 August 1859, p. 1 (Consulted photocopy of this material found in the collection of Field Horne in Saratoga Springs, N.Y.)

78. Kasson, *Rudeness and Civility,* 130. For more on dress and manners of working-class women see Peiss, *Cheap Amusements* and Elizabeth Ewen, *Immigrant Women in the Land of Dollars* (New York: Monthly Review Press, 1985).

79. *New York Times,* 8 August 1875, p. 1.

80. *New York Times,* 28 June 1885, p. 3; 23 August 1865, p. 2.

81. [L.C. Lillie], "The Catskills," *Harper's New Monthly Magazine* 67 (September 1883): 533.

82. Some vacationers worried about being included and making friends once they arrived at their designated vacation spot. Kate Fontaine, for example, confided to her friend Lucy Braxton in 1853 that a stay at White Sulphur might be "tiresome unless I went in a large party and had a great many acquaintances, and I have heard it is not easy to make acquaintances at the White Sulphur, there is so much ceremony." Kate Fontaine to Lucy Braxton, 19 August 1853, Beaverdam, Meade Family Papers, VHS.

83. A.H. Wharton, "The Courtesies of Summer Resorts," *Lippincott's* 44 (1889): 127, 128. For discussion of the unfriendly, haughty environment at Newport and White Sulphur see *New York Times,* 22 August 1860, p. 2; *New York Times,* 26 July 1875, p. 1.

84. *New York Times,* 7 July 1875, p. 1.

85. *New York Times,* 16 August 1885, p. 3.

86. "Our Saratoga Correspondence," *Harper's Weekly* 3 (3 September 1859): 563.

87. Karen Halttunen, *Confidence Men and Painted Women: A Study of Middle-Class Culture in America, 1830–1870* (New Haven: Yale University Press, 1982), 157, 166. See also Kasson, *Rudeness and Civility,* 176.

88. For discussion of these parlor theatricals see Halttunen, *Confidence Men and Painted Women,* ch. 6.

89. "Our Saratoga Correspondence," 563.

90. See chapter 1.

91. *New York Times,* 18 July 1870, p. 2. By the late 1860s Long Branch had its Pennsylvania Club, a sumptuous establishment where roulette, faro, cards, and dice tempted male guests, including President Grant. Other popular gaming places at Long Branch included the New York Club and a gambling establishment on the second floor of the Mansion House. Harold F. Wilson, *The Story of the Jersey Shore* (Princeton: D. Van Nostrand Company, 1964), 75.

92. *New York Times,* 30 July 1880, p. 3. See also *Chicago Tribune,* 28 July 1870, p. 4

for a description of Chamberlaine's sumptuous gambling casino in Long Branch, New Jersey.

93. *New York Daily Tribune,* 9 August 1865, p. 1.

94. "People and Things at Saratoga—Sketches of Life," *New York Daily Times,* 15 August 1856, typescript, SSPL.

95. *New York Times,* 6 July 1865, p. 1.

96. *New York Times,* 16 August 1885, p. 3. Some journalists maintained that the ebb and flow of life at fashionable resorts rested on the success or failures of such romantic encounters. Writing from Long Branch in late August of 1885, a correspondent observed: "This is the time when usually the young woman who has exhibited all her new Summer costumes and has exhausted her resources in trying to bring that long-winded flirtation with Smithers to a satisfactory issue begins to think about leaving the seaside and betaking herself for a brief spell to the quiet seclusion of the mountains or to the solid comfort of a Saratoga hotel. Yet thus far no one seems inclined to move." *New York Times,* 23 August 1885, p. 3.

97. *New York Daily Tribune,* 14 August 1865, p. 1.

98. *New York Times,* 20 August 1875, p. 1. At Newport in 1860, according to one journalist, the marriage market had become less effective: "American watering-place life . . . no longer facilitate[d] matrimonial arrangements." The reason, however, was not because the environment of fashionable resorts discouraged flirtations, rather that the "the promiscuous gatherings, the fast habits and the delusive excitements" scared off "sensible men" who sought "wives in a more secluded and domestic atmosphere." *New York Times,* 22 August 1860, p. 2.

99. For a review of republican ideas see Gordon S. Wood, *The Radicalism of the American Revolution* (New York: Alfred A. Knopf, 1991).

100. [emphasis added] *Chicago Tribune,* 21 August 1870, p. 2.

101. [T.A. Richards], "Saratoga," *Knickerbocker* 54 (September 1859): 246.

102. *New York Times,* 28 July 1865, p. 3.

103. "Southern Summer Resorts," *The Southern Bivouac* 2 (October, 1886): 269.

104. *New York Times,* 1 July 1870, p. 2.

105. *New York Times,* 12 August 1865, p. 5.

106. *New York Times,* 25 July 1880, p. 1.

107. Oscar Lovell Shafter, *Life Diary and Letters of Oscar Lovell Shafter,* ed. Flora Haines Loughead (San Francisco: Blair Murdock, 1915), 225–26.

108. "Saratoga: The American Baden-Baden," 261.

109. *New York Times,* 18 August 1870, p. 6.

110. See chapter 8.

111. See chapter 1.

112. Stilgoe, *Alongshore,* 335.

113. Peiss, *Cheap Amusements.*

114. For a discussion of dress and manners in the nineteenth century see Halttunen, *Confidence Men and Painted Women* and Kasson, *Rudeness and Civility.*

115. Kate Chopin, *The Awakening* (New York: Barnes and Noble, 1995), 17 and passim.

Chapter 4

1. Eva Moll, Diary, 18 August 1883, CHT.

2. *New York Times,* 17 August 1870, p. 8.

3. *New York Times,* 1 August 1870, p. 3.

4. *New York Times,* 1 August 1870, p. 3.

5. *New York Times,* 1 August 1870, p. 3.

6. *New York Times,* 17 August 1885, p. 8.

7. *New York Times,* 29 August 1885, p. 8.

8. R.M. Warren, *Chautauqua Sketches: Fair Point and the Sunday-School Assembly* (Buffalo: H.H. Otis, 1878), 69.

9. *Indianapolis Freeman,* 22 August 1891, p. 5.

10. *Indianapolis Freeman,* 9 August 1890, p. 5.

11. Ellen Weiss, *City in the Woods: The Life and Design of an American Camp Meeting on Martha's Vineyard* (New York: Oxford University Press, 1987), 30–31, 64.

12. Weiss, *City in the Woods,* 34.

13. For an excellent analysis of the camp meeting/vacation resort at Wesleyan Grove and Oak Bluffs see Dona Brown, *Inventing New England: Regional Tourism in the Nineteenth Century* (Washington, D.C.: Smithsonian Institution Press, 1995), ch. 3; Weiss, *City in the Woods,* 77–79.

14. During the summer of 1873 an estimated 25,000 people came to Ocean Grove. Harold Wilson, *The Story of the Jersey Shore* (Princeton, N.J.: D. Van Nostrand Co., 1964), 51.

15. *New York Times,* 3 August 1895, p. 5. Glenn Uminowicz, "Recreation in a Christian America: Ocean Grove and Asbury Park, New Jersey, 1869–1914," in *Hard at Play: Leisure in America, 1840–1940,* ed. Kathryn Grover (Amherst, Mass.: The University of Massachusetts Press, 1992), 8–38.

16. *New York Times,* 3 August 1895, p. 5.

17. *New York Times,* 16 August 1925, pp. 14–15.

18. *New York Times,* 3 August 1895, p. 5.

19. Wilson, *Jersey Shore,* p. 51–52; Uminowicz, "Recreation in Christian America," 25.

20. *New York Times,* 16 August 1925, pp. 14–15.

21. Around the turn of the century the question of whether alcohol should be sold at Asbury Park became a hot topic for debate. For more on this see chapter 8.

22. Wilson, *Jersey Shore,* 52.

23. *Rehoboth Beacon,* July 1873, p. 1, Rehoboth Historical Society, Rehoboth Beach, Delaware.

24. *Act of Incorporation and By-Laws of the Rehoboth Beach Camp Meeting Association of the M.E. Church* (Wilmington, James & Webb Printers, 1873), 3–4, 11, 17–18. In 1875 the Michigan Camp Ground Association opened a summer campground/resort at Bay View in northern Michigan. Keith J. Fennimore, *The Heritage of Bay View, 1875–1975* (Grand Rapids, Mich.: William B. Eerdmans Publishing Co., 1975).

25. *New York Times,* 27 June 1875, p. 5.

26. Quoted in Richard Fox, "The Discipline of Amusement," in *Inventing Times Square: Commerce and Culture at the Crossroads of the World,* ed. William R. Taylor (New York: Russel Sage Foundation, 1991), 90; Laurence Moore, *Selling God: American Religion in the Marketpace of Culture* (New York: Oxford University Press, 1994), 160–62.

27. Frederick A. Norwood, *The Story of American Methodism: A History of the United Methodists and Their Relations* (New York: Abingdon Press, 1974), 254–55, 259.

28. In 1874, for example, Presbyterians began to develop a resort near Cape May, New Jersey. Called Sea Grove, it received financial support from wealthy Philadelphia retailer John Wanamaker. Sea Grove never achieved the success of its

Methodist counterparts. It remained a small community and by the turn of the century was in decline. See George E. Thomas and Carl Doebley, *Cape May, Queen of the Seaside Resorts: Its History and Architecture* (Philadelphia: Art Alliance Press, 1976), 30–31; *New York Times*, 17 July 1875, p. 5.

29. Larry E. Burgess, *Mohonk: Its People and Spirit: A History of One Hundred Years of Growth and Service* (New Paltz, New York: Mohonk Mountain House, 1980), 15–20.

30. Mrs. F.R. Brunot to A. K. Smiley, 15 August [n.d.], Verona, MMH.

31. Albert G. Hook to Albert K. Smiley, 24 August 1871, New York, MMH.

32. An 1876 announcement for the Camp Ground at Bay View, Michigan, maintained that it would be "a resort, which it is believed, cannot be surpassed in healthfulness, accessibility, picturesqueness of scenery and inexpensiveness, anywhere in our country." A visitor could board at the association boarding house at Bay View for $5 a week. A 9 × 12 tent "including a board floor and putting up in good order" cost $5 a week or $7 for two weeks. Quoted in Fennimore, *Heritage of Bay View*, 28, 34.

33. Moses Hoge to Bessie, 2 September 1870, Berkeley Springs, Hoge Family Papers, VHS.

34. Benjamin Elberfield Atkins, *Extracts from the Diary of Benjamin Elberfield Atkins: "A Teacher of the Old School,"* ed. Emma D. Atkins and Jas. W. Atkins (Gastonia, N.C., privately published, 1947), 57, and passim.

35. Dona Brown has found that those who built cottages at Wesleyan Grove in the 1860s were from the lower end of the middle class, primarily shopkeepers and artisans. But Oak Bluffs attracted richer Methodists who built larger and more elaborate summer cottages. Brown, *Inventing New England*, ch. 3. Within a few years of its opening, the camp ground at Bay View, Michigan, sported "very neat" cottages, some of which cost "from $200 to $600." Fennimore, *Heritage of Bay View*, 61.

36. See chapter 2.

37. See chapter 3.

38. Dona Brown has found that similar motives and impulses explain the development and success of Oak Bluffs on Martha's Vineyard. See Brown, *Inventing New England*, ch. 3.

39. Rebecca Richmond, *Chautauqua: An American Place* (New York: Duell, Sloan Pearce, 1943), 59; Theodore Morrison, *Chautauqua: A Center for Education, Religion, and the Arts in America* (Chicago: University of Chicago Press, 1974), 32–33; John Vincent, *The Chautauqua Movement* (Freeport, N.Y.: Books for Libraries Press, 1971, first published 1885), 6; Alfreda Irwin, *Three Taps of the Gavel: Pledge to the Future: The Chautauqua Story* (Chautauqua, N.Y.: The Chautauqua Institution, 1987), 12–16.

40. Quoted in Foster Rhea Dulles, *America Learns to Play: A History of Popular Recreation, 1607–1940* (New York: Appleton-Century Co., 1940), 92.

41. Quoted in Carl Bode, *The American Lyceum: Town Meeting of the Mind* (Carbondale: Southern Illinois University Press, 1968), 11–12.

42. Joseph F. Kett, *The Pursuit of Knowledge Under Difficulties: From Self-Improvement to Adult Education in America, 1750–1990* (Stanford: Stanford University Press, 1994), 38–39.

43. Kett, *Pursuit of Knowledge*, 45–47, 65–67, 75–77. Moreover, those who attended were not necessarily searching for information that would translate specifically into vocational or career advancement. Rather, the desire for knowledge and the hope for general self-improvement apparently motivated those who attended these lectures.

44. Kett, *Pursuit of Knowledge*, 146–47.

45. See chapter 1 for more on this distinction and on the clergy's efforts to deal with the problem of leisure.

46. Lawrence W. Levine, *Highbrow Lowbrow: The Emergence of Cultural Hierarchy in America* (Cambridge, Mass.: Harvard University Press, 1988), ch. 1; Elliot Gorn and Warren Goldstein, *A Brief History of American Sports* (New York: Hill and Wang, 1993), ch. 3; David Nasaw, *Going Out: The Rise and Fall of Public Amusements* (New York: Basic Books, 1993).

47. Vincent, *Chautauqua Movement*, 35; Morrison, *Chautauqua: A Center*, 34; Richmond, *Chautauqua*, 60.

48. Morrison, *Chautauqua: A Center*, 47; Irwin, *Three Taps*, 13.

49. "Editor's Notebook," *The Chautauquan* 1 (March 1881): 283.

50. *New York Times*, 27 July 1885, p. 2.

51. While some of these may have served primarily as literary circles, others clearly functioned as educational resorts. Vincent, *Chautauqua Movement*, 41–42.

52. Louisa Roberts, *A Biographical Sketch of Louisa Roberts* (Philadelphia: Press of Alfred J. Ferris, 1895), 189–90.

53. Fennimore, *Heritage of Bay View*, 78.

54. Benjamin W. Griffin, "Csardas at Salt Springs: Southern Culture in 1888," *The Georgia Review* 26 (spring 1972): 53–54, 58.

55. W. Stuart Towns, "The Florida Chautauqua: A Case Study in American Education," *The Southern Speech Communication Journal* 42 (spring 1977): 228–45.

56. *Report of the Commissioner of Education for the Year 1891–1892* (Washington D.C.: Government Printing Office, 1894) 2:937–45.

57. Hjalmar Hjorth Boyesen, "The Chautauqua Movement," *Cosmopolitan* 19 (May 1895): 147.

58. Boyesen, "The Chautauqua Movement," 151.

59. Inez Harris Robinson, Memoir, CHT; *The Chautauqua Assembly Herald*, 9 August 1878, p. 1; *The Chautauqua Assembly Herald*, 4 August 1879, p. 1.

60. Ida Tarbell, *All in the Day's Work: An Autobiography* (New York: Macmilllan, 1939), 68.

61. R.M. Warren, *Chautauqua Sketches: Fair Point and the Sunday-School Assembly*, (Buffalo: H.H. Otis, 1878), 107.

62. *New York Times*, 27 July 1885, p. 2.

63. *Indianapolis Freeman*, 3 June 1893, p. 8; *Indianapolis Freeman*, 4 August 1894, p. 3.

64. Henry Berkowitz, "The Jewish Chautauqua Society," *The Chautauquan* 38 (July 1904), 447–48; *New York Times*, 22 July 1900, p. 15; 24 July 1900, p. 12.

65. Vincent, *Chautauqua Movement*, 53–54. Chautauqua pioneered in home extension reading courses through the Chautauqua Literary and Scientific Circle and even experimented for a few years with trying to become a degree-granting university. Morrison, *Chautauqua: A Center*, 48–54.

66. Vincent, *Chautauqua Movement*, 53.

67. "Chautauqua, 1887," *The Chautauquan* 7 (May 1887): 510–11. In 1886 the Chautauqua Assembly at Bay View, Michigan, offered, along with religious curriculum, a range of secular choices. There was a school of music, elocution, art, and cooking, as well as the Chautauqua Literary and Scientific Circle round tables. And apparently the cooking school was the most popular. The Bay View Assembly announced that its goal was to combine "with the recreational delights of a summer school at this peerless resort, the stimulating influence of a summer school." Fennimore, *Heritage of Bay View*, 81, 100.

68. Moll, Diary, 18 November 1884; 27 March 1887, CHT.

69. Barbara Miller Solomon, *In the Company of Educated Women: A History of Women and Higher Education in America* (New Haven: Yale University Press, 1985), 633–34.

70. Charlotte Perkins Gilman, "A Sensible Vacation," *The Independent* 60 (7 June 1906): 1338–39.

71. *Report of Commissioner of Education*, 940–41.

72. *Indianapolis Freeman*, 3 June 1893, p. 8; see also 18 June 1898, p. 2.

73. For more on the African-American middle class in the late nineteenth and early twentieth century see Glenda Gilmore, *Gender and Jim Crow: Women and the Politics of White Supremacy in North Carolina, 1896–1920* (Chapel Hill: University of North Carolina Press, 1996); Evelyn Brooks-Higginbotham, *Righteous Discontent: The Women's Movement in the Black Baptist Church, 1880–1920* (Cambridge, Mass.: Harvard University Press, 1992); Janette Thomas Greenwood, *Bittersweet Legacy: The Black and White 'Better Classes' in Charlotte, 1850–1910* (Chapel Hill: University of North Carolina Press, 1994); Willard B. Gatewood, *Aristocrats of Color: The Black Elite, 1880–1920* (Bloomington, Indiana University Press, 1990).

74. *Indianapolis Freeman*, 2 July 1910, p. 2; 1 June 1912, p. 4.

75. *New York Times*, 9 August 1875, 2–3.

76. Morrison, *Chautauqua: A Center*, 37; Warren, *Chautauqua Sketches*, 47.

77. Moll, Diary, 18 November 1884, CHT; "Chautauqua, 1887," *The Chautauquan* 7 (May 1887): 510–11.

78. *The Chautauqua Assembly Herald*, 9 August 1886, p. 1.

79. Boyesen, "The Chautauqua Movement," 150–52.

80. [emphasis added] Chancellor Vincent, "Going to the Assembly," *The Chautauquan* 11 (August 1890): 588–90; *The Chautauqua Assembly Herald*, 5 Aug. 1885, p. 1.

81. Moll, Diary, 27 March 1887, CHT.

82. "The Summer Assemblies," *The Chautauquan* 6 (July 1885): 603.

83. *Indianapolis Freeman*, 3 June 1893, p. 8.

84. *Indianapolis Freeman*, 18 June 1898, p. 2.

85. *New York Times*, 27 July 1885, p. 2; Morrison, *Chautauqua: A Center*, 46; Warren, *Chautauqua Sketches*, 79.

86. Albert S. Cook, "Chautauqua: Its Aims and Influence," *The Forum* 10 (August 1895): 690.

87. Lewis, in fact, admitted to enjoying a "toddy with his father until his church became politically active in the temperance movement." Morrison, *Chautauqua: A Center*, 22.

88. Tarbell, *All in the Day's Work*, 67.

89. Inez Harris Robinson, Memoir, CHT.

90. Warren, *Chautauqua Sketches*, 53–55.

91. *The Chautauqua Assembly Herald*, 26 July 1891, p. 1.

92. Boyesen, "The Chautauqua Movement," 147. For a description of fashionable resorts, see chapter 3.

93. Boyesen, "The Chautauqua Movement," 151–52, 156. For more on the Bayview Assembly see Fennimore, *Heritage of Bay View*.

94. Tarbell, *All in the Day's Work*, 67.

95. "Chautauqua as a Summer Resort," *The Chautauquan* 7 (July 1887): 612.

96. S.R. Stoddard, *Lake George and Lake Champlain* (Glen Falls, N.Y.: Published by the Author, 1891), 35–36.

97. The original Chautauqua, by 1903, could accommodate 10,000 to 12,000

summer residents at any one time. George Vincent, "Summer Schools and University Extension," in *Monographs on Education in the United States,* ed. Nicholas Murray Butler (St. Louis, Mo.: Division of Exhibits, Department of Education, Universal Exposition, 1904), 844.

98. *The Chautauqua Assembly Herald,* 21 August 1885, p. 1.

99. "Bicycling at Chautauqua," *The Chautauquan* 33 (June 1901): 311–12. In 1904 the board of the Bay View Assembly apparently discussed the possibility of buying adjoining piece of land and building a golf course, but never followed through. Fennimore, *Heritage of Bay View,* 184.

100. Stephen M. Dale, "What People Do at Chautauqua," *Ladies Home Journal:* 21 (July 1904), 8.

101. Cook, "Chautauqua: Its Aims and Influences," 690.

102. Dale, "What People Do at Chautauqua," 8.

103. *The Chautauqua Assembly Herald,* 13 August 1895, p. 1.

Chapter 5

1. Jeremiah C. Harris, *An Old Field School Teacher's Diary,* ed. Charles W. Turner (Verona, Va.: McClure Press, 1975), 62–63.

2. See, for example, Dona Brown, *Inventing New England: Regional Tourism in the Nineteenth Century* (Washington, D.C.: Smithsonian Institution Press, 1995); John Jakle, *The Tourist: Travel in Twentieth-Century North America* (Lincoln: University of Nebraska Press, 1985); Earl Pomeroy, *In Search of the Golden West: The Tourist in Western America* (New York: Alfred A. Knopf, 1957); Dean MacCannell, *The Tourist: A New Theory of the Leisure Class* (New York: Schocken Books, 1976).

3. Josiah Quincy would in 1823 become mayor of Boston and six years later assume the presidency of Harvard. M.A. De Wolfe Howe, ed., *The Articulate Sisters: Passages from Journals and Letters of the Daughters of President Josiah Quincy of Harvard University* (Cambridge, Mass.: Harvard University Press, 1946), 35–36.

4. Brown, *Inventing New England,* ch. 1.

5. David Prale, "Journal of a Jaunt from New York to Niagara in the Company with Chas. Bostwick & Capt. Forman," July 1821, NYHS.

6. For an excellent, recent book on Niagara see William Irwin, *The New Niagara: Tourism, Technology and the Landscape of Niagara Falls 1776–1917* (University Park, Pa: Pennylvania State University Press, 1996).

7. Esther Moir, *The Discovery of Britain: The English Tourists, 1540 to 1840* (London: Routledge & Kegan Paul, 1964), 139; James Buzard, *The Beaten Track: European Tourism, Literature, and the Ways to 'Culture,' 1800–1918* (New York: Oxford University Press, 1993), 20.

8. For a discussion of the impact of British aesthetic theories on American tourism see John Sears, *Sacred Places: American Tourist Attractions in the Nineteenth Century* (New York: Oxford University Press, 1989), 14–15; Buzard, *Beaten Track;* Moir, *Discovery of Britain,* chs. 8–11; Brown, *Inventing New England,* chs. 1, 2. For more on Niagara as an early tourist sight see Patricia Jasen, "Romanticism, Modernity, and the Evolution of Tourism on the Niagara Frontier, 1790–1850," *Canadian Historical Review* 71 (September 1991): 283–318.

9. Brown, *Inventing New England,* 57–59.

10. Buzard, *Beaten Track,* 102; Moir, *Discovery of Britain,* 3. See also Jeremy Black, *The British and the Grand Tour* (London: Croom Helm, 1985).

11. Buzard, *Beaten Track,* ch. 2.

12. Sears, *Sacred Places*, 4–5.

13. Carol E. Hoffecker, ed., "The Diaries of Edmund Canby, A Quaker Miller, 1822–1848," *Delaware History* 16 (October 1974): 89.

14. Sidney George Fisher, *A Philadelphia Perspective: The Diary of Sidney George Fisher Covering the Years 1834–1871*, ed. Nicholas B. Wainwright (Philadelphia: Historical Society of Pennsylvania, 1967), 82–83, 197. Christopher Baldwin, a lawyer from Worcester, made a trip with his father to the White Mountains that convinced him that Worcester, his home town, was "the handsomest, largest, and most flourishing town in our journey." Christopher Columbus Baldwin, *Diary of Christopher Columbus Baldwin, Librarian of the American Antiquarian Society: 1829–1835* (Worcester, Mass.: Published by the Society, 1901), 27.

15. Catharine M. Sedgwick, *Life and Letters of Catharine M. Sedgwick*, ed. Mary E. Dewey (New York: Harper & Bros., 1871), 129.

16. Catharine Sedgwick used the term "grand tour" to describe her trip to Niagara in 1821. Sedgwick, *Life and Letters*, 125. Catherine Clarkson used the same term in her diary as she described a similar trip in 1833. Catherine Clarkson, "Sort of a Journal of the Grand Tour," [n.d.], NYHS. Historian Dona Brown uses the term "fashionable tour" to describe this trip. Brown, *Inventing New England*, ch. 1.

17. Brown, *Inventing New England*, chs. 1, 2; Irwin, *New Niagara*, ch. 1.

18. Clarkson, "Sort of a Journal of the Grand Tour," NYHS.

19. See, for example, Edward Wagenknecht, ed., *Mrs. Longfellow: Selected Letters and Journals of Fanny Appleton Longfellow 1817–1861* (New York: Longmans, Green and Co., 1956), 10–14; James McDonald, Diary, 26 October 1837, NYHS.

20. Sedgwick, *Life and Letters*, 140; Prale, "Journal of Jaunt from New York to Niagara in the Company of Chas. Bostwick & Capt Foreman," July 1821, NYHS; Clarkson "Sort of Journal of the Grand Tour," NYHS.

21. Hoffecker, "Diaries of Edmund Canby," 87–89.

22. Richard Henry Dana Jr., *The Journal of Richard Henry Dana, Jr.*, ed. Robert F. Lucid (Cambridge, Mass: The Bellknap Press of Harvard University Press, 1968), 1:239, 251. See also Thomas Hubbard Hobbs, *The Journals of Thomas Hubbard Hobbs*, ed. Faye Acton Axford (Tuscaloosa: University of Alabama Press, 1976), 48–49 and Isaac Mickle, *The Diary of Isaac Mickle, a Gentleman of Much Promise*, ed. Philip English Mackey (Philadelphia: University of Pennsylvania Press, 1977), 2:391–92.

23. Catherine Clarkson (Mrs. Henry M. Stevens), Diary, June 1835, NYHS.

24. Hoffecker, "Diaries of Edmund Canby," 116–18.

25. Baldwin, *Diary of Christopher Columbus Baldwin*, 26, 77, 359–64.

26. Sears, *Sacred Places*, 191–208.

27. Mary Moragne, *The Neglected Thread: A Journal from the Calhoun Community*, ed. Delle Mullen Craven (Columbia: University of South Carolina Press, 1951), 174–80.

28. Mickle, *Diary of Isaac Mickle*, 1:202–08, 2:388–97.

29. See, for example, Hobbs, *Journals of Thomas Hubbard Hobbs*, 48–49, 116; Dana Jr., *Journal of Richard Henry Dana, Jr.*; Randal W. McGavock, *Pen and Sword: The Life and Journals of Randal W. McGavock*, ed. Herscel Gower (Nashville: Tennessee Historical Commission, 1960).

30. Dana, *Journal of Richard Henry Dana, Jr.*, 1:80.

31. Dana, *Journal of Richard Henry Dana, Jr.*, 1:119–21.

32. Historian Patricia Cline Cohen has found ample evidence of women traveling alone, journeying, for example, to visit relatives or to find employment. Patricia Cline Cohen, "Safety and Danger: Women on American Public Transport,

1750–1850," in *Gendered Domains: Rethinking Public and Private in Women's History,* ed. Dorothy O. Helly and Susan M. Reverby (Ithaca, N.Y.: Cornell University Press, 1992), 109–22.

33. Gayle Thornborough, ed., *Diary of Calvin Fletcher* (Indianapolis: Indiana Historical Society, 1972) 1:171, 172–73.

34. Mickle, *Diary of Isaac Mickle,* 2:395.

35. Dana, *Journal of Richard Henry Dana, Jr.,* 1:237; Hobbs, *Journals of Thomas Hubbard Hobbs,* 49. See also Rutherford B. Hayes, *Diary and Letters of Rutherford Birchard Hayes,* ed. Charles Richard Williams (Columbus: Ohio State Archeological and Historical Society, 1922–1925), 1:529.

36. Harris, *An Old Field School Teacher's Diary,* 53–54.

37. John D. Long, *The Journal of John D. Long,* ed. Margaret Long (Rindge, N.H.: Richard R. Smith, Publishers, 1956), 96, 99.

38. Mary Lydig Daly, *Diary of a Union Lady,* ed. Harold Earl Hammond (New York: Funk & Wagnalls Co., 1962), 235–37.

39. William Plumer Jacobs, *Diary of William Plumer Jacobs,* ed. Thornwell Jacobs (Oglethorpe University, Ga.: Oglethorpe University Press, 1937), 248–50.

40. Hugh DeSantis, "The Democratization of Travel: The Travel Agent in American History," *Journal of American Culture* 1 (spring 1978): 1–17.

41. Piers Brendon, *Thomas Cook: 150 Years of Popular Tourism* (London: Secker & Warburg, 1991), 105.

42. Quoted in Brendon, *Thomas Cook,* 161.

43. Brendon, *Thomas Cook,* 162–63.

44. T.J. Lamm to W.F. Simons, 18 March 1884, Jacksonville, Fla, Tourism, Warshaw Collection of Business Americana, NMAH.

45. Earl Spencer Pomeroy, *In Search of the Golden West; The Tourist in Western America* (New York: Alfred A. Knopf, 1957), 13–14; DeSantis, "The Democratization of Travel," 5; Brendon, *Thomas Cook,* 78.

46. *Raymond's Vacation Excursions, 5 Grand Summer Trips in August* (1887), Tourism, Warshaw Collection of Business Americana, NMAH.

47. Pomeroy, *In Search of the Golden West,* 15.

48. Louisa J. Roberts, *Biographical Sketch of Louisa J. Roberts with Extracts from her Journal* (Philadelphia: A.J. Ferris, 1895), 152–61. The monument in Cleveland was a memorial to Commodore Perry's 1813 victory in the battle of Lake Erie, which was fought at the Put-In-Bay Islands at the mouth of the Detroit River in Lake Erie. *Appletons' General Guide to the United States and Canada, Western and Southern States* (New York: D. Appleton and Company, 1888), 283. *Appletons' Hand-Book of American Travel. Western Tour* (New York: D. Appleton & Company, 1871), 5.

49. Sedgwick, *Life and Letters of Catharine M. Sedgwick,* 354, 356–57.

50. Anne Farrar Hyde, *An American Vision: Far Western Landscape and National Culture, 1820–1920* (New York: New York University Press, 1990), 108.

51. *New York Times,* 21 June 1875, p. 2; Hyde, *An American Vision,* ch. 3, 4; Pomeroy, *In Search of the Golden West.*

52. Sears, *Sacred Places,* 130, chs. 6, 7; Pomeroy, *In Search of the Golden West,* ch. 1; Alfred Runte, *National Parks: The American Experience* (Lincoln: University of Nebraska Press, 1979), ch. 1.

53. *Raymond's Vacation Excursions . . . Three Grand Trips to the Yellowstone National Park* (1888), Tourism, Warshaw Collection of Business Americana, NMAH. Raymond and Whitcomb was also offering six-day tours to Niagara and Saratoga for forty dollars. See "Raymond's Vacation Excursions," August 1887, Tourism, Warshaw Collection, NMAH.

54. Pomeroy, *In Search of the Golden West*, 7 and ch. 1.

55. Quoted in Brendon, *Thomas Cook*, 107. Cook recorded that the train trip from Philadelphia to Baltimore was particularly interesting because "it brought us into contact with the first views we had of the scenes of the late war." Quoted in Edmund Swinglehurst, *Cook's Tours: The Story of Popular Travel* (Dorset: Poole, Blandford Press, 1982), 58.

56. *Rockbridge Baths* (Baltimore: Selby & Dulany, 1868), p. 40, UVA. The two important institutions of learning were Virginia Military Institute and Washington and Lee College.

57. *New York Times*, 24 July 1870, p. 2.

58. Chesapeake & Ohio, *Blazings: A Route Marked for Tourists, Pleasure Seekers, and Searchers for Health* (Buffalo, N.Y.: Printing House of Matthews, Northrup & Co., 1884), 14. Important historic markers of the early nineteenth century continued, as well, to be popular attractions. The Saratoga battleground and the numerous battle-fields and forts around Niagara remained tourist attractions in the late nineteenth century. See R.F. Dearborn, *Saratoga and How to See It* (Albany: Weed, Parsons, 1873); *The Visitor's Guide to Saratoga Springs* (1876 copyright, published 1884 in this edition); *Gollner's Pocket Guide to Saratoga Springs* (New York, 1881); *New York Times*, 27 June 1875, p. 2.

59. Elizabeth Porter Gould, "A Trip Around Cape Ann," *The New England Magazine* 4 (March 1886): 268–75.

60. *Appletons' Hand-Book of American Travel. Northern and Eastern Tour* (New York: D. Appleton and Company, 1873), 146–47.

61. Frank M. Trexler, *The Diary of Judge Frank M. Trexler*, ed. Edwin R. Baldrige (Allentown, Pa.: Proceedings of the Lehigh County Historical Society, 1982), 134. Dr. Frank Kellogg, who took frequent touring vacations in the 1880s, 1890s, and early 1900s, visited "Sleepy Hollow Cemetery on a beautiful hill, in which [were] the graves of the Hawthornes, Thoreau, Alcotts and Emersons." David S. Kellogg, *A Doctor at all Hours: The Private Journal of a Small-Town Doctor's Varied Life*, ed. Allan S. Everest (Brattleboro, Vt.: Stephen Greene Press, 1970), 192.

62. Sears, *Sacred Places*, 191–208.

63. Baldwin, *Diary of Christopher Columbus Baldwin*, 359; Moragne, *The Neglected Thread*, 177–78.

64. John Sears offers an insightful analysis of how tourists were, as well, able to fashion Mauch Chunk into a picturesque sight and therefore to frame "the grandeur of American accomplishment" within the "magnificence of American nature." There is little doubt that Sears is correct and that Mauch Chunk served this function. But it is also true that numerous other places of work—both industrial and nonin-dustrial—attracted American tourists, and in many of these cases there was little of the picturesque to be had. Sears, *Sacred Places*, 199 and ch. 8.

65. MacCannell, *The Tourist*, 62, 57.

66. Matthew P. Deady, *Pharisee Among Philistines: The Diary of Judge Matthew P. Deady, 1871–1892*, ed. Malcolm Clark Jr. (Portland: Oregon Historical Society, 1975), 1:266.

67. For a discussion of the quest for authentic experiences see T. J. Jackson Lears, *No Place of Grace: Antimodernism and the Transformation of American Culture, 1880–1920* (Chicago: University of Chicago Press, 1981). As Daniel T. Rodgers has brilliantly explained, the late nineteenth-century middle class struggled to reconcile their belief in the moral value of labor with the reality of work in an industrialized culture. Some looked to leisure, rest, and consumption as alternatives to a world of degraded labor and industrial overproduction. Others tried to find substitutes—

handicrafts, strenuous sports—that would function as work did, building character and developing virtue. Daniel T. Rodgers, *The Work Ethic in Industrial America, 1850–1920* (Chicago: University of Chicago Press, 1978).

68. Everett Waddey, *Seaside and Mountain Resorts of the Old Dominion,* 1884, UVA. The Norfolk and Western Railroad's 1882 guide for "Tourists and Excursionists" in "the Mountains of Virginia" spent a few pages describing Lynchburg as "one of the most progressive and prosperous cities of the south . . . it supports two iron furnaces, about sixty tobacco factories. . . ." Norfolk and Western Railroad, *Tourists and Excursionists Guide Book to Summer Homes in the Mountains of Virginia on the Lines of the Norfolk and Western Railroad* (Philadelphia, 1882), 9, UVA.

69. Gould, "A Trip Around Cape Ann," 274.

70. *Appletons' General Guide to the United States and Canada, Western and Southern States* (New York: D. Appleton and Co., 1888), 308.

71. *Raymond's Vacation Excursions . . . Three Grand Trips to the Yellowstone National Park* (1888), Tourism, Warshaw Collection of Business Americana, NMAH.

72. See Pomeroy, *In Search of the Golden West,* 66–67 for descriptions of some of the "discomfort and even pain" that "regularly attended visits to many of the wonders mandatory on the grand tour" of Yosemite.

73. Trexler, *The Diary of Judge Frank M. Trexler,* 131–34.

74. See chapter 2 for more on the costs of various resorts.

75. It was perfectly possible to get to some not-too-distant summer resort from a major eastern city for as little as $5 roundtrip. The cost of transportation varied, depending upon how far a vacationer wanted to travel, but in the 1890s someone traveling from Boston could get to Bennington, Vermont, for $7.25 round trip on the Fitchburg Railroad, but only had to spend $3.25 if he or she wanted to summer at one of the hotels in Athol, Mass, about eighty-two miles from Boston. See *Summer Excursions via Fitchburg Railroad, for the season of 1897,* Railroads, Warshaw Collection of Business Americana, NMAH. Similarly, a vacationer could get from Harrisburg, Pa., to Atlantic City and back for about $6.25, or to Cape May and back for $8.00. See Philadelphia & Reading Railroad, *Excursion Routes to Summer Resorts, Season of 1878,* Railway Guides, Warshaw Collection of Business Americana, NMAH.

76. *Raymond's Vacation Excursions, 5 Grand Summer Trips in August 1887,* Tourism, Warshaw Collection of Business Americana, NMAH.

77. Philadelphia & Reading Railroad, *Excursion Routes to Summer Resorts, Season of 1878,* 28–30, Railway Guides, Warshaw Collection of Business Americana, NMAH.

78. Robert W. Rydell, *All the World's a Fair: Visions of Empire at American International Expositions, 1876–1916* (Chicago: University of Chicago Press, 1984), 2, 10. Historian James Gilbert estimates that as many as 10 percent of the American population visited the Chicago fair in 1893. James B. Gilbert, *Perfect Cities: Chicago's Utopias of 1893* (Chicago: University of Chicago Press, 1991), 1, 121.

79. Rydell, *All the World's a Fair,* 4; see also Gail Bederman, *Manliness and Civilization: A Cultural History of Gender and Race in the United States, 1880–1917* (Chicago: University of Chicago Press, 1995), ch. 5.

80. Gilbert, *Perfect Cities,* 83.

81. Franklin H. Williams, *Diary, From 1852–1891* (Sunderland, Mass.: Published by the Williams Family, 1975), 63.

82. David S. Kellogg, *A Doctor at all Hours: The Private Journal of a Small-Town*

Doctor's Varied Life, ed. Allan S. Everest (Brattleboro, Vt.: Stephen Greene Press, 1970), 112.

83. Marian Lawrence Peabody, *To Be Young Was Very Heaven* (Boston: Houghton Mifflin, 1967), 52.

84. At the Philadelphia Centennial Exposition, in addition to the main buildings, there were seventeen state buildings and nine foreign government buildings. Rydell, *All the World's a Fair*, 11.

85. Gilbert, *Perfect Cities*, 105–6.

86. Rydell, *All the World's a Fair*, 11; *Visitors' Guide to the Centennial Exhibition* (Philadelphia: J.B. Lippincott & Co., 1876), 12, World's Exposition, Warshaw Collection of Business Americana, NMAH.

87. Richard Lee Strout, ed., *Maud* (New York: Macmillan, 1939), 564.

88. Charles G. Dawes, *A Journal of the McKinley Years*, ed. Bascom N. Timmons (Chicago: The Lakeside Press, R.R. Donnelley & Co., 1950), 30.

89. When Walt Whitman visited the fair he "ordered his chair to be stopped before the great, great engine . . . and there he sat looking at this colossal and mighty piece of machinery for half an hour in silence . . . contemplating the ponderous motions of the great machinery man has built." Quoted in Rydell, *All the World's a Fair*, 15–16.

90. *Visitors' Guide to the Centennial Exhibition and Philadelphia* (Philadelphia: J.B. Lippincott, 1876), 14, World's Expositions, Warshaw Collection of Business Americana, NMAH.

91. Gilbert, *Perfect Cities*, 114; *Visitor's Guide to Centennial Exhibition and Philadelphia*, 19, World's Expositions, Warshaw Collection of Business Americana, NMAH; Rydell, *All the World's a Fair*, 38–71; Bederman, *Manliness and Civilization*, 31–41.

92. Quoted in Gilbert, *Perfect Cities*, 119.

93. *Visitors' Guide to the Centennial Exhibition*, 3, World's Expositions, Warshaw Collection of Business Americana, NMAH.

94. *A Week at the Fair* (Chicago: Rand, McNally and Co., 1893), World's Expositions, Warshaw Collection of Business Americana, NMAH.

95. *Visitors' Guide to the Centennial Exhibition*, 35, World's Expositions, Warshaw Collection of Business Americana, NMAH; Franklin H. Williams, *Diary*, 61.

96. *A Week at the Fair*, 21, World's Expositions, Warshaw Collection of Business Americana, NMAH.

97. A visitor could buy a fifteen-day round-trip ticket from New York to Philadelphia for from $4 to $5. A one-day, second-class excursion ticket could cost as little as $2. *The Centennial Exhibition and the Pennsylvania Railroad, 1876* (Rand, McNally & Co., Printers and Engravers), 33, World's Expositions, Warshaw Collection of Business Americana, NMAH.

98. Gilbert estimates that two weeks at the 1893 Chicago fair cost about $55 plus train fare. Gilbert, *Perfect Cities*, 121.

99. Mrs. M.D. Frazar, "Private Parties for the World's Fair," World's Expositions, Warshaw Collection of Business Americana, NMAH. Mrs. Frazar also offered European tours, so she was obviously catering to an upscale clientele. The Boston and Maine Railroad ran trips to the Chicago fair from Boston for $100, which included traveling expenses, a week's board and room at the Bay State Hotel, and admission to the fair. Boston and Maine Railroad, "Twenty-Five Trips to the World's Columbian Exposition," World's Expositions, Warshaw Collection, NMAH.

100. *Indianapolis Freeman,* 3 June 1893, p. 7; 19 August 1893, p. 8; 20 August 1904, p. 8.

101. Rydell, *All the World's a Fair,* 84–85; Edward L. Ayers, *The Promise of the New South: Life After Reconstruction* (New York: Oxford University Press, 1992), 322–26.

102. *Indianapolis Freeman,* 25 June 1905, p. 1. For a discussion of similar problems for African Americans at the 1896 Atlanta's Cotton States and International Exposition see Ayers, *The Promise of the New South,* 322–24.

103. Daniel Boorstin, *The Image: A Guide to Pseudo-Events in America* (New York: Harper Colophon Books, 1961), 79–80.

104. Many scholars have examined the negative view of tourism and the inauthenticity of the tourist experience. See, for example, Buzard, *The Beaten Track;* Boorstin, *The Image;* MacCannell, *The Tourist.*

Chapter 6

1. F.R. Stockton, "Camping out at Rudder Grange," *Scribner's* 16 (May 1878): 104–5.

2. Hans Huth, *Nature and the American: Three Centuries of Changing Attitudes* (Lincoln: University of Nebraska Press, 1957), chs. 8, 9; Alfred Runte, *National Parks: The American Experience* (Lincoln: University of Nebraska Press, 1979), ch. 1; Roderick Nash, *Wilderness and the American Mind* (New Haven: Yale University Press, 1967), ch. 9 and passim. See also Peter J. Schmitt, *Back to Nature: The Arcadian Myth in Urban America* (New York: Oxford University Press, 1969), 188–89 for an examination of the early twentieth-century interest in and appreciation of nature.

3. For an interesting discussion of hunting see Stuart A. Marks, *Southern Hunting in Black and White* (Princeton, N.J.: Princeton University Press, 1991).

4. Nash, *Wilderness and the American Mind,* ch. 2.

5. For a discussion of the relationship of nature to early nineteenth-century Americans see Huth, *Nature and the American;* Nash, *Wilderness and the American Mind;* Henry Nash Smith, *The Virgin Land: The American West as Symbol and Myth* (Cambridge, Mass.: Harvard University Press, 1950); Leo Marx, *The Machine in the Garden: Technology and the Pastoral Ideal in America* (New York: Oxford University Press, 1964); Schmitt, *Back to Nature;* Roy Rosenzweig and Elizabeth Blackmar, *The Park and the People: A History of Central Park* (Ithaca: Cornell University Press, 1992).

6. Nash, *Wilderness and the American Mind,* 57–62. One good example would be Charles Lanman, *A Tour to the River Saguenay, in Lower Canada* (Philadelphia: Carey and Hart, 1848). Another would be Henry David Thoreau, *Walden,* ed. J. Milnor Dorey (New York: Charles E. Merrill Co., 1910).

7. Thomas Wentworth Higginson, *Letters and Journals of Thomas Wentworth Higginson, 1845–1906,* ed. Mary Thacher Higginson (Boston and New York: Houghton Mifflin Co., 1921), 117–19.

8. William James Stillman, *The Autobiography of a Journalist* (Boston: Houghton Mifflin and Co, 1901), 239–40, 247.

9. Stillman, *Autobiography,* 248.

10. Stillman, *Autobiography,* 248–50; Frank Graham Jr., *The Adirondack Park: A Political History* (Syracuse: Syracuse University Press, 1984), 20–22. While Stillman did not specifically mention the duties of a guide, William Murray, another early advocate of camping, did. See the discussion on p. 161 and William Murray's *Adventures in the Wilderness; or, Camp-Life in the Adirondacks,* ed. William K. Verner and Warder H. Cadbury (Syracuse: Syracuse University Press, 1970).

11. David Strauss, "Toward a Consumer Culture: 'Adirondack Murray' and the Wilderness Vacation," *American Quarterly* 39 (summer 1987): 270–286.

12. Murray, *Adventures*, 11–15.

13. Murray, *Adventures*, 15.

14. Murray, *Adventures*, 18–19.

15. Murray, *Adventures*, 19, 58–59.

16. Murray, *Adventures*, 32–33.

17. Quoted in Cadbury introduction to Murray, *Adventures*, 52.

18. *New York Times*, 11 July 1870, p. 4.

19. "Camp Lou," *Harper's New Monthly Magazine* 62 (May 1881): 865.

20. George Miller Beard, *American Nervousness: Its Causes and Consequences* (New York: Putnam, 1881).

21. Robert E. Strahorn, "A Summer Outing on Northwestern Waters," *Cosmopolitan* 21 (September 1896): 473.

22. Cadbury introduction to Murray, *Adventures*, 40–48; Graham, *Adirondack Park*, 23–30.

23. Quoted in Cadbury introduction to Murray, *Adventures*, 53.

24. The exact numbers are difficult to determine. A letter written to the *New York Tribune* in August of 1869 claimed that as many as two to three thousand people stormed the Adirondacks that summer. The Racquette Lake House—deep in the wilderness—registered over 400 guests that summer, twice as many as the summer before. Hotels on the fringes may have also experienced a similar increase of people who were perched to make camping forays into the woods. Cadbury introduction to Murray, *Adventures*, 70; Graham, *Adirondack Park*, 28–30.

25. Murray, *Adventures*, 25.

26. See chapter 2.

27. *New York Times*, 17 August 1890, p. 10.

28. William Dix, "Summer Life in Luxurious Adirondack Camps," *The Independent* 55 (July 1903): 1556. See also Graham, *Adirondack Park*, 43.

29. John Todd, *John Todd, The Story of His Life, Told Mainly by Himself*, compiled and edited by John E. Todd (New York: Harper & Brothers, 1876), 473–74.

30. Theodore Roosevelt, *Theodore Roosevelt's Diaries of Boyhood and Youth* (New York: Charles Scribner's Sons, 1928), 250.

31. *New York Times*, 11 August 1875, p. 2.

32. L. Rosencrans, "A Glimpse of the Adirondacks," *Catholic World* 24 (1876): 264.

33. T. Addison Richards, "A Forest Story, II: The Adirondack Woods and Waters," *Harper's New Monthly Magazine* 19 (September 1859): 461; Rosencrans, "A Glimpse of the Adirondacks," 261–69.

34. John B. Bachelder, *Popular Resorts and How to Reach Them* (Boston: John B. Bachelder Publisher, 1875), 17–19.

35. In 1877 Major John Gould, for example, published a manual on *How To Camp Out* that Godkin praised highly in *The Nation*. Huth, *Nature and the American*, 110–11.

36. Roosevelt, *Diaries of Boyhood and Youth*, 250.

37. T. Addison Richards, "A Forest Story, I: The Hunting Grounds of the Saranac," *Harper's New Monthly Magazine* 19 (August 1859): 310–23; Richards, "A Forest Story II: The Adirondack Woods and Waters," 455–66.

38. George Whitwell Parsons, *The Private Journal of George Whitwell Parsons* (Phoenix: Arizona Statewide Archival and Records Project, 1939): 24.

39. *New York Times*, 10 August 1880, p. 3.

40. See, for example, F.R. Stockton, "Camping Out at Rudder's Grange," *Scribner's* 16 (May 1878): 104–7.

41. Benjamin Hart Dally, *A Milwaukee, Wisconsin Diary (for the Year 1888) of Benjamin Hart Dally*, ed. Alexander Grant Rose III (Baltimore, Md.: Mimeographed and Copyright by the Editor, 1974), 68–69.

42. Runte, *National Parks*, 28, 46, and chs. 1, 2.

43. Mary Bradshaw Richards, *Camping Out in the Yellowstone 1882*, ed. William W. Slaughter (Salt Lake City: University of Utah Press, 1994), ix, xxviii.

44. Richards, *Camping Out in Yellowstone*, 12–14, 57, 96.

45. Richards, *Camping out in Yellowstone*, 38.

46. Richards, *Camping Out in Yellowstone*, 80, 83–88, 106.

47. The Mammoth Hot Springs Hotel opened in the summer of 1884. Eight years later there were three other substantial hotels offering rooms to guests: the Canyon Hotel, the Lake Hotel, and the Fountain Hotel. Richards, *Camping Out in Yellowstone*, xxiv.

48. Webner, Pocket Journal, 2 September 1887, UVA.

49. William James, "Vacations," *The Nation* 17 (7 August 1873): 90–91.

50. "With Rod and Reel: The New England Fishing Resorts. How to Reach Them. Costs," *The Boston and Maine Courier* 1 (May 1895): 3–4, Railroads, Warshaw Collection of Business Americana, NMAH.

51. "Camping Out for Women," *The Boston and Maine Courier* 1 (May 1895): 9, Railroads, Warshaw Collection of Business Americana, NMAH.

52. S.R. Stoddard, *Lake George and Lake Champlain* (Glen Falls, N.Y.: Published by the Author, 1891), 3.

53. Stoddard, *Lake George*, 3–4.

54. Isabel C. Barrows, "Summer Camping in the Woodland," *New England Magazine* 18 (August 1898): 736.

55. Walter Page et. al, "The People at Play," *World's Work* 4 (August 1902): 2421.

56. *New York Times*, 17 August 1890, p. 10.

57. W. Gerard Vermilye, "Camping Trips in Maine," *Country Life* 14 (June 1908): 173–75.

58. Lawrence Lewis, "A Fishing Camp on the Gunnison River," *Country Life* 14 (June 1908): 167.

59. Todd, *John Todd*, 473.

60. Newman Smyth, "The Lake Country of New England," *Scribner's Magazine* 8 (September 1890): 494.

61. See Nash, *Wilderness and the American Mind*; Huth, *Nature and the American*; Schmitt, *Back to Nature*.

62. Schmitt, *Back to Nature*, 70.

63. *New York Times*, 20 August 1875, p. 1.

64. [Emphasis added] James, "Vacations," 91.

65. H. Vane, "Adirondack Days," *Harpers New Monthly Magazine* 63 (October 1881): 679. Historian Peter Schmitt has discovered similar themes in children's fiction. The early twentieth century saw a rash of novels and series (the Bobbsey Twins and others) that set city children on vacation in the countryside where they learned "manliness, self-reliance, physical and mental health, strength of character, simplicity of desire and love of nature." These novels featured both female and male heros. In one, *The Camp Fire Girls at Pine Tree Camp*, the young Edna and her friends "dream of idle, fashionable crowds at summer resorts, and ignore the wonderful,

pine-scented vigor of the forest." But their experience at the camp persuades them "that this great everyday world is a place of love and beauty and not merely of clothes; that one does not need chiffons and laces and bon-bons and yachts and beaus." Schmitt, *Back to Nature*, 119.

66. Smyth, "The Lake Country of New England," 496. Describing the benefits of New England as a summer vacation place, Isabel Barrows asserted that "there are as yet enough spots in New England and the region round about where one can come close to the heart of nature and there find the peace that passes all understanding." The vacationer would *not* find them, however, at "the summer boarding houses nor the seaside hotels." After all, she asked, "who ever thought of finding 'Nirvana' at an August 'hop'?" Barrows, "Summer Camping in the Woodlands," 732.

67. William Dix, "Summer Life in Luxurious Adirondack Camps," *The Independent* 55 (July 1903): 1558.

68. Henry Van Dyke, "A Holiday in a Vacation," *Scribner's Magazine* 41 (January 1907): 1.

69. *New York Times*, 27 July 1885, p. 6.

70. Schmitt, *Back to Nature*, 99.

71. Murray, *Adventures in the Wilderness*, 18.

72. Vane, "Adirondack Days," 683, 687–88.

73. *New York Times*, 10 August 1880, p. 3.

74. Strahorn, "A Summer Outing on Northwestern Waters," 473–76.

Part Two

1. [emphasis added] Charles G. Dawes, *A Journal of the McKinley Years*, ed. Bascom N. Timmons (Chicago: The Lakeside Press, RR. Donnelley & Co., 1950), 443–49.

2. See, for example, David Nasaw, *Going Out: The Rise and Fall of Public Amusement* (New York: Basic Books, 1993); Lewis Ehrenberg, *Steppin' Out: New York Nightlife and the Transformation of American Culture 1890–1930* (Chicago: University of Chicago Press, 1981).

3. Robert S. Lynd and Helen Merrell Lynd, *Middletown: A Study in Modern American Culture* (New York: Harcourt, Brace & World, 1929), ch. 18; Jacqueline Dowd Hall, "Disorderly Women: Gender and Labor Militancy in the Appalachian South," *Journal of American History* 73 (September 1986): 354–82.

Chapter 7

1. Philip G. Hubert Jr., "Camping Out for the Poor," *Century* 22 (July 1892): 633–34.

2. Hubert Jr., "Camping Out," 632–34.

3. Stuart A. Marks, *Southern Hunting in Black and White* (Princeton, N.J.: Princeton University Press, 1991).

4. Edward Hungerford, "Our Summer Migration," *Century* 42 (August 1891): 569–70.

5. See, for example, Roy Rosenzweig, *Eight Hours For What We Will: Workers & Leisure in an Industrial City, 1870–1920* (Cambridge, England: Cambridge University Press, 1983); Kathy Peiss, *Cheap Amusements: Working Women and Leisure in Turn-of-the-Century New York* (Philadelphia: Temple University Press, 1986); Joanne Meyerowitz, *Women Adrift: Independent Wage-Earners in Chicago, 1880–1930* (Chicago:

University of Chicago Press, 1988); Elliot J. Gorn and Warren Goldstein, *A Brief History of American Sports* (New York: Hill and Wang, 1993).

6. John Kasson, *Amusing the Million: Coney Island at the Turn of the Century* (New York: Hill and Wang, 1978); Francis G. Couvares, *The Remaking of Pittsburgh: Class and Culture in an Industrializing City, 1877–1919* (Albany: SUNY Press, 1984), 122.

7. *New York Times*, 20 July 1885, p. 5; 27 July 1885, p. 1; 16 August 1880, p. 8.

8. Peter J. Schmitt, *Back to Nature: The Arcadian Myth in Urban America* (New York: Oxford University Press, 1969), 96–97.

9. *New York Times*, 28 August 1890, p. 8.

10. Schmitt, *Back to Nature*, 96–99.

11. *New York Times*, 18 June 1885, p. 4.

12. *New York Times*, 12 June 1895, p. 16. See also Rose Cohen, *Out of the Shadow* (New York: George H. Doran and Company, 1918), 260–65.

13. *New York Times*, 18 June 1885, p. 4; 12 June 1895, p. 16; 19 June 1895, p. 16.

14. *New York Times*, 19 June 1895, p. 16.

15. Annie E.S. Beard, "Summer Outing Camps," *World To-Day* 11 (July 1906): 726.

16. Beard, "Summer Outing Camps," 725. See also *New York Times*, 16 June 1885, p. 8; 19 June 1900, p. 6.

17. For Progressive reformers operating in part out of a desire to assert "social control" over immigrants and workers see Robert H. Wiebe, *The Search for Order 1877–1920* (New York: Hill and Wang, 1967), 165–76.

18. Schmitt, *Back to Nature*, 97–98.

19. Beard, "Summer Outing Camps," 725.

20. *New York Times*, 6 June 1880, p. 5.

21. Theda Skocpol, *Protecting Soldiers and Mothers: The Political Origins of Social Policy in the United States* (Cambridge, Mass.: Harvard University Press, 1992), ch. 6.

22. Sanford Jacoby, *Employing Bureaucracy: Managers, Unions, and the Transformation of Work in American Industry, 1900–1945* (New York: Columbia University Press, 1985), 52, 59–60.

23. [Gertrude Beeks] to George DeForest, 10 July 1909, [New York], Welfare Department, National Civic Federation Papers (NCF), NYPUB. Various women were, as well, giving speeches under the auspices of the NCF about the necessity of providing recreational opportunities, athletic fields, vacations, and summer excursions for women workers. See "Address of Mrs. M. Frank Mebane," Richmond, Virginia, 10 April 1911, Women's Department, National Civic Federation Papers, NYPUB.

24. *New York Times*, 4 July 1900, p. 16.

25. Hugh Thompson, "The Vacation Savings Movement," *Munsey's Magazine* 49 (May 1913): 257–59; Amy E. Spingarn, "Summer Vacations for Working Girls," *The Survey* 22 (3 July 1909): 517–21.

26. Gertrude Robinson Smith to Ralph Easley, 8 January 1912, New York, Welfare Department, NCF, NYPUB.

27. John Oskison, "A New Way to Finance the Vacation," *The Delineator* 82 (August 1913): 10; Hugh Thompson, "The Vacation Savings Movement," *Munsey's Magazine* 49 (May 1913): 257–59.

28. Spingarn, "Summer Vacations for Working Girls," 517–21.

29. Harriet T. Comstock, "The Working-Girls' Vacation Society," *The Outlook* 92 (7 August 1909): 862. *New York Times*, 12 July 1910, p. 7; 31 July 1910, p. 7. See also Janet Schulte, "'Summer Homes': A History of Family Summer Vacation Communi-

ties in Northern New England, 1880–1940," (Ph.D. diss., Brandeis University, 1993), 150–54, for a discussion of the vacation programs and houses run by the National League of Women Workers.

30. The camp, boasting a branch of the public library, a bathing beach, and a donated graphophone, hosted from 45 to 100 women a week. Not all of these working women were enjoying a week's vacation, about half commuted from camp back into the city to work each day. Bertha M. Stevens, "Vacations Through an Employment Bureau," *The Survey* 26 (22 July 1911): 610–12. In Chicago, the Eleanor Clubs operated a summer camp for working women. Pearl Harris MacLean to Gertrude Beeks, 15 November 1911, Chicago, Welfare Department, National Civic Federation Papers, NYPUB. Gertrude Beeks to Mrs. M. Haddon MacLean, 20 November 1911, [New York], Welfare Department, NCF, NYPUB.

31. *New York Times*, 3 July 1910, sec. 3, p. 5.

32. Spingarn, "Summer Vacations for Working Girls," 519.

33. *New York Times*, 25 June 1905, p. 3.

34. Gertrude Beeks to Helen Snow, 2 October 1911, New York, Welfare Department, NCF, NYPUB. See also Bowman & Co. to National Retail Dry Goods Association, 20 February 1913, Harrisburg, Pa., Welfare Department, NCF, NYPUB.

35. Spingarn, "Summer Vacations for Working Girls," 520.

36. Gertrude Beeks to Miss Edith Conant, 21 October 1912, New York, Welfare Department, NCF, NYPUB.

37. Spingarn, "Summer Vacations for Working Girls," 521.

38. See Elizabeth Israels Perry, *Belle Moskowitz: Feminine Politics & the Exercise of Power in the Age of Alfred E. Smith* (New York: Oxford University Press, 1987), 45–54; Peiss, *Cheap Amusements*; Meyerowitz, *Women Adrift*.

39. Beard, "Summer Outing Camps," 729.

40. Cohen, *Out of the Shadow*, 261–62.

41. Thompson, "The Vacation Savings Movement," 257.

42. Perry, *Belle Moskowitz*, 47.

43. For a discussion of reformers' interest in helping women see Skocpol, *Protecting Soldiers and Mothers*.

44. Jacoby, *Employing Bureaucracy*, 49.

45. Samuel Crowther, *John H. Patterson: Pioneer in Industrial Welfare* (New York: Doubleday, Page & Co., 1923), 196–97, and ch. 12.

46. Jacoby, *Employing Bureaucracy*, 61–62.

47. Vacation Policy, 1960, NCR.

48. The company apparently paid the fare and admission fees to the fair for 1,000 of the people, half the fare "of all other employes and part of the fares of the wives of the Men's Welfare Work League members who made the trip." It is unclear which employees merited full subsidization and which only got half. "N.C.R. Forces at World's Fair," *The N.C.R.* 27 (September 1905): 151–52, NCR. Charles M. Steele to National Civil Federation, 3 December 1906, Dayton, Ohio, Welfare Department, National Civic Federation Papers, NYPUB. Crowther, *John Patterson*, 195.

49. See Rosenzweig, *Eight Hours*, chs. 4, 5, 6.

50. No doubt prompted by the single-minded and somewhat eccentric ideas of John Patterson, NCR continued to pursue the idea of workers' vacations. In 1906 Charles M. Steele, the assistant head of the publications department at NCR, wrote to the National Civic Federation requesting "any information regarding vacation outings for factory employees." He reminded the National Civic Federation that NCR had "for the last three years" conducted "vacation outings, in 1904 going to

the St. Louis Worlds Fair, and in 1905 and 1906 conducting a vacation camp at the Lakes." Charles M. Steele to National Civic Federation, 3 December 1906, Dayton, Ohio, Welfare Department, National Civic Federation Papers, NYPUB.

51. "How Long Should a Man's Vacation Be," *New York Times Magazine*, 31 July 1910, p. 3.

52. "How Long Should a Man's Vacation Be," *New York Times Magazine*, 31 July 1910, p. 3.

53. [Gertrude Beeks] to George DeForest, 10 July 1909, New York, Welfare Department, National Civic Federation Papers, NYPUB; Gertrude Beeks, "Welfare Work," Welfare Department, National Civic Federation Papers, NYPUB; Report, 18 November 1911, Welfare Department, National Civic Federation Papers, NYPUB.

54. Thompson, "The Vacation Savings Movement," 259.

55. "The Annual Vacation," *NCR News* 1 (July 1914): 2, NCR.

56. Jacoby, *Employing Bureaucracy*, ch. 6.

57. Until the 1920s, however, such welfare policies were implemented only in a very small numbers of companies. See Jacoby, *Employing Bureaucracy*, 192–97.

58. Charles M. Mills, *Vacations for Industrial Workers* (New York: Ronald Press Co., 1927), 64.

59. "Vacation as a Business Asset," *Current Opinion* 60 (April 1916): 289.

60. J.D. Hackett, "Vacations with Pay for Factory Workers," *The Survey* 44 (16 August 1920): 626.

61. "Vacations with Pay for Workers," *The Literary Digest* 66 (11 September 1920): 37.

62. "Vacations for Factory Workers," *Monthly Labor Review* 13 (August 1921): 212–13; for similar arguments see State of New York, Department of Labor, *Vacation Policies in Manufacturing*, July 1925, Special Bulletin No. 138, pp. 14–15, DOL; Annette Mann, "Vacations with Pay for Production Workers," Cincinnati, Ohio, May 1926, DOL.

63. For more on Walter Camp see Gorn and Goldstein, *A Brief History of American Sports*, 153–64.

64. Walter Camp, "The Nose and the Grindstone," *Collier's* 68 (30 July 1921): 15; see also *New York Times*, 12 July 1925, sec. 8, p. 11.

65. "Vacation Policy," 1960, NCR. In 1922 there were 541 ten- and twenty-year factory employees who received vacations with pay. All "straight time and salaried employees," as well as "one year women employees," also received one week's vacation with pay. Ten-year employees were awarded one week, twenty-year employees enjoyed two weeks. "Ten and Twenty Year Employees Who Received Vacations With Pay," *NCR News* 8 (September 1922): 24–25, NCR.

66. "A Vacation Message," *NCR News* 8 (July-August 1922): 1, NCR.

67. Grace Pugh, *Vacations with Pay for Vacation Workers*, Consumer's League of Eastern Pennsylvania, May 1923, DOL.

68. Some of the other questions that businessmen raised were: How long should the vacations be? Should there be eligibility requirements? Should all employees receive the same amount of vacation, or should vacation time be graded based on seniority or service? When should employees receive their vacation pay—before the vacation, after the vacation, or at the end of the year? How should a company determine the vacation pay for hourly or piece rate workers? Should a company that pays workers for legal holidays also offer its employees vacation pay? Should workers be required to contribute money or time toward the cost of their vacation? Mills, *Vacations for Industrial Workers*, 51–61.

69. New York Dept. of Labor, *Vacation Policies,* 12–13, DOL.

70. New York Dept. of Labor, *Vacation Policies,* 10, DOL. Metropolitan Life Insurance Company, *Vacations for Industrial Workers* (New York: 1929), 9–12, DOL.

71. "Vacations with Pay for Production Workers," *Monthly Labor Review* 23 (July 1926): 35–36; see also "Nesday Chemical Company," *Harvard Business Reports* (Chicago: A.W. Shaw Co., 1927) 4:162–70.

72. *New York Times,* 12 July 1925, sec. 8, p. 11.

73. Armour and Company, for example, required women to have three years and men five years of service before becoming eligible for a week's paid vacations. Metropolitan Life, *Vacations for Industrial Workers,* 10, DOL.

74. David William Moore, "'Two Weeks'—Or Bust!" *The Outlook* 134 (August 1923): 669; Grace Pugh, "Vacations with Pay," *The Survey* 50 (15 July 1923): 435–36; "Taking a Vacation," *Catholic World* 117 (August 1923): 682–83; *New York Times,* 12 July 1925, sec. 8, p. 11.

75. Paul E. Johnson, *A Shopkeeper's Millennium: Society and Revivals in Rochester, New York, 1815–1837* (New York: Hill and Wang, 1978); Ryan, *Cradle of the Middle Class,* ch. 3; Rosenzweig, *Eight Hours,* chs. 4–6; Schmitt, *Back to Nature,* 73–74.

76. Hackett, "Vacations with Pay for Factory Workers," 626–27. In 1921 the Chicago Council of Industrial Relations Association of America conducted a survey of sixty-three firms and discovered that those with vacation policies for factory workers recognized "the need for employees spending their vacations in a beneficial way." "Vacations for Factory Workers," *Monthly Labor Review* 13 (August 1921), 213.

77. "Vacation Season is at Hand," *NCR News* 2 (August 1915): inside back cover, NCR.

78. "Vacations with Pay for Wage Earners," *Monthly Labor Review* 22 (May 1926): 3–4.

79. "The Vacation Problem in America," *The Playground* 18 (March 1925): 695–96.

80. "A Vacation Message," *NCR News* 7 (July-August 1921): 1, NCR.

81. "Now Comes Vacation," *NCR News* 9 (July-August 1923): 26, NCR.

82. *New York Times,* 12 July 1925, sec. 8, p. 11.

83. "Outdoor Recreation for Industrial Employees," *Monthly Labor Review* 24 (May 1927): 10–12. The Von Hoffman Press of St. Louis provided an "elaborate" facility—a 3,600 acre camp "in the Ozark Mountains where employees and their families may spend one week vacation." Cabins were furnished free. The camp also offered horses, a hunting preserve, and streams stocked with trout. "The food cost is $1.00 a day for each employee and each child up to 14 years of age, and $2.00 a day for guests." Metropolitan Life, *Vacations for Industrial Workers,* 15, DOL.

84. Mills, *Vacations for Industrial Workers,* 6, 9, 51–52, 58, 276–77. By 1927 Standard Oil of New Jersey, for example, was awarding a week's vacation to employees who had completed one year of service. A company official held that the "purpose of the vacation plan . . . is the two fold purpose of preparation for another year and reward for faithful performance of work already done." "Vacations with Pay for Industrial Workers," *Monthly Labor Review* 24 (May 1927): 36.

85. Donna Allen, *Fringe Benefits: Wages or Social Obligation? An Analysis with Historical Perspectives from Paid Vacations* (Ithaca: Cornell University Press, 1964), 66.

86. According to Jacoby, "between 1923 and 1927 unemployment rates in industry were higher than for any other five year period since 1900, excluding depression years." Jacoby, *Employing Bureaucracy,* 167–68, 171–72, and ch. 6.

87. Mills, *Vacations for Industrial Workers*, 15, 36, 39, 70–71, 141–42. Some of the other locals across the country that had negotiated contracts that included paid vacations were engine and steam operators, electrical workers, meat cutters, teamsters, and street and electrical railway workers. "Typical Local Union Agreements in the United States Containing Vacations Regulation," Agreements covering the years 1924–27, DOL.

88. Benjamin Kline Honeycutt, *Work Without End: Abandoning Shorter Hours for the Right to Work* (Philadelphia: Temple University Press, 1988), 80–83, 142, and passim.

89. Daniel J. Tobin, "Vacations with Pay," *American Federationist* 34 (July 1927): 794–96.

90. Quoted in "Vacations with Pay for Industrial Workers," *Monthly Labor Review* 24 (May 1927): 36.

91. Mills, *Vacations for Industrial Workers*, 70.

92. "Hawthorne Force Gets Mass Vacations—With Pay," *The Business Week* (30 July 1930): 16; *New York Times*, 29 June 1930, sec. 3, p. 5.

Chapter 8

1. Hiram Johnson, *The Diary Letters of Hiram Johnson*, ed. Robert E. Burke (New York: Garland Publishing Inc., 1983) vol. 3. (Pages are not numbered, these are facsimile of the following letters: Hiram Johnson to My Dear Boys, 20 August 1921, Atlantic City; Hiram Johnson to Hiram Johnson and Archibald Johnson, 10 September 1921, Washington, D.C.).

2. Whether or not to consider these African Americans "middle class" is a question that historians continue to debate. Most of these people represented the elite rather than the middle of African-American society. They did, however, subscribe to many of the cultural values and standards of the white middle class. See Glenda Elizabeth Gilmore, *Gender and Jim Crow: Women and the Politics of White Supremacy in North Carolina, 1896–1920* (Chapel Hill: University of North Carolina Press, 1996); Janette Thomas Greenwood, *Bittersweet Legacy: The Black and White 'Better Classes' in Charlotte, 1850–1910* (Chapel Hill: The University of North Carolina Press, 1994); Evelyn Brooks Higginbotham, *Righteous Discontent: The Women's Movement in the Black Baptist Church, 1880–1920* (Cambridge, Mass.: Harvard University Press, 1993); Willard B. Gatewood, *Aristocrats of Color: The Black Elite, 1880–1920* (Bloomington: Indiana University Press, 1990).

3. As early as 1905 Atlantic City, for example, could already "comfortably . . . accommodate and entertain a half million visitors" at one time. *New York Times,* 11 June 1905, sec. 4, p. 6. One million people visited resorts in the state of Michigan alone in 1920, adding more than $5,000,000 to the coffers of resort owners. John M. Hepler, "Sanitation Problems in Resorts and Tourist Camps," *American Journal of Public Health* 14 (November 1924): 925–30. National parks welcomed an increasing number of vacationers. In 1915 50,000 people visited Yellowstone. In 1916 400,000 people toured the national parks; by 1929 the number had grown to more than 3 million. Anne Farrar Hyde, *An American Vision: Far Western Landscape and National Culture, 1820–1920* (New York: New York University Press, 1990), 267. *New York Times,* 24 August 1920, sec. 3, p. 1.

4. See pp. 209, 229, 244–46 for more on the impact of cars. See also Warren Belasco, *Americans on the Road: From Autocamp to Motel, 1910–1945* (Cambridge, Mass.: MIT Press, 1979).

5. Alden Hatch, *American Express: A Century of Service* (New York: Doubleday &

Co., 1950), 93. Hugh DeSantis, "The Democratization of Travel: The Travel Agent in History," *Journal of American Culture* 1 (spring 1978): 10.

6. Ritter to Colt, 3 December 1912, New York, Tourism, Warshaw Collection of Business Americana, NMAH.

7. T.J. Jackson Lears, *No Place of Grace: Antimodernism and the Transformation of American Culture, 1880–1920* (Chicago: University of Chicago Press, 1983); John Higham, "The Reorientation of American Culture in the 1890s," in *Writing American History: Essays on Modern Scholarship*, ed. John Higham (Bloomington: Indiana University Press, 1970), 73–102; John F. Kasson, *Amusing the Million: Coney Island at the Turn of the Century* (New York: Hill and Wang, 1978).

8. "Strictly Personal," *NCR News* 1 (August 1914): 3, NCR.

9. "Up the Stillwater," *NCR News* 2 (July 1915): 10, NCR.

10. Robert S. Lynd and Helen Merrell Lynd, *Middletown: A Study in American Culture* (New York: Harcourt, Brace, Jovanovich, 1957), 251–56; Belasco, *Americans on the Road,* 106–7.

11. "Toolmaking Department," *NCR News* 6 (October 1919): 11, NCR. See also "Attention Vacationists," *NCR News* 9 (July-August 1923): 4; "Those Good Old Vacation Days," *NCR News* 9 (September 1923): 39, NCR.

12. "Screw No. 1 Department," *NCR News* 6 (October 1919): 24–25, NCR.

13. Historian Warren Belasco has written perceptively about the development of automobile touring among the middle class in the early twentieth century, but he has given less attention to the role of automobiles in the development of working-class vacations. Belasco suggests that a growing number of working-class autocampers, unable to afford the price of hotels, were staying at free municipal campgrounds that began to open in the late 1910s and early 1920s. See Belasco, *Americans on the Road,* 112–13 and passim.

14. "Cutter Dept.," *NCR News* 6 (September 1920): 50, NCR.

15. "An Ideal Vacation," *NCR News* 8 (July-August 1922): 28, 31, NCR.

16. "Dont's For Vacation Motorists," *NCR News* 12 (July-August 1926): 7, 18, NCR. D. M. Waggonner, an employee in the punch press department, described his 3,300 mile, two-week automobile trip west. He visited places in Colorado (Pikes Peak, the "famous Mineral Springs"), continued into Wyoming where he "took in a little of the Rodeo, or Frontier Celebration," and "enjoyed every minute" of the 13½ days. "3,300 Miles in 13½ Days—A Wonderful Trip," *NCR News* 14 (July-August 1928): 10, NCR.

17. "Attention Vacationists," *NCR News* 9 (June 1923): 46, NCR.

18. "Where You Can Go . . . ," *NCR News* 13 (July-August 1927): 7–8, NCR.

19. Janet Schulte, "'Summer Homes': A History of Family Summer Vacation Communities in Northern New England, 1880–1940," (Ph.D. diss., Brandeis University, 1993), 191–92 and ch. 3.

20. Walter Page et. al. "The People at Play," *World's Work* 4 (August 1902): 242.

21. Schulte, "Summer Homes," 133–35, 183–85, ch. 3.

22. Belasco, *Americans on the Road,* ch. 5.

23. Schmitt, *Back to Nature,* 162.

24. Wm. F.. Gossel to W.H. Taft, 10 May 1909, Butte, Montana, Entry 6, Yellowstone, Complaints, National Park Service Records, Record Group 79, NA.

25. Charles E. Funnell, *By the Beautiful Sea: The Rise and High Times of That Great American Resort, Atlantic City* (New Brunswick, N.J.: Rutgers University Press, 1983), 93.

26. Records Relating to *Women's Bureau Bulletin* No. 74: 7–10–24, *Immigrant Women and the Job* (1930), Record Group 86, NA. Many thanks to Eileen Boris for bringing this case to my attention.

27. "A Good Vacation Tip," *NCR News* 7 (June 1921): 46, NCR.

28. The *Indianapolis Freeman* reported in 1892 that in Atlantic City the "Afro-American boarding houses all seem to be doing a good business." *Indianapolis Freeman*, 16 July 1892, p. 7). The Thompson Cottage in Saratoga, "one of the finest in the city owned by any colored lady," was in 1901 apparently accommodating about 10 people who were "all pleasantly domiciled at this haven of rest, being carefully looked after by the proprietress, Mrs. Marshall." *Indianapolis Freeman*, 3 August 1901, p. 6. Caesar A. A. Taylor described spending two weeks in Saratoga, "the world's greatest watering place," where he stayed at the Howell House, owned by Dr. S. Howell. *Indianapolis Freeman*, 9 September 1893, p. 6. African American newspapers like the *Indianapolis Freeman* and the *Baltimore Afro-American* frequently reported on members of the community who were spending their vacation at Atlantic City or Cape May, and by the early twentieth century were running frequent ads for boarding houses and hotels in both seaside resorts. See, for example, *Baltimore Afro-American,* 10 August 1895, p. 4; 31 August 1895, p. 3; 13 June 1896, p. 2; Gatewood, *Aristocrats of Color,* 200–02.

29. *Indianapolis Freeman,* 7 July 1900, p. 7; 28 July 1900, p. 7; 13 July 1901, p. 3.

30. *Indianapolis Freeman,* 14 August 1915, p. 1. *Baltimore Afro-American* 10 July 1915, p. 6 described Sea Isle, New Jersey, this way: "This little haven for those seeking a brief respite from work during the summer presented a gala appearance from Friday to Tuesday, hundreds of persons coming to enjoy the brief holiday period [July 4]. The mecca of the race was the Ocean House, a modern hostelry with accommodations for 100 guests and situated right on the boardwalk. The spacious and well-appointed dining room directly overlooks the ocean, thus adding zest to the meal as one sniffs the salt air. An orchestra enlivens things, smartly-gowned women and well groomed men, all with evident air of refinement and education, tend to make the surroundings desirable. . . . A reception . . . and a grand hop took place at the Ocean House Monday night. The visitors were lavish in their praise of the fittings of the Ocean house, which is said to be one of the best on the Atlantic Ocean run by colored people."

31. *Baltimore Afro-American,* 30 May 1896, p. 1. See also "Vacation Days," *The Crisis* 4 (August 1912): 186.

32. *New York Times,* 15 August 1905, p. 1. See also *New York Times,* 10 August 1890, p. 10.

33. *Indianapolis Freeman,* 4 July 1908, p. 7.

34. "Vacation Days," 187; *Indianapolis Freeman,* 31 August 1907, p. 6.

35. *Baltimore Afro-American,* 7 August 1909, p. 5.

36. Advertisements for the Hotel Dale in Cape May appeared repeatedly in the *Indianapolis Freeman* in the early 1910s. See, for example, *Indianapolis Freeman,* 10 June 1911, p. 2; 17 June 1911, p. 3; 15 June 1912, pp. 1, 3; 6 July 1912, p. 3; 27 June 1914, p. 8; 4 July 1914, p. 8; 15 August 1914, p. 8.

Advertisements for new hotels in Atlantic City appeared in African-American newspapers, as did ads for black hotels in Sea Island, N.J.; Harper's Ferry, W. Va; Averne, a beach community on Long Island; and at Mt. Clements, Mich. See, for example, *New Pittsburgh Courier,* 27 May 1911, p. 3; *Baltimore Afro-American,* 30 May 1914, p. 2; 6 June 1914, p. 5; *Indianapolis Freeman,* 29 May 1915, p. 8; *Baltimore Afro-American,* 28 June 1918, p. 2; 5 July 1918, p. 6; *Indianapolis Freeman,* 22 June 1907, p. 5; 18 July 1908, p. 3; *New Pittsburgh Courier,* 22 May 1911, p. 5.

37. *Indianapolis Freeman,* 8 August 1908, p. 7; 27 August 1910, p. 1; 19 August 1911, p. 6; 26 July 1913, p. 7.

38. *New Pittsburgh Courier,* 4 August 1923, p. 11.

39. *New Pittsburgh Courier,* 18 June 1927, sec. 2, p. 1. During the 1920s increasing numbers of summer hotels and boarding houses for African Americans opened in places as diverse as Buckroe Beach on the Chesapeake Bay in Virginia, the Pocono Mountains of Pennsylvania, in the mountains at Asheville, North Carolina, New Cumberland in West Virginia, and in Middletown, New York. *Baltimore Afro-American,* 30 May 1924, p. 2; *New Pittsburgh Courier,* 5 June 1926, p. 2; 4 June 1927, p. 7; "Vacation Days," 186–88.

40. *Indianapolis Freeman,* 29 July 1916, p. 7.

41. Shirlee Taylor Haizlip, "The Black Resort," *American Legacy* 2 (summer 1996): 11–21; Marsha Dean Phelts, *An American Beach for African Americans* (Gainesville, Fla.: University Press of Florida, 1997).

42. Carroll Greene Jr., "Summertime—In the Highland Beach Tradition," *American Visions* 1 (July 1986): 46–50; Mary Church Terrell, *A Colored Woman in a White World* (Washington, D.C.: Ransdell, Inc., 1940): 239–40.

43. Jacqueline L. Holland, "The African American Presence on Martha's Vineyard," *The Dukes County Intelligencer* 33 (August 1991), 3–26; Adelaide M. Cromwell, "The History of Oak Bluffs as a Popular Resort for Blacks," *The Dukes County Intelligencer* 26 (August 1984): 3–26. Telephone conversation with Dorothy West, Martha's Vineyard, July 1994.

44. John Fraser Hart, "A Rural Retreat for Northern Negroes," *The Geographical Review* 1 (April 1960): 156–58.

45. Alice Rhine, "Race Prejudice at Summer Resorts," *The Forum* 3 (July 1887): 523–31. Stephen Birmingham, *"Our Crowd": The Great Jewish Families of New York* (New York: Harper and Row, 1967), ch. 18. Stefan Kanfer, *A Summer World* (New York: Farrar Straus Giroux, 1989), 40–42.

46. Birmingham, *Our Crowd,* 164; *New York Times,* 2 June 1885, p. 7; Alf Evers et. al. *Resorts of the Catskills* (New York: St. Martin's Press, 1979), 82–83.

47. Philips to A.T. Bell, 25 February 1916, Mohonk, MMH; Bell to M.C. Phillips, 26 February 1916, Atlantic City, MMH.

48. Annual Report of the Secretary, 1917, MMH; Annual Report of Secretary to Mr. Smiley, 1918, MMH. Throughout the 1920s the Annual Report of the House Manager continued to report on the number of "Hebrews" who somehow managed to get in. For example, the 1921 report admitted: "As always, a few Hebrews . . . got in, sometimes by subterfuge; but usually only three-quarters of a day was needed to interest them in other places. One Mr. Levy (a very decent fellow) walked in and remained a week." Annual Report of the House Manager, 1921, MMH.

49. *New York Times,* 23 June 1895, p. 12; 30 June 1895, p. 13; 10 July 1910, p. 5.

50. Abraham Cahan, *The Rise of David Levinksy* (New York: Penguin Books, 1993), 403–5.

51. N.B. Fagin, "East Siders in the Mountains," *The Survey* (15 July 1923): 443–44. See also Harry Gersh, "'Kochalein': Poor Man's Shangri-La," in *Commentary on the American Scene: Portraits of Jewish Life in America,* ed. Elliot Cohen (New York: Alfred A. Knopf, 1953), 161–77.

52. "Refugees from New York," *The Survey* (15 July 1923): 443.

53. *Justice,* 8 June 1923, p. 11.

54. *Justice,* 5 July 1919, p. 8.

55. *Justice,* 23 June 1919, p. 7; 21 June 1919, p. 8; 5 July 1919, p. 8.

56. *Justice,* 19 June 1920, p. 3.

57. *Justice,* 9 June 1922, p. 5; 16 June 1922, p. 1; 14 July 1922, p. 10.

58. Throughout the 1920s members of the ILGWU could vacation there for about $17 a week, while members of other unions paid about $5 more. *Justice,* 23 July 1922, p. 1. General Secretary Treasurer to Mr. Julius Portnoy, 2 February 1925, Records of the ILGWU, Martin P. Catherwood Library, Cornell University, Ithaca, N.Y. *Justice,* 24 July 1925, p. 8; 5 July 1919, p. 8; 22 July 1921, p. 6; 24 July 1925, p. 8; 15 Aug. 1927, pp. 1–2.

59. Susan Stone Wong, "From Soul to Strawberries: The International Ladies' Garment Workers' Union and Workers' Education, 1914–1950," in *Sisterhood and Solidarity: Workers' Education for Women, 1914–1984,* ed. Joyce L. Kornbluh and Mary Frederickson (Philadelphia: Temple University Press, 1984), 41.

60. *Justice,* 17 July 1920, p. 5.

61. *Justice,* 19 August 1927, pp. 5,7.

62. "What fills Unity House," Bertha Mailly wrote, "is a sense of comradeship and it finds expression in constant singing together and walking together." *Justice,* 2 July 1920, p. 6.

63. *Justice,* 23 June 1922, p. 10; 24 July 1925, p. 8; 10 June 1927, p. 6.

64. *Justice,* 17 June 1925, p. 4; 10 June 1927, pp. 1–2.

65. *Justice,* 17 June 1925, p. 10.

66. *Justice,* 10 June 1927, pp. 1–2.

67. Myra Beth Young Armstead, "The History of Blacks in Resort Towns: Newport, Rhode Island and Saratoga Springs, New York," (Ph.D. diss., University of Chicago, 1987).

68. David Nasaw, *Going Out: The Rise and Fall of Public Amusements* (New York: Basic Books, 1993), 1–2.

69. Max Siepereman to Secretary of Interior, 16 July 1920, New York; T.H. Martin to Toll, 2 August 1920, Longmire, Washington; Entry 6, Mt. Rainier Complaints, National Park Service Records, Record Group 79, NA.

70. E.E. Sykes to Mr. Cammerer, 17 May 1923, New Orleans; [Ambrose?] to Cammerer, 5 June 1923, Kansas City, Mo., Entry 6, Grand Canyon Complaints, National Park Service Records, Record Group 79, NA.

71. A.H. Thompson to Dept. of Interior, 9 August 1920, Vancouver, Wash., Entry 6, Mt. Rainier Complaints, National Park Service Records, Record Group 79, NA.

72. For ptomaine poisoning incident see Annual Report of House Manager's Department, 1923, MMH. The problems with bed bugs, roaches, red ants, and other vermin appeared almost yearly in the house manager's reports throughout the 1910s and 1920s.

73. John M. Hepler, "Sanitation Problems in Resorts and Tourist Camps," *American Journal of Public Health* 14 (September 1924): 925–26.

74. *New York Times,* 9 July 1925, p. 18.

75. *New York Times,* 17 July 1925, p. 16.

76. See Kathy Peiss, *Cheap Amusements: Working Women and Leisure in Turn-of-the Century New York* (Philadelphia: Temple University Press, 1986).

77. See chapter 3.

78. Flora Ward to Dept. of Interior, 27 July 1909, Entry 6, Yellowstone, Complaints, National Park Service Records, Record Group 79, NA.

79. *New York Times,* 19 August 1905, p. 7; 29 July 1905, p. 7.

80. Recollections of Willie S. Martin, Lake Mohonk, 1912–13, MMH.

81. Annual Report of Secretary of Mr. Smiley, 1917, MMH.

82. Annual Report of House Manager's Department, 1921, MMH.

83. *New York Times*, 8 August 1910, p. 1; 9 August 1910, p. 1; 10 August 1910, p. 9, 10.

84. *New York Times*, 10 August 1910, p. 9, 10; 8 August 1910, p. 1; 9 August 1910, p. 1.

85. Anna Steese Richardson, "Etiquette at a Glance: Some Vacation Pointers," *Woman's Home Companion* 54 (July 1927): 40. See also Margaret Sangster, "Summer Holidays," *Woman's Home Companion* 32 (July 1905): 26; *New York Times*, 26 August 1910, p. 6; "As To Vacations," *The World Today* 8 (June 1905): 569–70; Harvey M. Wiley, "Vacation Vaticinations," *Good Housekeeping* 63 (July 1916): 80–84.

86. Ruth Harger, "Vacation Experiences: On a Mountain Shelf," *The Independent* 68 (2 June 1910): 1196–97.

87. For an excellent and thorough discussion of autocamping see Warren Belasco, *Americans on the Road*.

88. "Vacation Experiences: Symposium," *The Independent* 66 (2 June 1909): 1222–23.

89. See, for example, J.R. Vedder, "Our Gypsy Vacation: Real Vacations for Little Money," *Woman's Home Companion* 41 (August 1915): 18; "Vacation Days: Seven on Four Wheels," *Colliers* 45 (9 July 1910): 16; "The Business Girls' Two-Weeks' Vacation," *Ladies Home Journal* 27 (May 1910): 32; "Vacation Experiences: Six Hundred Miles in a Buggy," *The Independent* 68 (2 June 1910): 1182; "Where to Spend Your Vacation," *Woman's Home Companion* 40 (August 1913): 22.

90. George E. Walsh, "A Motorboat Vacation," *Country Life in America* 18 (May 1910): 110. See also Herbert Whyte, "Vacation in a Canoe," *The Outing Magazine* 56 (June 1910): 382–84; Edward I. Pratt, "A Three-Dollar Houseboat Vacation," *Country Life in America* 18 (June 1910): 210–11; "Vacation Experiences: In a Canoe," *The Independent* 68 (2 June 1910): 1191–92.

91. "Vacation Experiences: In Bonnie Maryland," *The Independent* 72 (6 June 1912): 1227–28. See also Beatrice Griswold, "Vacations Days on a Houseboat," *Craftsman* 24 (July 1914): 402–9; "Vacation Experiences: Canoe Cruising," *The Independent* 74 (5 June 1913): 1273–74; Herbert Whyte, "Vacations in a Canoe," *The Outing Magazine* 56 (June 1910): 382–84; Edward I. Pratt, "A Three-Dollar Houseboat Vacation," *Country Life in America* 18 (June 1910): 210–11; W.P. Stephens, "The Vacation Cruise," *Country Life in America* 18 (September 1910): 546–47.

92. Four women camping alone apparently attracted some attention. Foye recorded that "people were much interested in us and watched us load our packs and start off. The hotel man was very kind and gave us all the water we could drink and filled our canteen for us." In general they found other campers and vacationers "so kind and obliging, so willing to give advice about roads, shortcuts, etc. They think our trip is fine and that we are very brave to start out without any men in the party . . ." Eva N. Foye, "On Their Own in Yosemite," *Sierra* 64 (May/June 1979): 18–26.

93. See, for example, H.W. Dewey, "Vacations for Everybody," *Woman's Home Companion* 39 (May 1912): 47; "New Ways to Take a Vacation," *Women's Home Companion* 40 (July 1913): 31; "Delightful Vacations at Little Cost," *Women's Home Companion* 40 (May 1913): 25–26; "Real Vacations for Little Money," *Woman's Home Companion* 41 (August 1915): 18; "Vacations as a Business Asset," *Current Opinion* 60 (April 1916): 289–96.

94. See, for example, "An Enforced Vacation," *The Outlook* 114 (20 September 1914): 152–54.

95. Harger, "On a Mountain Shelf," 1196–97.

96. "New Ways to Take a Vacation," *Woman's Home Companion* 40 (July 1913): 31.

97. "The Business Girls' Vacation," *Woman's Home Companion* 41 (July 1914): 5, 40.

98. "Vacation Experiences: In the Sugar Bush," *The Independent* 70 (1 June 1911): 1170. First prize in the *Independent's* 1914 essay contest went to Minnie Leona Upton who described going home for "maple sugar time." "Best Vacation Day," *Independent* 78 (1 June 1914): 353.

99. "Vacation Experiences: A Factory Girl's Vacation," *The Independent* 72 (6 June 1912): 1215; "A Factory Girl's Vacation," *The Literary Digest* 44 (June 1912): 1309–11.

100. "Delightful Vacations at Little Cost," 25–26.

101. "Vacation Experiences Symposium: A Haying Vacation," *The Independent* 66 (3 June 1909): 1218.

102. Frederick Brush, "Vacation Days: The Hayin'," *Colliers* 49 (10 July 1909): 9.

103. See, for example, "Delightful Vacations at Little Cost," 25–26; "Ways and Means of Taking a Vacation: A Dozen Contributions from the Companion Contest," *Woman's Home Companion* 41 (June 1914): 8; "Vacation Days," *Colliers* 57 (5 August 1911): 16–19; "Good Times that Cost Next To Nothing," *Woman's Home Companion* 41 (August 1914): 22; "The Business Girls Vacation," 40; "Plan Your Vacation Early," *Women's Home Companion* 41 (May 1914): 35; "New Ways to Take a Vacation," *Women's Home Companion* 40 (July 1913): 31.

104. "Ways and Means of Taking a Vacation: A Dozen Contributions from the Companion Contest," 8.

105. "Vacation Days: Changing Workshops," *Colliers* 47 (5 August 1911): 19.

106. "Vacation Days: Seven on Four Wheels," *Colliers* 45 (9 July 1910): 16.

107. Leonard Hatch, "Billy Gets Back to Work," *Colliers* 70 (9 September 1922): 28.

108. See, for example, Floyd W. Parsons, "Everybody's Business," *The Saturday Evening Post* 195 (6 May 1922): 34; "Longer Vacations," *The New Republic* 27 (10 August 1921): 286–87; Wallace Meyer, "After All, This is World for Well People," *The Magazine of Business* 54 (August 1928): 140–44; "A Vacation for Farmers," *The Playground* 17 (January 1924): 574–75; *New York Times*, 13 July 1925, p. 2; William S. Sadler, M.D. "Getting Away from the Grind," *The American Magazine* 103 (June 1927): 29, 181–85.

Chapter 9

1. Benjamin Kline Hunnicutt, *Work Without End: Abandoning Shorter Hours for the Right to Work* (Philadelphia: Temple University Press, 1988), 1. Hunnicutt offers an excellent analysis of the shortening of work hours during the depression.

2. "Should Ministers Have a Vacation?" *Literary Digest* 110 (8 August 1931): 21–22.

3. William E. Leuchtenburg, *Franklin D. Roosevelt and the New Deal, 1932–1940* (New York: Harper and Row, 1963), 1.

4. *New York Times*, 18 August 1935, sec. 10, p. 12. Sociologist Jesse Steiner, who conducted a study on recreation during the depression for the Social Science Research Council, found that "seasonal hotels, which rely largely upon the patronage of tourists and vacationists, showed a decline of 75 per cent in receipts between 1929 and 1933." Jesse F. Steiner, *Research Memorandum on Recreation in the Depression* (New York: Social Science Research Council, 1937; reprinted by Arno Press, 1971), p. 95.

5. Bulletin, 6 September 1932, Bulletin, 6 July 1932, Entry 7, Yellowstone, National Park Service Records, Record Group 79, NA.

6. Joseph Joffe, Outlook Bright for 1935 Yellowstone Park Travel, Department of Interior, Yellowstone National Park, Entry 7, Yellowstone, National Park Service Records, Record Group 79, NA.

7. Grand Canyon, File 550, Part 1, Entry 7, National Park Service Records, Record Group 79, NA.

8. Mohonk Mountain House, Annual Report, 1930, MMH; Mohonk Mountain House, Annual Report, 1931, MMH. In 1931 the prices at Mohonk were $42 to $49 for a single, doubles with bathrooms went for $84 to $98 per week.

9. Mohonk Mountain House, Annual Report, 1931, MMH.

10. Mohonk Mountain House, Annual Report, 1933, MMH.

11. Grand Canyon, File 504, Part 3, Entry 7, National Park Service Records, Record Group 79, NA.

12. *New York Times*, 9 June 1935, sec. 10, p. 1.

13. Steiner, *Research Memorandum on Recreation in the Depression*, 64.

14. *New York Times*, 9 June 1935, sec. 10, p. 1. See also 30 June 1935, sect., 11, p. 1. Sociologist Jesse Steiner found that "... pleasure travel was one of the first forms of recreation to show a decided upward trend. By the year 1935 travel had increased to the point where transportation agencies were beginning to face the problem of crowded passenger accommodations." Steiner, *Research Memorandum on Recreation in the Depression*, 95.

15. *New York Times*, 11 August 1935, p. 9. See also 5 August 1935, sec. 10, p. 1.

16. *New York Times*, 18 August 1935, sec. 10, p. 12

17. Yellowstone, Press Release for 1936 and 1937, File 501.03, Entry 7, National Park Service Records, Record Group 79, NA; Yellowstone, Press Release, 15 August 1939, File 501.03, Part II, Entry 7, National Park Service Records, Record Group 79, NA. Similarly Grand Canyon saw an upturn after 1933. In 1935 206,018 tourists visited Grand Canyon, and two years later the numbers had reached almost 300,000. Grand Canyon, File 550, Part 1, Entry 7, National Park Service Records, Records Group 79, NA.

18. Mohonk Mountain House, Annual Report, 1938, MMH; Mohonk Mountain House, Annual Report, 1939, MMH. The management credited their decision not to raise the rates in 1934 with the 15 percent increase in volume of business and a 13 percent increase in revenue over 1933. By 1937 their total receipts equaled $335,541, although they fell slightly over the next two years.

19. *New York Times*, 2 June 1930, p. 24. That same month New York state health offices and public health nurses assembled at Saratoga for their annual conference where Governor Franklin Roosevelt addressed the opening session. *New York Times*, 22 June 1930, sec. 2, p. 2. In 1935 Atlantic City hosted 8,000 people for the joint meeting of the American and Canadian Medical Associations while 2,000 doctors, nurses, and lay people attended a joint meeting of the American Sanitorium Association and the National Tuberculosis Association at Saranac Lake, New York. *New York Times*, 9 June 1935, sec. 2, p. 4; 23 June 1935, sec. 2, p. 7. Montana bankers, Business and Professional Women's clubs, and various sororities held conventions in Yellowstone at Old Faithful and Canyon Hotels. Joseph Joffee, "Outlook Bright for 1935 Yellowstone Park Travel," Yellowstone, File 501.04, Entry 7, National Park Service Records, Record Group 79, NA.

20. "The American Vacation," *Fortune* 17 (July 1936): 158, 161.

21. "Even in the midst of the depression in 1933, the decline from 1929 represented a drop of only 36% [in expenditure for vacation travel] ... compared to a drop of 49% for recreational services and 61% for recreational products." Julius

Weinberger, "Economic Aspects of Recreation," *Harvard Business Review* 15 (summer 1937): 448–63. For more on the importance of automobiles in vacationing in the 1930s, see pp. 244–46.

22. The *Fortune* survey did show that the "the length of vacation rises as you mount the [economic] scale," but that "still, half of the prosperous have only two weeks or less." "The American Vacation," 158, 161.

23. See, for example, *New York Times,* 8 June 1930, sec. 9, pp. 13–22; 14 June 1930, p. 21; 15 June 1930, sec. 2, p. 5; 29 June 1930, sec. 8, p. 10; 6 July 1930, sec. 8, p. 9; 6 June 1935, p. 18. During the summer of 1935 the *New York Times* sometimes included travel sections of 22 pages or more. See 9 June 1935, sec. 10; 30 June 1935, sec. 11; 7 July 1935, sec. 10; 14 July 1935, sec. 10; 21 July 1935, sec. 10.

24. Harold Ickes, *The Secret Diary of Harold Ickes* (New York: Simon and Schuster, 1954), 2: 178–79. See also G. William Domhoff, *The Bohemian Grove and Other Retreats: A Study in Ruling-Class Cohesiveness* (New York: Harper and Row, 1974).

25. Winifred Woodley, *Two and Three Make One* (New York: Crown Publishers, 1956), 53, 70, and passim.

26. Telephone interview with Selma Squires, 10 June 1997.

27. Ann Marie Low, *Dust Bowl Diary* (Lincoln: University of Nebraska Press, 1984), 86–88 and passim.

28. *NCR News* 16 (July-August 1930): 15–16, NCR.

29. *NCR News* 16 (July-August 1930): 15, 16; *NCR News* 16 (September 1930): 7; *NCR Factory News* 3 (August 1935): 1, 6–8; *NCR Factory News* 4 (September 1936): 7, NCR.

30. *NCR News* 16 (July-August 1930): 42, NCR. The company organized a variety of summer excursions for its employees—in 1934 to the Chicago World's Fair, in 1935 to Washington, D.C., and in 1936 to New York City. The 1936 trip to New York included 537 people riding in "the largest industrial excursion train that every pulled into Pennsylvania Station." One member of the group described his experience—visiting the Empire State Building, Rockefeller Center, the NBC studios, the Cathedral of St. John the Divine, and the Statue of Liberty. He maintained, however, that "the most interesting were the trips through Harlem, Chinatown, and the Ghetto. It certainly is impressive to see how and under what condition some people exist." Before returning to Ohio the group sailed up the Hudson, stopped to tour West Point, and continued on to Niagara. *NCR Factory News* 4 (July-August 1936): 13; *NCR Factory News* 4 (September 1936): 6–7, NCR.

31. As budgets studies of the 1930s have discovered, even people who faced severe economic constraints did what they could to maintain "their previous standard of living." Some families took advantage of the decline in food prices and scraped together funds to keep up payments on a car, to attend the movies, and generally to try to maintain pre-depression levels of consumption. Daniel Horowitz, *The Morality of Spending: Attitudes Toward the Consumer Society in America, 1875–1940* (Baltimore: Johns Hopkins University Press, 1985), 153–61.

32. And the amount spent increased with the slight economic upturn of 1935, when "vacation travel—85 percent of it by car—accounted for over half of the total estimated expenditures for all recreational purposes, $1,788 million out of $3,316 million." Warren Belasco, *Americans on the Road: From Autocamp to Motel, 1910–1945* (Cambridge, Mass.: MIT Press, 1979), 142–43. The vast majority of tourists to national parks traveled by car. In 1932 only 821 people arrived in Grand Canyon on the train, while 4,648 cars entered. Four years later 3,000 people came by train but almost 11,000 cars arrived at the park. Each car, of course, was likely to contain

many vacationers. Grand Canyon, File 550, Entry 7, National Park Service Records, Record Group 79, NA. By the 1930s African American vacationers could consult *The Negro Motorist Green Book*, a publication listing the hotels, camps, road houses, and restaurants that accomodated African Americans. *The Negro Motorist Green Book* (N.Y.: Victor H. Green, 1938).

33. "The American Vacation," 158, 161.

34. Belasco, *Americans on the Road*, 152.

35. Belasco, *Americans on the Road*, 152, 144. In 1935 the *New York Times* offered a somewhat higher estimate. 16 June 1935, sec. 11, p. 15.

36. *New York Times*, 16 June 1935, sec. 11, p. 15.

37. Belasco, *Americans on the Road*, 150–51.

38. *New York Times*, 21 July 1935, sec. 10, p. 1.

39. *New York Times*, 28 July 1935, sec. 11, p. 10.

40. *New York Times*, 9 June 1935, sec. 10, p. 1.

41. "A Report Prepared by the Industrial Bureau, the Merchant's Association of New York," 21 July 1932, DOL. "Vacation Practices and Policies in New York City in 1932," *Monthly Labor Review* 35 (September 1932): 533–34. "'Wageless' Vacations Help to Keep Payrolls Down," *The Business Week* (6 July 1932): 10.

42. "Vacations with Pay for Wage Earners," *Monthly Labor Review* 40 (June 1935): 1494–99. *Vacations With Pay for Wage Earners* (New York: National Industrial Conference Board, 1935), 9–10. The study discovered that as companies shortened hours in response to decreased industrial demand, many executives felt vacations were no longer necessary. The Conference Board, however, pointed to the importance of vacations as a means of "making possible a period of complete freedom in which the employee may get away from customary tasks and surroundings and secure a new point of view, as well as relaxation and rest . . . ." The authors felt that since at this particular moment "more thought is being given to maintaining cordial relations with employees, a vacation policy merits consideration, since it is certain to arouse spontaneous approval of employees."

43. *Vacations With Pay*, p. 31.

44. National Industrial Conference Board, Conference Board Information Services: Domestic Affairs Series, "Selected Plans of Companies Granting Vacations with Pay to Wage Earners: Memorandum No. 48," 1936, DOL. "Vacations with Pay for Wage Earners," 1496. "Vacations in Manufacturing Industries in New York," *Monthly Labor Review* 32 (April 1931): 189–90. Donna Allen, *Fringe Benefits: Wages or Social Obligations?* (Ithaca, New York: Cornell University Press, 1964), 66.

45. U.S. Bureau of Statistics, U.S. Department of Labor, *Vacations with Pay in Industry, 1937* (Washington, D.C.: U.S. Government Printing Office, 1939), 8, 2.

46. U.S. Dept. of Labor, Division of Labor Standards, *Reports of Committees and Resolutions Adopted by Third Annual Conference on Labor Legislation: Report of Committee on Vacations with Pay* (Washington, D.C.: Government Printing Office, 1936), 23, DOL.

47. Jacoby, *Employing Bureaucracy*, 233, 253–54, chs. 7, 8.

48. Allen, *Fringe Benefits*, 80, 77, ch. 4.

49. Allen, *Fringe Benefits*, 76.

50. For labor's interest in regularizing work, see Ron Schatz, *The Electrical Workers: A History of Labor at General Electric and Westinghouse, 1923–60* (Urbana: University of Illinois Press, 1983), 150.

51. Allen, *Fringe Benefits*, 73, 84.

52. International Labour Conference, *Holidays With Pay* (Geneva: International Labour Office, 1935), 97–102.

53. Allen, *Fringe Benefits*, 79–88.

54. Hunnicutt, *Work Without End*, ch 3.

55. Henry Pratt Fairchild, "Exit the Gospel of Work," *Harper's* (April 1931): 567. See also "The New Leisure, *The New Republic* 137 (19 November 1933): 610–11; Bertrand Russell, "In Praise of Idleness," *Harper's Magazine* 165 (October 1932): 558. In *The Challenge of Leisure*, Arthur Newton Pack held: "It would be a rash prophet who denies the possibility that this generation may live to see a two-hour day." Arthur Newton Pack, *The Challenge of Leisure* (New York: Macmillan, 1934), 11.

56. Hunnicutt, *Work Without End*, chs. 5–8.

57. See, for example, Jesse Frederick Steiner, *Americans At Play: Recent Trends in Recreation and Leisure Time Activities* (New York: McGraw Hill, 1933); George A. Lundberg et. al., *Leisure: A Suburban Study* (New York: Columbia University Press, 1934); Jesse F. Steiner, *Research Memorandum on Recreation in the Depression* (New York: Social Science Research Council, 1937); Pack, *The Challenge of Leisure*, "Coming: The Age of Leisure," *Literary Digest* 112 (January 16, 1932): 26; Fairchild, "Exit the Gospel of Work," 566–73; Walter Lippmann, "Free Time and Extra Money," *Woman's Home Companion* 57 (April 1930): 31–32; F. H. Allport, "This Coming Era of Leisure," *Harper's Magazine* 163 (November 1931): 641–52; A. Pond, "Out of Unemployment, Into Leisure," *Atlantic* 146 (December 1930): 784–92; H.I. Phillips, "Have a Good Time," *Collier's* 93 (21 April 1934): 20; Russell, "In Praise of Idleness," 552–59.

58. See, for example, Richard Wightman Fox and T.J. Jackson Lears, ed., *The Culture of Consumption: Critical Essays in American History 1889–1980* (New York: Pantheon Books, 1983), ix–xiii.

59. Fairchild, "Exit the Gospel of Work," 567.

60. "National Recovery Administration Acts to Teach Workers to Play," *Recreation* 27 (December 1933): 403.

61. Nicholas Murray Butler, "Leisure and Its Use," *Recreation* 23 (August 1934): 219.

62. Pack, *The Challenge of Leisure*, 58–59 and ch. 3. Professor of sociology Jesse Steiner explained the problem this way: "When leisure was merely a brief respite from long hours of exacting toil, it was valued chiefly as a time for rest and for relaxation through pleasurable diversions. As leisure expands, it provides opportunity for self-improvement and public service as well as for sports and games. One of our serious problems is the development of leisure time attitudes and habits that will be satisfactorily adjusted to an era that enjoys long hours of leisure." Steiner, *Research Memorandum on Recreation in the Depression*, 112. Writing in *Harper's* in 1931, Henry Pratt Fairchild, admonished: "The god of work must be cast down from his ancient throne, and the divinity of enjoyment put in his place." Fairchild cautioned, however, that "leisure . . . must be immeasurably more than mere idleness." Like many others, Fairchild advocated leisure spent in "the realization and enlargement of personality." Such pursuits could range from amateur photography, cabinet making and gardening, to "art, or philosophy, or research, or the breeding of Chow dogs or dahlias." Fairchild, "Exit the Gospel of Work," 570, 572.

63. Pack, *Challenge of Leisure*, 51.

64. "Time for Play," *Collier's* 92 (12 August 1933): 50.

65. Lippmann, "Free Time and Extra Money," 31–32.

66. "Time for Play," 50.

67. "Organizing for Leisure," *The Survey* 62 (December 1933): 405.

68. Anna Steese Richardson, "These Changing Vacations," *Woman's Home Com-*

panion 64 (July 1937): 6; Marese Eliot, "Why Not a Stay-at-Home Vacation?" *Recreation* 31 (May 1937): 91–92, 115–16.

69. Clara Ingram Johnson, "The Homemaker's Vacation," *Ladies Home Journal* 47 (August 1930): 74.

70. Leon Meadow, "Double Dividends from Sunshine Preferred," *Popular Science Monthly* 119 (July 1931): 4–5.

71. "Pack Up Your Family and Go!" *Ladies Home Journal* 49 (July 1932): 12–13. See also Frank J. Taylor, "Tips for the Two-Week Vacationists," *Better Homes and Gardens* 9 (June 1931): 13.

72. Mrs. Franklin D. Roosevelt, "By Car & Tent," *Woman's Home Companion* 61 (August 1934): 4.

73. Grace Higgins, "Match Yourself to a Vacation," *Ladies Home Journal* 48 (June 1931): 17, 126.

74. William Lyon Phelps, "Don't Sleep Through the Summer," *The Delineator* 118 (May 1931): 9, 101. To those who could not afford to leave home, Phelps recommended taking advantage of numerous opportunities for self-improvement available, especially in large cities: ". . . there are many opportunities to hear either free, or at a very low price, symphony orchestras playing splendid music in a public park or in a stadium. . . . If the motion pictures and talkies are carefully chosen, they may minister to education as well as to amusement. If one has a radio it may be turned into a source of true culture, instead of softening the brains of the household and destroying the character of the neighbors."

75. "Holiday Time," *Nature Magazine* 17 (June 1931): 361. "The Challenge of the Vacation," according to a 1934 article in *Hygeia,* "is in doing something that we have long wanted to do but for some reason could not accomplish." While not diminishing the importance of using vacation time to "recuperate physically," the author emphasized vacationing as an opportunity to do "some of the things that [one's] soul craves to do." This could mean learning a new language ("just for fun"), experimenting with color photography, or fixing up a "dilapidated farm." "The Challenge of the Vacation," *Hygeia: The Health Magazine* 12 (January–December 1934): 652.

76. *New York Times,* 3 August 1935, p. 12.

77. *New York Times,* 23 June 1935, sec. 10, p. 1.

78. The little theater movement was an effort to bring serious drama and theater to a broader cross section of the population and to revitalize theater in America. Joseph Kett explains that the little theaters "reacted against the Broadway commercial theater's enshrinement of profit, presentations of long-running shows that destroyed repertory, typecasting that checked the development of actors, and hostility toward experimentation." Joseph F. Kett, *Pursuit of Knowledge Under Difficulties: From Self-Improvement to Adult Education in America, 1750–1990* (Stanford, CA.: Stanford University Press, 1994), 381–89.

79. *New York Times,* 23 June 1935, sec. 10, p. 1.

80. *New York Times,* 25 June 1933, p. 1–2. These included theaters at Saratoga Springs, Newport, Long Beach, Spring Lake (New Jersey), Ogunquit (Maine), Putney (Vermont), and Abingdon (Virginia), among others.

81. *New York Times,* 23 June 1935, sec. 10, p. 1.

82. See Barbara Melosh, *Engendering Culture: Manhood and Womanhood in New Deal Public Art and Theater* (Washington, D.C.: Smithsonian Institution Press, 1991); Jane De Hart Matthews, *The Federal Theatre, 1935–1939: Plays, Relief, and Politics* (New York: Octagon Books, 1980).

83. Kett, *Pursuit of Knowledge,* 370–71.

84. "Summer Has Its Springs of Learning," *New York Times Magazine* (6 July 1930), 11.

85. Kett, *Pursuit of Knowledge*, 391; *New York Times*, 8 June 1930, sect. 2, p. 5.

86. "Summer Has Its Spring of Learning," 19.

87. Kett, *Pursuit of Knowledge*, 391.

88. *New York Times*, 8 June 1930, sec. 2, p. 5.

89. *New York Times*, 16 July 1930, p. 1.

90. Dr. Walter Eddy, "Why Is a Vacation?" *Good Housekeeping* 105 (August 1937), 86–87.

Epilogue

1. *The Washington Post*, 30 June 1998, sec. E, p. 1, 11.

2. Juliet B. Schor, *The Overworked American: The Unexpected Decline of Leisure* (New York: Basic Books: 1991), 82.

3. Walt Disney Travel Co., "Walt Disney World Vacations," 1998.

4. "The Disney Institute," 1998 Vacation Guide.

5. Official Elderhostel Home Page, http:///www.elderhostel.org.

6. Outward Bound Web Page: http:///www.outwardbound.org/index2.html

7. IST Cultural Tours Brochure, "Collectibles for the Inquisitive Mind"; Canyon Ranch Brochure.

Index